JAPAN'S AGING PEACE

CONTEMPORARY ASIA IN THE WORLD

David C. Kang and Victor D. Cha, Editors

This series aims to address a gap in the public-policy and scholarly discussion of Asia. It seeks to promote books and studies that are on the cutting edge of their disciplines or promote multidisciplinary or interdisciplinary research but are also accessible to a wider readership. The editors seek to showcase the best scholarly and public-policy arguments on Asia from any field, including politics, history, economics, and cultural studies.

For a complete list of books in the series, see page 369.

Japan's Aging Peace

*Pacifism and Militarism
in the Twenty-First Century*

TOM PHUONG LE

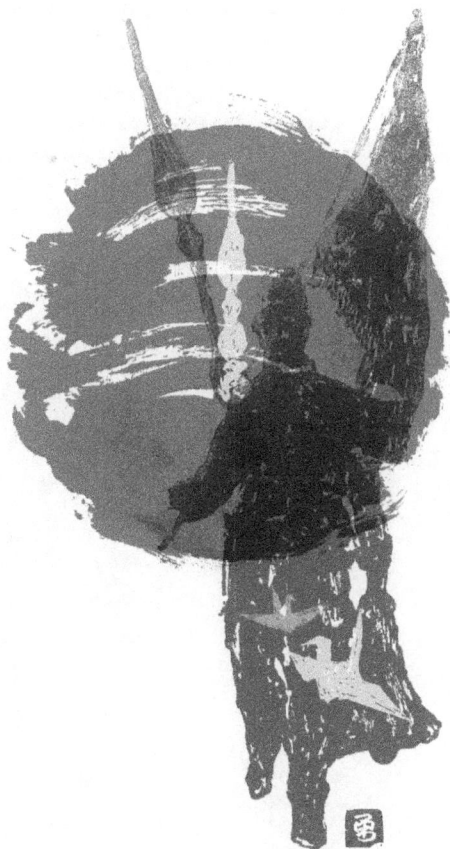

Columbia University Press
New York

Columbia University Press
Publishers Since 1893
New York   Chichester, West Sussex
cup.columbia.edu

Library of Congress Cataloging-in-Publication Data
Names: Le, Tom Phuong, author.
Title: Japan's aging peace : pacifism and militarism in the twenty-first century /
    Tom Phuong Le.
Other titles: Pacifism and militarism in the twenty-first century
Description: New York : Columbia University Press, [2021] | Includes bibliographical
    references and index.
Identifiers: LCCN 2020051786 | ISBN 9780231199780 (hardback) | ISBN 9780231199797
    (trade paperback) | ISBN 9780231553285 (ebook)
Subjects: LCSH: Militarism–Japan. | Pacifism–Japan. | National security–Japan–Public
    opinion. | Public opinion–Japan.
Classification: LCC UA845 .L42 2021 | DDC 303.6/60952–dc23
LC record available at https://lccn.loc.gov/2020051786

Cover image: © Yuji Baba, *Soldier Returns*, 2020.
Cover design: Lisa Hamm

To my darling, Erika.

Contents

Figures and Tables

FIGURES

TABLES

Preface

I t is not easy to pinpoint the exact date and location that this book began. As is common among first-time authors, the initial pieces of the puzzle appeared in graduate school. Japan watchers in academic and policy circles seemed obsessed with what made Japan so peculiar. I did not know any better than any of these fantastic scholars. Still, I was equally dissatisfied with how much Japanese security policy did not match the predictions in academic literature, opinion editorials, and news reports. Despite the volatile regional and international contexts, the government of Japan had failed to amend the Constitution, significantly increase defense expenditures, and convince the public of the need to normalize.

Piecing together the puzzle came in fits and spurts. Between my first trip in 2005 as a study abroad student and my most recent research trip in early 2020, I have completed a little more than two dozen trips to Japan, totaling approximately 2.5 years of on-the-ground time. During this period, Japan experienced three monumental events that revealed the character of its people—the 3/11 Tōhoku triple disaster, the awarding of the 2020 Olympics, and the 2020 COVID-19 pandemic. The international community marveled at the Japanese industriousness that rebuilt a country ravaged by natural disasters, soft power that drew the world's attention, and a robust welfare state that contained a pandemic far better than the West. The Japanese public held its government to a much higher standard—criticizing its slow reaction, waste of resources, and odd faith in the power of two face masks. There was an apparent disconnect between what the Japanese public and the outside world expected of the government.

In the hundreds of conversations with friends about the state of their country, the aging and declining population kept coming up. They wondered when they would be able to have children? How would they support them? When could they retire, given the uncertainty of the pension system? How would they take care of their aging parents? Young Japanese men and women had little time for the high politics of power balancing. If anything, given that Japan enjoyed such peace and prosperity in domestic and global affairs, my friends found my framing of security in terms of a rising China and nuclear North Korea strange, maybe even American. What came naturally to me was abnormal for them. Hence, my focus shifted from understanding security policy to understanding how different societies think about security.

The first "aha!" moment may have occurred in 2013 during a homestay in Hiroshima. In addition to taking peace studies courses at Hiroshima City University, I spent dozens of hours playing *Super Smash Bros.* with my two host brothers, looking for Subaru WRX parts with my host father, and chatting about the differences between living in a big city and the countryside with my host mother. I purposely avoided talking about research and politics because it would have been rude and, at worst, boring. It is quite rewarding and enjoyable to just observe and listen. On one morning before I left for class, a Japan Self-Defense Forces commercial played on the television. I was taken aback because I had never seen one live before, not in Tokyo or Yokohama, where I had previously lived. How effective would the commercial be in the famed peace city of Hiroshima?

The commercial's content and tone were not very interesting; it checked all the boxes of the atypical Japanese militarism that Western anthropologists and political scientists found so curious—smiling faces, upbeat music, and not a gun to be found. My host mother's reaction? Now that was interesting. In a somewhat panicked fashion, she told me that she was surprised to see the commercial herself, and she went to great lengths to assure me that such commercials must be an anomaly and that I should not worry. Her reaction provided direction for this book. It became clear that security needed to be understood within the context of those who experience it, and that the literature was lacking in this regard. How could Japan remilitarize when poor demographics constrained the economy, and the public showed no interest in testing the Constitution's limits? Politics is the art of the possible, and that possible is determined by the physics and biology of the material world as well as the ideas held by society. In fleshing out different conceptions of militarism and how states pursue security given the constraints, I could grapple with how we justify violence in international relations when Japan's case suggests that its brand of antimilitarism offers a more peaceful path forward.

I have many people to thank for making this book possible. To begin, I am very grateful to the many interviewees who graciously gave their time, patience, and expertise to a Vietnamese-American with few connections to elite policy circles. Engrossing conversations in Kesennuma *snakku*, Tokyo *izakaya*, Hiroshima parks, Teshima museums, Iwaishima homes, and cafes and offices across the country taught me so much about Japanese politics, life motivations, and greatly underappreciated diversity.

I proudly give my gratitude to my research assistants, Don Chen, Lucy Onder-wyzer Gold, Sophia Han, Audrey Jang, Sarah Kim, Ryan Levy, Jacob Merkle, Anupriya Nag, Yuki Numata, Divya Ryan, Haruka Sano, Erika Sato, Hina Tanabe, Kirara Tsutsui, Michelle Tunger, April Xu, Daphne Yang, David Yu, and Nina Zhou, whose countless hours hunting data, catching typos, and debating ideas improved this book significantly. Most importantly, they made the research fun! We spent far more time laughing than stressing over research obstacles. I look forward to their future work that will surely surpass my own. I would also like to thank Christopher Rand, and the many other donors to the Summer Undergraduate Research Program, that make these opportunities possible for our students.

As many within the academy know, we work in an exploitive industry that relies on the boundless generosity of terribly busy people to read messy drafts, recommend resources, help secure interviews, and provide critical observations. Hence, I am indebted to Aoi Chiyuki, Neil Chaturvedi, Aurélie Deganello, Josh Gellers, Peter Harris, Masaaki Higashijima, Kaihara Kentaro, Leonard Kosinski, Christopher Lamont, Gregory Noble, Graham Odell, Gene Park, Kyle Reykalin, Andrew Oros, Soul Park, Kikuma Shigeru, and Ryo Hinata-Yamaguchi.

I greatly benefited from the Young Leaders Program at Pacific Forum, the U.S.-Korea NextGen Fellowship sponsored by the Korea Foundation and CSIS, and the Japan Foundation Summer Research Program. Through these networks, I met scholars, policymakers, military personnel, and researchers whose insights and conversations pushed me to consider different perspectives and seek new data. The enjoyable conversations, insightful feedback, support, and friendship provided by Rachel Aden, Kent Boydston, Darcie Draudt, Julia Cunico Gardner, Hanmee Kim, Akira Igata, Takashi Kawamoto, Gibum Kim, Sohee Kim, Robin Lewis, Takehiro Masutomo, Jonathan Berkshire Miller, Masashi Murano, Crystal Pryor, Jun Pyon, Sean Quirk, Meredith Shaw, Aiko Shimizu, Ariel Stenek, and Shuhei Yoshimura truly made me reach further.

Similarly, I am grateful for the emotional and professional support of my peers and mentors in the Faculty Development and Diversity Success Program—Margaret Anderson, Kathi Harp, Andrew Kwok, and Melanie Morten. For generous access, advice, and mentorship, I thank Victor Cha, Karl Ian Cheng Uy Chua, Bridget Coggins, Ralph Cossa, Brad Glosserman, Brien Hallet, Robert Hellyer, David Kang, Mire Koikari, David Leheny, Michael Segal, and Andrew Yeo. A little extra shoutout to Robert Hellyer for giving me the title, *Japan's Aging Peace*. I am of mixed emotions that I have received more compliments for those three words than the remaining 120,000 that make up this monograph. If I were a better writer and more skilled researcher, I would have pursued my dream of becoming a historian like Robert.

Maybe the real treasure was the friends we made along the way. With great joy, I thank Hidemi Chen, Ikuko Kanno, Genny Ki, and Wilfred Wan for letting me crash in their homes in Japan, which allowed me to stretch that research dollar.

Speaking of research dollars, generous financial support for this book was provided in part by the Fulbright Program and Pomona College Steele Leave grant. The Pacific Basin Institute, Asian Studies Program, International Relations Program, Politics Department, and Dean's Office also provided funding to complete this book. Travel and lodging support was also provided by the American Friends of the International House of Japan Fellowship. The Sasakawa Peace Foundation Non-Resident Fellowship and Japan Foundation Summer Program allowed me to search for answers at conferences and conduct fieldwork throughout Japan. The support of Matthew Sussman and Ito Miyuki at the Japan-U.S. Education Commission was critical in the early stages of this book. Affiliations with Hiroshima City University and the PRIME Institute at Meiji Gakuin University provided two bases of operations. I am in tremendous debt to Furuzawa Yoshiaki, Mike Gorman, Robert Jacobs, Meguro Toshio, Nishida Tatsuya, Takahara Takao, Ulrike Woehr, Charles Worthen, and Yuasa Masae for their guidance. Also, many thanks to Okane Yasuko, Watanabe Tomoko, and Ogura Keiko for sharing their resources and time during my fieldwork in Hiroshima.

As a first-generation college graduate who did not know that the SATs were a requirement for admission, my professors' mentorship was invaluable. At the University of California, Davis, Michael Saler convinced me to pursue a career in academia. Emily Goldman and Larry Berman oversaw my first major research project during the UCDC program. Yoshii Atsushi helped me conduct field research for the first time in Japan at Meiji Gakuin University. Robert Uriu and Patrick Morgan were supportive advisers at the University of California, Irvine. I am grateful to Cecelia Lynch, who provided support long after graduation and through whom I can trace my intellectual roots back to the very foundation of constructivism.

I would also like to thank Paul Midford, who has provided great mentorship over the last few years—something he did not volunteer to do nor probably knows he did. I hope this book takes me closer to reaching the standard he set as an international relations scholar and teacher.

Much gratitude is due for the support provided by my colleagues at the Claremont Colleges. Thank you, Mietek Boduszyński, David Menefee-Libey, and Heather Williams, for reading early drafts. The support, mentorship, and friendship of Nicholas Ball, Angela Chin, Phillip Choi, Michael Diercks, Erica Dobbs, Martina Ebert, Lorn Foster, Amanda Hollis-Brusky, Pierre Englebert, Heidi Haddad, Nina Karnovsky, Zayn Kassam, Mark Kendall, Evelyn Khalili, Lisa Koch, Kyoko Kurita, Richard Lewis, Lisa Maldanado, Stephen Marks, Rebecca McGrew, Susan McWilliams, Lynne Miyake, Albert Park, Kacie Ross, Sara Sadhwani, Tomás Summers Sandoval, John Seery, Richard Worthington, Feng Xiao, Samuel Yamashita, and Patricia Zurita helped me see this project through. So was the encouragement of Dean Audrey Bilger, Associate Dean Nicole Weekes, President David Oxtoby, and President Gabi Starr.

Columbia University Press has been the perfect press, providing incredible—almost reckless—support and flexibility for a first-time author at the periphery of elite academic and policy circles. Columbia University Press's generosity is also why I was able to commission art from Yuji Baba for this book's cover. Yuji perfectly captured the themes of peace, aging, and the long shadow of militarism that this book aims to convey. I hope readers noticed the minute hand just 100 seconds to midnight on the *hinomaru*.

Readers can thank Caelyn Cobb and Monique Briones at Columbia University Press, whose guiding hands provided polish, order, and focus to an unruly manuscript barely holding together at the seams. Karen Stocz had the unenviable job of copyediting this manuscript, for which all readers should be grateful. Ben Kolstad managed the production for KGL. Moreover, the anonymous reviewers' generous and insightful comments ensured that I could deliver a better product. Of course, credit for the book's strengths should be divided among all the individuals previously mentioned. All errors should be attributed to my stubbornness not to heed all of their advice.

I give my heartfelt love and thanks to my family, Chi, Nga, Cuong, Stephanie, Timothy, Tony, ClaraJo, Ted, Irene, and Dick for the tremendous support and tolerance, for my selfish pursuit of an academic career. Despite the popular perception that first-gen graduates "make it" through personal sacrifice and gumption, none of it is possible without family who put in extra hours at work so I could put in extra hours towards my studies. With utmost modesty, I can confidently say that no one is prouder of this book than my family.

Not once was this academic journey difficult or lonely, a blessing that not all enjoy in an industry that can be so unforgiving and competitive. I can first attribute that to my son, Soren. Soren actually did not do much work, but he sure made the journey fun and increased the pressure to get the book done quicker—I should thank his daycare teachers. It is not possible to adequately thank my wife, Erika. She took risks and made sacrifices only to give me unending support, love, and humor, which kept me humble and confident. Erika read drafts, fixed problems before they even occurred, and provided the vital common-sense check that academic research sorely needs. This book was a joy to write because Erika brought joy. Thank you for your faith in me. Now on to our next adventure.

Note on Names and Currency

Asian names are written in the following order: family name (surname) followed by given name, except in those cases when the individual publishes primarily in English. Diacritics are used for locations but are omitted for places that are typically rendered in English (e.g., Tokyo).

The value of the Japanese yen fluctuates over a wide range. Although in some discussions amounts are given in U.S. dollars, most values are given in yen. A useful shorthand for the reader might be to assume that one dollar equals approximately one hundred yen.

Japan's Aging Peace

CHAPTER ONE

Japan's Aging Peace

International and domestic conditions may force Japan to finally abandon over seventy-five years of restrained security policy. Policymakers are increasingly concerned with terrorism, cyberattacks, piracy, unpredictable alliances, and Japan's irrelevance in international affairs. In East Asia, a rising China, nuclear North Korea, and assertive Russia are potential threats to Japan's security in the near future. Domestically, conservatives led by long-serving Prime Minister Abe Shinzō have capitalized on feelings of insecurity caused by three decades of economic stagnation and fierce competition from Japan's neighbors to push a more ambitious security agenda. If Japan were ever to remilitarize, now seems more likely than ever.

If the notion of a remilitarizing Japan sounds familiar, it is because it has been predicted before. For decades, scholars and East Asia neighbors believed it was only a matter of time before a booming economy, swelling national pride, and foreboding claims of Japanese exceptionalism would lead to Japan's reemergence as a world power.[1] As a world power, Japan would increase its power projection capabilities, disrupt the regional power balance, and exert its military power in international security affairs. In other words, Japan would display "normal" security behavior.[2] Such predictions were never quite realized.

Historians and political scientists of the constructivist tradition argued that Japan's unwillingness to remilitarize was due to a culture of antimilitarism generated by the devastating loss of World War II.[3] This culture produced institutions, laws, norms, and a "security identity" that made it difficult for conservative politicians to pursue "normal" security policy.[4] In the postwar era, Article 9 of the Peace Constitution has been a bulwark against militarization by serving as a unifying symbol of pacifism for activists in Japan and around the world.

Although few would still maintain that Japan is "number one,"[5] realists interpreted its lack of ascendance as only a setback. Some believed Japan would be punished if it remained an anomaly in the international system and would eventually normalize, including acquiring indigenous nuclear weapons capabilities. Others argued that Japan was biding its time and would normalize at a moment's notice if required. More tempered predictions concluded that Japan would play a greater role in international relations within a U.S.-led framework.[6] Undeniably, since 1991 several bright lines have been crossed, such as the dispatch of the Japan Self-Defense Forces (JSDF) overseas for peacekeeping operations (PKO), upgrade of the Japan Defense Agency (JDA) to the more powerful Ministry of Defense (MOD), creation of the National Security Council (NSC), and modification of the longstanding Three Principles on Arms Exports that limited growth in the arms industry. As illustrated in figure 1.1, the scope and magnitude of these

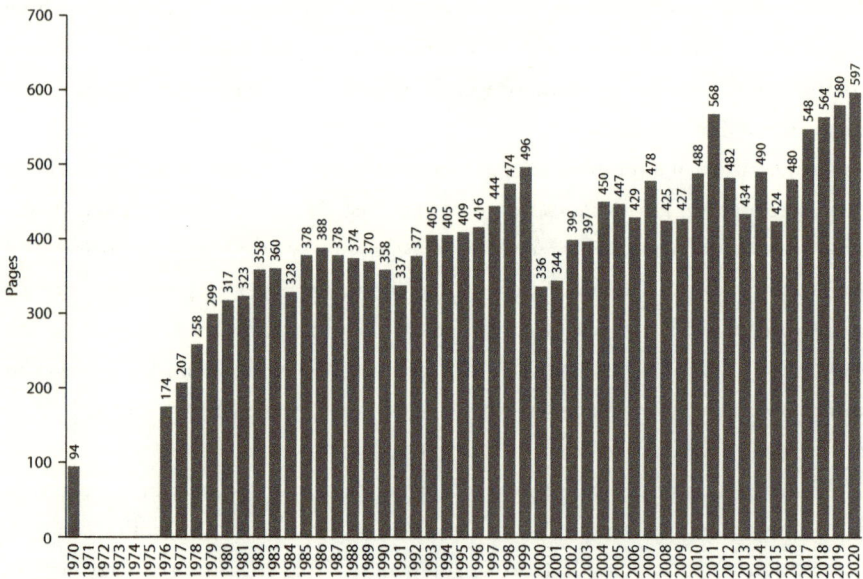

FIGURE 1.1 Defense of Japan page count (Japanese Print Edition), 1970–2020.

Source: Ministry of Defense, *Bōei Hakusho* (defense white paper; Tokyo: Ministry of Defense, 1970–2020). Bōei Hakusho 2020 entry represents the digital edition.

changes are made apparent by the length of Defense of Japan white papers, which has increased markedly over the last thirty years.

The increased sophistication of security discussions, evidenced by more detailed analysis of a wider range of topics in white papers, demonstrate a concerted and robust modernization of Japanese security policy—what Andrew Oros has called a "security renaissance."[7]

This book engages the question that has vexed many since the end of the Cold War: Why is Japan not a normal country? More specifically, this book addresses the question: What determines the content and direction of Japanese security policy? However, my objective is not to settle whether internal or external forces shape Japanese security policy—they both do—but to reevaluate how militarism and the use of force are discussed and justified in debates about security. This reevaluation of militarism is a worthy endeavor not only for Japan enthusiasts but also for all interested in how state-sanctioned violence is negotiated at home and abroad. Militarism is not just the tools and politics of warfare but the institutions that determine their appropriateness and pervasiveness.

Japan's restrained security policies over the past seventy-five years are a remarkable demonstration of the proposition that states have far greater range for choice in international politics than realists predict. That is, states have wider latitude for avoiding aggressive militaristic policies without being punished by the anarchical system. "Normal" and "abnormal" are not best defined by what scholars believe a state should do but by why and how a society chooses to respond to threats. Thus, this book reintroduces to the international relations field the idea that security policy is *normative*. Foundational scholars in the realist tradition such as Thucydides, Niccolò Machiavelli, and Hans Morgenthau were immensely concerned with justice, virtue, prudence, and wisdom in politics and foreign affairs.[8] Thucydides's account of the Peloponnesian War is rife with lessons about how the sense of justice can motivate states to go to war, defend allies, mask self-interests, and ultimately shape international relations. Machiavelli's *The Prince* and Morgenthau's *Politics Among Nations* provide guidance for not only how to survive in a conflict-prone world but also how to do it without violating rules and norms that invite unnecessary conflict. Machiavelli's objective, for example, "was to counter the ignorance of rulers by spelling out the consequences when rules are ignored."[9] Embedded in Morgenthau's argument is a statesperson's *responsibility* to the people. Neorealists abandoned normativity altogether in favor of rational-choice calculations for state survival. By rejecting the second image, or the importance of domestic politics, neorealists ignored how the legal and moral authority granted to the government by the people to act in their best interests is what makes survival an interest in the first place. Second-generation constructivists reintroduced normativity into the scholarship as "norms." However, they gave the concepts incredible causal power "without asking whether, to what degree, and how" norms were normative.[10]

This book builds upon these foundational debates by explaining the complex intersections among the material forces and ideational forces that shape policy preferences. The content and direction of Japanese security policy are not entirely intentional, nor are they entirely within the power of the government of Japan (GOJ) and the public to control. Beyond strategic and ideological reasons, Japan's limited security footprint is an inevitable byproduct of material constraints. The physical world is a significant component in the construction of the ideas that create and reject policy possibilities. Aging serves as a useful metaphor for the relationship between the material and ideational. How Japan addresses the process of aging and its consequences has far-reaching impacts for regional and global security.

Aging can be interpreted in a number of ways. For one, aging can imply that something is becoming weaker and lacking the vigor that is commonly attributed to youth. This may be the case with Japan, the world's first hyperaged society. By 2050, over 40 percent of the Japanese population will be over the age of sixty-five, which severely inhibits the MOD's ability to recruit new JSDF members and maintain force readiness. Unable to meet recruitment quotas for decades, the MOD has been forced to pursue creative policies to make up the shortfall. The government will also find it increasingly difficult to extract resources from a shrinking and highly-taxed population to support the JSDF. Despite a universal acknowledgment among security experts that China and North Korea have substantially augmented their power projection capabilities, Japan has been unwilling and unable to keep pace. Defense officials must also be mindful of the resources required to prevent current capabilities from falling into decline. Aging has compromised Japanese defense equipment and infrastructure as much as it has Japanese bodies. Japan's underdeveloped defense sector requires significant and immediate investment before these hardware deficits can be adequately addressed.

Aging may also lead one to be out of date, where one's values are no longer reflective of the times. This may be true for Japanese antimilitarism, which appears antiquated with the emergence of a myriad of threats unique to the twenty-first century. Former prime minister Abe sought to amend the Constitution, believing Japan's one-nation pacifism was no longer viable, and the nation's security was tied to the international community. Article 9's most influential defenders, pacifists who cut their teeth in the 1960s and 1970s, are aging themselves and will soon pass away. Can the next generation successfully take up their cause without having first-hand knowledge of the consequences of war? The massive protests against nuclear power and constitutional amendment following the March 11, 2011 triple disaster and introduction of the 2015 security bills suggest they can. Student-led grassroots movements such as Students Emergency Action for Liberal Democracy (SEALDs) are a powerful reminder that antimilitarism is strongest when most threatened.

Aging brings wisdom, confidence, and caution. Over seven decades of peace have turned Japan from a war-torn imperial power into the third-largest economy and one of the freest countries in the world. Polling data regularly indicates that the Japanese public believes in peace through diplomacy and is skeptical of the effectiveness of the use of force in international relations.[11] Like with fine wine or aged cheese, the passage of time can bring out the best qualities. Japan's democratic institutions, well-defined antimilitarism principles, soft power, and peace identity are hallmarks of a nation that has realized its unique place in the world.

Aging forces one to confront the past, take stock of the present, and prepare for the future. This book will explore how the Japanese government and public have navigated this process.

ARGUMENT IN BRIEF

What determines the content and direction of Japanese security policy? The rich academic and policy literature rightly sheds light on factors such as the regional environment, power balance, perceptions of insecurity, domestic politics, and desire for prestige that can lead to the remilitarization of Japan.[12] However, the preoccupation with reasons *for* remilitarization sacrificed nuanced consideration of *if* change is possible and *how* change is implemented. Explanations of security policy remain incomplete without consideration of how pull factors influence push factors.

This book's argument consists of two primary contentions. First, states operate within interrelated international and domestic environments that shape their security policies. These environments influence policymakers' decision making, but material constraints and ideational restraints within those environments govern security debates and limit policy change.[13] Concerning Japan, cultural, economic, and demographic forces have limited its embrace of conventional militarism as a tool of statecraft. This book treats the material and the ideational worlds not as wholly separated, but rather as intrinsically connected. I place particular emphasis on material constraints, however, because some constraints are independent of social constructs. In other words, the material reality out there matters. Demography, technological limitations, and finite resources simply *are*, and these material constraints significantly influence security policy. Ideational restraints such as norms, or what constructivist Nicolas Onuf calls "rules," govern how a society moves forward given those material constraints.

Second, antimilitarism institutions are reified through time, experience, and recurrent practices, and therefore they remain resilient and influential. Threats to Japanese security come and go, but the peace gained through restrained militarism has remained a constant in the postwar era. This book refers to this context as the Japanese "antimilitarism ecosystem." I adopt the term "ecosystem," as opposed to the terms "world" and "environment" found in the literature, to emphasize the interactions among living organisms and between those organisms and the physical environment. Although the Japanese people can influence the rate of population decline and invent new technologies and ideas, the laws of nature determine the limits of change.

Here, the user-and-computer model provides a useful metaphor for describing how material constraints and ideational restraints shape the content and direction of Japanese security policy. One can imagine the GOJ and the public are users, and the nation's security apparatuses, such as the JSDF and defense sector, are the computer. Analogous to a computer, a country's security apparatuses have hardware and software components. When a computer reaches its processing limits, the user can upgrade hardware components or replace the device entirely, although both options can be prohibitively expensive. In security terms, the GOJ may purchase new weapons systems to address hardware weaknesses.

Users also have software options, such as writing new software, overclocking the processor, and changing user behavior, that can extend the life of hardware. Similarly, introducing new security policies and relaxing use of force norms can be understood as implementing software changes to mitigate some of the hardware deficits. Users can operate the computer beyond the recommended limits of the hardware and software—but only for a limited time and not without costs. That is to say, the freedom of the user "depends on their ability to recognize the material and social limits that apply to them" and "to be able to evaluate the consequences of exceeding those limits."[14] Users have more freedom to negotiate social limits than they do material limits; however, if one can surpass a physical limit, then it was not a limit to begin with. In other words, the ideational world determines what is possible, and the material world determines what is impossible.

Scholars such as Andrew Oros have explored how the ideas and the environment shape security policy, writing that policies "were generated by an interactive dynamic of domestic political realignment with a shifting international environment, in conjunction with changed preferences more broadly in Japanese policy society and new political institutions as well—a 'perfect storm'—that has enabled the security renaissance of the past decade."[15] Other constructivists call into question the importance of an "*a priori* material reality 'out there' upon which the socially constructed world depends."[16] In *Constructivism in International Relations: The Politics of Reality*, Maja Zehfuss writes, "Even if material reality imposed a limit, what is significant is how we conceptualize this." Zehfuss presents the illustrative example of how material obstacles did not prevent the German government from deploying the *Bundeswehr* (Federal Defense Forces of Germany) because the "obstacles which might be construed as material were simply seen as problems to overcome, not as fundamental hindrance." Ultimately, according to Zehfuss, all material limits are political constructions and not "boundaries to which kinds of deeds or speech acts were possible."[17] Zehfuss's analysis sheds light on how asymmetrical power (privileges) influences constructions of reality, yet I contend even the most powerful actors cannot escape the influence of the material world on their constructions. The acknowledgment that material limitations *are* a problem to overcome demonstrates that the material world has shaped the discussion and therefore has tethered the construction to a starting point with defined boundaries.[18] Moreover, material resources are a source of power and privilege. The material and ideational realities are equally significant because "resources are nothing until mobilized through rules, rules are nothing until matched with resources to effectuate rule."[19]

To analyze the material and ideational dimensions of the Japanese antimilitarism ecosystem, this book turns to a foundational constructivist approach within the field of international relations that has thus far been underutilized by Japanese security experts, specifically Nicholas Onuf's concepts of "rules" and "rule." Rules constitute and regulate relations among states, and therefore create the condition of rule or the privileging of one group over another.[20] These rules "tell us how to play a game" and "guide play," which "make social life intelligible to those participating in it."[21] Agents, through deeds and speech acts, generate three types of rules: (1) directive rules that tell us what they must do and "provide information about the consequences of disregarding them"; (2) instruction-rules that "tell us how to proceed if we are to get the result we are hoping for"; and (3) commitment-rules that are "like contracts reciprocally undertaken to assure a mutually desired result."[22] Rules are normative because they tell agents what they *should* do with the information and resources they possess.

Concerning the content and direction of Japanese security policy, rules influence how the GOJ and the public conceptualize security and justify the use of force in international relations. The antimilitarism ecosystem has cultivated a unique strain of Japanese militarism that prevents the GOJ from investing significantly in the JSDF's power projection capabilities while simultaneously promoting the deployment of JSDF to achieve nontraditional security objectives. For many within the Japanese public, it is commonsensical that the use of force should be limited to self-defense and the protection of human security. Security policy is therefore normative because rules provide justifications for the *proper* use and nonuse of force.

Material Constraints and Ideational Restraints

Table 1.1 outlines the social-structural and technical-infrastructural hardware constraints and political and normative software restraints that comprise the Japanese antimilitarism ecosystem. Constraints are material variables that limit the JSDF's power projection capabilities. Restraints are self-imposed restrictions on the JSDF's implementation of its capabilities. Antimilitarism rules govern the interaction among these variables, and through repeated

TABLE 1.1 Constraints and restraints on Japanese militarism

Strength of constraint and restraint	Type of constraint	
	Social-structural	*Technical-infrastructural*
Strong *Change possible with the implementation of new cultural and economic practices*	• Aging and declining population	• Underdeveloped military-industrial complex
Moderate *Change possible with the implementation of new policies*	• No conscription (Article 18) • Weak recruitment	• Lack of combat experience • Outdated infrastructure
Weak *Change possible with the modifications of current policies*		• Defense-oriented technologies

	Type of restraint	
	Political	*Normative*
Strong *Change possible with the rejection of current dominant rules*		• Peace constitution (Article 9) and related laws
Moderate *Change possible with the reframing of current rules*	• U.S.-Japan alliance • Reassurance policy • Japanese neutrality	• Nonnuclear principles • Antinuclear/Antimilitarism lobby [public, media, academia]
Weak *Change possible with the intro- duction of new rules*	• International stigma	• 1% of GDP cap on defense expenditures • Arms export principles

interactions and practices, material constraints and ideational restraints become path-dependent.[23]

Constraints and restraints possess varying degrees of strength. Strong constraints are almost impossible for policymakers to overcome. Moderate constraints significantly influence security policy but can be mitigated by adept policymakers working in a deliberate and sustained manner. Weak constraints operate more like restraints in that they exist as long as policymakers believe overturning them would not be politically cost-prohibitive.

In practice, strong restraints, such as the antimilitarism norm, can be as durable as a strong constraint. For example, legally Article 9 can be amended at any time, but this is unlikely because antimilitarism is so interwoven with national identity that hawkish politicians are unable to obtain the support necessary for an amendment in a national referendum as required by Article 96 of the Constitution. Moderate restraints are durable due to decades of reiterated practices but can weaken when material conditions change. Weak restraints are violated regularly within the parameters that antimilitarism rules allow. All restraints can be unraveled by a shock to the system that unsettles the underlying logic of current rules, such as invasion or total alliance collapse. Even in such circumstances, strong restraints remain in a residual form.

Social-structural constraints are the human resource limitations on the JSDF. Although modern warfare has placed a premium on technology, the importance of raw manpower cannot go understated. Latent power and military effectiveness will always be partially tied to boots on the ground, because the upper limit of a nation's military strength is intrinsically linked to the population's willingness to fight and support a war effort.[24] The aging and declining population significantly impact the JSDF at the tactical and operational levels, which ultimately shape the GOJ's security policy discussions. Tsuchiya Motohiro, a cybersecurity expert and professor at Keio University who served on the 2019 National Defense Program Guidelines (NDPG) *kondankai* (advisory group), provides valuable insight on these internal discussions. The advisory group developed a *yonjin* (four persons) concept to mitigate the impact of the demographic crises on the JSDF.[25] The four persons included, (1) *mujin* (literally means "unattended," but implies automation or autonomous systems), (2) *shōjin* (implies saving manpower), (3) *rōjin* (old people, which implies reemploying retired people), and (4) *fujin* (women, which implies increasing the recruitment of women). The MOD has increased its reliance on technology, such as robotics and artificial intelligence (AI) while seeking ways to decrease human resource requirements, such as considering smaller crew size when commissioning new destroyers. However, since automation cannot replace many JSDF personnel duties, the MOD has modified retirement policies, developed policies to increase the recruitment of women, and increased the age limit of new enlistees from twenty-six to thirty-two in October 2018, the first increase in twenty-eight years.

Broadly, the GOJ has sought to address the population and workforce crises through economic policy, most recently under the "third arrow" of Abenomics, but has been unsuccessful due to social, economic, and normative factors. Addressing the demographic crises requires rewriting the rules that contribute to population decline, such as patriarchal government and workplace cultures that provide women few opportunities to flourish in the public sphere and raise families at home simultaneously. The impact of the demographic crises on the JSDF is further exacerbated by the public's lack of enthusiasm for joining the JSDF. Many Japanese hold indifferent or antagonistic views of military service due to a popular attitude—reinforced by peace education—that blames the military for hijacking the nation and leading it down a destructive path in World War II.[26] As a result, the JSDF is understaffed, and this weakness limits the strategic options of the MOD. These social-structural constraints endure because overcoming them requires significant social engineering that is beyond the power of the government.

The MOD has also pursued a strategy of capacity building to overcome its human resource problems. Capacity building can be achieved through conscription, improving technology (quality and costs effectiveness), high-level training, and increasing the number of bases and outposts. However, due to decades of constrained militarism, Japan has not invested the necessary financial and political resources for the rapid expansion of the JSDF. This infrastructure lag is the technical-infrastructural constraint, exemplified by old bases, defense-oriented technology, and weak military-industrial complex, that limits Japan's power projection. For most of the post–World War II era, the MOD has struggled with finding locations and the resources to build new bases, which has made it difficult to introduce and test new defense technologies.

Moreover, the lack of infrastructure stalls the rearrangement of force structures that is necessary for adapting to the rapidly changing regional security environment. These limitations are exacerbated by normative restraints, such as the 1 percent of GDP soft cap on the defense budget, Three Principles on Arms Exports (recently lifted but still heavily regulated), and Article 9 of the Constitution. Normative restraints also contribute to the suboptimal development of the defense sector. For decades, defense contractors relied on a small domestic arms market because they lacked access to the international market. Exclusion from the international market not only prevented the defense sector from growing but made future growth more difficult because it severed access to valuable data, joint-development projects, networking, and goodwill that is necessary for a company to survive in an ultra-competitive industry. Due to the domestic defense sector's inability to meet the aspirations of the Abe administration, the MOD has increasingly relied on foreign military sales (FMS), which completes the nonvirtuous cycle of lack of investment in the Japanese arms industry.

Political restraints are the regulating behavior that hinders militarization. Instruction-rules and commitment-rules lead the GOJ to adopt a policy of reassurance to signal to former colonies and the international community that Japan has no intent to possess capabilities beyond the bare minimum necessary for self-defense. These rules also allowed East Asian leaders and the Japanese public to use Japan's colonial history to pressure the GOJ to forgo policies that strengthen the JSDF. The GOJ is well aware of the security dilemma and is therefore careful not to take actions that disrupt regional stability. Alone, political restraints are weak because a change in leadership can undo decades of positive relations. However, the political restraints have allowed the social-structural and technical-infrastructural constraints to solidify and the normative restraints to germinate—creating an antimilitarism ecosystem that increases the resilience of political restraints.

Normative restraints are the norms, practices, laws, rules, and institutions (collection of rules) that govern how the Japanese address insecurity.[27] Peace activists, educators, and the media cultivate antimilitarism attitudes in the public and protect Article 9, the Three Nonnuclear Principles, and related laws. Peace education has made antiwar attitudes commonsensical, but due to weaknesses in the peace movement, security policies are not entirely shaped by antimilitarism norms. Moreover, the antimilitarism norms are expressed in varied and sometimes contradictory and contested ways. Contestation ensures that antimilitarism norms not only reach a wider audience but also opens the space for the justification of the use of force. Since rules are continually debated and transformed, antimilitarism norms are pervasive and enduring but not hegemonic.

Antimilitarism endures because it is reified through time and experience—that is to say, "constituted in and through recurrent practices."[28] For three quarters of a century, antimilitarism—often expressed as *heiwa bunka* (peace culture)—made the avoidance of conflict the starting point in security policy discussions.[29] Satoh Haruko suggests that the postwar state "gave rise to a peculiar body politic *incapable* of recognizing security as a legitimate (and arguably central) concern of any state. Such a body politic obviously cannot engage in a 'normal' security discourse, let alone conceive one."[30] Antimilitarism provided the rules that determine the parameters of debates concerning the character and direction of the nation and the logic to which actors can understand the content discussed. The ideational roadblocks posed by antimilitarism sometimes made security conceptually incomprehensible to the degree that the concept of national security remained ambiguous to even the government, what Satoh has referred to as "mutated security discourse."

National security debates shed light on the interactive effects between material constraints and ideational restraints. For example, the declining population and technical limits of the JSDF create conditions in which antimilitarism norms are not challenged. Since the GOJ is unable to strengthen the capabilities of the JSDF through recruitment or capacity building, it lacks opportunities to demonstrate a credible alternative to the restrained security posture that has benefited the public. Similarly, the weak military-industrial complex strengthens antimilitarism culture. The absence of Japanese-made weapons at home and abroad reaffirms Japan's commitment to be a "peace-loving nation."[31] Equally, ideational restraints influence how Japan ranks the material threats to its security. Polling data have shown that the Japanese public does not believe regional security threats are more important than other national objectives, such as health care and a sustainable pension system.[32] In short, material and ideational factors are mutually constitutive.

Material and ideational factors are "co-constituted," in that material structures "reinforce or undermine existing norms and beliefs" and ideational factors guide agents' interaction with the material world.[33] Put differently, military strength—measured by defense spending and arms procurement—matters so much as norms allow. The mutual constitution of the material and the ideational worlds has been underappreciated by realism and mainstream constructivism since the foundational works of Onuf and Friedrich Kratochwil, especially in security studies of Northeast Asia. The combination of the material and ideational factors has led to Japanese security behavior that the current literature would not describe as "normalization." Norms, or "rules by another name,"[34] determine appropriate and inappropriate behavior by way of their *normativity*.

Japanese antimilitarism is uncritical and simplified—it is an instinctive feeling that war is bad and must be avoided. This instinctive feeling, what Japan Institute of International Affairs (JIIA) senior fellow Kotani Tetsuo refers to as "ambiguous pacifism," is difficult for the GOJ to overcome because it is so fundamental.[35] Conservatives have expended significant resources to broach the discussion of increasing the capabilities of the JSDF, introduce new security bills, and convince the public of their necessity, but cold hard facts and figures have little impact on a public distrustful of any attempt to normalize. As a result, the content and direction of security policy are less reflective of threat and more of the limits imposed by an ecosystem that finds increasing the possibility, even slightly, of going to war unacceptable.

Rules regulate and constitute behavior at the same time.[36] Take for example the term "peace-loving nation"—which seems to be employed more often in government speeches than in daily conversation—simultaneously provides boundaries and generates new roles in security policy debates. The concept grounds security debates in fundamental questions, such as, Does the use of force violate the fundamental character of the nation? What does a "peace-loving" nation *do*? and How does Japan's achieve security without a reliance on the use of force?

In sum, Japan has not normalized as many have predicted because in many ways it *cannot* and in some ways, it *will not*. As a result, Japan has avoided the aggressive militarization that defined it during the pre–World War II era, and many states during the Cold War. In the post–Cold War era, instead of remilitarization, Japan has adopted a unique minimal-use militarism, which allows for the limited use of force to uphold security domestically and to promote human security internationally. This type of militarism does not easily fit into the conventional understanding of normal security behavior. However, the concept of militarism, as used in the literature, may be too constraining. In a rapidly changing world where militaries are expected to do more than defend state sovereignty, such as combating terrorism, promoting democracy, and providing disaster relief, sharper analytical differentiation among militarisms is necessary.

MULTIPLE MILITARISMS

"Militarism," "remilitarization," and "normalization" are often vaguely defined. Japan observers regularly cite disputes over islands, historical revisionism, military build-up, and hawkish politicians as indicators of remilitarization, but they do not specify what exactly is militarism.[37] Is contemporary Japanese security policy mimicking World War II-style militarism, or is it imitating present-day U.S. foreign policy? This book proposes an expanded conception of militarism to more accurately account for the factors that shape, direct, and comprise Japanese security policy. That is, there are multiple militarisms.

Militarism is discussed in opaque terms because it has been conceptualized as a dichotomous or ordinal variable with pacifism on one side and militarism on the other side of a spectrum (see figure 1.2). In practice, security policies rarely fit neatly in either category. To measure militarism, scholars rely on data such as defense expenditures and military equipment acquisition. Such an approach makes comparative analysis exceedingly difficult. In describing this difficulty, Onuf writes, "Insofar as war is avoided because its outcome is predictable, the measure of military capabilities substitutes for war as a medium of measurement. Global comparison turns 'power' into a common medium for the measurement of standing and disallows, sometimes radically, its use as a means to achieve other interests."[38] Furthermore, "even if an expenditure of military capability enhanced one's security with respect to an adversary because military engagement costs the latter even more than it costs oneself, one's standing would still be reduced in

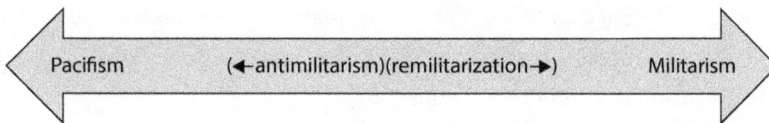

FIGURE 1.2 Conventional conceptualization of militarism.

comparison to all those in the system not making such expenditures."[39] Moreover, the cost of using force differs among states. For countries with small defense budgets, each weapon is relatively more expensive to deploy. Superpowers are not only financially more able to use their weapons, but they are also less likely to face international sanctions for the use of taboo weapons or overkill because of their hard power and soft power. Hence, conventional metrics of power are more descriptive than analytical because they do not take into account the debates, double-talk, rationalizations, and political relationships that are also defining elements of a state's militarism.

Consider for example, if a state increases the defense budget to augment disaster relief capabilities—is it more or less militaristic? If the head of state pursues military expansion but fails because of strong opposition, was the country militarizing? Or how does one compare the level of militarization among states? Is China, with the largest defense budget in East Asia, more militaristic than North Korea, which possesses the largest standing military in the world? Measuring militarism is a Sisyphean exercise.

This book utilizes comparative analysis of conventional metrics to describe military power but pays close attention to the myriad of motivations, justifications, and orientations of security policy in modern Japanese history. Within the last 150 years, Japan has practiced at least four types of militarism. This book develops the concept of multiple militarisms to explain these differences and provide a more nuanced analysis of security policy across cases.

ALTERNATIVE EXPLANATIONS

Literature concerning Japanese security policy change, or lack thereof, can be organized into three levels of analysis: (1) international-level explanations emphasizing the balance of power, (2) domestic-level explanations emphasizing political interests, and (3) ideational explanations emphasizing norms and culture.

Despite well-defined intellectual camps, many scholars acknowledge that to some degree each level of analysis explains elements of security policy. Yet, even an amalgamation of competing schools of thought creates an incomplete understanding of Japanese security policy when fundamental assumptions remain unchallenged.

To begin, realists have routinely misconstrued constructivist analyses of anti-militarism. Within the literature, terms such as "pacifism" and "antimilitarism" are used interchangeably, and critiques of the former are equivalent to disproving the latter. Pacifism is the deontological rejection of war and violence as accept-able tools of statecraft. Although there have been prominent pacifists in Japan's postwar history, antimilitarism more accurately reflects mainstream attitudes that deem military force is often not the best method for achieving peace and stability. Antimilitarists believe the use of force is justifiable for self-defense and, under certain conditions, for protecting vulnerable populations outside of Japan. This difference is important. Pacifism and antimilitarism have had vastly differ-ent effects on Japanese security policy. The oversimplification leads to narrow assessments of data, but more importantly, it underappreciates security behavior that does not neatly fit into concepts within the traditional literature.

Constructivists have been careful not to exaggerate claims concerning the causal effect of norms, a disclaimer that is often overlooked. Over time, norms erode, change, and are replaced by competing norms.[40] Constructivists account for security policy change by identifying when and why norms erode and when competing norms become dominant forces in security debates. Norms shape how the Japanese interpret threats and the legitimacy of military force. Hence, norms are more than variables that are taken into consideration by leaders and the pub-lic when dealing with external threats; they shape how threats are assessed, limit policy options, and produce novel ways of addressing security concerns.

The misinterpretation of constructivism is due to a fundamental shortcoming of realist-informed international relations theory; there are limited analytical or linguistic tools to discuss norms without sacrificing the integrity of fundamental realist claims. According to a strict interpretation of realist tenets, norms do not exist, or they are epiphenomenal to the political process.[41] Paradoxically, when realists seek to disprove the antimilitarism norm, they argue Japanese pacifism and antimilitarism have eroded, indicating these ideational factors had previ-ously influenced security policy.[42]

Due to the centrality of states and elites in international relations scholarship, realists have also overlooked the critical role of nonstate actors and grassroots movements in constructing norms.[43] In the postwar period, Japan has become a vibrant democracy with an active civil society that produces and disseminates security norms, such as the anti-*Anpo* (anti-Treaty of Mutual Cooperation and

Security) movement of the 1960s, the antinuclear movement of the 1970s, the Teshima antidumping movement of the 1980s, the Okinawa antibase movement of the 1990s, and the SEALDs movement of the 2010s.[44]

Last, realist lenses tend to focus on the causes of security policy change while minimizing variables that make change difficult, such as demography and technological limitations. Consider security policy change as a three-step process. First, leaders recognize threats and respond accordingly. On occasion, government leaders expand the purpose and capabilities of the armed forces to justify military expansion. Second, policymakers overcome political, normative, and institutional obstacles to convert their policy objectives into law. Third, these policy initiatives are implemented. The third step has been under-analyzed within security studies literature. Due to over seven decades of constrained security policy, among other factors, implementing new policy measures is difficult. Overcoming path-dependent obstacles requires not only political and normative change but also technical and social change as well.

International-Level Explanations

Neorealists contend the anarchic international system compels states, most importantly great powers, to continually seek power to ensure their survival. Since states are rational actors and are uncertain of the intentions of others, they pursue security via internal and external balancing.[45] Accordingly, Japan as a traditional economic, political, and military great power, is likely to increase its power projection capabilities when threats arise and when the power balance in the international system shifts.

Realists regularly cite the rise of China, North Korea's nuclear and intercontinental ballistic missile (ICBM) programs, poor relations with South Korea, and stateless threats such as terrorism as the causes of more autonomous and militarized Japanese security policy.[46] Historian Kenneth Pyle, for example, argues, "Japan is on the verge of another sea change in its international orientation," and "over more than half a century of national pacifism and isolationism, the nation is preparing to become a major player in the strategic struggles of the twenty-first century."[47] Daniel Kliman echoes these conclusions, writing, "Tokyo has experienced a distinct turning point in its security strategy, as the erosion of normative restraints has markedly accelerated."[48]

Policymakers have undeniably been vigilant at identifying threats to Japanese security and have responded accordingly. However, as Waltz reminds, structural realism is insufficient for understanding foreign policy because it does not explain the internal dynamics of the state.[49] Due to structural realism's emphasis on theoretical parsimony and focus on the international system, it has difficulty explaining domestic and normative variables that shape Japanese security policy. It has been over twenty-five years since Christopher Layne predicted Japan would become a normal nation, yet it is unclear if this has been the case.[50] Recent research continues to claim Japan is normalizing without any indication of when the process of normalization would be completed or what the end product would entail.

Miyashita Akitoshi has raised the important question, "Where do norms come from?" to illustrate that the strength of Japanese antimilitarism is tied to the security environment.[51] Through the analysis of public opinion polling data, Miyashita concludes that the constructivist attention to Japan's historical experience alone cannot account for policy change and that the absence of an American security guarantee would lead to the erosion of pacifism. This argument, however, succumbs to the agent-structure fallacy in that it draws an overly rigid line between norms and the physical environment. Japanese pacifism, or more accurately antimilitarism, is a fundamental aspect of the U.S.-Japan alliance and the regional power balance. Here, "rules" would be the more accurate term in describing how norms operate. Antimilitarism rules constrain and shape Japanese security behavior while they are practiced and challenged. Hence, rules do not come from the international environment or the domestic environment but from their mutual constitution.

Similarly, Jennifer Lind argues Japan pursues a strategy of "buck-passing" and when the U.S.-Japan alliance weakens, Japan seeks more autonomous security policies.[52] Lind's research is a significant contribution to Japanese security studies in that it demonstrated multiple methods of analyzing defense expenditures and brought renewed attention to the importance of clarifying what defense technologies entail for regional power balances. Although convincingly disproving the myth that Japan is militarily weak, Lind's reexamination of Japanese military power, evidence of buck-passing, and conclusion of a "dramatic transformation" of security policy merit some reconsideration.

Lind contends the normative 1 percent of GDP cap on defense expenditures is inconsequential given the quality of JSDF technology and training. Even if this were true, it deflects from the question: Why has the 1 percent cap endured when buck-passing threatens the U.S.-Japan alliance, and Japan can afford to spend more to increase its independent capabilities? The 1 percent figure is rather arbitrary, and therefore incredibly informative. The informal policy is *customary* and not tied to a strategic calculation of capabilities, and thus provides little insight on how the GOJ makes a rational-choice buck-passing calculation. Buck-passing is an inexact strategy that can lead to imprecise conclusions about how and when certain technologies are adopted.

Additionally, in comparing Japan with traditional European military powers, Lind draws attention from a more instructive indicator of the direction of Japanese security policy—limited growth in comparison to East Asian militaries. If Japan were to adopt a balancing strategy, it would correspond with China, North Korea, Russia, and to a lesser extent South Korea and Taiwan. A brief examination of defense expenditures in East Asia over the last two decades makes clear that not only has Japan not balanced, but it has increasingly fallen behind (see figure 1.3).

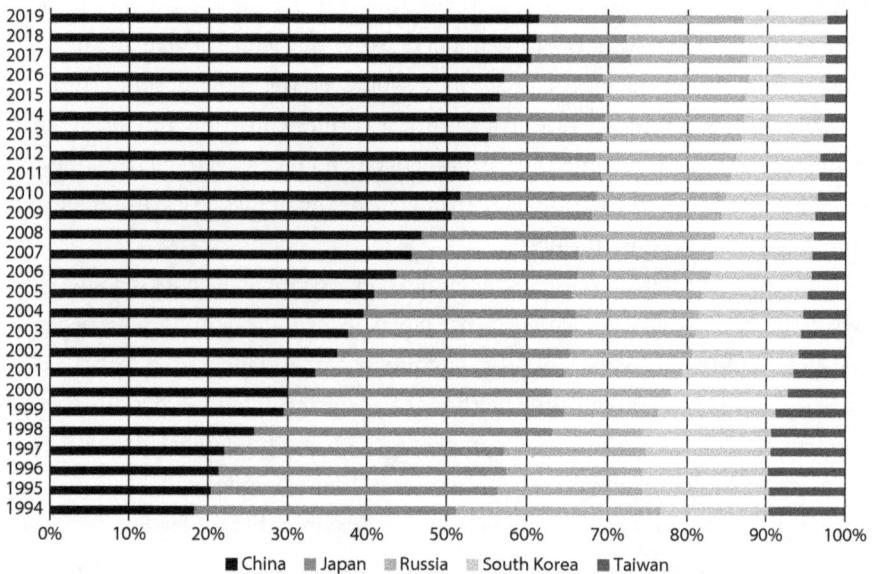

FIGURE 1.3 Percentage share of East Asia defense expenditures, 1992–2019.

Source: Stockholm International Peace Research Institute, "SIPRI Military Expenditure Database," accessed November 30, 2020, https://www.sipri.org/databases/milex.

In the 1970s Japan's defense expenditures increased significantly due to the unprecedented growth of its miracle economy. Between 1970 and 1980, Japan's GDP increased by five times over, from 200 billion to 1 trillion, while military expenditures rose from 2 billion to 22 billion.[53] Japan's dominance peaked between 1991 and 1998 when its share of regional defense expenditures was 10 percent greater than the next highest spender. During the short period, Japan comprised 40 percent of East Asia defense expenditures, although the figure provides an incomplete picture, as the fall of the Soviet Union accounts for Japan's higher share. Beginning in 1999, Japan's share of regional defense expenditures declined, and by 2005 China became the top spender in the region. Russia overtook Japan two years later. This period is notable because the shift occurred during Prime Minister Koizumi Junichiro's term, a period considered the start of rising nationalism and recommitment to the U.S.-Japan alliance. For nineteen of the next twenty years, Japan's share of regional spending declined and reached a low of 10.7 percent in 2019. Sceptics of this measure would argue Japan's decreased share of regional defense spending is due to the significant increase of China's defense budget. However, Russia and South Korea's regional share increased over the last twenty years, and in 2019, Japan and South Korea's regional share was equal. In other words, Japan's defense expenditures are more in line with middle powers in the region than its great power rival.

It is also questionable if Japan buck-passed given the high cost of its current security strategy. To offset the costs of a more independent security posture, Japan liberally provides Official Development Assistance (ODA) throughout the world and takes on the economic and social burdens of hosting U.S. bases.[54] Moreover, by linking its security strategy to the United States, Japan has jeopardized its neutral position in international relations, created tensions in East Asia, and sacrificed autonomy in security matters.

Although descriptive analysis makes clear that the JSDF possesses significant capabilities, there is no rubric for determining what constitutes dramatic change. Typical of most policy measures, the MOD has implemented incremental changes to the capabilities of the JSDF over the last few decades.[55] Qualitative and quantitative military strength is difficult to gauge, especially concerning states that do not fight wars.

Some scholars have turned to defensive realism and neoclassical realism to account for idiosyncrasies in Japanese security policy. Paul Midford argues Japan's limited security policy is not derived from a domestic pacifism but a rational response to the anarchical system.[56] Japan balances against threat and, therefore, maintains a low profile to reassure its neighbors—avoiding a security dilemma. In *Rethinking Japanese Public Opinion and Security*, Midford expounds on the argument through a careful analysis of public opinion polls, which show the Japanese public supports the defensive use of the JSDF while expressing less enthusiasm for offensive activities.[57] Similarly, Kawasaki Tsuyoshi contends, "Japan's overall strategic goal is to reduce the intensity of the security dilemma in Northeast Asia. To achieve this goal, Japan maintains its alliance with the United States and its modest and defensive military capabilities."[58]

This book builds upon conclusions drawn by neoclassical realists in chapter 5. However, as neoclassical realists such as Kawasaki claim constructivists underestimate the influence of the security dilemma,[59] neoclassical realists underestimate the importance of rules in shaping security behavior and discourse. Leaders are less likely to utilize military force to address threats not only because it can send the wrong signals or is ineffective, but also because the public finds military buildup an affront to its beliefs and national identity. Rational-choice calculations are made within the context of norms and rules. Many Japanese believe imperialism was immoral. And notwithstanding die-hard revisionists, many attribute Japan's monumental defeat in World War II not to counterbalancing but to poor elite decision making that dragged the nation into an unwinnable war.

The security dilemma cannot explain why Japan actively participates in PKOs and assertively pursues a seat on the UN Security Council, actions that undoubtedly alarm distrustful neighbors. Reassurance is not a costless strategy, because it leads to enduring policies and institutions that handcuff Japan's ability to independently defend itself. Japan's lack of self-reliance, immense trust in the U.S.-Japan alliance, and hope that suspicious East Asian states will find its signals reassuring challenges a core realist assumption—that states are never certain of the intentions of others.

Domestic-Level Explanations

Domestic-level explanations focus on how domestic politics and the U.S.-Japan alliance shape security policy. Richard Samuels's detailed investigation of the relationship between regional threats and shifts in domestic politics provides valuable insight concerning how and why Japanese leaders respond to threat. International threats are filtered through domestic debates, resulting in distinct groups vying for control of security policy.[60] Samuels concludes the external environment and political failures of socialists marginalized pacifism. As a result, Japan's "goldilocks consensus" grand strategy leads to hedging between China and the United States and a security posture that is neither too big nor too small.[61] Keiko Hirata finds a different combination of actors, and contends pacifists, mercantilists, normalists, and nationalists vie for the national consciousness. Up to the end of the Cold War, mercantilists were the dominant force, but they have since been overtaken by normalists, led by Prime Minister Abe.[62]

Elite policies provide an incomplete picture of domestic politics. Public opinion, NGOs, and grassroots movements shape the environments in which elites operate. The failures of the Japan Socialist Party and Japan Communist Party are well documented and illustrate why pacifists are marginalized in Japanese politics. However, the influence of pacifism in Japanese politics has been too quickly dismissed. For example, Kōmeitō, which often utilizes antimilitaristic rhetoric and is closely associated with the Buddhist peace organization Sōka Gakkai, regularly checks the Liberal Democratic Party's (LDP) efforts to significantly change security policy. Moreover, the pervasive pacifist discourse in newspapers, radio, symposiums and conferences, music concerts, textbooks, manga (comics), and museum exhibitions influences the public's views of the legitimacy of violence as a tool of statecraft.

Some scholars link the domestic and international levels. David Arase argues, "Aside from the generational change, a new alignment of factors at the levels of international structure, domestic institutions, and national identity after 9/11 has encouraged Japan to change its security posture; it has done so with unprecedented scope and speed."[63] Arase predicted these trends to continue as leaders "cast off the weakness and deference that characterized Japan after World War II in order to claim the rights and respect that Japan's accomplishments have earned."[64] Kevin Cooney contends politicians utilize the "myth" of *gaiatsu* (foreign pressure) to justify a "normal nation" agenda.[65]

There are several shortcomings to attributing security policy solely to leadership and politics. First, leadership in the postwar period has been erratic. From 1947 to 2020, only seven of thirty-one prime ministers remained in office for more than one thousand days. This is particularly remarkable given Japanese prime ministers can call elections when their party is popular, thus increasing the likelihood they can extend their time in office. Of the seven prime ministers to hold office for more than one thousand days, only Nakasone Yasuhiro, Koizumi, and Abe sought to normalize the JSDF. Prime Minister Kishi Nobusuke cemented the Treaty of Mutual Cooperation and Security between Japan and the United States as the cornerstone of Japanese foreign policy but was forced to resign due to significant public backlash. Prime Minister Abe reached the one-thousand-day milestone on September 18, 2014 (combining both terms) and was moderately successful in enacting policy change. Strong leaders can be very influential in determining the direction of security policy, but rarely has a Japanese prime minister secured enough time and support to implement transformational security policies. On the other hand, Prime Minister Yoshida Shigeru and Prime Minister Satō Eisaku very successfully established many antimilitaristic principles and institutions, partly because they enjoyed an early-mover advantage. Prime Minister Ikeda Hayato eschewed controversial security initiatives in favor of improving the economy, which have defined Japanese politics for the greater part of the last century.

Second, civilian control is a fundamental feature of the Constitution (discussed in chapter 6). Many bureaucrats believe they are the final check on over-zealous politicians and oppose efforts to increase the capabilities of the JSDF by obstructing unwanted policy platforms through loosely interpreting policy directives and creative legal drafting. Third, the impact of the U.S.-Japan alliance on elite decision making is much more complicated than unwanted foreign pressure. Abe, for example, believed the U.S.-Japan alliance created the opportunity for Japan to proactively contribute to peace, while others argued it is a questionable cornerstone of Japanese security policy because it can lead to regional isolation and being drawn into U.S. conflicts. Given the United States' declining influence, costly wars in the Middle East, and the increasing importance of China, some leaders are reconsidering the prudence of relenting to U.S. pressure.

Ideational-Based Explanations

Ideational-based explanations examine how nonmaterial factors such as ideas, norms, culture, and identity influence security policy. In the literature, the most commonly cited ideational forces are nationalism, antimilitarism, pacifism, and prestige.

Realists and the popular press frequently cite nationalism—fueled by conservative pride of Japanese culture, lack of war guilt, desire for prestige, and racism—as the impetus for more aggressive Japanese security policy. Sasada Hironori argues, "As the antipathy toward Japan has intensified in China and Korea, the Japanese have countered with their own nationalistic turn, marked by increasing support for more assertive national defense policies and an uncompromising stance toward its hostile neighbors."[66] Sasada continues, writing, "Today Japanese people, including the young population who used to advocate pacifism enthusiastically, favor nationalistic policies more than ever before, and the public is leading Japan away from its post–World War II pacifist tradition."[67] Prime minister visits to the Yasukuni Shrine and historical revisionism in some Japanese textbooks are notable examples of nationalism that draw the attention of former colonies.[68]

Linking nationalism to increased militarism is problematic. To begin, the majority of the security measures pursued in recent years are defense oriented. Since it is generally accepted, even in East Asia, that Japan has the right to self-defense, policies that increase Japan's ability to protect its territories are a far cry from aggressive nationalism. Japan also participates in Track I and Track II bilateral and multilateral negotiations, and other confidence-building measures (CBM) concerning disputed territories and security matters, which is hardly an uncompromising stance toward potential rivals. Lastly, conservative groups primarily focus their attention on reinterpreting Japan's colonial past and rarely propose specific policy recommendations.

It is difficult to determine whether nationalism leads to militarism, because nationalism is as elusive a concept as militarism. Historian Kevin Doak contends there are several types of competing nationalisms originating from different segments of society.[69] Scholars, however, have mistakenly followed the "time-honored means of explaining both Japan's economic successes and political crimes over the course of the twentieth century" by underscoring "the role of the state in historical accounts of national identity in modern Japan."[70] This approach treats nationalism as a single hegemonic force when, in practice, ethnic-centered and state-centered nationalisms propagated and challenged militaristic policies. The tensions among nationalisms are relevant in the postwar period because some Japanese intellectuals hailed ethnic nationalism as "a critical ingredient in anti-imperialism and decolonization movements in ways that reconnected to the post-Meiji popular disenchantment with the modern capitalist state."[71] Ethnic nationalism, which can complement conservative movements, is one of several nationalisms that vie for the soul of modern Japan. During the U.S. occupation, elites promoted a specific brand of nationalism, which espoused:

> Whether achieved through democratic labor unions or American banking methods, the fundamental policy included an encouragement of a liberal democratic nationalism that would support the liberal, capitalist Japanese state. This democratic nationalism rested on a concept of the Japanese people as a sovereign *kokumin*, the key concept of postwar national citizenship that would now include women and that was explicitly joined to the civic values of the new constitution. This belief in the values of a liberal, civic nation was not merely a rejection of class as more fundamental to social life than the nation but a clear alternative to the pervasive concept in wartime Japan of the Japanese as a distinct ethnic nation (*minzoku*) among its fellow members of the Asian race (*jinshu*).[72]

Nationalism, and the militarism that may derive from it, is diverse and is continuously negotiated in society. When political scientists predict the rise of Japanese militarism, it is unclear if it is due to patriotism, jingoism, or nationalism. "Nationalism" and "militarism" have become catch-all terms for dangerous and treacherous. Because Japan was a defeated enemy nation in World War II, its history has served as a scarlet letter in international relations and academic debates.[73] This has prevented critical analysis of the complex nationalisms that influence Japan.

Many constructivists, on the other hand, call attention to the role of norms, culture, and identity in constraining militarism.[74] Thomas Berger argues the physical and emotional devastation of World War II led to the belief that, "The military is a dangerous institution that must be constantly restrained and monitored lest it threaten Japan's postwar democratic order and undermine the peace and prosperity that the nation has enjoyed since 1945."[75] According to some estimates, 2.7 million Japanese died as a result of the war, or approximately 3 to 4 percent of the population in 1941.[76] Hundreds of cities were destroyed, Hiroshima and Nagasaki suffered the only use of atomic bombs on humans in history, the state and empire collapsed, and the mythical status of the emperor was completely discredited. In other words, the war was not just the destruction of physical Japan; it unraveled a century-long and elaborately constructed national identity. The shock of this monumental defeat laid the foundation for enduring institutions and ideologies that constrain aggressive forms of militarism. Berger concludes, "The primary reason for Japan's reluctance to do so [normalize] is not to be found in any structural factor, such as a high degree of dependence on trade or the absence of any potential security threats, but rather is attributable to Japan's postwar culture of anti-militarism."[77]

Andrew Oros observes how this antimilitarism can take the form of a "security identity" that emphasizes three central tenets: (1) no traditional armed forces, (2) no use of force by Japan except in self-defense, and (3) no Japanese participation in foreign wars. A security identity is "a set of collectively held principles that have attracted broad political support regarding the appropriate role of state action in the security arena and are institutionalized in the policy making process."[78] This security identity influences organizational design, provides the boundaries to which security policy is debated, and establishes limits to what policy options are available. Izumikawa Yasuhiro further complicates the antimilitarism norm, writing, "Japanese antimilitarism is not a monolithic concept. Rather, it consists of three elements: pacifism, anti-traditionalism, and the fear of entrapment."[79]

This book builds upon these contributions and addresses several shortcomings. First, much of the constructivist literature explains restraints in security policy decision making while neglecting material factors that are vital to that process. Second, constructivist literature examining Japanese security policy prioritizes elites over other equally relevant actors and forces, such as grassroots movements, education, and NGOs. This book brings to light contemporary peace discourses to determine how antimilitaristic messages are propagated throughout society. Revisiting how antimilitarism came to be and, more importantly, how it is sustained for over seven decades can shed light on security policy change.

Third, constructivists have not adequately accounted for substantial shifts in security policy. Within the last fifteen years, Japan has loosened the arms export ban, increased the role of JSDF officers in security decision making, and adopted collective self-defense. These policy shifts suggest that other norms also influence security policy.

Fourth, the antimilitarism norm has not been adequately scrutinized. Norms are often renegotiated when the public and government face changing security and ideological environments. An under-analyzed dimension of the evolution of the antimilitarism norm is the increasing importance of human rights and humanitarian intervention norms. This book examines how international norms are localized and reshape Japanese beliefs concerning the appropriate use of force in international relations.

Fifth, constructivists have not addressed the weaknesses of antimilitarism norm advocates. This book examines bureaucratic, strategic, and cultural weaknesses of peace groups and addresses why the antimilitarism norm is not a hegemonic force. Lastly, constructivists have focused on the 1960s and 1970s to explain the peak of the antimilitarism norm and developments in the 1990s to explain its moderate decline. This book updates the literature through an in-depth examination of several developments in the past decade that significantly impacted security policy. The seventieth anniversary of World War II, the declining *hibakusha* (atomic bomb survivors) population, new NDPGs, and National Security Strategy (NSS), among other topics, are worthy of investigation.

INTELLECTUAL MERIT AND CONTRIBUTION

East Asia is the center of world politics. In 2019, East Asia (including the United States) comprised 57 percent of the global economy, 62 percent of defense spending, and 60 percent of the world population. The popular media regularly calls attention to the dynamism of the region, such as China's blistering economy and immense military power, *hallyu* (Korean Wave), and North Korea's emergence as a nuclear power. The region is also defined by stagnation, made apparent by the aging and declining populations and historical disputes. The United States' renewed interest in Asia and the seventy-fifth anniversary of the end of World War II introduced opportunities for significant change in regional relations. How Japan, as the world's third largest economy and oldest democracy in East Asia, responds to the region's dynamism and difficulties provides valuable lessons for the rest of the world, which will face similar obstacles in the near future.

This book is written with academics, policymakers, and the general public in mind. First, it contributes to the growing literature on Japanese security culture. Utilizing original interview data collected over two years of field research in Japan, this book explains how the security culture has evolved, paying particular attention to the changing international and domestic material and ideational contexts. Second, this book further develops a central concept in international relations, militarism. Although this book challenges some of the core beliefs about militarism, it builds upon the traditional literature that outlines why states remilitarize. Third, the book contributes to our understanding of how the government and public negotiate militarism in the context of international norms. By analyzing how Japan manages competing militarisms, this book addresses broader questions of how violence as a tool of statecraft is accepted and how states localize dominant international norms. Last, this book provides valuable lessons for policymakers and NGOs. The findings of this book will help policymakers identify weaknesses in security forces that stem from demography and technological limitations. A more accurate understanding of constraints and restraints will illustrate how weaknesses at the operational level and at the tactical level can affect the security policymaking process. NGOs will benefit from analysis explicating how civil society impacts policy and why they sometimes fail to meet their objectives. Both groups would gain from a better understanding of how their objectives align.

CASES, DATA, AND METHODOLOGY

This book carefully examines over seven decades of the content and direction of Japanese security policy. This longitudinal approach avoids exaggerating the effects of policy changes that are not enduring, and helps differentiate between true watershed moments, or critical junctures, and anomalous events. Some scholars observe that significant debates over security policy take place in roughly ten-year intervals.[80] Lieutenant General Yamaguchi Noboru contends, in order to understand security policy now, one should not look at what is being spent today but what has been spent over the last twenty years.[81] These estimates may vary quite significantly, but they illustrate that it takes years to understand the full implications of new policies.[82]

The public's discussion concerning security policy and identity also requires some time to appreciate. Peace activists plan their activities to coincide with major events, such as war anniversaries, Treaty on the Non-Proliferation of

Nuclear Weapons (NPT) meetings, and government press releases. Between these events, activists host and attend numerous academic and public events to advocate their positions. Understanding Japanese security policy not only requires analysis of watershed moments but also the day-to-day activities leading up to the adoption of a policy.

I utilize process-tracing to analyze change over time. Process-tracing "attempts to identify the intervening causal process—the causal chain and causal mechanism—between an independent variable (or variables) and the outcome of the dependent variable."[83] Process-tracing is useful for detangling complex phenomena that take place over long periods. Sequencing and long-term processes are important to illustrating that "causal analysis is intrinsically historical—the order of events or processes is likely to have a crucial impact on outcomes."[84] For example, had the LDP been in power during the 3/11 triple disaster, it is unlikely that Abe would have the opportunity to pursue his Proactive Contribution to Peace agenda. Abe also learned from the failures of his first term in 2007.[85] His departure served as an important learning moment, and Abe returned better prepared to deal with the obstacles to his security agenda. Context, unrelated to power balancing, has a significant impact on security policy.

The primary case examined in this book is postwar Japan (1945-present), with a particular emphasis from 1991 to 2020. Within this single-nation case study, this book also examines three additional temporal cases—the Meiji period, interwar period, and World War II. Additionally, this book utilizes context-driven analysis by briefly comparing Japan's military size and policies with countries in East Asia. Lastly, this book analyzes the U.S.-Japan alliance, PKOs, and humanitarian assistance/disaster relief (HA/DR) operations cases to illustrate the direction and content of Japanese security policy.

To determine the content and direction of Japanese security policy, this book examines the rules that govern how the government and public conceptualize and pursue their security objectives. Understanding how elites conceptualize security is fruitful in investigating Japan's foreign policy because dominant interpretations "are construed and reproduced most frequently by those in power."[86]

In total, I analyze over one thousand prime ministers and ministers of foreign affairs speeches, policy statements, and press releases to ascertain elite opinion.

Additionally, I conducted over seventy semistructured interviews with politicians, bureaucrats, JSDF personnel, scholars, members of the media, museum directors, peace activists, and NPO leaders for this book. Supplementing these on-record interviews are hundreds of off-record conversations with relevant stakeholders at Track II workshops, government press conferences, and security-related events. Lastly, data for this book was also drawn from government white papers and reports, company financial reports, and political advertisements.

To understand public opinion and expressions of peace and militarism, I analyzed newspaper articles and editorials, physical monuments, polls and surveys, museum signage and exhibits, textbooks, films, video games, and comics. I also observed protests, attended peace group meetings, and visited historical peace-related sites. By utilizing diverse "high" and "low" data, this book triangulates Japan's shared conception of security policy.[87]

To assess the meaning behind visual and textual data, I utilize discourse analysis.[88] Discourse analysis is useful because it reveals how often specific themes and terminologies appear in policy statements, speeches, and interviews and illustrates how security conceptions are constructed, justified, and propagated. Discourses are not only expressions of policy preferences but also acts of power that can impact social practices and how security is understood and pursued. As Richard Price argues, "discourses produce and legitimize certain behaviors and conditions of life as 'normal' and serve to politicize some phenomena over others."[89] In the case of Japan, the antimilitarism ecosystem frames how security is debated and negotiated between the public and the government. When unpopular security policies are adopted, government approval ratings drop, and the public becomes more adamant at maintaining the status quo. In other words, counterfactual occurrences do not necessarily indicate norms go away; norms change, are contested and are expressed in different ways at different times.

OUTLINE OF BOOK

The rest of the book is divided into seven chapters. Chapter 2 develops the multiple militarisms concept through an analysis of several types of militarism practiced by Japan since the Meiji period. The multiple militarisms concept provides the framework for contextualizing the constraints and restraints on Japanese militarism. The chapter denatures some of the assumptions about militarism and explains how the use of force is legitimated.

Chapter 3 and chapter 4 examine the material hardware constraints on the JSDF. Specifically, chapter 3 examines the strongest hardware constraint, demographics. The aging and declining population have direct and indirect effects on Japan's ability to project power and the policies the GOJ can adopt. The chapter also elucidates underlying rules, particularly gender norms, that make material constraints so difficult to overcome. Chapter 4 discusses the technical-infrastructural constraints on the JSDF, many of which are byproducts of antimilitarism norms. The technical-infrastructural constraints reveal not only the GOJ's efforts to overcome the demographics problem but also the obstacles it faces. The difficulties in fostering an indigenous defense industry, developing new defense technologies, and investing in a robust infrastructure demonstrate the embeddedness of the political and normative restraints on defense policymaking.

Chapter 5 and chapter 6 explore the software restraints in detail. Chapter 5 analyzes the various political restraints on the GOJ's ability to significantly change security policy. Although the international security environment has changed, U.S.-Japan relations and Asia-Japan relations have not. The political costs of change remain, and in many ways, have increased due to over seven decades of peace. Chapter 6 evaluates contemporary peace movements and their effect on the famed peace institutions commonly attributed to pacifism by many scholars. This chapter analyzes peace discourses—material and ideational—to illustrate how antimilitarism has evolved while maintaining core ideas formed in the early-postwar period.

Chapter 7 explores the constitutive effects of antimilitarism rules, namely the JSDF's adoption of PKOs and HA/DR operations to increase its stature at home and abroad. Japan has developed a comprehensive security approach that relegates the use of force as last resort for defense, while allowing for a circumscribed mobilization of the JSDF for international security.

Chapter 8 concludes the book with a brief discussion of Prime Minister Abe's Proactive Contribution to Peace and some final thoughts on the role of scholars in international relations.

AN OLD LOGIC AND THE NEW NORMAL

The Teaching, Research and International Policy survey of international scholars found that Alexander Wendt is considered to have the greatest influence on the field of International Relations in the past twenty years. Wendt's 1992 article, "Anarchy is What States Make of It: The Social Construction of Power Politics" challenged the hegemonic realist school of thought, forced scholars to reconsider the causal effects of structure, and solidified constructivism's place among the big three International Relations theories. Constructivism was always a much more ambitious approach to studying international relations. Nicholas Onuf's first book is titled *World of Our Making*. Embedded in constructivist theory is an emphasis on the agency of individuals to *act* upon the world in which they reside. In other words, we do what we are, and we are what we do and aspire to be.

The question of how to act within those worldly constraints lays before Japan. How long can the peace-loving nation survive in an increasingly insecure world? It seems that Japan is at a crossroads and many believe it will do what normal nations do, and remilitarize. However, this crossroads presents a false dichotomy. The content and direction of Japanese security policy are not determined by a single force, whether it is the international security environment or domestic antimilitarism norms. Security policy is a reflection of the environment in which it is debated and reconciled. Japan's antimilitarism ecosystem is comprised of social-structural, technical-infrastructural, political, and normative constraints and restraints that determine the upper limits of the nation's power projection capabilities, and the manner in which security is pursued. Change will occur, but the antimilitarism ecosystem ensures that it will be at the margins. The remainder of the book will explore how Japan balances between adopting a new normal of the international security environment and the old logic of antimilitarism that has provided over seven decades of peace and prosperity.

CHAPTER TWO

Multiple Militarisms

S cholars and policymakers have long predicted Japan's eventual return to normal security behavior, mainly differing over whether international threats or domestic forces would undo Japanese pacifistic attitudes and institutions. Embedded in these predictions is the belief that normal states are militaristic. This chapter unpacks some of the underlying assumptions within the study of international relations theory that inform such thinking and, in doing so, establishes a more comprehensive understanding of how the use of force is legitimized.

The current militarism analytical framework is inadequate for understanding Japanese security policy because it oversimplifies complicated—and seemingly contradictory—security practices, which leads to misinterpretation of Japanese security motives. For example, although scholars readily acknowledge that present-day Japanese security policy is not akin to 1930s-style militarism, they do not precisely articulate what contemporary *remilitarization* entails, nor do they specify the standards by which it would be considered normal. This lack of specificity forgoes critical analysis of why Japan would not return to its more aggressive colonial past, a shortcoming that regularly fuels open-ended alarmist predictions. Most states accept the legitimacy of the use of force in a conflict-prone world, and therefore they are militaristic. However, states address insecurity in vastly different ways.

An expanded conceptualization of militarism is necessary to accurately reflect how the interactive effects among the international security environment, domestic politics, and norms shape security policy. Japan's decision not to return to more aggressive forms of militarism is not only due to a lack of desire but also because the present context lacks many of the institutions and socioeconomic variables that allowed for imperialistic militarism to arise in the early nineteenth century. Although nationalism and militarism exist in the present day, their influence, in degree and character, is determined by the rules of a given period.

This chapter proceeds as follows: First, it examines historical cases of Japanese militarism to elucidate consistent and divergent themes among the cases. These cases demonstrate that although Japan has been militaristic over the last 150 years, it has adopted vastly different security policies due to material and ideational conditions. Second, this chapter reexamines the meaning of militarism and discusses the content and utility of the multiple militarisms concept.

JAPAN'S MULTIPLE MILITARISMS

Although regularly referenced, there is a lack of nuanced analysis on what militarism *means* in international relations. This deficiency is due to the absence of an analytical framework that differentiates among types of militarism. Consequently, vastly different cases are described as "nationalism," "militarization," and "remilitarization," and these terms are often used interchangeably. Scholars are frequently overly reliant on basic indicators of militarization, such as defense spending and technology acquisition, and therefore reify narrow conceptions of security that dominate international relations scholarship. The orthodox realist view assumes that security policy begins and ends with the state, ignoring non-state actors utilizing innovative methods for achieving peace and curtailing more aggressive forms of militarism.

Given the significance of Japan's militaristic past and anxiety over its current security policy, it is surprising that the concept of militarism has not been more critically examined. Sociologist Martin Shaw contends that the term "militarism" is not often used in international studies because it denotes a political opposition to military force and is therefore not scientific.[1] One can also attribute the hesitation to critically examine the term to the positionality of scholars, many of whom reside in the United States. The United States often serves as the reference point within security studies and criticisms of militarism, and therefore the United States itself could be interpreted as politically charged and controversial. The United States' primacy in international relations provides some insight on the limitations within the literature concerning Japanese security policy.

Since the United States frequently responds militarily to international threats, the starting assumption regarding change to security policy is that it must be tied to threat. When scholars contend that Japan is normalizing, militarizing, or remilitarizing, they emphasize motivations for change while neglecting the character and direction of change. Not all motivations are acted on or converted to corresponding security measures. Inaction can reveal more about a security doctrine than action. Furthermore, analysis of security behavior is often framed as bidirectional—states are either increasing power projection capabilities or decreasing power projection capabilities. However, the Japan Self-Defense Forces (JSDF) is most often mobilized for peacekeeping operations and humanitarian assistance/disaster relief missions, activities that do not fit neatly into power projection calculations or conventional understandings of militarism.

U.S. foreign policy also shapes how scholars interpret security behavior. Since the United States is often criticized for what are perceived to be politically motivated nation-building agendas, the assumption that security policies must have ulterior motives is prevalent in international relations scholarship. Nonetheless, such ulterior motives are normal if they fit within a narrow realist conception of self-interest.

Although realism focuses on why states adopt militaristic security policies, the theory tacitly acknowledges not all militarisms are the same. Within neorealist debates, disagreement over offensive, defensive, and free-riding strategies suggests that although state survival is most important, states differ in how best to secure it. As war technologies become more advanced and accessible, after a certain threshold, the differences are negligible among states. Most countries possess an air force, a navy, and an army, yet few scholars would suggest they practice the same *kind* of militarism. Since World War II, the United States has spent more on defense than any other country, possesses bases in foreign territories, and has fought several wars—sometimes unilaterally. However, U.S. militarism is unlike the militarisms of the British Empire, Nazi Germany, the Mongol Empire, and other hegemons. The current literature implicitly understands militarisms are different but has not integrated this understanding into the analysis of security policy.

According to Cynthia Enloe, militarism is "a compilation of assumptions, values, and beliefs."[2] The compilation of ideas are rules that inform a society whether the use of force is a legitimate tool of statecraft. Militarization involves the "encroaching of military forms, personnel and practices upon civilian institutions or social orders."[3] Militarization is a mutually-constituted process where the more "militarization transforms an individual or society, the more that individual or society comes to imagine military needs and militaristic presumptions to be not only valuable but also normal."[4] In other words, militarism is a collection of rules that informs a society when, why, and how force is utilized. Several scholars have called attention to the all-encompassing nature of the concept, where everyday life is transformed by militarism and militarism is supported by things that may not be obviously military.[5] External threat is one potential cause of militarization but not a sufficient explanation for how militarism is pursued or what character militarism takes. Militarism stands contrary to absolute pacifism, which argues that the use of force is illegitimate in all circumstances. Most states are militaristic—undoubtedly postwar Japan has been and is. This book builds upon these root definitions and the arguments of previous scholars by shifting the focus from determining *if* militarism exists to *what* kind of militarism exists. Moreover, this book argues militarization is shaped not only by institutions that allow it to flourish but also by conditions that constrain it.

Several indicators illustrate the degree of militarization and type of militarism. The power dynamic between civilian and military forces in government reveals the direction of security policy. If military officers possess disproportionate influence, states are more likely to utilize force to settle international disputes. Another indicator is the prevalence of militaristic symbols. In many communist states, statues and murals propagate party narratives about national history and identity. In North Korea and Russia, for example, statues of war heroes are often displayed in roundabouts, and political murals blanket major cities. These discourses are public, unabashed, and uncritical of the military. Another indicator of militarism is how history is portrayed in places of education, such as textbooks, museums, and monuments. For many in East Asia, the Yasukuni Shrine is commonly associated with Japanese militarism. An investigation of not only the contents of museums but also their popularity and relationship with the government can be informative. In Japan, the portrayal of the military, whether positive or negative, in novels, movies, comics, and television elucidate how the public's opinion of the JSDF is influenced. How comfortable is the public with military symbols? Are there certain taboos that the public and media avoid? Are JSDF personnel respected in society? The pervasiveness (or lack thereof) and type of symbolic and physical manifestations of militarism among states can illustrate different militarism types.

A Brief History of Japanese Militarisms

During the Edo period (1603–1868), the Tokugawa Bakufu (shogunate) ruled Japan from Tokyo. Tokugawa Ieyasu consolidated power through war, but what followed was 250 years of peace and stability. The intrusion of Western powers, most notably by Commodore Matthew Perry who sailed into Yokohama Bay in 1853 with his infamous black ships, led to the steady decline in power of the Tokugawa Bakufu, signaling the beginning of the end the Edo period. The United States followed the international relations playbook and swiftly forced unequal treaties upon Japan. The erosion of Japanese sovereignty was a rude awakening, and the bitter lessons of great power politics have informed government leaders since. Though Japan's most iconic symbol of militarism, the samurai, is often associated with the Edo period, in reality, they were a minority group. Many of this elite warrior class, most notably from Satsuma and Chōshū, would play an important role in the development of the succeeding Meiji government; however, they were valued more for their bureaucratic skills than their ability to wield a sword. Japanese security policy moving forward was as much influenced by the norms of the Western powers as any militaristic tradition at home.

The Meiji Period (1868–1912)

Capturing all of the significant societal changes during the Meiji period is a herculean, if not impossible, endeavor. As such, this section focuses on four issue areas that most directly relate to militarism: (1) legitimacy of the state, (2) state religion (3) armed forces, and (4) foreign policy.

The Meiji Restoration is regarded as the beginning of modern Japan. After successfully overthrowing the Tokugawa Bakufu, Meiji leaders quickly sought to address international and domestic problems. In international affairs, the government renegotiated the unequal treaties signed with Western powers. China, for centuries the nexus of power in East Asia, was a shadow of its former self after just a few decades of Western semicolonialism. The balance of power in international relations had a significant impact on domestic and foreign policy. Simultaneously, domestic debates over cultural identity, race theory, and direction of the nation shaped foreign policy. Japan sought recognition as a modern and equal nation to the Western powers. This motivation was not only due to strategic power balancing but also due to a desire for prestige and respect. To avoid China's fate and regain its sovereignty, the Meiji government adopted the philosophy of *fukoku kyōhei*, or "rich nation, strong army." Japan internalized the "rules of the game" in international relations, what historian Harry Harootunian describes as "overcome by modernity."[6] To ensure Japan's survival, the Meiji government worked toward legitimizing its rule, modernizing its economic policies and legal codes, and building a cohesive national identity.

Though the imperial line dated back to antiquity, the emperor was rarely the center of Japanese economic and political affairs. During the Edo period, *daimyō* (feudal lords) governed autonomous domains and held allegiance most strongly to the Tokugawa Bakufu. Based in Kyoto, the emperor was the final authority in political affairs yet effectively remained isolated from state affairs. While he was considered the legitimate ruler of Japan, rarely did the emperor serve in an active role as a uniting symbol for the public. Meiji government leaders understood that in order to legitimatize their newfound authority and effectively exercise power, the emperor had to be restored as the ultimate symbol of authority of the nation. Historians have referred to the elaborate and, at times, forceful implementation of restoring imperial rule as "internal colonization."[7] The young Meiji emperor toured the four main Japanese islands to unite the public under a single powerful symbol. Before the Meiji Restoration, the emperor rarely made public appearances. By having a presence across the countryside, yet remaining physically separated by an imposing entourage, the emperor established a visceral link to the common person while maintaining an aura of divinity. The locations the emperor visited became public spaces where Japanese congregated and celebrated the nation. Historian Takashi Fujitani carefully details these "mnemonic sites," or "material vehicles of meaning that either helped construct a memory of an emperor-centered national past that, ironically, had never been known or served as symbolic markers for commemorations of present national accomplishments and the possibilities of the future."[8] These sites later served as locations for celebrating military victories during the interwar period.

Establishing a state religion was also critical to legitimizing the Meiji government and constructing a national identity. The emperor had long been considered a "living deity with magical powers," and according to some accounts, during imperial processions, villagers gathered dirt-covered pebbles kicked up by imperial horses believing that they would bring good luck and a plentiful harvest.[9] The government aggressively promoted Shinto as the state religion and foundation of the educational system. Before the Meiji Restoration, Shinto and Buddhism were highly syncretic, sharing places of worship across a decentralized network of shrines and temples. The government established the *jingikan* (Department of Divinities) to separate the two religions, solidifying Shinto as a unifying force of Japanese cultural identity. What followed was a "frenzied move to suppress Buddhism, and consequently, many Buddhist artifacts were damaged, or destroyed."[10] The violence instigated by the government under the guise of religion is telling of how militarism developed over the following five decades. Japan's colonial expeditions were supported by the divinity of the emperor, and thus, the righteousness of the mission.

Establishing a modern military was a priority for the government, which was concerned with encroaching Western powers and domestic instability. In April 1871, three years into the Meiji period, the government established an imperial army of approximately ten thousand soldiers recruited from restoration forces.[11] By 1873, Japan had instituted universal conscription, which required three years of active service and four years of reserve service from all males of age.[12] Conscription is important for understanding militarism in modern Japan. Though Japanese soldiers have been portrayed as zealous practitioners of Bushido up to World War II,[13] conscription was an unpopular and contested policy. To former samurai elites, conscription represented the end of the class system that privileged their abilities and afforded them numerous rights not provided to the majority of the population. In other words, the rules that governed society changed, and so did their rule. On the other hand, nonelites rejected what they believed was a "blood tax," and numerous protests against the new government policy broke out throughout the country.[14] Thus, "the strong discipline and fierce loyalty shown by Japanese soldiers in the later decades were by no means timeless traditional elements of Japan's 'national character.' "[15] Regardless of time period, the majority of the population does not draw their lineage from the warrior samurai class.[16] The establishment of several elite military schools and war professionalized the military and normalized a national standing force as an essential feature of the state. As Onuf reminds, "exercising choices, agents act on, and not just in, the context within which they operate, collectively changing its institutional features, and themselves."[17] In short, the institutionalization of the military militarized the civilian population.

The government aggressively spent and distributed technologies to remake the private sector into an independent and sustainable military-industrial complex. Kōzō Yamamura contends "the 'strong army' policy, combined with the wars, was the principal motivation behind creating and expanding the arsenals and other publicly-financed shipyards and modern factories which acted as highly effective centers for the absorption and dissemination of Western technologies and skills."[18] Participation in foreign wars generated demand, helping the struggling private shipbuilding, machinery, and machine tools industry.[19] The sheer speed of Japan's economic growth was astounding. Within a decade of the Meiji Restoration, the government had developed four major arsenals with satellite plants and three government shipyards that were "fully engaged in supplying the needs of a modern military force."[20] The strong links between government and industry were critical to the growth of militarism. Through the Ministry of Construction, the government ensured the efforts of the private sector closely complemented security policy. For example, on the eve of the First Sino-Japanese War, government-supported arsenals went into "a 24-hour production schedule to increase the output of ships, guns, shells, and other military needs, and the largest private shipyards, such as Ishikawajima and Kawasaki, were also called upon to upgrade their technological competence and increase production."[21]

The international environment also influenced the Meiji government. Meiji leaders were preoccupied with two main issues, establishing a greater presence in Korea and renegotiating unequal treaties. Japan's first major foreign policy success on the Korean Peninsula was the Treaty of Kanghwa in 1876. It gave Japan access to key trading ports and, more importantly, a footprint on the continent to challenge Chinese and Russian influence in Korea. For Meiji leaders such as Prince Yamagata Aritomo, Korea was critical to the security strategy of establishing a colonial buffer zone ("zone of advantage") necessary for protecting mainland Japan ("zone of sovereignty").[22] Over the next few decades, the government and public intellectuals grappled with the ethics and ideologies of who and what comprised the nation. By the early 1920s, colonial possessions became integral components of the empire, thus expanding Japan's zone of sovereignty. This fueled the government's anxiety over its security and fueled legitimization of security policies seeking to establish more zones of advantage. Consequently, the independence, prestige, and boldness of the military increased. These issues would arise a few decades later during the Manchurian Incident when the Kwantung army manufactured an invasion of Northeastern China. Just a few decades prior, military officials were "relatively cautious" and resisted popular jingoistic attitudes.[23] It was not until the euphoria of later military successes did Japan dedicate its resources to full-scale imperialism.

The next major foreign policy victory for Japan was the Treaty of Shimonoseki, which was signed following the 1894–1895 Sino-Japanese War. After achieving an unexpected lopsided victory, Japan gained territorial concessions, development rights, sizable war reparations, and most importantly the respect of the international community. Japan's rising status fueled an enormous outpouring of domestic support and national pride. Japan's incursions in Korea and China established a pattern of the press and political opponents of the government propagating Korean independence from China under the "guise of Asia-wide (pan-Asian) solidarity," followed by the government limiting but not sanctioning such movements as "it moved cautiously in a similar direction."[24] Similar to the strategy of establishing the divinity of the emperor, pan-Asianism was an elaborate tool utilized by nationalists and military forces to justify aggressive militarism. Japan's military successes during the Meiji period reached its zenith after its remarkable victory over a Western power in the Russo-Japanese War. Securing victory in September 1905, Japan gained some territorial possessions, but most significantly, dominion over Korea, later formally colonized in 1910.

Its aggressive policies in East Asia provided the leverage the government needed to renegotiate the unequal treaties with the Western powers. During the Iwakura Mission of the early 1870s, Japan was a voracious student looking to mimic Western political, military, economic, and cultural institutions. Over the next few decades, the government slowly regained rights over tariffs, territories, and trade. Eventually, Japan forced unequal treaties upon Asian countries, and it annexed Korea, which went unchallenged by the West. The fact that its early military successes allowed the government to renegotiate treaties and gain a prominent position in world affairs certified its belief that what it was doing was justified.

The Meiji period provides several important insights concerning Japanese militarism. First, colonialism did not begin with Korea—it started at home. The first territories the Meiji government gained were Ezo (Hokkaidō) and the Ryūkyū Islands (Okinawa). Additionally, the imperial processions allowed the emperor to establish sovereignty over the main Japanese islands, with each step analogous to placing a flag in the ground of unclaimed territories. Early Meiji leaders sought to remake society, one obedient and loyal to the divine emperor, and hardworking to build a rich nation and strong army. This brand of militarism was not initially expansionist. The government and public intellectuals were in the process of constructing fundamental characteristics of Japanese identity and had not yet developed a colonial doctrine of empire and race. Hence, militarism during the early Meiji period was defensive and inward looking. This survival militarism was defined by the government's creation and control of the military to fulfill the goals of a vulnerable developing nation. Even with several military successes, the public was not ready to support empire building. The public suffered from war fatigue as often as it was overtaken by the deliria of victory. Government coffers were pushed to their limits by questionable international excursions, and Japan endured significant losses in the Russo-Japanese War. Up to the Meiji period, the common person did not pay the costs of war so directly.

Second, it was not only the distribution of power that fueled the rich nation, strong army ideology but also the feeling that Japan was unmodern and backward. These sentiments would eventually be overtaken by feelings of pride in Japanese uniqueness and anti-Western attitudes. Nationalism in the Meiji period sought to *mimic* the West. Japan's evolving ideologies led to different types of militarism during the interwar and World War II periods; militarisms defined by racism, military control of the state, and arrogance. Meiji institutions and ideologies served as fertile ground for the imperial war machine in the succeeding period; the war machine did not create Meiji institutions and ideologies.

Interwar Period (1918–1939)

By the end of the Meiji period, Japan had fully transformed from a developing state to an expansionist empire, possessing colonies (Korea, Taiwan, and the southern half of the Sakhalin Islands), a strong military, a modern economy, relatively equal treaties with the West, and unequal treaties with East Asia. The path toward empire and confrontation with the West was not a foregone conclusion. During the interwar period, Japan was divided between democratic internationalism and fascist isolationism, with the latter eventually winning the day.

The Taishō period (1912–1926), often referred to as the Taishō democracy, was the model for democracy and modernity in the non-Western world and yet, it was here that militarism took hold of the state. This period demonstrates the extreme sides of Japan, a nation torn between cooperating with status-quo powers and placing faith in its ability to independently progress through power projection. The militarists were able to wrest the nation from internationalist forces because of weak democratic institutions, subterfuge, and eventually popular support. Interwar period militarism is defined by two contradictory beliefs: (1) Japan could carve out a space for itself among the Western powers; and (2) Japan could not be accepted by the West and thus must prepare for an inevitable war. Neither a defensive nor offensive realist account of the Taishō period completely captures this internal struggle. Japan went to war not because the capabilities of the West were fundamentally more threatening, but because Japan's conceptions of the West and itself changed.

During the Taishō period, the Japanese government was an emperor-centered democracy, a hybrid form of government full of compromise and contradictions. Here, it is worth considering the difficulties faced by developing democracies. For most of world history, the majority of people were not free citizens who possessed inalienable rights. The Meiji Constitution was passed only twenty-three years before the beginning of the Taishō period, and during the 1920s Japan was in the process of remaking a population of previously nonpolitical peasants into modern citizens, albeit imperial subjects. Prior to the Meiji period, society was divided into a four-class system consisting of samurai, farmers, artisans, and merchants. Only samurai possessed substantive rights; the rest of the population was trapped in hereditary positions. However, half a century after the end of the Edo period, it was possible for a farmer born in the countryside to commute to a factory owned by foreigners in the city and work alongside members of all social classes. The Meiji and Taishō governments not only established basic rights but also wholly remade the Japanese economy, technology, and society. However, democracy was ultimately disrupted by a combination of shocks, namely "economic depression, intense social conflict, military expansions, and the assassination of prime ministers and leading capitalists."[25] The depression provided an opportunity for military leaders to seize the nation.

The strength of democracy was inversely related to the strength of the military. During the Taishō period, military officials were deeply involved in the policymaking process. Militarists took advantage of public discontent over rising rice prices, inflation, and a weak economy to justify their expansionist agenda and to marginalize government officials. Militarists argued, "Japan's economic difficulties could be resolved by moving into Manchuria and other parts of China where supposedly unlimited reservoirs could be tapped."[26] Ambassador Kitaoka Shinichi summarizes this expansionist mentality by stating, "The idea that a country could not make headway without sufficient territory, and that military force could be used to create such a territory, began to grow. It was this approach that Japan ended up endorsing."[27] With each military success, militarists grew bolder and sought to extend their reach further. After the Russo-Japanese War, they aggressively pressed the government to increase the size of the military. As Onuf states, "Institutionalizing expediates the assignment of value to and through rules offering instruction."[28] And instruct they did. During this period, military spending comprised over 30 percent of the national budget and would increase to over 70 percent beginning in 1937, the start of the Second Sino-Japanese War.[29] The increasing size and prestige of the military allowed Japan to expand the scope of its colonial aspirations. Under the pretense of supporting the Anglo-Japanese alliance, Japan entered World War I with intentions of increasing its international standing and taking hold of German possessions in China.[30] In 1918, Japan inserted itself in the Siberian intervention with far more troops than requested by its allies and stayed two years after the other powers had abandoned the mission.[31] The government utilized the military to increase its colonial possessions, international prestige, and maintain domestic stability, hence the government and military were mostly aligned in these early expeditions.

Over time, the military became increasingly uncontrollable. In 1931, two Kwantung army officers plotted to take Manchuria from Chinese nationalists in the name of the Empire of Japan. They reasoned that taking Manchuria was vital to protecting Japan from Russia, provided valuable resources for the economy, and ultimately good for Mongolians.[32] On September 18, 1931, a small cabal within the Kwantung army blew up a small section of the South Manchurian

Railroad and used this opportunity to blame China and increase hostilities. Following the attack, the Kwantung army occupied all of southern Manchuria in an independent and illegal military campaign.

The government in Tokyo was powerless during the entire fiasco. Before the Manchurian Incident, the emperor expressed concern over the rogue military leaders, leading Minister of War Minami Jirō to dispatch General Tatekawa Yoshitsugu to rein in the Kwantung army.[33] The army acted before Tatekawa arrived. During the Kwantung army's incursions into southern Manchuria, Foreign Minister Shidehara Kijūrō desperately tried to settle the dispute with China. The army rebuffed Shidehara's efforts, claiming that their actions were protected by the "independence of the supreme command." Moreover, the army received enthusiastic public support, further limiting the power of the government. Even the emperor could do little to control the army. Prime Minister Inukai Tsuyoshi contemplated asking the emperor for assistance in stopping the rebels but did not out of fear that the army's independence would reveal the throne's weakness.[34] The Inukai cabinet ultimately yielded to the military's demands, sending two army divisions into Shanghai to quell anti-Japanese demonstrations against the illegal activities. On March 9, 1932, the army formally established the state of Manchukuo. This episode demonstrates that the military was beginning to make independent political and strategic decisions on behalf of the government; not on its orders. This was a new kind of militarism; one defined by the *manufacturing* of opportunities instead of responding to threats.

The boldness of the military is apparent in attempted coups and assassinations of opposition forces, sometimes referred to as "government by assassination." The military coups in 1932 and 1936 resulted in the assassinations of Prime Minister Inukai, several prominent politicians, and opposition military leaders. Although both coups were suppressed, the light punishment of the rebels and boldness of the military signaled the end of effective civilian control of the government.

Japan's relationship with the West deteriorated significantly during the interwar period. Following the Allies' victory in World War I, Japan pressed China with the infamous Twenty-One Demands. Up to this point, the West was relatively accepting of Japan's intrusions into China's affairs. However, Japan suffered an embarrassing blow to its status when the British and Americans sided with the Chinese on some demands, resulting in significant modifications to the original proposal. Though Japan gained control of German possessions in China and railway rights, this event laid credence to the belief that the West was the ultimate adjudicator of its foreign affairs. Another conflict between Japan and the West arose during negotiations of the Treaty of Versailles. Japanese leaders advocated for a racial equality clause in the founding charter of the League of Nations but were denied. This defeat drudged up memories of the humiliating Gentlemen's Agreement of 1907. The Immigration Act of 1924 would expand on the limits of the Gentlemen's Agreement and banned Japanese immigration altogether. The end of World War I was not the beginning of a more egalitarian era.

In 1922, several Japanese leaders denounced the 5:5:3 tonnage ratios for the United Kingdom, United States, and Japan that were established at the Five-Power Naval Limitation Treaty of Washington. Though the agreement was favorable to Japan in that it artificially limited the arms production of the United States—a two-ocean power—and provided relief to a Japanese economy stretched thin by war, nationalists saw the conference as a clear sign of Japan's secondary status in the international community. They found the London Naval Treaty of 1930 equally insulting. Following the Manchuria Incident, the League of Nations responded with the Lytton Commission report criticizing Japanese aggression. The report outlined a plan that would result in limited control of the new state, to which Japan responded by leaving the League of Nations altogether.[35] These series of conflicts led many to believe that coexistence with the West was impossible and war was inevitable.

The interwar period highlights the difficulty the literature has with analyzing militarism. In one sense, the period is an example of Japanese democracy at its zenith before World War II. Increased enfranchisement, improved standard of living, and cooperation with the West according to the rules of the game indicated Japan was becoming a more peaceful nation. On the other hand, it was increasingly reckless and antagonistic. Was Japan more or less militaristic than in previous eras? The conventional indicators of militarism, such as military expenditures, reveal little. In the 1920s, the government cut force size, arms, and defense spending.[36] Yet Japan was not less expansionistic in objectives and practice. As the government cut defense spending, it fostered military education curricula in middle schools and high schools and refined its increasingly racist worldview. War capabilities retracted while the logic of war expanded. What is apparent is that the material and ideational conditions had changed. Kitaoka concludes that the growing population led to the idea that not only was expansion necessary but also that "expansion of the nation meant national glory, and that expansion was good."[37] That is, "interests are recognizable to us as the reasons we give for our conduct."[38] The *idea* that expansionism was necessary was only as powerful as it could be justified to the public. The rules of the international system, which allowed for Western imperialism and stymied Japanese growth, made those justifications easier to make.

World War II Japan (1937–1945)

At first glance, it seems that colonial expansion, end of cooperation with the West, and attack on Pearl Harbor are natural progressions of Japanese militarization of the previous five decades. A realist analysis of Japan's security behavior would conclude that the international system compelled it to engage in balancing behavior. Indeed, foreign policy before World War II was decidedly realpolitik. On September 27, 1940, Japan formed one-third of the Tripartite Pact and proceeded to sign the Japanese-Soviet Neutrality Pact on April 13, 1941. Japan was preparing for war.

However, Japanese security policy did not follow a linear trajectory, nor was it ideologically coherent. As demonstrated in the Meiji and Taishō periods, the government sought ways to cooperate with the West and rein in the military. Had it possessed the ability to control the military and cooperate with the West, militarism would have been very different.

World War II militarism was markedly different from preceding types. Japan's actions were hyperaggressive, risky, and excessively cruel. A simple rubric describing war expenditures and listing body counts provides little insight into motivations and practices. Structural-based arguments have difficulty explaining security behavior leading up to World War II because the international distribution of power was increasingly favorable to Japan as it became stronger. Realism can account for the West's response to Japanese expansion, but it cannot explain why Japan was so willing to put itself at odds with clearly militarily superior nations that, for the most part, accepted its rapid growth.[39] Japan's changing perceptions of the West and its increasingly racist ideology compelled the government to remake the rules of the game.

Following the establishment of Manchukuo, Japan dedicated its resources to total war. The Sino-Japanese War was followed by the colonization of several regions in China, French Indochina, the Philippines, and several other territories in Asia. The expansion of territory alone provides an important, but incomplete, story of security policy. Japan's behavior within the colonies *defined* World War II militarism. "Total war militarism" was the extreme manifestation of ideologies and strategies of the previous eras.

Japan believed it was the center of a Greater East Asia Co-Prosperity Sphere. The Kyoto School philosophy developed the foundations of this belief in the 1920s. Leading intellectuals such as Tanabe Hajime propagated a theory of the "logic of species," arguing for a multiethnic nation under a single Japanese identity.[40] According to Naoki Sakai, "Tanabe's Logic of Species was a response to such needs of Japanese Imperialism and it represented a philosophical attempt to undermine ethnic nationalism."[41] This philosophy found a following with empire proponents in government. One government document, titled "An Investigation of the Global Policy with the Yamato Race as Nucleus," outlines the racial hierarchy in East Asia. This report guided policymakers and propagated "the subordination of other Asians in the Co-Prosperity Sphere," an "unfortunate consequence of wartime exigencies, but the very essence of official policy."[42] Japan's hierarchical view of the world reflected a lack of confidence in its security and cultural strength, which it tried to rectify via comparison with the poorer and weaker East Asia countries. Historian Robert Eskildsen explains:

Japanese colonialism happened concurrently with and contributed much to Japan's modernizing process. The discourse on civilization and savagery that gained popularity at the time of the Taiwan Expedition points to a similar pattern. Even before Japan established a formal colonial empire, debates about using Japanese military power overseas drew heavily on the imagery and rhetoric of Japan's own efforts at modernizing. Despite being shot through with contradictions and ambivalence, the idea of exporting the Western civilizing impulse to the indigenous population of Taiwan helped justify, naturalize, and explain the concurrent effort to modernize Japan. Mimesis of Western imperialism, in other words, went hand in hand with mimesis of Western civilization.[43]

Colonialism was modern and natural. Military leaders such as Colonel Ishiwara Kanji developed "an apocalyptic view of the international scene through his idiosyncratic studies of Buddhism and world history," predicting that a "cataclysmic 'final war' loomed inevitably between Japan and the United States."[44] The public was "indoctrinated to see the conflict in Asia and the Pacific as an act which would purify the self, the nation, Asia, and ultimately the whole world."[45] Japanese security policy was not only a strategic rebalancing of power in the international system but also the practice of establishing an ideological racial hierarchy. Remaking the world required transformation at home.

The militarization of education became especially pronounced after 1941. Japanese elementary schools were reorganized as *kokumin gakkō* (National People's Schools), where they implemented a form of highly regimented and militarized education that took both its name (a direct translation of *Volksschule*) and inspiration from Nazi Germany.[46] Students were rebranded as "little nationals" and provided war-related training—boys were taught martial arts and girls were trained to use *naginata* (traditional Japanese pole weapon) and in nursing. The Ministry of Education implemented a curriculum that ensured "selfless dedication" to the emperor and nation. For example, one elementary school textbook included a flowery narrative about the honor of dying for one's country and being enshrined at Yasukuni.[47] Students were bombarded with propaganda describing enemy combatants as "beasts" and "devils" and the homeland as pure.[48] The indoctrination of youth was best symbolized by *hinomaru bentō* (rising sun lunch boxes), comprised of rice and a red plum arranged to resemble the Japanese flag.[49] The boxes instilled loyalty to the nation, built solidarity with the military, and fostered unity. The pervasiveness of militarization extended to the playground, where students played war games instead of tag, and children's magazines glorified war. Students were wholly mobilized for the war effort. All middle school students committed one year to building munitions at factories and regularly worked in the most dangerous air raid areas digging firebreaks. When students came of age and entered the war, their mothers sewed one thousand stitches in the shape of tigers into their clothing for their safe return and success for the empire. The parallels with Spartan mothers sending their sons to war and expecting them to return with or on their shields are more than apparent.

The full mobilization of the public, young and old, led to the most extreme violations of acceptable war conduct.[50] Although realism can account for the scope of Japanese expansionism during World War II, it has difficulty outlining the logic of its scale and character. The wanton violence did little to secure the homeland and only invigorated opposition forces. Its actions were often irrational and not strategic. Japanese "prejudices affected their war conduct: the way they evaluated, and frequently misjudged, Allied capabilities; the attitudes and policies they adopted toward other Asians within the Co-Prosperity Sphere, and how they fought and died."[51]

Under the doctrine of the Greater East Asia Co-Prosperity Sphere, many believed they were freeing Asia from the "many years of tyranny under white rule."[52] The Japanese held a genuine belief that they were on a divine mission to create regional solidarity. This mentality was an amalgamation of warped religious and modernity philosophies and self-serving economic interests. Japan did not simply replace one colonizer with another. Japanese dehumanized their colonial subjects and enemy combatants. The list of Japan's war crimes is lengthy. From 1937 to 1945, it colonized several countries, killed hundreds of thousands of noncombatants (Nanjing Massacre, Manila Massacre, and Bataan Death March), and killed millions indirectly (the Vietnamese famine of 1945). Many of those who survived the initial fighting became forced laborers. Japan violated dozens of warfare norms, such as torture, execution of prisoners of war, human experimentation, and use of chemical and biological weapons. The government also operated a vast network of "comfort stations," forcing between 10,000 to 200,000 *ianfu* (comfort women) to provide sex for its soldiers.[53] In total, approximately fifteen million Chinese, four million Indonesians, one million Vietnamese, and several hundred thousand Malaysians and Filipinos were killed.[54]

The Japanese paid for their extremism as well. Thousands of soldiers died fighting in unwinnable battles and one-way kamikaze attacks. Civilians were coerced into believing that they had to fight to the death, and many did. The fighting in Iwo Jima and Okinawa was particularly intense and tragic. Firebombing leveled almost every major city, and Hiroshima and Nagasaki suffered the only use of nuclear weapons on a human population in history, resulting in 140,000 and 70,000 deaths, respectively. In total, approximately 2.1 million soldiers and civilians died, about 3 percent of the total population.[55] The six million soldiers who returned home faced the stark reality that they had fought an unjust war that had led to the end of an imperial line that dated back millennia.

Japan's conduct in World War II cannot be entirely explained by the orientation of the international system, external threats, or internal politics. Ideology shaped how Japan treated its colonial subjects and operated in the wider world. Thus, when scholars discuss Japanese remilitarization, what kind of militarization do they mean? Militarism in the Tokugawa period and the first half of the Meiji period sought to create *internal* security. The Meiji government's chief objective was creating modern citizens. From the second half of the Meiji period to the end of World War II, Japanese militarism sought not only to increase its security from outside forces but also to remake the international order. In the postwar period, the government adopted antimilitarism to increase *external* security. More recently, the government of Japan has pursued the concept of proactive contribution to peace that leverages a combination of military, economic, and diplomatic tools to combat causes of international insecurity. In the span of 150 years, the role of the military, the public's view of the use of force in statecraft, and Japan's place in the international community have undergone remarkable changes. To treat all militarisms as the same sacrifices the valuable lessons that can be drawn from Japan's many mistakes and successes, and it is a disservice to the countless individuals who stood in the way of tyranny.

Postwar Japan (1945–Present)

The remaining chapters in this book investigate the content and direction of Japanese security policy in the postwar period. Therefore, the following section is limited to analysis of the connections and cleavages of different types of militarism before and after World War II.

One of the core features of various militarisms from the Meiji period onward was the primacy of religion. The government prior to and during the war years utilized state Shinto to legitimize its claim to power, justify colonial expansion, construct ethnic and culture-based nationalisms, and garner fanatical devotion to the state. Today, religion is no longer closely linked to politics, removing a critical element of the militarisms of the past. Japan would have difficulty returning to older forms of militarism, and any new type of militarism would have to derive its strength from another source of unity.

The removal of religion from politics was a purposeful attack on militarism. State Shinto was abolished by the Supreme Commander for Allied the Powers (SCAP) in 1945. Soon after, the Shinto Directive abolished Shinto as the official state religion, the Yasukuni Shrine was "demobilized, Shinto altars (*kamidana*) and the Imperial Portrait were removed from all schools, the worship of the

Imperial Palace from afar, imposed upon pupils in Japan and its overseas territories was banned, and visits to Shinto shrines were prohibited."[56] The democratization of Japan, specifically freedom of religion, ensures that the government cannot monopolize religion for political purposes. Whatever links remained between the state and Shinto were met with protests and civil rights litigation. Currently, many local and former national shrines are independently affiliated with the Association of Shinto Shrines.[57]

According to Masako Shibata, education of State Shinto "has never been revived in publicly funded schools since World War II," and "even some hardline nationalist cabinets, which attempted to restore the old notions of national identity and national traditions in education, have been hesitant to stir up the old memory of State Shinto."[58] The Japanese are quite distrustful of religion. In one survey about confidence in seventeen social institutions, "only 13 percent of the respondents in Japan indicated some level of trust in religious groups, putting religious institutions at the bottom of the list," which "reflects a high level of distrust toward religious groups across the board."[59] State Shinto is now associated with the militaristic state, and new religions are often met with skepticism. Religion is unlikely to have a significant role in politics again.

Nevertheless, many in East Asia contend Japan is whitewashing history and remilitarizing. No site is more contested by Japan's former colonies than the Yasukuni Shrine, which has been used to highlight Japan's victimhood during World War II.[60] The Yasukuni Shrine has minimized Japan's colonization of East Asia in the mid-nineteenth and early twentieth centuries and serves as a rallying point for nationalistic groups. Nationalists have used the shrine to encourage antiforeign attitudes and to stand out among a typically apolitical public. These groups seek to restore Japan's former glory and instill pride among the Japanese youth. Several prominent politicians, such as Prime Minister Koizumi and Prime Minister Abe, have visited the shrine in official and unofficial capacities. Indeed, since the 1980s, the Yasukuni Shrine controversy has created tension in East Asia and increased the chance of conflict. However, outsiders usually overstate the importance of the Yasukuni Shrine in Japanese politics and society. Much of the controversial discourse associated with the Yasukuni Shrine is not actually located in the shrine but at the Yūshūkan that shares the same grounds.[61] When politicians visit the shrine to pray, they rarely go into the Yūshūkan, the museum that propagates a whitewashed version of war history. Furthermore, since Japan is a democratic country with strong freedom of speech protections, there is little the government can do to change the narratives propagated by the Yūshūkan.

Many Japanese visit the Yasukuni Shrine to pray for those who died fighting for the nation. According to theologian William Woodard, Japanese "feel guilty about enjoying post-war prosperity by surviving the war and by receiving a state stipendiary for the sacrifice of the death of their sons. They are normally regarded as pacifists and even anti-nationalists, but they also want a healing sanctuary in the shrine supported by the state for which their sons died."[62]

The emperor system has also changed significantly since World War II. During the war eras, the emperor was the symbolic force behind colonialism. Historians debate the centrality of the Shōwa emperor in World War II, but the role of the emperor in contemporary politics is clear—he does not have meaningful influence on politics and security policy. Under the postwar Constitution, the emperor of Japan is "the symbol of the State and the unity of the People, deriving his position from the will of the people with whom resides sovereign power."[63] The end of World War II demystified the emperor's status as a living god, and as a result, proponents of reviving World War II-style militarism can no longer use him to further their agendas.

Takashi Fujitani contends that the emperor system has significantly changed since the end of World War II, highlighting the importance of "radical transformations" and "historical discontinuities" within the emperor system that reveal "which operations of power change over time."[64] Understanding the changing role of the emperor in modern Japan helps differentiate militarisms over the past one hundred years. The emperor system was an elaborate mix of material and ideational discourses that formed an environment conducive to aggressive militarism. According to Fujitani, during the prewar era:

Tokyo underwent massive physical transformations as political elites within the new national and Tokyo governments as well as the Imperial Household Ministry reconstructed it to become a central and open theater for performance of spectacular national pageants. In that age of rising mass nationalism, the masses and the emperor were brought together to Tokyo's new public spaces, the most important being the Imperial Plaza, for enormous ritualized celebrations for themselves and their communion.[65]

In the past, the public was an active participant in constructing the divine status of the emperor and the exceptionalism of the Japanese state. Today, the Constitution separates the emperor from public affairs.

The "de-auratization" of the emperor system was facilitated by communication technologies that not only laid the emperor's humanity bare, but it also "comes long after the Shōwa emperor's self-proclaimed renunciation of divinity in 1946 and the formal, legal/ideological repositioning of political sovereignty from the monarch to the people."[66] In other words, the locus of power no longer sits with the emperor; the public uses the emperor system for their secular purposes. Fujitani's analysis of the Shōwa emperor's funeral and ascension of the Heisei emperor finds that the emperor system highlights the progressive changes in the postwar period and a convenient forgetting of the past. During the enthronement of Akihito, the emperor (now emperor emeritus) emphasized his status as a symbol and an upholder of Japan's "Peace Constitution." Fujitani argues, "despite the charges from the left that the mystery surrounding the *daijosai* [enthronement of the Japanese emperor] threatened a return to the divine emperor of prewar days, media coverage accomplished quite the opposite. Rather than enhancing the monarch's cult value, mystery coupled with titillation and these snatched glimpses completely deauratized him. No longer, as in imperial Japan, did the emperor's panoptic gaze discipline the masses."[67] The emperor's increased presence in society has led to the opposite effect that it had during the Meiji period.

Another significant development regarding the emperor and politics is that all three emperors following the end of World War II have made it difficult for conservatives to utilize the throne for their causes. After the enshrinement of the fourteen Class A war criminals at the Yasukuni Shrine, the Shōwa emperor stopped visiting the shrine. The emperor emeritus Akihito never visited the shrine during his thirty-year tenure. Akihito is also quite the nontraditionalist—acknowledging the imperial family's Korean ancestry, speaking in plain language, apologizing for Japan's colonial history, and marrying a commoner. Akihito's son, emperor Naruhito has maintained a low profile but shares the same liberal and global outlook. On rare occasions and prior to his enthronement, Naruhito has made oblique statements about the need to look back at the past humbly and correctly. The naming of the last two eras, Heisei (creating peace) and Reiwa (auspicious peace), highlight the general ethos of the Chrysanthemum Throne after

World War II. Modern nationalism, and the militarism that can derive from it, clings to a dehistoricized notion of the emperor and imaginary past. Yet nationalists are marginalized by the very symbols that they rally behind.

Japan is also a long-established and robust democracy with firm civilian control of the military. Americans did not introduce democracy to Japan during the occupation. The Meiji period and early Taishō period showed signs of a healthy party system and expanded the franchise to millions. Japan was not a complete democracy because the emperor was the source of political power and the military sabotaged the democratic process, but within 150 years it had evolved from an extremely stratified class system, where the vast majority of the population were peasant subjects, to a country with full suffrage, free and fair elections, religious freedom, academic freedom, and freedom of press.

The strength of democracy goes hand-in-hand with civilian control of the military. Civilian control is the "distribution of decision-making power in which civilians have exclusive authority to decide on national politics and their implementation."[68] Moreover, it is "civilians alone who determine which particular policies, or aspects of policies, the military implements, and the civilians alone define the boundaries between policy-making and policy implementation."[69] In East Asia, Japan enjoys the highest amount of civilian control in the areas of elite recruitment, public policy, internal security, national defense, and military organization—what political scientist Aurel Croissant has referred to as "civilian supremacy."[70]

Concerning military practices Croissant states, "While a certain degree of autonomy is necessary for the military to fulfill its missions and roles, civilian control requires the ability of civilians to define its range and boundaries"[71] This is best exemplified in the current debates around Article 9. Critics of the Abe administration argue reinterpreting Article 9 is tantamount to remilitarization. However, this effort to expand the role of the JSDF is not coming from the military but from a civilian prime minister. Moreover, the reinterpretation is a significant concession; Abe sought a constitutional amendment in his first term. Abe extended deliberation in the Diet hoping to clarify to the public the legal limitations of collective self-defense and provide adequate time to consider the merits of his policy recommendations.

The separation between the military and the government is clearly outlined in the Ministry of Defense (MOD) guidelines and white papers. The prime minister of Japan, a civilian, is the commander-in-chief of the JSDF. Military authority then proceeds to the minister of defense (civilian) of the MOD. The prime minister and minister of defense are advised by the chief of staff (military) of the Joint Staff Council and the National Security Council (civilian officials from the Ministry of Foreign Affairs and MOD), which was established in 2013. Military officers do not have a direct link to the prime minister and must go through the normal channels of communication; the system is designed to have several layers between the prime minister and the military. This is vastly different from the 1920s, when high-ranking army and navy officers had direct access to the emperor via the mechanism of the "independence of the supreme command."[72]

MILITARISM WITH ADJECTIVES

From the Tokugawa period to the present, Japan has pursued a myriad of militaristic policies and ideologies with significant consequences domestically and internationally. The diverse security motivations, practices, and justifications of the government and the public suggest militarism is much more complicated than currently depicted in the literature. The standard pacifism-militarism analytical framework fails to provide deeper insight into the creation and consequences of policies reflective of unique individuals, relationships, and historical contexts. Comparative analysis of militarism across temporal and geographic cases would be a fruitful exercise in determining the content and direction of contemporary Japanese security policy. This book proposes a multiple militarisms analytical framework to achieve sharper analytical differentiation among militarisms.

This framework denaturalizes the prevailing assumptions about militarism and provides some basic guidelines for analyzing security policy. Historian Ingo Trauschweizer argues it is problematic to rely on normative definitions based on the most extreme historical examples.[73] The term "militarism" is commonly associated with interwar-period Japan, Nazi Germany, and present-day North Korea. Though these cases are surely examples of militarism, further scrutiny reveals diverse motivations and practices. The United States, for example, has fought more wars and acquired many more destructive weapons than the aforementioned cases, but one would be hard-pressed to conclude it is similarly militaristic. The United States' democratic values, civilian control of government, and general acceptance in the international community legitimatize its security behavior.

To begin, the multiple militarisms framework does not assume militarism is aggressive, immoral, or singular. Sanitizing the term allows for the examination of security policy according to a case's unique context and circumvents normative biases. Second, the multiple militarisms analytical framework encourages analysis of how force is used. Is the military used for defensive or offensive purposes? Does the military represent a single state, or does it participate in multilateral missions? Does it participate in nontraditional security missions, such as reconstruction, disaster relief, or election monitoring? Addressing these questions illustrates the types of militarism states practice. Third, empirical data, not theory, should guide analysis. Realism assumes states, as rational actors, engage in balancing behavior because of tangible and perceived threats. This assumption is built on normative prescriptions of what theorists believe states *should* do. Analysis of weaponry, defense budgets, and elite rhetoric should focus on actual practices and less on predicted outcomes or unsaid motivations. Fourth, an eclectic approach utilizing *only* the complementary elements of different theories in the field of international relations is problematic and should be avoided. Although both material and ideational variables shape militarism, researchers should avoid cherry-picking hypotheses from competing schools of thought to fill in gaps in theory. For example, one cannot assume that a culture of antimilitarism explains constrained security policy while also arguing that international anarchy compels states to always balance against threats. The assumptions regarding the permanence of the international system and the lack of actor agency are ontologically incompatible with arguments highlighting the malleability of interests and impacts of ideational variables on state behavior. In other words, theories of absolutes are not compatible with theories of change. Fifth, beyond the examination of data related to security, such as the military-industrial complex and defense expenditures, careful attention should be paid to the general environment that cultivates or represses militarism. Demographic, economic, political, and ideational variables significantly impact a state's willingness and *ability* to pursue certain kinds of militarism.

These general guidelines are not a definitive list of what can comprise a multiple militarisms analytical framework. Depending on the case, one may need to examine other dimensions of security policy. I propose this framework to reverse the conventional logic. Instead of the question, Have material and ideational environments caused militarism? one asks, What kind of militarism has a state adopted, if at all, given the material and ideational environment? Before militarism type can be determined, a baseline understanding of the core elements of militarism is needed.

Although a recurring topic in international relations scholarship, political scientists have not critically examined militarism. In the foundational book, *History of Militarism: Civilian and Military*, historian Alfred Vagts reasons that militarism is not the opposite of pacifism, but "more, and sometimes less than the love of war," as it can exist and even flourish in peacetime.[74] Militarism "presents a vast array of customs, interests, prestige, actions, and thought associated with armies and wars and yet transcending true military purposes. . . . Its influence is unlimited in scope. It may permeate all society and become dominant over all industry and arts."[75] In this classic definition, the commonly understood dimension of militarism is emphasized, the encroachment of military forces into the civilian world. Yet, as demonstrated in the Meiji period, militarism draws much of its strength from discourse and motivations not entirely related to matters of war. Besides, this definition suggests that the causal arrow is unidirectional; militarism reshapes the nonmilitary world and not the other way around. The public can be as culpable as military elites in shaping and propagating militaristic ideologies and practices.

Ingo Trauschweizer contends that militarism "may best be understood as the connection of militarization of the state and of society. It requires a strong military ethos, a social system threatened with rupture, a mythical reading of the nation's past, and a sense of fear—of one's neighbors or of ideological foes—that subsumes political culture."[76] Trauschweizer suggests the concept of militarism is not static, and that the meaning can evolve depending on the strategic and political needs of those who brandish the term. For example, one reason why Nazi Germany and Imperial Japan are typically considered ideal types of militarism is because these countries lost World War II. If the Axis powers had won the war, one could assume British and American war conduct would be severely criticized in the present day. How states understand the relationship between military force and state formation has changed over time. In the late nineteenth century, many Europeans measured national greatness in military strength and colonial possessions.[77] During the Cold War, militarism took on a different connotation depending on the ideological orientation of the concept holder. Marxists believed militarism was a result of capitalistic societies, and the West argued it was about the failure of civilian control.[78] By the end of the Cold War, states rapidly decolonized, and the worth of a nation was measured by how much it could protect and promote democracy. The use of the military and the concept of militarism drastically changed within a hundred-year span. Militarism is derived from different contexts, comes in different forms, and requires careful analytical differentiation.

Martin Shaw contends that militarism should be specified not in terms of "how military practices are regarded, but how they *influence* social relations in general."[79] Furthermore, militarism "denotes the penetration of social relations in general by military relations; in militarization, militarism is extended, in demilitarization, it contracts."[80] Richard Kohn proposes utilizing the term "militarization" instead of "militarism" to avoid the political connotations of the latter.[81] Militarization is "the degree to which a society's institutions, politics, behaviors, thought, and values are devoted to military power and shaped by war."[82] However, analyses focusing on degree instead of type leads to counting instances of militarism and an overreliance on the indicator, military expenditures. Determining the degree of militarization is crucial to understanding the strength of a militarism type, but the concepts are distinct. Additionally, this definition's focus on evidence of militarism neglects scenarios where militarism was rejected or modified. The tenets of militarism that a state adopts, or rejects, can illustrate the kind of militarism it has constructed.

This book defines militarism as the following: (1) the acceptance of the use of violence as a legitimate tool of statecraft; (2) the merging of government, military, and public ideologies of war; and (3) the spread of militaristic discourse throughout the physical and ideational dimensions of a civilization, such as through art, physical sites, and public education. This broad definition salvages much of the literature identifying militarism in states while requiring the researcher to provide additional analysis to clarify type.

From this baseline definition, one can identify militarism type. Where to begin? Due to the dearth of analysis within international relations scholarship on the subject, I look toward other fields of research, namely democracy studies, to construct the multiple militarisms framework. In identifying democracy sub-types, Collier and Levitsky call attention to the challenge that researchers face in constructing typologies, the tension between increasing analytical differenti-ation and maintaining conceptual validity. One method of creating subtypes is to utilize Sartori's ladder of generality. As one moves up the ladder of generality, one finds more cases of the root concept, and as one moves down, fewer cases exist.[83] This approach is useful for identifying cases of militarism but requires an additional step to determine type. Hence, Collier and Levitsky propose the use of diminished subtypes, accomplished by removing attributes from the base-line concept to explain each case. This approach is insufficient for our purposes because it assumes there is an ideal type of militarism. For example, one can have an "illiberal democracy" but not a "illiberal militarism."

Unlike the concept of democracy, where procedures and institutions are eas-ily identifiable indicators of an ideal type, militarism is a broader concept that lacks similar indicators. The researcher can create a minimum list of militarism indicators to establish a root concept but should be transparent on how the list was determined and acknowledge that subtypes of this root concept reflect a normative bias. Another method is "precising" the definition by adding defin-ing attributes to the root concept.[84] Precising allows for finer analytical differ-entiation because the additional attributes illustrate the uniqueness of each case. However, this method risks overly modifying the root concept and creating types far removed from the original concept. Colin Elman shows the usefulness of explanatory typologies, which are "multidimensional classifications based on an explicitly stated theory."[85] Explanatory typologies "invoke both the descriptive and classificatory roles of typologies," defining compound concepts and assigning case type.[86]

In determining militarism type, this book proposes the method of utilizing the ladder of generality (abstraction) to determine the existence of militarism, precising type by identifying defining attributes, and utilizing explanatory typo-logical analysis to confirm the content and direction of that militarism type. The researcher starts with a case that demonstrates the baseline definition of "mili-tarism" and proceeds to add identifying descriptors to illustrate type. In other words, militarism with adjectives.

There are several strands of research within political science, sociology, and history that can help identify militarism types. Neorealists, for example, have debated the prudence of offensive and defensive security postures. Constructivists such as Daisuke Akimoto utilize Andrew Oros's security identity framework to classify four kinds of security identity—a pacifist state, a UN peacekeeper, a normal state, and a U.S. ally.[87] Bhubhindar Singh has supplemented realist works with identity-based analysis, contending that Japan has shifted from a "peace state" to an "international state."[88] Leif-Eric Easley draws a difference between unilateral and multilateral defense postures in addition to considering the "pacifism" versus "extensive use of force" traditional model.[89] Martin Shaw identifies at least two forms of militarism, classical modern militarism (industrialized total warfare) and contemporary militarism (global surveillance warfare).[90] Historian Andrew J. Bacevich calls attention to "misleading and dangerous conceptions of war, soldiers, and military institutions" that have come to define an American militarism.[91] Sociologist Michael Mann writes extensively of this American militarism that is far too reliant on its military power given its ideological, economic, and political strengths.[92] Adrian Lewis argues that the increased professionalization of the military and end of conscription changed the very nature of American citizenship, where citizens eliminated themselves from the conduct of wars and offered support for the troops in lieu of selfless service,[93] what this book would call bystander militarism. Lastly, Pierre Hassner warns of a growing modern militarism where the indirectness of conflicts sanitizes violence and dehumanizes the enemy, thus blurring the "normal" and the "extreme."[94]

This extensive literature across disciplines allows for the construction of multiple militarisms that do not fit neatly in a pacifism-militarism framework. Consider protectionist militarism in present-day Turkey and Thailand, where the military believes it serves as a check on government corruption. New defense technologies born out of the Revolution in Military Affairs (RMA) may be leading to a techno-militarism that replaces boots on the ground with drones and hackers. Some terrorist groups practice a religion-based militarism whose objectives extend far beyond gaining territory. And some states have begun to explore privatized militarism, relying on mercenaries and private security contractors to circumvent international law and domestic criticisms. What may be the most controversial claim in this book, antimilitarism is another type of militarism that emphasizes diplomacy over the use of force, yet finds the use of force *legitimate* in some circumstances. These militarisms are constructed differently and have far-reaching and diverse consequences.

PACIFISM AND MILITARISM IN THE TWENTY-FIRST CENTURY

Predictions of a foreboding return of Japanese militarism and nationalism are built on assumptions of what states *should* do. This approach to analyzing security policy is incomplete at best and alarmist at worst. As this chapter sought to demonstrate, militarism has held different connotations for different people at different times. Impressive economic growth, fear of the West, and sense of superiority in Asia were the main forces behind the zealous imperialism of the late Meiji period and interwar period. During World War II, militarism was defined by fanaticism and wanton violence. Over the last three decades, Japanese nationalism has been fueled by insecurity brought on by economic decline and poor demographics. In each period, movements and countermovements, novel justifications and deeply embedded practices, and the material world and ideational world clashed and melded to form a distinct militarism reflective of the time. The next chapter begins the exploration of the material conditions that shape Japanese security policy by examining the consequences of an aging and declining population.

CHAPTER THREE

Who Will Fight? The JSDF's Demographic Crises

Conventional wisdom would have one believe that the United States should have won the Vietnam War. The United States possessed superior firepower, technology, air and naval capabilities, economic resources, and latent power compared to the Viet Cong and North Vietnam. The United States did not restrain its overwhelming might; during the war, over seven million tons of bombs were dropped on Vietnam, Laos, and Cambodia—more than twice the amount dropped on Europe and Asia in World War II.[1] To this day, leftover ordnance maims and kills hundreds of Southeast Asians every year. Although they lacked symmetrical military capabilities, the North Vietnamese refused to surrender, and the United States was forced to leave by the end of 1973. Armed with weapons of war designed to challenge superpowers, the United States was unprepared for the North Vietnamese use of guerilla-style tactics. The United States fell victim to what sociologist James William Gibson refers to as the false logic of the "technowar," which he describes in the following quote:

> For the military as well as civilian policymakers, the enemy becomes a mirror image of ourselves, only "less" so. Military strategy becomes a one-factor question about technical forces; success or failure is measured quantitatively. Machine-system meets machine-system and the largest, fastest, most technologically advanced system will win. Any other outcome becomes *unthinkable*.[2]

Technology does not win the war over hearts and minds. The United States pulled out of Vietnam because the public, and ultimately Congress, were not prepared to "accept thousands of body-bags for what appeared to be a lost cause."[3]

For every foreign soldier sent to Vietnam, there were scores of native Vietnamese who knew every inch of their homeland and were willing to give their lives to defend it. Absent the political will, the United States simply lacked the boots on the ground to establish a long-term presence, firmly hold onto territory, and defeat the enemy. While technology can supplement human resources and reduce the number of soldiers needed, technology is not divorced from the individuals that operate it nor the contexts in which it is implemented. As one senior government official makes clear, "War is a very simple thing. A kind of naked violence. I am not a hundred percent sure we can preserve our deterrence by only relying on technology. It is not only about technology, but also our psychology. Deterrence is about psychology, ultimately."[4]

Political scientists, like government leaders, can be seduced by the neatness of the technowar narrative in which, with the right tools, warfare becomes a solvable problem. Consequently, when scholars discuss power projection, ability to balance against regional threats, and eventual Japanese remilitarization, their lens of analysis narrows in on the strengths of the Japan Self-Defense Forces (JSDF), particularly its technological capabilities and training. But the logic of the technowar obscures the existence of other important variables that contribute to military power.

The technowar logic has framed the realist narrative concerning Japanese security policy. Its proponents have remained fixated on disproving the constraining power of norms while misguidedly ignoring the difficulties of adopting more aggressive security policies and practices once those norms erode. The logic goes that if Japan were truly threatened, the government would overcome the normative and political restraints imposed on the JSDF by the public and pursue more normalized security policies. In other words, realists believe the JSDF's weaknesses are a matter of choice. However, in war and politics, the easy things are difficult, and the difficult things can be next to impossible. Government leaders may have preconceived notions of what, when, and how they will pursue their agendas, but successful implementation is far from guaranteed. Despite the myriad of threats abroad, improvements to the capabilities of the JSDF have not met the ambitions of defense hawks.

The will to normalize, if it does exist in Japan, does not necessarily mean there is a way. The JSDF is significantly constrained by demographics and capacity. This chapter investigates the demographic social-structural hardware constraint and argues that even if the government of Japan (GOJ) can overcome the high political, normative, and budgetary hurdles, the JSDF's power projection capabilities will still be limited by force size and defense infrastructure. The JSDF's weak recruitment is most directly tied to the aging and declining population, but normative forces, such as the public's aversion to joining the military and legal prohibition of conscription, further exacerbate the consequences of poor demography. As a result, the Ministry of Defense (MOD) regularly makes compromises to its security policy, and the JSDF chronically operates under suboptimal conditions.

The chapter is organized as follows: First, it outlines the current responsibilities of the JSDF. Second, the chapter compares East Asian military force sizes. The size and youth of the JSDF have an outsized impact on Japan's ability to counter international threats, project power, and respond to natural disasters. Third, the chapter discusses the impact of the aging and declining population on the JSDF. This section also analyzes the MOD's efforts to increase recruitment and the GOJ's efforts to address the demographic crises. The GOJ's use of female images and bodies reveal deep-seated cultural issues that obstruct the radical transformation necessary for unlocking Japan's latent power. This chapter concludes with an examination of how normative forces exacerbate the demographics problem. The content and direction of Japanese security policy is heavily shaped by social-structural constraints that affect the JSDF at the tactical and operational levels. The human resource problem is path dependent and reinforced by normative, cultural, political, and economic factors, all of which form the environment in which security and militarism are understood.

CONTEXTUALIZING PEOPLE AND POWER IN EAST ASIA

Military power can be measured in numerous ways, such as defense spending, infrastructure, defense industrial base, and RDT&E (research, development, test, and evaluation) institutions.[5] Nevertheless, a military is only as strong as the individuals that comprise it. In warfare, it is preferable to have a preponderance of power than to have just enough, and absolutely preferable to have enough power to not enough. The importance of force size is particularly evident when discussing power projection, which implies force strength beyond defense.[6] The effectiveness of technology on the battlefield is heavily influenced by how it is implemented and operated by the combatants. With all else being equal, a state would want the largest military possible because it would provide more raw power and flexibility on the battlefield; more operations can be conducted simultaneously, and fewer compromises need to be made. Boots on the ground are essential for holding onto occupied territories, protecting assets, and limiting enemy combatants' mobility. Simply put, human resources matter.

The relationship between demographics and security has long been a topic of interest across disciplines. Economist Thomas Robert Malthus and ecologist Garrett Hardin warned of the dangers of overpopulation and poor resource management for global stability.[7] Political scientists directed their attention toward how demographics relate to conflict. Mark Haas, for example, argues that an aging population can lead to increased stability in the international system over time because the costs of conducting war become prohibitively expensive for aging societies.[8] Others have called attention to a quiet revolution where population decline among nations disrupts the balance of power and stability in the current world order.[9] Population distribution is also consequential, especially when an excess of unmarried, single, and young men coupled with a deficit of opportunities often lead to domestic and international instability.[10] The literature makes clear, however, that demographics alone do not determine the level of state volatility. Political and socioeconomic conditions can mitigate, or exacerbate, the consequences of aging and declining populations. Japan is no exception to these trends, as its demographics have played a defining role in its security trajectory over the last century.

From the Meiji period to the end of World War II, the Empire of Japan was not only built on impressive technological advancements but also on a large and growing population, government policies promoting Japanese emigration to colonized territories throughout Asia, and effective mobilization of the public for warfare. From 1920 to 1945, the population of Japan grew from 55,963,053 to 71,998,104 at a rate of 5.6 percent to 7.9 percent annually.[11] The population was predominantly young, with over half of the population under the age of thirty and approximately 6 percent over the age of sixty-five.[12] Millions—many young and impoverished—left Japan to work the lands across the empire and beyond. Japan's power projection was synonymous with the occupation, and expansion, of colonial territories in order to protect the Japanese mainland. This expansion ultimately stretched Japan too thin, and the government was forced to make sacrifices concerning which territories it could protect. In World War II, the United States exploited Japan's human resource limitations by utilizing a strategy of island hopping, or leapfrogging, to avoid pockets of Japanese military power. Although Japan possessed the largest battleships in World War II, technological strengths and almost fanatical willpower could not mitigate the lack of boots on the ground. The size of the Japanese population was not large enough to hold onto the empire but was sufficient for convincing American policymakers that an invasion of the mainland would be incredibly costly. The war was ended by the first and only use of nuclear weapons on a civilian population.

In the postwar period, Japan became an economic powerhouse that possessed significant latent power. However, this economic power was never converted to aggressive militaristic policies due to strategic, legal, and normative reasons. Moreover, unlike the prewar period, Japan was a thriving democracy fully embedded in the international system. Japan had little reason to remilitarize, even if it could. Over the last decade, Japan's latent power has diminished as the population aged and declined. According to one government official, "It is inconceivable that Japan is taking an expansive and aggressive foreign military policy. A declining birthrate encourages the tendency to preserve the status quo. Our mindset of national security is overly defensive. Very defensive. We just want to preserve our current territory."[13]

The Great and Growing Responsibilities of the JSDF

The JSDF possesses diverse responsibilities, and its effectiveness requires a large standing force. But with major changes in the regional balance of power, the emergence of new threats, a weakening domestic economy, and unbalanced demographics, the JSDF has to do more with less. The Japanese archipelago is comprised of 6,852 islands spanning 378,000 square kilometers. The JSDF and Japan Coast Guard (JCG) are responsible for protecting 29,751 kilometers of coastline and patrolling 4,470,000 square kilometers of territorial and exclusive economic zone (EEZ) waters, which is roughly twelve times the size of Japan's land area. As an island nation, Japan enjoys natural defense advantages but also endures several vulnerabilities. During war, blockades can sever Japan's access to vital resources and trade, which is especially problematic because it is resource poor. Japan's unique geography make defense officials particularly concerned with Chinese antiaccess and area denial strategies that could limit the effectiveness of the U.S.-Japan alliance.

The JSDF deploys the majority of its forces to protect the main islands, strategic islets, airspace, and surrounding waters. Over the past few decades, North Korean abductions, illegal fishing in Japanese territorial waters, and Chinese and Russian intrusions into Japanese airspace have made it clear that the JSDF's capacity and capabilities are increasingly stressed. Pressure on the JSDF has become more glaring as China's strength and boldness grows. Since 2006, Japan Air Self-Defense Force (ASDF) scrambles against Chinese aircraft increased year-over-year, peaking at 851 in 2016. Chinese incursions decreased to five hundred in 2017 but scrambles against Russian aircraft increased by 89 times compared to the previous year. The reprieve was short-lived, as total scrambles increased to 999 against foreign military aircraft in 2018, the second highest on record since Japan implemented the measures against airspace violations in 1958.[14] In November 2013, the Chinese government unilaterally declared the "East China Sea Air Defense Identification Zone," which includes airspace over the disputed Senkaku Islands. Since Japan "nationalized" the Senkaku Islands in September 2012, Chinese vessels have intruded into Japanese territorial waters over one hundred times.[15] Japan is locked in territorial disputes with countries to its north, east, and south, forcing the JSDF to be vigilant across diverse territories and against formidable militaries.

The area in which the JSDF operates has increased with its growing global responsibilities. Prominent conservative politicians have sought to increase Japan's security roles abroad, including playing a greater role in the U.S.-Japan alliance, adopting collective defense, and addressing new threats such as terrorism and piracy. For example, since the end of the first Gulf War, Japan has dispatched over twelve thousand personnel on twenty-seven missions, including fourteen UN PKO missions.[16] Under Prime Minister Abe's proactive contribution to peace doctrine, the JSDF will likely continue to increase its activities abroad in noncombat but labor-intensive operations.

The JSDF also has nontraditional security responsibilities at home that require significant human resources. Authorized by General Douglas MacArthur, the JSDF originated as a National Police Reserve (NPR) on September 8, 1950 and has slowly adopted additional security roles over time. The SDF law was adopted in 1954 and has been amended 163 times (as of December 2020)[17] to meet the changing and growing needs of the JSDF. Beginning in the 1990s, the JSDF was most often deployed to conduct disaster relief operations, which was not the original intent of the Japanese or American governments.[18] The GOJ has been particularly willing to mobilize the JSDF for disaster relief and public works projects because it has found these activities effective in improving the image of the JSDF and maintaining positive relations with communities most impacted by bases and military exercises.[19] Between 1951 and 2011, the Ground Self-Defense Force (GSDF), and its predecessors the NPR and the National Safety Force, were deployed to disasters approximately twenty thousand times and dispatched approximately fourteen million personnel.[20] Perhaps the most notable operation was the deployment of more than one hundred thousand JSDF personnel to the Tōhoku region of Japan following the great Tōhoku earthquake, tsunami, and Fukushima nuclear disaster in 2011, which was its biggest disaster relief effort in Japanese history.[21] In 2014, JSDF personnel were deployed to Hiroshima after devastating mudslides and to Mount Ontake after a volcanic eruption. Thousands of JSDF personnel were again dispatched to the southwestern region of Japan in 2018 after another major flood. Due to the increased frequency and magnitude of environmental disasters caused by climate change, it is likely that these nontraditional security operations will comprise the majority of JSDF missions going forward.

The JSDF's admirable work in disaster relief serves as a reminder of just how active the forces have been in nontraditional security activities in the last twenty years (discussed in chapter 6). Consequently, according to one senior MOD official, the entire "security apparatus" has grown and both the "civilian component and uniform services" will require "greater policy oversight."[22]

Numerically, the JSDF is rather large. With 247,150 authorized personnel (150,850 GSDF, 45,350 Maritime Self-Defense Force (MSDF), 49,950 ASDF), the JSDF ranks eighteenth in the world in force size.[23] In terms of overall force size (including regular and nonregular military), the JSDF drops to thirty-third in the world.

Japan's forces are much smaller than its regional rivals (see figure 3.1). China possesses the world's largest standing military with 2.03 million active personnel. Japan's forces are smaller than those of North Korea, Russia, South Korea, and Taiwan, and the second lowest ratio of military personnel (including reserve and paramilitary) to civilians in East Asia, with 2.49 JSDF members per 1,000.[24] China

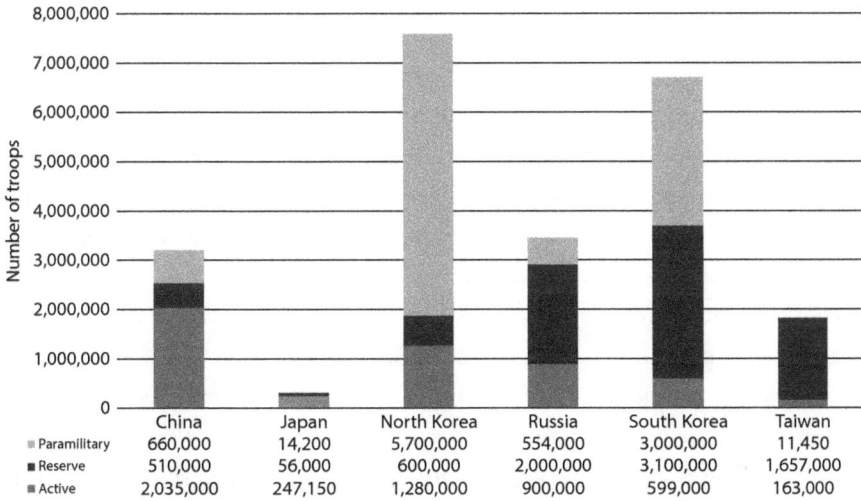

	China	Japan	North Korea	Russia	South Korea	Taiwan
▪ Paramilitary	660,000	14,200	5,700,000	554,000	3,000,000	11,450
▪ Reserve	510,000	56,000	600,000	2,000,000	3,100,000	1,657,000
▪ Active	2,035,000	247,150	1,280,000	900,000	599,000	163,000

FIGURE 3.1　(Authorized) Armed forces size in East Asia.

Source: International Institute for Strategic Studies, *The Military Balance* (London: Routledge, 2020).

ranks lower with a 2.27:1,000 ratio due to its large population (1.39 billion). North Korea (297.6:1,000), Russia (23.98:1,000), South Korea (131.9:1,000), and Taiwan (79.71:1,000) possess much higher ratios due to conscription.

Japan's reserve forces are also meager. China (0.51 million), North Korea (0.6 million), South Korea (3.1 million), Taiwan (1.65 million), and Russia (2 million) maintain reserve forces larger than the entire JSDF. These figures indicate that states routinely possess significant latent power because the majority of their forces are on reserve. On the other hand, Japan only possesses 56,000 reserve forces and 13,740 paramilitary (forces that train approximately five days a year). Unlike its regional rivals, Japan is fully utilizing its human resources; there is no untapped potential. For Japanese power projection, what you see is what you get.

THE DEMOGRAPHIC CRISES AND FAILED REFORM

The MOD's difficulty with addressing the force size problem reflects a convergence of demographic, normative, economic, and cultural forces. The public aversion to joining the JSDF ebbs and flows with the strength of peace movements, the effectiveness of government recruiting efforts, the perception of regional threats, and sensitivity to occupational hazards. However, population decline and the aging of society are constant constraining forces that are difficult to overcome because of economic and cultural realities that have developed over decades. Moreover, ideational forces, such as gender norms, impact the content and direction of government policies that address the demographic crises and their impact on the JSDF. The GOJ has pursued two interrelated objectives: (1) institute measures to increase the fertility rate, and therefore the supply of potential recruits; and (2) promote the JSDF as an admirable and nonmilitaristic entity to gain popular support and increase enlistment.[25]

According to the National Institute of Population and Social Security Research (IPSS), based on medium fertility rate projections, Japan is entering into a long period of population decline (see figure 3.2). The population is expected to decrease to approximately 119.1 million by 2030, to 101.9 million in 2050, and to 88.1 million by 2065. The projections for 2060 vary widely—from

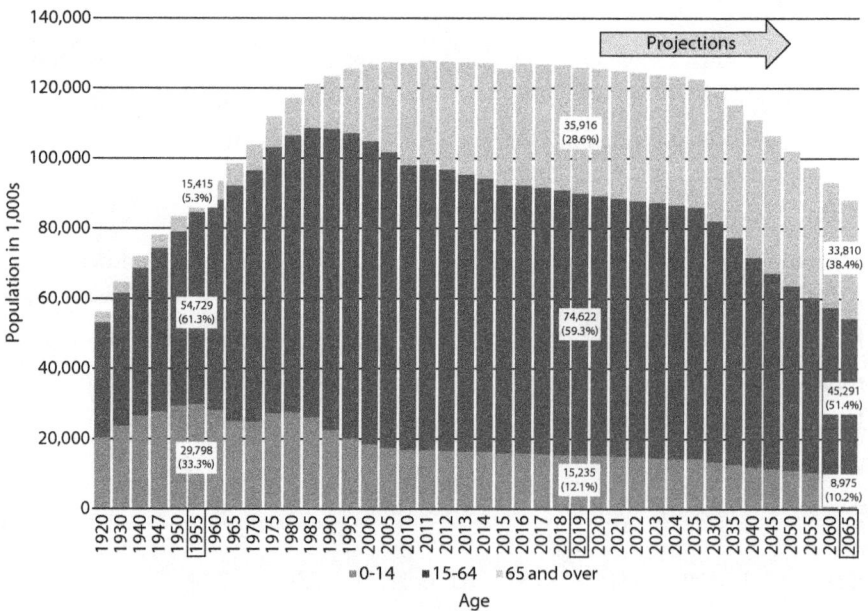

FIGURE 3.2   Population projections of Japan, 1920–2065.

Source: National Institute of Population and Social Security Research, "Social Security in Japan 2014," accessed November 30, 2020, http://www.ipss.go.jp; and Statistics Bureau of Japan, "Search Statistics Surveys and Data," accessed November 30, 2020. https://www.stat.go.jp/data/jinsui/new.html.

82.1 million to 94.9 million; the more pessimistic scenario would result in a 35 percent decrease in population since 2010.

Japan has long been under the population replenishment rate threshold due to its anemic fertility rate, which fell below 2.1 in 1974, where births slightly outnumbered deaths. Though the precipitous drop was momentarily halted in 2005, and the replenishment rate slightly rebounded to 1.41 in 2012, the cause is unclear, and few officials believe the rate will increase to a level necessary for sustaining population equilibrium. The 981,000 births in 2016 marked the first time the figure fell below one million since such data was first compiled in 1899. This figure amounted to less than half the annual births of 1973, when signs of population decline began to emerge. In 2016, 1,296,000 deaths were recorded—the highest number since the end of World War II—a startling figure given that the Japanese enjoy the longest average life expectancy in the world. The full impact of the declining population will be even more apparent in a few decades when today's children become adults. The under-fifteen population has decreased from 27 million in the early 1980s to 15.1 million in 2020. The IPSS projects that the population of young Japanese will be only 8.9 million by 2065, which is one-fourth the size of Japanese over retirement age. Even the most bullish government estimates predict a fertility rate of 1.8, still short of replacement level. The demographic crises are uniquely pronounced because Japan never enjoyed a prolonged population surge like most industrialized states. The average age of the population increased by twenty years between 1947 and 1970, but the *dankai no sedai* (baby boom generation) lasted only four years due to the Eugenic Protection Act passed in 1948 that made abortion legal, among other factors.[26] As a result, Japan's birthrate dropped 40 percent. The GOJ is thus seeking to reverse a trend that has been developing for the majority of the postwar period. One can look toward the struggles of China, where even the most authoritarian social engineering measures have not reversed the consequences of the one-child policy.

The low fertility rate is not purely a numbers game. Strongly embedded cultural practices in both public and private spheres, such as declining marriage rates, a corporate culture not conducive to a healthy work-life balance, and a stubborn aversion to immigration, mitigate the effectiveness of government policies. Although bureaucrats predicted the decline in fertility rate early on, it was not until the 1.57 shock of 1989 that a sense of urgency about stemming the oncoming crisis emerged.[27] This precipitous drop has been attributed to a greater proportion of never-married women in their twenties and early thirties and a decline in marital fertility rates. Following a boom in the 1970s, which saw ten marriages per thousand, marriage rates have halved to 4.8 per thousand in 2019 (598,965 couples). According to the Ministry of Health, Labour, and Welfare, the mean age of women on first marriage was 29.6 in 2019, up 3.7 years from 1990. Moreover, the mean age of women on the birth of the first child was 30.7, up 3.7 years over the same twenty-eight-year period.[28] The reasons for later marriages vary. Some individuals simply prefer to remain single and avoid marrying unsuitable partners.[29] Others would like to get married but only once they are financially stable, a status increasingly delayed in Japan's stagnant economy. Later marriages decrease the chances of having multiple children because the window of opportunity for childbirth is smaller. Of course, women can have children outside of marriage, but societal stigma in Japan makes it an uncommon occurrence, with only 3 percent of children born out of wedlock. There are many reasons why some women choose not to have children, including financial concerns, career aspirations, and personal preference.

In response to the low fertility rate, government leaders and bureaucrats (mostly middle-aged men) scrambled to institute policies to incentivize women to have more children. In 1994, the government adopted the Angel Plan, which created additional childcare spaces with extended hours, and it established consultation centers to support new mothers.[30] Since the initial Angel Plan, various new programs have been implemented, such as modest subsidies for childbirth and childrearing, couples counseling, and measures to assist female labor force participation after childbirth. However, these policies have been misguided and ineffectual.

First and foremost, coaxing women with monetary incentives to have more children to support the economy, and ultimately Japan's security, is really not within the purview of government—particularly when it is predominately men who design these family planning programs. Concerning the relationship between the birth rate and national security, one government official concludes, "The population question is a matter of personal freedom. You do not have to have babies if you do not want to. If you want babies, you can do it and the government will support it. But to argue that we have to increase the birthrate because of our national security, it is a very difficult thing to put in the right context."[31] Finding the right context is exceedingly difficult when women are not at the forefront of the policymaking process. In 2018, women made up less than 15 percent of policymakers in the Diet, and when they speak on the demographic crises, they are occasionally met with sexist derision.[32] During Abe's last year in office, only two members of his cabinet were women. The current Suga Yoshihide government has only one woman serving in the cabinet. Treating the low fertility rate as a state problem and not as a problem of inequality results in a disconnect between policy objectives and women's rights. Policies designed to improve the position of women in society have insufficiently addressed fundamental weaknesses in a patriarchal system. Despite all the discussion of work-life balance, there have not been significant improvements to family care infrastructure, mainly regarding childcare and senior nursing, where women take up a disproportionate amount of responsibility. Yashiro Naohiro, an economist and councilor for the Council on Economic and Fiscal Policy during the Abe and Fukuda Yasuo administrations, argues that Japan's protected welfare system has made it difficult for the government to make industries both cost-effective and attractive to new workers.[33]

Second, changes to the work, welfare, and family-planning cultures require a degree of social engineering far beyond the capabilities of the government. In 2002, the Plus One Plan was introduced to alleviate some of the household work burdens on women. It called on employers to offer parental leave immediately after a child is born. The objective was for fathers to bond with their newborns and to establish a commitment to raising the child over the succeeding months and years. The policy was adopted, but few firms promoted the "daddy week," and only about 10 percent of fathers participated in the program.[34] The reluctance of fathers to utilize the plan and to do more housework reveals how deeply embedded gender roles are in Japanese society. As Sasaki Kaori, businessperson and CEO of ewoman, Inc., puts bluntly, "changing the law can only do so much; our value system has to change, too. When we rebuilt the economy after the war, our society forged a powerful 'boys network,' with a common set of goals and values."[35] Indeed, much of Japan's economic woes can be attributed to a rigid work culture that developed during the economic boom. Men are expected to be *sararīman* (salaried workers), or the breadwinners, and they take for granted that women are responsible for the unpaid household and care work—regardless of their commitments to the public workforce. Maintaining a healthy work-life balance remains difficult, where 70 percent of working women quit their jobs either at marriage or at their first birth.[36] For women who remain in the public workforce, they are essentially doing double the work if men are not doing their fair share at home. Without changing these expectations, there is a "market failure" where the "asymmetry in the consequences of marriage by gender has brought about a trade-off for women between work and marriage."[37] When women are forced to quit their jobs at marriage or at childbirth, a vicious cycle forms where companies are reluctant to employ or promote women out of fear that they will take parental leave. Without equal opportunities—Japan has the third highest gender pay gap among OECD countries—women are more likely to give up their jobs than their partners. This vicious cycle is completed, according to Yashiro, "when a company hires a man, they are also hiring the spouse in the sense that she must remain at home and take care of all house duties so that her husband can work long hours at the office, sometimes living separated from the family.[38] Yashiro concludes it would be culturally difficult for Japan to change its economic structure because of "fixed social roles for men and women, both at work and at home."[39]

Immigration and What It Means to Be Japanese

A potential solution to the population crisis is immigration. According to a survey of over 42,300 employers in forty-three countries, Japanese firms reported the highest difficulty in filling jobs, at 86 percent.[40] The world offers a ready supply of young workers who can contribute to the economy and possibly join the JSDF, although the latter is unlikely given the citizenship requirements of the JSDF and Japan's strict citizenship laws. Japan's restrictive policies have led political scientist Michael Strausz to conclude, "Japan is unusual as an advanced industrialized country in that it hosts comparatively few labor migrants, virtually no refugees, and relatively small number of foreign residents who migrated for other reasons."[41] The scale of the GOJ's policies have not matched the demands of the private sector nor the long-term economic and security needs of the nation.

In 2019, 2,933,137 registered foreign nationals resided in Japan, or 2.3 percent of the total population.[42] In the past five years, the GOJ has instituted policies to increase so-called high-skilled and middle-skilled labor to increase the competitiveness of the Japanese economy and to fulfill needs in the care and service industries. It should be noted, however, that these policies seek to import labor, not people, because long-term residency and citizenship are still difficult to obtain for migrants. For example, the Japanese language exam failure rate of immigrants in the critical area of nursing was so high that the GOJ was forced to ease the requirements and provide test takers with additional time.[43] Recent graduates face similar difficulties securing employment. In 2007, only 11,000 of

130,000 foreign students studying in Japan found jobs.[44] Ten years later, a record 25,900 out of 298,980 foreign students landed a job.[45] Although Japan has been successful attracting more international students—experiencing approximately 10 percent annual growth between 2013 and 2018—employment figures have not kept pace. The percentage of students securing a job only increased by one-fifth of a percent over the last decade. Liberal immigration policies would likely face significant opposition, especially from more conservative rural prefectures. In five surveys conducted of Diet members between 2009 and 2016, not once did support for increasing foreign labor rise above 40 percent.[46] More importantly, support for increasing labor has been extremely volatile among LDP Diet members,[47] demonstrating a lack of long-term and sustained support necessary for the transformative immigration policy reform required for meeting Japan's diverse needs. More conservative parties, such as Jiseidai no Tō (Party for Future Generations), have been more discriminatory. It proposed a bill in 2014 that aimed to exclude non-Japanese residents, many born in Japan or had lived there for most of their lives, from receiving welfare benefits. The unpopular far-right party rebranded as Nippon no Kokoro (Party for Japanese Kokoro, or Heart of Japan) in 2015, and eventually dissolved in 2018, however some of its members found a home with the LDP. Moreover, although it was considered a fringe party, prominent politicians such as Osaka mayor Hashimoto Tōru and Tokyo mayor Ishihara Shintarō were members.

Japan has a history of making life difficult for individuals who do not fit preconceived notions of "Japanese." In the 1980s and 1990s, the GOJ instituted programs that repatriated Brazilian-Japanese to fulfill labor shortages in the manufacturing sector. The effort was a spectacular failure. Language barriers and discrimination made it difficult for Brazilian-Japanese to integrate smoothly into mainstream Japanese society. Some Japanese held prejudices and believed the immigrants were lazy and troublesome.[48] One can find similar right-wing propaganda against immigrant workers in Japan today, where they inflate crime rates of migrants from Southeast Asia. When the economy slowed, the Japanese government sought ways to send the immigrants back to Brazil, even offering large sums for them to pack up and leave.[49] This episode left many Japanese wary of immigrants because if *Japanese* could not assimilate, how could non-Japanese? This narrow framing on what it means to be Japanese reveals deep-seated biases that result in policies that seek to gain everything from immigrants *but* the person themselves.

It is unlikely that Japan can adopt immigration on the scale necessary to mitigate the population crisis. According to the former director of the Tokyo Immigration Bureau, Sakanaka Hidenori, Japan can pursue two policy options; a small option that restricts immigration and pursues a "compact society," or a big option that welcomes immigration and a restructuring of Japanese society to its core.[50] The big option would require 20 million immigrants over fifty years, or 400,000 a year, which according to Sakanaka, would be difficult for Japan to take in such a large number so suddenly. This figure would be more than four times the current rate of migration, which would lead to migrants comprising 20 percent of the total population by 2030.[51] Such an approach would require Japan to "transform itself into a land of opportunity, building an open, fair society which guaranteed equal opportunity, judged people on their merits, and allowed everyone to improve their social status regardless of origin or ethnicity."[52] For many, this transformation may be prohibitively expensive. To assimilate immigrants—which by no means is the only or optimal model of immigration—the GOJ would need to provide language training, social welfare benefits, and assimilation programming not just for immigrants but for native Japanese as well.

Age Is Just a Number, Until It Is Not

Given these difficulties addressing the shrinking population, the GOJ has settled on managing a graceful decline over meaningful growth. Optimists argue that population decline is manageable because even the most conservative projections would leave Japan with more people than it had in the 1960s when the economy was doing well. However, Yashiro reminds us that Japan's "economy and society implicitly depend on increasing the size of the population, particularly the working age population."[53] Although the current population size would be the same as in the 1960s, it would be significantly older and decreasing in size.

The aging population poses the most immediate obstacle to the GOJ's efforts to bolster the economy and to increase the JSDF's force power. Demographers consider a society aging when 7 percent of the population is older than sixty-five, and aged when 14 percent of the population is older than sixty-five.[54] Japan has the dubious distinction of being the world's first hyper-aged society, where 20 percent of the population is of retirement age. Figure 3.3 illustrates Japan's increasingly constrictive population pyramid. A desirable expansive population

1965

Male

Female

100
90
75
80
65–74
70
60
50
40
15–64
30
20
10
0–14
0 Age

130 120 110 100 90 80 70 60 50 40 30 20 10 0   0 10 20 30 40 50 60 70 80 90 100 110 120 130
Population (10 thousands)

2020

Male

Female

100
90
80   75+
70   65–74
60
50
40   15–64
30
20
10   0–14
0 Age

130 120 110 100 90 80 70 60 50 40 30 20 10 0   0 10 20 30 40 50 60 70 80 90 100 110 120 130
Population (10 thousands)

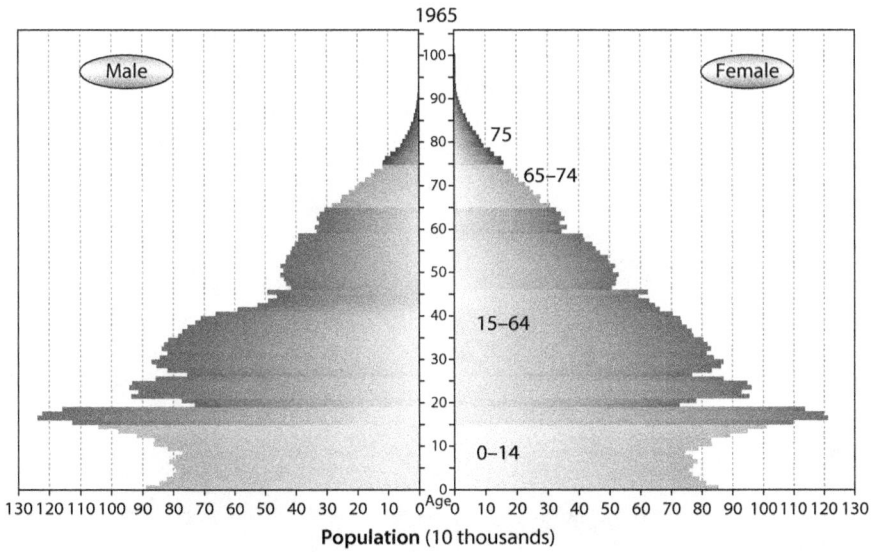

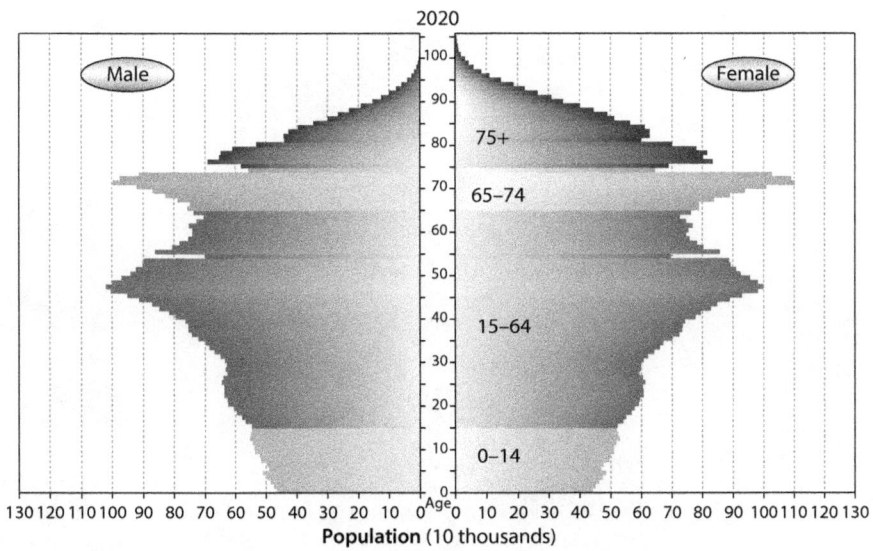

FIGURE 3.3 Population projections of Japan, 1965; 2020; 2030; 2065.

Source: Census (1965–2015) and National Institute of Population and Social Security Research, "Population Projection for Japan: 2016–2065" (Medium-fertility [medium-mortality] projection), 2017, http://www.ipss .go.jp/index-e.asp.

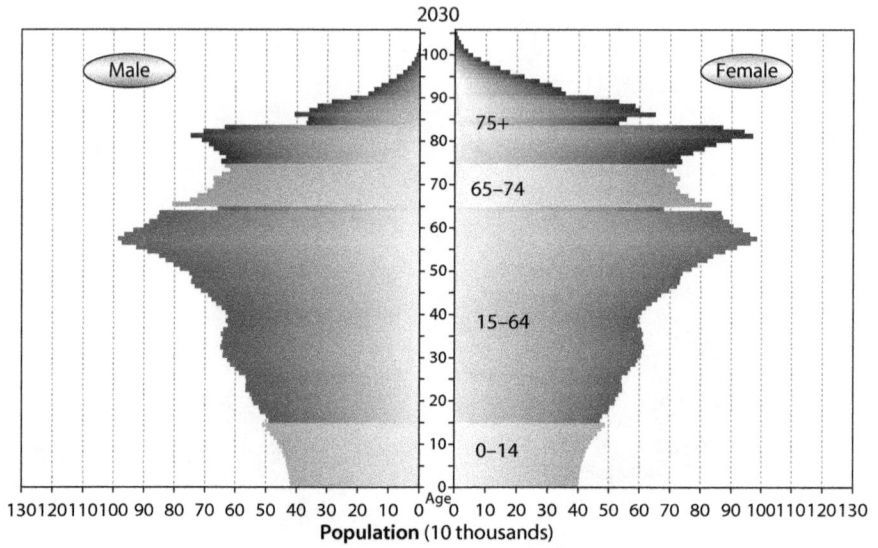

2030

Male / Female

75+
65–74
15–64
0–14

130 120 110 100 90 80 70 60 50 40 30 20 10 0 | Age | 0 10 20 30 40 50 60 70 80 90 100 110 120 130
Population (10 thousands)

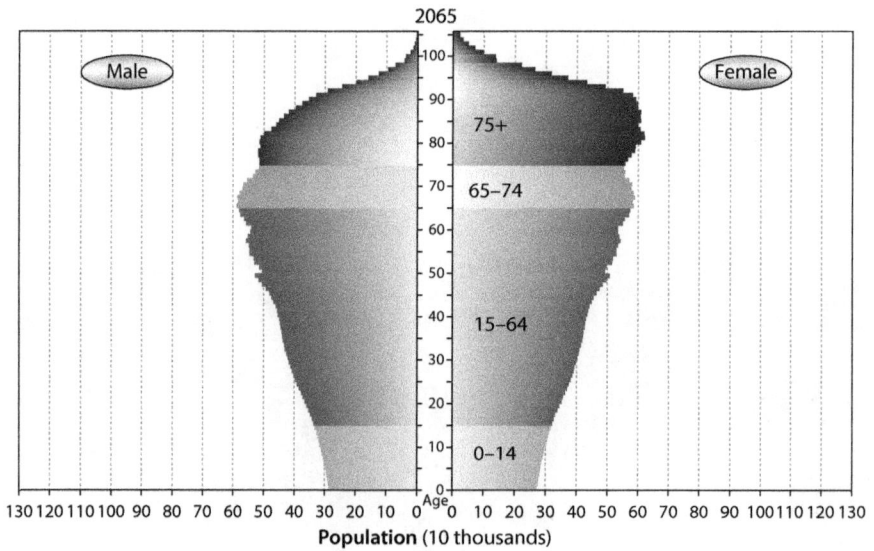

2065

Male / Female

75+
65–74
15–64
0–14

130 120 110 100 90 80 70 60 50 40 30 20 10 0 | Age | 0 10 20 30 40 50 60 70 80 90 100 110 120 130
Population (10 thousands)

FIGURE 3.3 (*Continued*)

pyramid is one in which the majority of the population is of working-age or younger, a constrictive pyramid has fewer people contributing to the economy and more people drawing social welfare benefits. In 2020, 35.12 million Japanese were of retirement age, or 27.7 percent of the population. By 2060, close to 40 percent of the total population will be over the age of sixty-five. As a result, the increasingly small working-age population will be burdened with upholding the economy while caring for the large retirement-aged population. By 2060, the age dependency ratio, which measures the burden of support on the working-age population, will be 1.36 workers for each person over the age of sixty-five.[55] It seems fitting that Japan's population pyramid resembles an urn.

The financial stress of these trends will have broader adverse economic effects than simply straining labor-intensive and already understaffed industries such as healthcare.[56] Banks, already doing the heavy lifting to keep the Japanese economy afloat, will lose valuable investment capital when the elderly dip into their savings for nursing care and medical services—increasingly common practices driven by the disruption of the nuclear family and declining confidence in the social safety net. Ongoing population decline will lead to decreased consumption and place acute pressures on GDP growth and wages.[57] The increased competitiveness in industries that Japan once dominated, such as automobiles and consumer electronics, will further squeeze the economy, making it less attractive to foreign investors and removing yet another valuable tool for economic recovery.[58]

In sum, the impacts of the aging and declining population are profound, far-reaching, and difficult to overcome. In matters of national security, poor demographics is an acute vulnerability.

IMPACTS ON THE JSDF

The impacts of the aging and declining population on the strength of JSDF are substantial. The most immediate crisis for the MOD is recruitment. According to defense white papers, the general recruitment climate has become severe, and the recruitable population has decreased in size due to the declining birthrate and increasing university enrollment.

Following an initial boom shortly after its establishment due to the weak economy, beginning in the mid-1950s, the JSDF began to fall far short of its recruiting targets.[59] The poor showing forced the JSDF to lower admissions requirements, and thus, many personnel lacked enthusiasm or were illiterate.[60] By 1991, when the Japanese economy reached its peak, the JSDF met only 85.5 percent of its recruitment target. JSDF recruits struggled to finish training, while officers experienced a drop in the quality of training. The military academies endured severe faculty shortages because soldiers quit their posts for jobs in the economy.[61] Although conditions have improved, actual force size is approximately 90 percent of authorized personnel quotas (see figure 3.4).

The JSDF has struggled to replace the required twelve to thirteen thousand noncommissioned officers (NCOs) each year.[62] In 2018, the JSDF was only able to recruit 77 percent of its 9,734 quota, marking the fourth consecutive year of missing its target.[63] Since 1994, there has been a 40 percent drop in people eligible for enlistment. This pool is expected to shrink by another 30 percent, to 7.2 million, over the next forty years. Traditionally, the JSDF has drawn most of its recruits from rural areas, which have been hit hardest by demographic trends. While researching for this book, I came across a striking example of population decline during a trip to Iwaishima, an island in Yamaguchi prefecture with a population of 350. The average

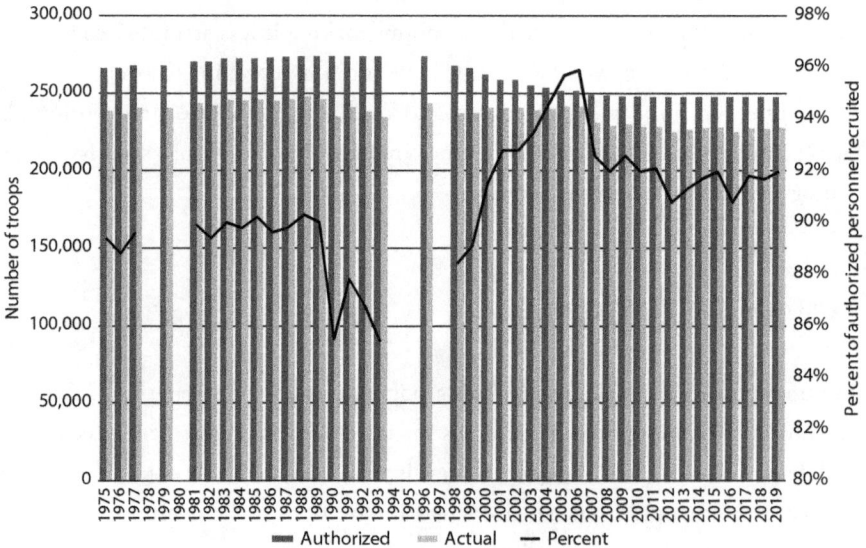

FIGURE 3.4   JSDF force size (authorized and actual), 1976–2019.

Source: Ministry of Defense, *Bōei Hakusho*.

age of the Iwai islander was seventy-eight. During an interview with some local fishermen, I learned, to my great surprise, that the locals considered anyone under seventy young. When asked about islanders under thirty-four, the fishermen named all twenty-four individuals. Only three residents residing in Iwaishima were under the age of ten, which led to the closure of the local elementary school. Iwaishima's predicament is less of an extreme than one imagines; many communities in rural areas are facing extinction. Reviving the populations outside the major cities includes not only increasing the fertility rate but also revitalizing the infrastructure to support the population. In other words, Japan's demographic problems are not evenly distributed across the country, thus requiring highly tailored policies.

A lack of job opportunities has stimulated urbanization, which has hastened the demise of the countryside. Japan is the second most urbanized country in the world, with 93 percent of the population living in cities.[64] Major cities offer attractive competing job opportunities for would-be recruits. Tokuchi Hideshi, former Vice-Minister of Defense for International Affairs, summarizes the pressure of population decline on JSDF recruitment with the following assessment:

> If you look back at the history of the Japan Defense Forces development, recruitment was always a big headache for the defense forces. The biggest source of recruitment is high school graduates at the age of eighteen. Last year, the number of newborn babies was less than one million, which means that in eighteen years, high school graduates will be less than one million. However, the Japan Defense Forces have to recruit around ten thousand per year. So, one high school graduate has to join the military out of a hundred. Actually, that's very high. It's very challenging. If the population keeps decreasing, it is becoming harder and harder. Of course, you can rely on machines, or AI, those kinds of things and the defense forces have been expanding their recruitment toward females. However, those kinds of efforts have limits. And, the military needs people, particularly the Ground Self-Defense Force because one of the main missions of the Japanese Defense Forces is disaster relief, and search and rescue operations in particular cannot depend on machines. Actual human power is indispensable for search and rescue.[65]

Contrary to expectation, two decades of economic stagnation has not led to increased enlistment in the JSDF. The declining population has all but eliminated excess labor. The unemployment rate peaked at 5.5 percent in June 2002 but dropped to 2.2 percent in May 2018, the lowest since 1992. Even in the midst of the 2020 COVID-19 global pandemic that saw the U.S. unemployment rate jump from 4.4 percent to 14.7 percent between March and April,[66] Japan's unemployment rate inched up to only 2.6 percent. These figures do not tell the whole story of just how uncompetitive the JSDF is in attracting potential recruits. Although the unemployment rate is low, 21.65 million Japanese (31 percent of the labor force and 19.5 percent of the population fifteen years or older) are underemployed as part-time or temporary workers in 2019.[67] *Arubaito* (part-time or temporary employment), are low-pay, nonbenefit jobs that offer little long-term stability. Nonetheless, despite the JSDF's respectable pay and benefits, the MOD continues to struggle to meet recruitment quotas.

A smaller pool of potential recruits decreases the overall quality of the JSDF. In countries such as the United States, recruitment is highly targeted in order to extract the full potential of available recruits. For example, advertisements are tailored to direct potential recruits toward the branch of the armed forces that best matches their strengths and life goals. In East Asia, conscription provides the armed forces access to every qualified male, allowing for maximum flexibility in how they are designed and organized. Conversely, the MOD relies on a generic message of peace to capture the broadest population possible. Instead of receiving enlistees with specific interests and skills, or having access to all people in the country, the MOD must mold a shrinking pool of talent into a force that must punch far above its weight class.

An aging population also exacerbates the troop quality problem. War is a young person's game: even with the increased reliance on technology, combat is physically and mentally strenuous. Soldiers carry heavy equipment, complete hundreds of training hours, memorize innumerable tactics, operate increasingly sophisticated weapons technology, and engage in combat in severe environments. The average age of a JSDF member is thirty-five, about ten years older than the average age of soldier in the rest of East Asia. This age gap would be even greater if the MOD did not retire personnel much earlier than the general workforce, with many retiring in their mid-fifties to keep the JSDF at peak performance.[68] Whereas East Asian militaries have limitless potential because they enlist healthy young men in their prime, the JSDF is scraping together whomever it can get and hoping technology fills the gaps.

In recent years, the MOD has accepted that the aging of the JSDF is an inevitability and has slowly adjusted its recruitment policies to address the demographics crises.[69] Aiming to increase the size of the recruitment pool, in October 2018, the MOD increased the maximum age for enlisted personnel and NCO applicants from twenty-six to thirty-two.[70] This change increased the recruitment pool by 7.76 million, or 41 percent.[71] Moreover, due to the JSDF's increasing disaster relief responsibilities, the MOD increased the upper age limit for recruitment of privates and lower SDF Reserve Personnel from under thirty-seven to under fifty-five. The MOD also expanded the band of service years by increasing the upper age limit for continued appointment from under sixty-one to under sixty-two.[72] It is too soon to determine if these policy changes will have a significant impact, but staffing *fell* by a tenth of a percentage point the following year.

An older armed forces in and of itself is not problematic for a defense-oriented security posture. JSDF personnel are highly trained and offer decades of service, even if they enlist in their early thirties and retire in their mid-fifties. However, the strength of the JSDF remains compromised because a top-heavy age distribution negatively affects the training and experience of all of its members. There are nine main methods of recruitment in the JSDF, but the bulk of the force can be divided into two main categories—NCOs and commissioned officers. NCOs in the GSDF enlist for two years, and NCOs in the MSDF and ASDF enlist for three years. Following the completion of the initial contract, some quit. Still, many personnel remain and develop long careers in the JSDF. Due to weak recruitment and retention, however, there are more senior officers than recruits. According to Lieutenant General Yamaguchi Noboru, "The ratio of senior NCOs to junior NCOs, and NCOs to privates, is extremely high that leaders among enlisted service members tend to have smaller numbers of juniors to lead."[73] This warped senior to junior officer distribution hinders leadership development and weakens morale because as Yamaguchi concludes, the "confidence of NCOs, junior NCOs in particular, is harmed because they are not given responsibilities to make their job seem important," and thus, "making the job increasingly undesirable."

The current condition of the JSDF is insufficient for maintaining extended operations in East Asia and beyond. Advanced technology may be adequate for defending the homeland or sufficient for fighting enemy combatants, but it would be insufficient for suppressing the reemergence of threats, preventing continued assault, or securing far off territories. A defense of the mainland would also be highly taxing given the overwhelming number of troops possessed by regional rivals and Japan's understaffed armed forces. According one estimate, some GSDF frontline units are understrength by 20 percent, and some ships are undermanned by 30 percent.[74] In a war of attrition, Japan might do well *if* the government could mobilize the entire population to support the war effort, but this remains unlikely given the antimilitarism ecosystem. Nonoffensive operations, such as search-and-rescue and disaster relief, would also be difficult to maintain due to lack of human resources. The human resource problem has been on the radar of defense officials for at least a decade. Beginning in 1993, the MOD decreased the authorized force level of the GSDF but was forced to freeze the cuts in 2013 because it became apparent that there was a human resource deficit given the JSDF's responsibilities.

WHERE IDEATIONAL RESTRAINTS EXACERBATE THE RECRUITMENT CRISIS

Demographics alone, however, cannot explain anemic recruitment and enlistment. The authorized force size of the JSDF amounts to less than 2 percent of the recruitment population and less than .01 percent of the entire population. Despite the dire external threats to Japan's security—at least according to realists—the Japanese public has steadfastly refused to join or fully support the JSDF. In the last ten years, NCO applicants decreased from 47,907 to 28,310.[75] As illustrated in figure 3.5, the Japanese public are the least enthusiastic in East Asia when confronted with the possibility of having to go to war. According to a 2015 WIN/Gallop International survey, only 11 percent of Japanese would be willing to fight for their country, the lowest of sixty-four states surveyed. Similarly, the World Values Survey (WVS), found that Japanese respondents ranked last in "willingness to fight for your country" amongst East Asian states.[76] Since the 1980s, at most, only 21 percent of Japanese citizens state that they would be willing to fight for their country. This number has held steady at approximately 15 percent over the last twenty-five years, dropping to a historic low of 13 percent in 2019. The WVS Wave 7 indicated that, in comparison, approximately 89 percent of Chinese, 67 percent of South Koreans, and 77 percent of Taiwanese were

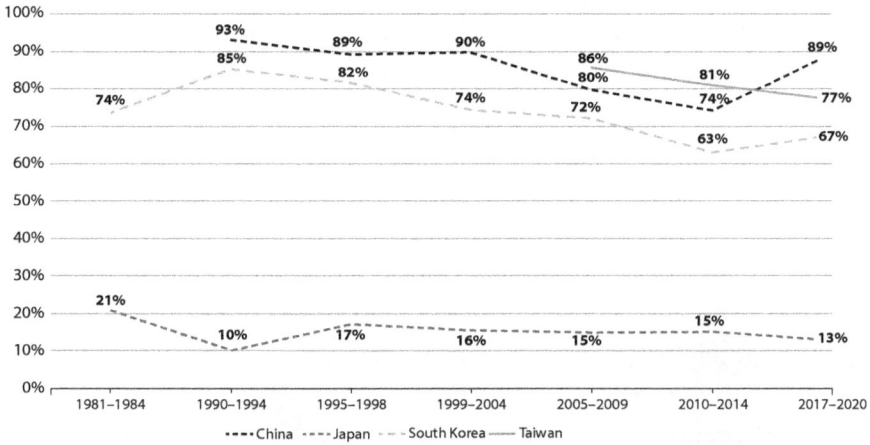

FIGURE 3.5 World Values Survey: Willingness to fight for your country survey.

Source: "World Values Survey" (data file and code book), various years, https://www.worldvaluessurvey .org/wvs.jsp.

willing to fight for their countries, with the former two showing an increase in percentage points from the Wave 6 survey. The lackluster willingness to defend the nation in times of war illustrates an enduring stigma against joining the JSDF among the Japanese public.

While the reputation of the JSDF has improved significantly since the 1990s, thanks to its humanitarian assistance and disaster relief work, the improved public image has not addressed the systemic biases against the armed forces that make recruiting high-quality candidates so difficult. According to Tsukamoto Katsuya, a research fellow at the National Institute for Defense Studies, the MOD's weak recruitment of top graduates is because the defense sector is not seen as a growth industry, and the military is not perceived to be suitable for "smart" people.[77] Even with higher salaries and greater benefits, Tsukamoto concludes, the MOD would still have difficulty recruiting good students.

Despite the public holding more favorable views of the JSDF, seventy-five years of peace has cultivated an antimilitarism ecosystem that is not conducive to recruitment. The armed forces are not a common element of the Japanese daily experience and visual landscape; JSDF members are rarely seen in public, military service is not a career path promoted in schools, few people have friends or relatives in the JSDF, and military service is not often openly praised. Consequently, young Japanese are unlikely to consider joining the JSDF because of perceived dangers and lack of support from their families and greater society. Although sometimes perceived as providing a respectable job with good benefits, serving in the armed forces is still believed to be a difficult and dirty occupation that does not instill any particular sense of pride.[78] In other words, few societal rules direct the average person to consider joining the JSDF.

Poor demographics also ensure that both strong and weak economies hinder recruitment efforts. Private companies pay more generous wages and offer greater opportunities than the JSDF. In the late 1970s and early 1980s, 90 percent of Japanese identified as middle class.[79] Thus, structural and economic drivers of military enlistment that are common in other countries did not develop in Japan. Even three decades of economic stagnation has not changed public perceptions—the majority of Japanese still do not consider the military a suitable place to seek employment. The MOD has sought to reshape such perceptions by actively promoting the JSDF as a career choice for high school graduates, particularly in Japan's underdeveloped countryside. Of the fifty Provisional Cooperation Offices in Japan, four are located in Hokkaidō and one in every other prefecture. The presence of the JSDF in Hokkaidō dates back to the early days following World War II, where it served as a major employer and played a crucial role in its development.[80] Coincidentally, Kyūshū is the largest source of recruitment for the JSDF. Tokuchi Hideshi surmises that the region's military history and vulnerability to natural disasters have led the people in Kyūshū to be "more accustomed to the military," and their "feelings about the military are different from people from other areas."[81] Tokuchi's conclusions highlight how the natural environment shaped the perception of the military in the social imaginary.

The absence of a school-to-armed services pipeline make it difficult for the JSDF to recruit university graduates. Most university students begin their job search in the first half of their third year and can generally secure employment upon graduation, especially as the labor pool has shrunk. New employees, usually twenty-one or twenty-two years old, begin employment at the start of the fiscal year in April. Students who study abroad or cannot gain employment during the regular hiring season often remain in college with the hope that they can land a job in the next year. Up until October 2018, the maximum recruitment age of NCOs was twenty-six, which meant the MOD had an approximately five-year window to recruit new graduates or individuals looking to make a drastic career change. Although the Japanese are more willing to switch occupations earlier in their careers than in the past, most will work for their initial company for at least a few years. When employees consider their first career move, companies usually offer their first promotion and significant pay hike, which disincentivizes a career change within the MOD's window of opportunity.[82]

The private sector also takes advantage of the MOD's strategy of increasing recruitment by offering recruits technological training. The ASDF, in particular, advertises that enlistees gain valuable skills that can lead to future job opportunities. This strategy may increase recruitment in the short term but has the adverse effect of decreasing retention rates. The private sector has historically headhunted engineers and highly-skilled JSDF personnel once their training is complete. The JSDF bears the cost of training, and then the private sector offers a salary the MOD cannot match. In recent years, even students of the prestigious National Defense Academy have reneged on their commitments to the JSDF and quit immediately after graduation. In the March 2020 graduating class, 35 of the 437 graduates refused their commissions in order to join the private sector. The MOD has lobbied for measures preventing poaching practices, but because the JSDF is an all-volunteer force, a consequence of the Peace Constitution, personnel are free to leave as they wish.

The JSDF's recruitment struggles also stem from a basic truth that all armed forces grapple with—the inability to offer a high quality of life. Quality of life concerns make the MSDF especially unpopular, according to former Minister of Defense Morimoto Satoshi.[83] While at sea, MSDF personnel are forbidden to use mobile devices because they may give away the locations of their ships. Morimoto surmises that young Japanese care more about freedom and promotion opportunities than salary and government perks, which make them even less likely to tolerate living on bases or being away from their families for months during missions, especially as the average amount of time a MSDF member spends away from home has increased in recent years.[84] Another senior MOD official concludes that the JSDF is "not stressed but there's a lot of strain, wear and tear" on defense equipment and personnel as "sailors are spending many, many days at sea."[85]

The conviction among senior MOD officials that financial incentives are insufficient enticement for new recruits seems plausible given that entry-level employees typically do not negotiate their salaries in Japan. Many do not even know their exact salary, sometimes for years. Even if salary played a more significant role in recruitment, the private sector can offer bonuses that JSDF personnel are not entitled to receive due to their status as special government employees. JSDF personnel technically work twenty-four-hours a day, and therefore, the government lacks mechanisms for providing overtime pay.[86]

The unpopularity of the MSDF has grown for decades and is more tied to the modernization of Japan than the perceived risks of a rising China or nuclear North Korea. Morimoto notes that in the 1960s, the MSDF was a popular branch of the JSDF because it offered a sense of adventure. For young Japanese men without opportunities in a postwar nation, the opportunity to travel to far off places for training exercises was a compelling incentive. However, now they can easily travel on their own.[87] Postgraduation travel is a common experience for young Japanese people because of the declining costs of transportation and increased globalism of the nation. According to the Japanese National Tourism Organization, overseas commercial aviation travel in Japan increased in forty-four of the last fifty-five years. In 1964, 128,487 passengers visited foreign countries, approximately .01 percent of the population. In 2019, 20,080,669, or 15.8 percent of the population, traveled overseas.

The JSDF is not only unable to offer competitive bonuses but military service also comes with drawbacks unlike any in civilian life. The stresses of the job are not limited to the soldier and extend to the family, as one would expect in such a difficult line of work. During an interview for this book, one JSDF officer remarked, "I do not see any drawbacks, but my wife thinks JASDF officers have a lot of job transfers. So it is difficult for us to buy a home if we would like to live together."[88] Moreover, many recruits fail to pass the initial enlistment stage because they do not meet physical and intellectual standards, or they quit when they realize the hardships of serving in the armed forces. When considering the prospects of participating in more than disaster relief operations, one JSDF member lamented, "I do not want to go to war," and "if it (the JSDF) was a military, I might not have joined it."[89]

Gone is the certainty that serving in the armed forces does not pose a credible threat to one's well-being. Even though the JSDF is forbidden to engage in overseas combat missions, 2,001 personnel have died in service of the country (as of November 2020),[90] most commonly from accidents and suicide. The suicide crisis was particularly pronounced after Japan participated, albeit in noncombat roles, in the War in Afghanistan and the Iraq War. Between November 2001 and January 2010, 1 in 562 JSDF members committed suicide. For personnel sent to Iraq, 1 in 280 GSDF members committed suicide, and 1 in 453 ASDF members committed suicide.[91] The U.S. Armed Forces, which are very active in hot wars, has a 39.2 per 100,000 suicide ratio. Under this metric, the suicide rate of JSDF personnel who participated in the Iraq mission was 220.8 per 100,000. In other words, JSDF personnel were 5.5 times more likely to commit suicide than a U.S. soldier.[92] If the Japanese have been unwilling to enlist in times of peace, they will be even less willing to do so if the GOJ pursued more aggressive security policies that would send the JSDF to dangerous missions abroad.

In sum, economic forces and normative rules exacerbate the demographic constraint and create a vicious cycle where weak recruitment worsens the conditions of serving in the JSDF. The strained conditions in turn make military service an even less desirable career path.

Lessons from the Colonial Era: East Asia and Conscription

How Japan's neighbors address their demographic crises provides valuable insight on the differing impacts of ideational restraints on the armed forces. Unimpeded by legalistic hurdles such as Article 9 of the Japanese Peace Constitution, all East Asia states practice conscription (see figure 3.6), a blunt yet highly effective tool for overcoming human resource deficits. Although conscription is not a popular policy, China, North Korea, South Korea, Russia, and Taiwan lack the normative aversion to military service that exists in Japan. The lesson the Japanese drew from World War II was that aggressive militarism led to Japan's monumental defeat; for other East Asians, their lack of military power led to Japanese colonization. This belief remains deeply embedded in East Asian countries, especially since they are still embroiled in conflicts that stem from World War II.

Mandatory military service cultivated environments where militarism is acceptable because every citizen is intimately tied to the security of the nation, whether through a brother, a husband, a son, a relative, or oneself.[93] Since the end of World War II, military service is not an expected responsibility of a Japanese citizen; for the majority of East Asians, sacrificing several years in military service of the country is an intrinsic part of national identity.

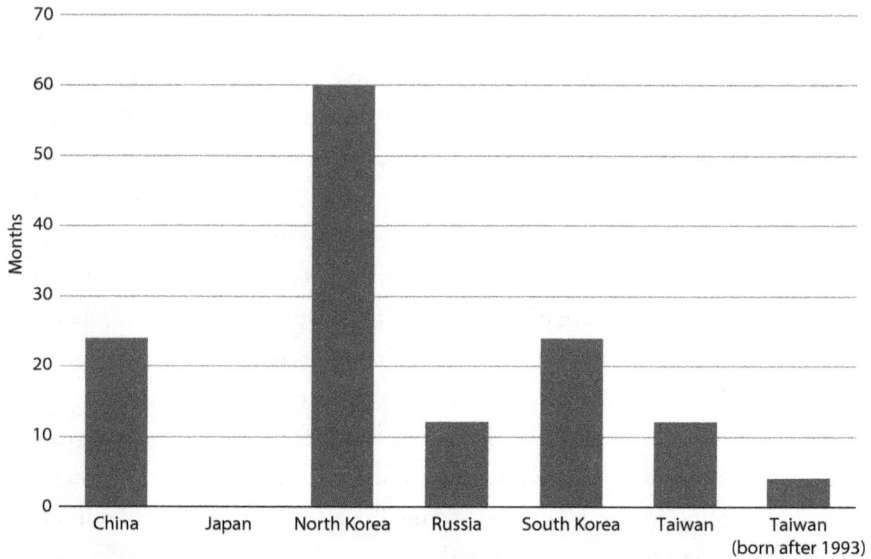

FIGURE 3.6   Conscription in East Asia.
Source: Central Intelligence Agency, *The World Factbook 2020–2021* (New York: Skyhorse, 2020).

The Korean People's Army requires the longest commitment of its citizenry, which ranges from 60 to 144 months. South Koreans must serve in the armed forces for twenty to twenty-four months. China does not enforce conscription because of sufficient volunteers for the People's Liberation Army—however, military service is expected when needed.[94] In practice, most Chinese receive some form of military training, typically during college where students must complete one to four weeks of training before graduation. Beyond allowing states to increase their immediate power, conscription helps maintain force readiness. South Korean conscripts commit three days of reserve duty a year until the age of thirty-three, Taiwanese conscripts have some obligations until the age of thirty, Russians until the age of fifty, and North Koreans serve part-time until forty followed by nominal commitments until the age of sixty.

Regular training not only augments military strength but also cultivates an environment conducive to public support of the military. The armed forces train soldiers to engage in behavior that is rare, if not altogether taboo, in civilian life. When confronted with danger, the natural human response is either flight or fight. Regardless, without proper training or combat experience, neither reaction will be tactical. Moreover, as historian Christopher Browning explains in his seminal book *Ordinary Men: Reserve Police Battalion 101 and the Final Solution in Poland*, military indoctrination can persuade the average person to commit the worst atrocities against the enemy. Training is an essential militaristic tool that prepares individuals to act strategically and calmly in times of crisis and confront the possibility of death.

Hence, conscription is a vital component of offense-oriented militarization that not only increases force size but also effective force mobilization. In Japan, conscription is a legal and political impossibility. Article 18 of the Constitution bans involuntary servitude, and an amendment would require the support of the majority of the public. The JSDF is an all-volunteer force, a feature the GOJ emphasizes to disassociate the current defense forces with the imperial military that the Japanese education system blames for leading the country down the wrong path. Even if the GOJ could force all eligible men to enlist through implausible fiat power, it would take time to develop the infrastructure and institutions to fully exploit the potential of the JSDF. Nearly every country in East Asia has prepared the majority of their population for warfare for the greater part of a century; Japan has not.

In sum, conscription mobilizes the entirety of society for war. In states that practice conscription, the education system and the general economy are built on the assumption that close to half of the population will take a multiyear break from civilian life to serve the nation. Conscripts and their families are accustomed to the idea that the use of force is legitimate, and since the blood tax is equally distributed among the population, governments within East Asia do not face the same level of scrutiny concerning the use of force abroad as does the GOJ. Whereas Japan's rivals have a steady supply of well-trained soldiers ready for duty at a moment's notice, Japan cannot fulfill a recruitment quota. Simply put, *virtually every male between the ages of eighteen and thirty-five have military training in East Asia, except Japanese men.*

A MORE WELCOMING DEFENSE FORCE: MOBILIZING WOMEN FOR THE NATION

In recent years, the MOD has pursued two innovative strategies to reframe how the JSDF is perceived, and consequently, increase enlistment in the JSDF. By portraying the JSDF as a more welcoming force and implementing more women-friendly policies, the MOD can increase the recruitment pool while the size of the population continues to decrease. In both strategies, the MOD leverages images of women to sanitize the controversial characteristics of the JSDF. An examination of MOD recruitment tactics, and their consequences, highlights how interactions between material and ideational forces significantly impede Japan's ability to pursue more aggressive forms of militarization.

In a groundbreaking study of the JSDF, anthropologist Sabine Frühstück's found that the MOD has sought to "symbolically 'disarm' " the JSDF through normalization and domestication, which would make the armed forces resemble other state-run service organizations, such as the railway and postal systems.[95] MOD recruitment campaigns mobilize idols, mascots, and anime characters to project a JSDF image that exemplifies the virtues of peace, love, and self-improvement.[96] These characters often fulfill popular Japanese animation tropes, such as *moe* (literally translated as "budding," and implies affection) and *kawaii* (cute), to attract young men and sanitize the aggressive imagery that is commonly associated with the military. One may find striking similarities between contemporary JSDF recruitment campaigns and airline advertisements from the 1970s, such as the notorious National Airlines "Fly Me" campaign that sexualized flight attendants to attract customers. In 2014, Shimazaki Haruka, of the popular idol group AKB48, starred in a JSDF commercial in which the beautiful and nonthreatening talent ends with the slogan "*koko de shika dekinai shigoto ga arimasu*" (there is a job that you can only do here). The ninety-second commercial features a video of JSDF members hugging children, conducting disaster relief operations, and using cool technology. Not once is the viewer shown the use of force, handling of weapons, or potential dangers of serving in the armed forces. In another advertisement, the all-girl group Morning Musume (Morning Daughters), smiling and dressed in summer outfits, present the slogan, "How cool is it that you work hard! GO! GO! PEACE!"

The MOD-published magazine, *MAMOR* (*mamoru* in Japanese, meaning "to protect"), follows the same tact where all but 11 of the 169 volumes (as of March 2021) have featured attractive female members of the JSDF or professional models (volume 144 combines multiple tropes and features an *anime* JSDF member; volume 20, which dates back to October 2008, is the only cover to feature a man). *MAMOR* is an effective public relations platform that normalizes civilian-JSDF interactions, most notably through *konkatsu* (marriage hunting) articles that offer marriage advice and feature single JSDF personnel.[97] The use of feminine imagery is almost an exact reversal of the hyper-masculine *yamato-damashii* (Japanese spirit) discourse that was integral to the Imperial Japanese Army in the late nineteenth and early twentieth centuries.[98] In fact, women have played a key role in rehabilitating Japan's reputation, willfully and otherwise, from the very onset of the postwar period. As Lisa Yoneyama discusses in her foundational book *Hiroshima Traces: Time, Space and the Dialects of Memory*, "accentuated feminine presence in formal politics, moreover, contributed to the demilitarization and emasculation of the nation's image, while consolidating the notion of peace as an icon of nationhood reborn."[99]

The MOD also publishes *Manga-Style Defense of Japan*, a Japanese-style comic book designed to introduce the JSDF to youths.[100] Through the use of anime and feminine imagery, the MOD hopes to erase the hyper-masculine characteristics that are commonly associated with the military and thus increase recruitment of women and men who would traditionally not consider the armed forces. One ASDF staff officer surmises that although the use of anime "lures younger people and tries to make the military more friendly and intimate (*shinkinkan*)," it "does not show the real military roles."[101] The staff officer's conclusion is held by many JSDF personnel interviewed for this book, who find the impact on recruitment of campaigns questionable and the warped portrayal of their service to the nation "strange," "embarrassing," and apt to attract the "wrong" type of person.

Former U.S. Secretary of Defense Donald Rumsfeld once stated, "you go to war with the army you have, not the army you might want or wish to have at a later time."[102] The JSDF remains eager for an army that at least meets authorized force size targets. Yet, the MOD remains hamstrung because strong antimilitarism norms make candid communication with the public nonviable as a recruitment strategy. The U.S. Armed Forces, for example, utilizes targeted recruitment strategies to enlist individuals who best fit the needs of each military branch, which ensures that recruits are less likely to quit once training begins.[103] One consequence of employing certain imagery to make the JSDF more palatable is that many perceive service in the JSDF as analogous to a regular government job. Hence, new recruits are often not prepared for the challenges and dangers of serving in the JSDF and quit soon after enlisting. These campaigns have also attracted *otaku* (a Japanese term for individuals with obsessive interests) who are drawn more to cute characters and video games than the defense of the homeland. For

individuals who desire to serve the nation, other civil service jobs, such as policing, provide such opportunities without the same degree of danger or historical
baggage. For everyone else in Japan, the sanitized depictions of military service
warp societal expectations of the military and decrease the overall understanding
of the armed forces, which create additional restraints on the GOJ's ability to
pursue policies that augment the capabilities and responsibilities of the JSDF.

Underappreciated Power: Women and the JSDF

The use of feminine imagery to sanitize the image of the JSDF has also gone hand-
in-hand with the MOD's effort to increase the recruitment of women to bolster
force size. Since returning to power in 2012, Prime Minister Abe aggressively promoted the mobilization of women for the economy and defense of Japan. As of
March 2020, the total number of female JSDF personnel was 16,863, or approximately 7.4 percent of the total number of JSDF personnel. Recruitment ratios of
female NCOs have significantly increased over the last decade, decreasing from 1
in 35.6 in 2010 to 1 in 6.7 in 2019. Overall recruitment ratios increased from 1 in 13.4
to 1 in 4.3 in the same period. Yet the meager 2.2 percent increase of total female
personnel over the last decade suggests that the MOD will have difficulty meeting
its modest goals of women comprising 9 percent of total force size and 3.1 percent holding the rank of field officer or higher by 2030. Although recruitment of
female NCOs has increased in the last five years, between 2001 and 2019, the MOD
recruited over 11.5 times more men than women across the three JSDF branches.[104]

The lack of women in the JSDF is not due to absence of awareness or policies.
In 1999, the Basic Act for a Gender-Equal Society went into effect, establishing
wide-ranging objectives to improve the position of women in society, empower
women, and increase participation in conflict prevention and peacebuilding.
In 2001, the GOJ established the Defense Agency Headquarters for the Promotion of Gender Equality. JDA initiatives sought to improve work-life balance
and facilities to more fully integrate female personnel into the forces. The Basic
Plan for Gender Equality, which was first formulated in 2000, has been revised
twice, with the Third Basic Plan for Gender Equality emphasizing economic and
societal revitalization through women's participation in the workforce. In 2015,
the GOJ completed the National Action Plan on Women, Peace and Security to
implement United Nations Security Council Resolution (UNSCR) 1325.

The MOD expanded on these initiatives in March 2011 and drew up the Basic Plan for Gender Equality in the MOD (2011–2015), which added measures to increase recruitment and promotion of female personnel.[105] Since April 2007, the MOD has set up workplace nurseries at six bases and in Ichigaya, where the MOD headquarters is located.[106] Starting in 2015, the MOD allocated additional funds for daycare facilities and services, expansion of training to change mindsets about gender roles in the workplace, providing maternity dresses as part of military uniforms, building facilities for female personnel, and researching how other countries integrate female personnel, including preventing sexual harassment and assault.[107] JSDF personnel have been receptive to these changes and the general position of women has improved in recent years, with notable examples including Rear Admiral Saeki Hikaru (MSDF), the first female flag officer in the JSDF; Captain Azuma Ryoko (MSDF), the first woman to command a warship division; and First Lieutenant Matsushima Misa (ASDF), the first woman to qualify as a fighter pilot. The examples of high-ranking women remain few, however, because of limited funding for these initiatives and deeply ingrained attitudes about women and the use of force.

Politics is either "who gets what, when, and how,"[108] or "the authoritative allocation of values."[109] Embedded in Harold Lasswell's and David Easton's classic definitions is the premise that a person or idea's importance can be measured in time and resources dedicated to them. Despite elite rhetoric extoling the importance of improving the conditions of women in the JSDF, the resources have simply not been there. In the past five years, the MOD allocated less than $20 million per year for the improvement of facilities and gender-equality initiatives. The financial support would need to substantially improve, especially regarding the creation of infrastructure such as barracks and retrofitting submarines and naval ships to ensure women have adequate lodging. The JSDF requires updates in mindsets in addition to hardware. It was not until 2015 that the ASDF lifted rules restricting women from operating fighter jets. In 2017, virtually all assignment restrictions were lifted. The situation, Morimoto Satoshi argues, is akin to that of the United States: "Women always get high test scores, are promoted to high ranks, are very hardworking, do the mission sincerely and honestly, and are very loyal to the mission. The problem is still there are limitations for women in combat operations."[110] Women have more job opportunities in the GSDF because of available noncombat duties, such as supply, maintenance, accounting, telecommunications, and general sections and personnel assignments. The ASDF and MSDF have had more difficulty placing women. Morimoto concludes that women can play important roles in disaster relief operations, particularly in providing medical care, nursing for the elderly and young, and distributing supplies.

Statements like these reveal the fundamental reason why the measures implemented to increase the recruitment of women will continue to have a marginal impact—because they are not *women-centered* policies. Gender norms concerning the division of labor and the so-called proper role of women in society continue to shape how the GOJ addresses the material constraints of the demographic crises. Within Defense of Japan white papers, only four to five pages of the five-hundred-plus-page reports are dedicated to the subject of gender equality and women's empowerment. Out of the 132 issues of *Japan Defense Focus* (as of February 2021 a MOD produced web-journal that includes officer interviews and JSDF activity highlights, only five mention women and gender subjects. The most substantive examination of women appeared in issue 56 (September 2014), which was also the first time women were mentioned in *Japan Defense Focus*. In a one-page article titled "Women Making a Difference at the MOD," "SDF Female Officer" Lieutenant Colonel Chizu Kurita is interviewed about her experiences as the first female officer sent to a PKO mission individually. Chizu believes she adds a female perspective, which allows local women to communicate with the JSDF because they can be reluctant to speak with the male officers. Chizu concludes the interview stating that her future goal is to raise awareness of gender equality in the MOD/SDF. Chizu is mentioned again in issue 59 (December 2014) concerning her dispatch to NATO Headquarters to give advice on integrating women in policies and PKO activities. Issue 68 (August 2015) has a one-page article on Major Takaaki Tanaka's participation in the Gender Field Advisor Course, and issue 69 (September 2015) briefly mentions Marriët Schuurman, NATO Secretary General's Special Representative for Woman, Peace and Security, visiting the MOD. Women are not mentioned again in the *Defense Focus* for another three and half years, when First Lieutenant Matsushima Misa was recognized for becoming the first woman to qualify as a jet fighter pilot.

Sociologist Sato Fumika, a specialist on women in the JSDF writes, "Since its creation, the SDF has sought to camouflage its military character by blending into the surrounding civil society. Women have played an important role in camouflaging the SDF in this manner."[111] Sato's research finds that women are rarely given equal opportunities and responsibilities, and they are often used for improving the image of the country as a "progressive and modern nation" and in increasing the recruitment of men, either through the use of their image in recruitment posters or their bodies in beauty contests.[112] Although women make up less than 10 percent of the JSDF, their imagery is used in the majority of recruitment campaigns.

The struggles of integrating women in the JSDF should come as no surprise given that other countries are similarly challenged. Feminist scholars have long established that the armed forces are spaces created by and for men. Maya Eichler, for example, introduces the concept of "militarized masculinities," defined as "the assertion that traits stereotypically associated with masculinity can be acquired and proven through military service or action, and combat in particular. When a state and military leaders aim to display strength through the use of military force or hope to recruit male citizens through appeals to their masculine identity, they are relying on and reproducing militarized masculinity."[113] Women can only take part in the military if they are given the right to serve and if they can prove they have the capacity to serve.[114] In the case of the JSDF, the motivation for integrating women is primarily to address human resource deficits, not to eradicate fundamental inequalities in society—although such a shift would greatly improve the MOD's ability to successfully carry out its policies. Here, it is worth reminding that "feminine" and "masculine" are social constructions—that is, rules that define individuals and guide, restrict, and generate their actions. Since women are not assigned combat roles, women can only serve a supplementary role in the armed forces, whether by providing logistics and support, or through the appropriation of their imagery and feminine features to dull the controversial, aggressive, and masculine features of the military. The barriers of overcoming these prejudices remain high because of external pressures. Female JSDF members must strike a delicate balance of degendering the armed forces to be treated as "equal," while also bringing attention to gender discrimination in the workplace and meeting societal expectations. In a series of interviews, Sabine Frühstück found that "female service members feel that their professional and social mobility is impeded by and their careers measured against social conventions that promote women's main goals as being wives and mothers."[115] The pressures on female service members to prioritize marriage and having children over their careers make clear the true priorities of the state.

The MOD's recruitment of women demonstrates how ideational forces, in this case gender norms and antimilitarism, can shape the policies that seek to address the material constraints posed by anemic recruitment. These rules limit the policy options that the MOD can pursue, which not only make it difficult to increase the force size of the JSDF but also ensure that the armed forces is unlikely to return to the more aggressive forms of militarism in the pre-World War II period.

THE BACK-END APPROACH: FIXING THE AGING AND DECLINING ECONOMY

Thus far, this chapter has examined the front-end impacts of poor demographics on force size. Ideational variables, such as gender norms, antimilitarism, and cultural practices exacerbate the recruitment problem by limiting the recruitment pool and the MOD's options for attracting new enlistees. This section examines the interactions between the material constraints and ideational restraints and how it impedes back-end strategies that seek to minimize the consequences of the demographic crises. The aging and declining population has weakened the Japanese economy, and thus the ability of the GOJ to extract resources from society to increase the defense budget and upgrade the capabilities of the JSDF.

Few countries punch above their economic weight more than Japan. Within four decades, the eleventh-largest population in the world rebuilt a nation devastated by war and created the second-largest economy in the world. The Japanese economic miracle was made possible by a combination of factors, including support from the United States, successful integration into the global economy, prudent industrial policy, and conservative foreign policies that avoided involvement in international conflicts. Central to Japan's growth and eventual decline was an unforgiving work culture that mobilized a large and young working population. The Japanese economy is built on the assumption that there would always be a domestic labor force willing to work more hours than any other country in the world. The GOJ rewarded the Japanese public for their hard work with a robust social welfare system, but they lacked the foresight to consider a future where there would not be enough people to support the retirement-age population. For three-quarters of a century, Japanese work culture shaped the relationship between the public and the economy and institutionalized work practices that are difficult to change. When the economic bubble burst in the late 1980s, the structural problems in the Japanese economy were laid bare, and Japan continues to struggle to find a path forward.

Although the Japanese are known for their work ethic—generating a phenomenon in which some literally die from work (*karōshi*)—one can only produce so much. The demographic crisis further strains the working-age population and has significant impacts on national productivity. According to Yashiro Naohiro, the present structure of the Japanese "economy and society implicitly depends on an increasing population, particularly of working-age population." Therefore, Japan must change its economic structures and practices to ease the impacts of population decline.[116] However, even if the GOJ can implement policies that increase productivity and grow the economy, "a significant portion of those gains would be offset by the effects of a declining population."[117] Due to the reduction of work hours and retirement of the elderly population, from 1995 to 2010 the workforce decreased by 3 percent while work hours decreased by 12 percent.[118] The decline in labor output, among other factors, resulted in lackluster economic growth, which averaged 1.1 percent between 1990 and 2018. In a study examining the impact of Japan's poor demographics on the economy, economist Robert Dekle writes, "Had Japanese labor grown at 1 percent annually (about the same rate as in the United States) instead, annual GDP growth in Japan would have averaged 2.5 percent."[119]In other words, Japan has been remarkably productive since the asset bubble burst, but the consequences of population decline are so severe that the nation's productivity has all but been erased. A less productive country would be drowning instead of treading water. Nevertheless, it is difficult to light the embers of war while barely keeping the economy afloat.

The weak economy has tied the hands of government leaders. In 2020, Japan's debt was 266 percent of the GDP, 59 percent higher than a decade earlier and the highest among advanced industrialized countries.[120] This debt will grow as the population grays. Social security expenditures accounted for 34.9 percent of government spending in 2020, more than double the amount in 1993. Entitlements will be almost unsustainable once Japan faces the 2025 problem in just half a decade, when the 6.5 million-person baby boom generation will be seventy-five or older. With a maximum income tax rate of 55.95 percent, a 10 percent flat residence tax, and 10 percent consumption tax, there is little left to extract from an overworked public. As a result, the GOJ will continue to finance itself through debt.

Optimists have downplayed the debt crisis because the Bank of Japan (BOJ) has aggressively purchased government debt, thus making debt essentially interest-free. As of December 2020, the BOJ owned 48 percent of the one quadrillion yen Japanese government bond (JGB) market and held assets collectively worth more than the entire GDP of Japan (JGB accounted for 76 percent of the BOJ's total assets).[121] Such aggressive quantitative easing policies are not without risk. If Japan finds itself in another financial crisis, the BOJ would be saddled with bad debt and few fiscal tools. The 2020 COVID-19 pandemic, for example, forced the BOJ to remove limits on government bond purchases to keep borrowing costs low. Nevertheless, Japanese-owned debt does not protect the economy when the value of the debt falls. Calling attention to the vulnerable social security system, which entirely depends on deficit financing, Yashiro argues "it is nonsense [that the debt does not matter] because although Japanese are borrowing from other Japanese, they do not keep the national debt for patriotic reasons, so if the price of the national debt goes too low, they will keep their own families' assets, and maybe turn to U.S. bonds."[122] If Japanese offload their debt elsewhere, the GOJ approaches a nightmare scenario that could destroy the social security system that has kept the nation stable during the last three decades of economic uncertainty.

Japan's antimilitarism ecosystem shapes how the demographic crises affect the GOJ's effort to strengthen the JSDF through economic means. According to Diet members from Japan's three largest political parties interviewed for this book, it would be a political impossibility to significantly increase the defense budget. For decades, defense expenditures have remained below 1 percent of the GDP. This level of spending has remained steadfast despite the rise of China and numerous North Korean nuclear tests (chapter 6 will discuss the normative dimension of this 1 percent spending cap in detail). Under the Abe government, the defense budget increased every year after eleven years of continuous decline, although budget increases have not kept up with inflation. Even modest increases would be difficult given the economic situation, especially since government leaders have been unable to develop a plan to justify a specific spending target.[123] The limited budget forces the MOD to choose between system upgrades and maintenance, weapons acquisition, salary increases and benefits, and recruitment.

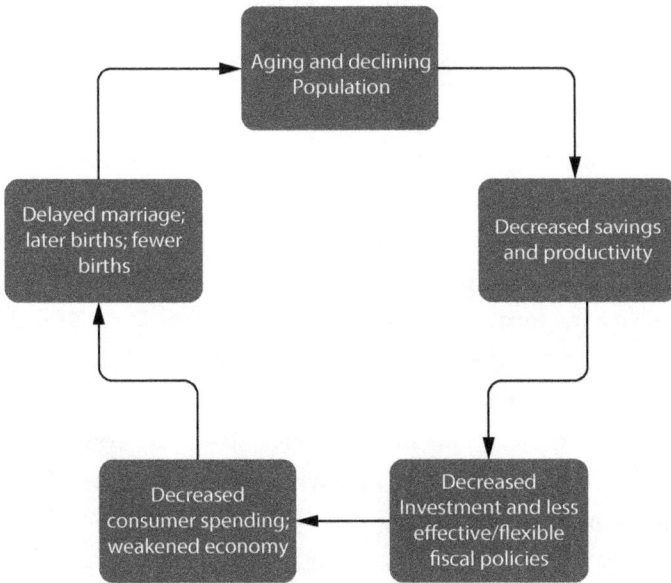

FIGURE 3.7 The impact of demographics on Japanese security.

As summarized in figure 3.7, these constraints, shaped by ideational restraints, form a vicious cycle that is difficult to break. Japan's demographic crises cuts across historical, economic, normative, and gender issue areas; policymakers will struggle to develop a panacea for vulnerabilities that have developed over decades. Thus far, the GOJ has slowly widened the intake valve to take in the minimum number of women and immigrants necessary to address its economic and security problems without disrupting the old way of life. A much more daring approach is required to address demographic crises, one that transforms the fundamental characteristics of the JSDF and Japanese society.

REPLACING OLD BODIES WITH NEW MACHINES

The JSDF's force size problem is a true dilemma; to tackle one underlying cause requires undoing deeply embedded social rules at the macroeconomic level, societal level, and individual level.

Rewriting rules is a lengthy process and can cause additional problems to the economy and security. Fumika Sato provides valuable insight on some of the most deeply embedded rules, which continue to shape not only the content and direction of Japanese security policy but also societal relations themselves—that of gender norms. Sato concludes, "the 'feminization' of the SDF has been caused by 'statist reasons' rather than 'feminist reasons.' "[124] This statist approach was imbued in the Abe government's policies that sought to mobilize women to jumpstart the economy and fill in the gaps of the JSDF. Yet, when policies do not address fundamental inequalities within society, whether in the armed services, workplace, or home, there is little reason why women would accept being mobilized *for* men and the state.

This chapter explored the demographics hardware constraint on the JSDF's power projection capabilities. Moreover, it highlighted how normative restraints, namely the public's unwillingness to join the JSDF and the obstacles toward reform, entrench and augment the constraints on JSDF force size. The GOJ has steadily increased the JSDF's capabilities and updated its security doctrines in the past few decades, resulting in an impression of grand changes. However the tangible alterations to Japan's security forces have been limited.

Some of the limits are self-imposed, but many are not. There is no silver bullet for the demographic crises; as much as they are a problem of numbers, addressing them requires grappling with knotty cultural, political, and normative practices. Seventy-five years of antimilitarism have worsened the demographics crises and limited Japan's ability to address them. Historically, Japan has shown a remarkable ability to overcome great disaster and strengthen itself through growth. However, the challenge today is not just lack of growth but decline as well. Overcoming regional threats in the twenty-first century may not require linear growth in power projection capabilities (if that is possible at all) but a new approach to security. Such a transformation will require not only novel ways of deterring threats abroad but also rethinking the norms at home, specifically how to weave disenfranchised groups into the Japanese national tapestry. This will be difficult. Yashiro Naohiro laments, "In Japan, reforms are always too small and too late. And so that is our structural problem."[125]

If social problems are hard to fix because people are creatures of habit, then the solution may come from technology, such as AI and robotics. The following chapter will examine the limits of this strategy by outlining the second set of hardware constraints, such as outdated infrastructure, lack of combat experience, defense-oriented technology, and immature military-industrial complex. Similar to the human resource problem, the acquisition and use of technology for defense is influenced by far more than the external security environment.

CHAPTER FOUR

Technical-Infrastructural Constraints and the Capacity Crises

The JSDF is no military pygmy. World-class fighters, cutting-edge submarines, and the eighth-largest defense budget in the world support the highly trained JSDF personnel. Furthermore, the GOJ has loosened the self-imposed ban on arms exports that hindered growth in the domestic defense industry. They did this with the hopes of mitigating the JSDF's demographic and technological weaknesses and augmenting its strengths to tackle the diverse challenges of the twenty-first century. Improved surveillance capabilities, acquisition of new defense technologies, increased combined exercises with the United States and like-minded states, and concerted effort to create a more seamless and logical defense force have led some scholars to conclude that recent developments are the thin end of a wedge and that Japanese militarization is well underway.

Such conclusions are new language for old practices. Since the inception of the JSDF, the MOD has implemented hundreds of incremental changes to improve its ability to defend the Japanese homeland.[1] The gradual changes to the JSDF, however, have not matched the sudden and significant changes in the global security environment. Efforts to normalize the JSDF have been stymied by legal obstacles, public resistance, and private sector indifference. Over the last seven decades, and for the foreseeable future, path-dependent technical-infrastructural constraints such as an outdated base infrastructure, lack of combat experience, defense-oriented arms procurement and production, and underdeveloped defense sector prevent significant change in Japanese security policy.

This chapter is organized as follows. It begins with a discussion of the difficulty in ascertaining the impact of arms procurement and security policy change.

It proceeds to elucidate the constraints imposed by outdated infrastructure and lack of combat experience on the JSDF. The chapter concludes with an examination of how antimilitarism rules reinforce these material constraints and lead to an underdeveloped indigenous defense industry.

THE DIFFICULTY WITH (RE)MILITARIZATION

In *Defense of Japan* white papers and National Security Strategy (NSS), government officials candidly identify changes in the regional and global environment as impetuses for modernizing the JSDF. Prime Minister Abe expended much of his political capital for revising the Constitution, increasing defense budgets, and changing longstanding policies that capped Japan's power projection capabilities. The introduction of collective defense and the relaxation of the arms export principles, among other developments, have led scholars to conclude that "pacifism is dead" and Japan is militarizing, if it has not done so already.[2]

Similar conclusions could have been drawn many times over the last three decades. The JSDF's first overseas deployment in 1992, the revision of the Guidelines for U.S.-Japan Defense Cooperation in 1997, the authorization of air-to-air refueling capabilities in 2000, and the deployment of the JSDF to assist in the reconstruction of Iraq in 2004 were met with anxiety by Japan's neighbors and with seemingly greater interest by scholars anxious to finally disprove the significance of antimilitarism norms. The regional power balance in East Asia did not change. China and North Korea continued to gain additional leverage as their powers grew, and concerned Japanese policymakers continued to argue for Japan to become a "normal nation."

The difficulty with projections is determining when meaningful change begins and ends. What seems like a sudden change could have been in development for decades, whereas an apparent game-changer can reinforce the status quo. Projections favor boundless imaginings of where a state's capabilities may go at the expense of appreciating where the capabilities have been and why it is difficult to move beyond where they are currently.

States regularly upgrade existing weapons systems and acquire new technologies, often due to economic necessity or the natural evolution of defense technology. Eventually it is economically and strategically sound to replace aging equipment because parts become difficult and expensive to procure. New acquisitions alone provide limited insight on intentions in the present or the future. When considering East Asia's power distribution, it is even more challenging to conclude that recent policies are significant. For example, in September 2012, China commissioned its first aircraft carrier, the *Liaoning*, while Japan simultaneously sought to upgrade its Atago-class destroyers with improved BMD technology. The *Liaoning* transformed the People's Liberation Army Navy from a green-water force to a blue-water force, while the MSDF remained defense-oriented. Even if China had not commissioned a new ship class, the MOD might have still sought to upgrade its aging fleet, as it has regularly pursued incremental upgrades throughout the postwar period. China has since introduced a second aircraft carrier and will complete two more within the decade. In the 2019 National Defense Program Guidelines (NDPG), the GOJ proposed retrofitting two Izumo-class helicopter destroyers into aircraft carriers capable of deploying F-35s. This upgrade may seem significant, but it is far from proportional. How is one to interpret the policy choice of upgrading over the commissioning of a new ship class? Realists use capability change as "an analytical shortcut to understanding foreign policy change,"[3] and consequently, overlook why specific policy outcomes are indicators of underlying constraints on Japan's ability to remilitarize and ultimately misinterpret its foreign policy altogether.

The more aggressive interpretations of MOD capacity building policies erroneously lead one to believe that such policies are game changers. A game changer qualitatively disrupts the balance of power or changes how warfare is conducted; otherwise, the game remains the same. The GOJ is sensitive to how Japan's neighbors interpret its defense policies because it does not want to change the game (discussed further in chapter 5). According to Nishida Jun, deputy director of the National Security Policy Division in the Ministry of Foreign Affairs, the GOJ has primarily sought to streamline communication among the three JSDF branches, improve efficiency, and unburden themselves of unnecessary complex legal codes so that they can make more significant contributions to humanitarian assistance and disaster relief (HA/DR).[4] If Japan has changed the game, it has done so with the support of the public that has become more receptive of deploying the JSDF for purposes beyond immediate national security, such as peacekeeping operations (PKOs) and HA/DR (discussed further in chapter 7). This type of militarism does not lend itself easily to the dichotomous pacifism-militarism analytical framework.

Projections of JSDF militarization also suggest that growth is linear and infinite, where one can conclude it is a "dramatic transformation" and "vigorous buildup."[5] The reality may be more piecemeal and patchwork. Not only has arms procurement not kept pace with regional neighbors, let alone other great powers, but the MOD has difficulty convincing the Japanese public of the necessity of procuring more advanced and expensive technologies. Even if the normative and legalistic hurdles are overcome, the MOD will struggle to continuously and significantly strengthen the JSDF because of the residual antimilitarism that is still deeply embedded in security practices and outdated infrastructure, that is infrastructural lag. In short, there is a tendency to compare the world's militaries of today to Japan's military of tomorrow.[6] Normalization of the JSDF requires more than acquiring new capabilities. It also requires undoing the constraints that are features of the antimilitarism ecosystem. As many scholars would have it, the JSDF is coming out of retirement to enter the game down twenty points, while nursing an ankle injury and having to guard Kobe Bryant in his prime. It is a big ask that will likely not end well.

Upgrades intended to mitigate the weaknesses of the JSDF also come with tradeoffs. For example, defense officials consider the tradeoff between increasing offensive capabilities and building female-only facilities when deliberating the acquisition of new destroyers and submarines. The demographic crises have also led defense officials to consider decreasing the size of new destroyers and submarines to reduce the complement necessary for their operation, especially since increased fleet size exacerbates the chronic personnel deficits. One senior MOD official summarizes the dilemma of achieving both, stating:

> Even if you have a ship with great capabilities, that ship cannot be in two places at once. So, you need a certain number, but at the same time, the requirements or needs, how to staff and man these ships are increasingly a problem. The current NDPG called for an increase of our surface competence from forty-eight to fifty-four and also the previous NDPG, which is the 2010 NDPG, called for the increase of our submarine fleet from sixteen to twenty-two, and we are in the course of accomplishing those goals. Increasing the number of surface vessels is especially challenging because of the shrinking population base and also increased demands on JSDF activities including ISR activities in the East China Sea.[7]

Decreasing crew size, or minimal manning, deprives the JSDF of critical redundancy. During warfare, redundancy allows the military to absorb injuries and casualties while continuing the operation of ships. Minimal manning also increases crew fatigue because sailors are deployed for extended periods, deployed more often, and worked nonstop in battle. Maintaining the bare minimum human resource requirements becomes a significant liability during warfare, which is the raison d'être of every military. Concerning fighter aircraft, Ono Keishi, a researcher at the National Institute for Defense Studies (NIDS) specializing in defense economics, concludes that during war, "Japan cannot maintain a 90 percent operation ratio, which is its pride in peace time and much higher than other armed forces. It will drop to 80, 70, 60 percent as the war lasts. The JSDF has no preparation as a whole system for dropping operational ratios. The most fatal problem is the lack of personnel for intensive round-the-clock operation for a long period."[8] Another tradeoff of introducing sophisticated weapon systems is the increase maintenance costs. This is especially true now, as the MOD has become increasing reliant on foreign military sales (FMS) and has less control over long-term costs. The inability to increase capabilities and human resources also signifies broader financial obstacles. The defense budget, which is informally capped at 1 percent by antimilitarism norms (discussed further in chapter 6), forces officials to choose between the expensive acquisition of new equipment and maintenance of current weapons systems. Defense procurement acquisitions are thus shaped by demographic constraints and normative restraints as much as they are by external threats.

The MOD has also increased investment in artificial intelligence (AI) and robotics to overcome the human resource deficits. According to Ono, such tools would "not cost as much as capital equipment such as warships and fighter aircraft," especially because these technologies are also developed in the commercial sector.[9] However, AI and robotics are primarily defensive technologies and designed to lessen the burden on the JSDF, not disrupt regional power balance. Ono reminds us that "China and Russia are also introducing AI and robotics, together with their huge amount of human workforce. So just a replacement [of current capabilities] is not enough."[10]

The gap between today's capabilities and tomorrow's possibilities is far larger than popular perception. Many recent developments in Japanese security policy are to *make up* power deficits that are the byproducts of a deeply entrenched antimilitarism ecosystem. It will take time and resources, both of which Japan lack, before the JSDF is remilitarized.

PEBBLES GROW INTO BOULDERS LUSH WITH MOSS: THE JSDF'S BASE ISSUE

Whether Japan is undergoing a security renaissance or not, policymakers are approaching security policy with sophistication and pragmatism. As one senior government official puts it, "we have been pragmatic all along. We were not pragmatic at all during the war. That is why we lost the war. But after the war, we have been pragmatic."[11] The heart of this pragmatism has not been unbridled militarism but an increased cognizance of the need to identify strategies and practices that are no longer conducive to the defense of Japan.

During the Cold War, approximately half of the JSDF's training grounds were concentrated in Hokkaidō to prevent attacks from the Soviet Union. However, the end of the Cold War necessitated a shift in strategy, from one designed to counter conventional forces to a more flexible war footing that includes acquiring antiballistic-missile systems, increasing synergy among the JSDF branches, and increasing interoperability between the JSDF and U.S. Armed Forces. To reinforce the ASDF air defense posture in the southwestern region, the MOD established the Southwestern Air Defense Force in 2014 and increased the number of fighter squadrons in the following years. In 2016, the MOD extended its surveillance network near the disputed Senkaku Islands by constructing a new radar observation station on Yonaguni Island and increasing the JSDF's presence in the Amami Islands. The movement of forces to the south, however, has been slowed by the lack of facilities, such as housing and training grounds.

Since the end of World War II, the GOJ has not significantly invested in the JSDF's bases, with many requiring upgrades to maintain current readiness and to meet major shifts in defense planning. According to Tokuchi Hideshi, acquiring new facilities is expensive, but the "biggest obstacles are local politics and getting the support and understanding of the local community."[12] The JSDF, like most militaries in democratic countries, struggle with acquiring land for new bases.[13] Antimilitarism norms, however, make the Japanese public especially cautious. Consequently, many JSDF bases are reclaimed pre-1945 bases that lack critical infrastructure and are co-operated with the local authorities. For example, runways are shared between ASDF aircraft and civilian aircraft at the Miho Air Base and Chitose Air Base. Japan's most substantial former imperial bases are controlled, operated, or shared with the United States. The lack of a ready-to-go infrastructure is a bottleneck in the MOD's efforts to adjust to shifting security environments. According to Colonel Jonathan C. Goff, the United States' first marine attaché to Japan, despite the construction of new facilities, there is still a need for training areas to practice amphibious operations and housing facilities to absorb the movement of forces into southern Japan.[14]

Base maintenance costs far surpass the financial resources that are dedicated to the construction of new facilities and base upgrades. A unique reason for this resource distribution is the frequency of earthquakes in Japan, which cause damage to the already undermaintained facilities.[15] As illustrated in figure 4.1, although the facility improvement budget increased by 89 percent between 2010 and 2020, it was only one-tenth of the total maintenance budget. Facility improvement expenditures dropped to 2010 levels in 2019, only to inch up

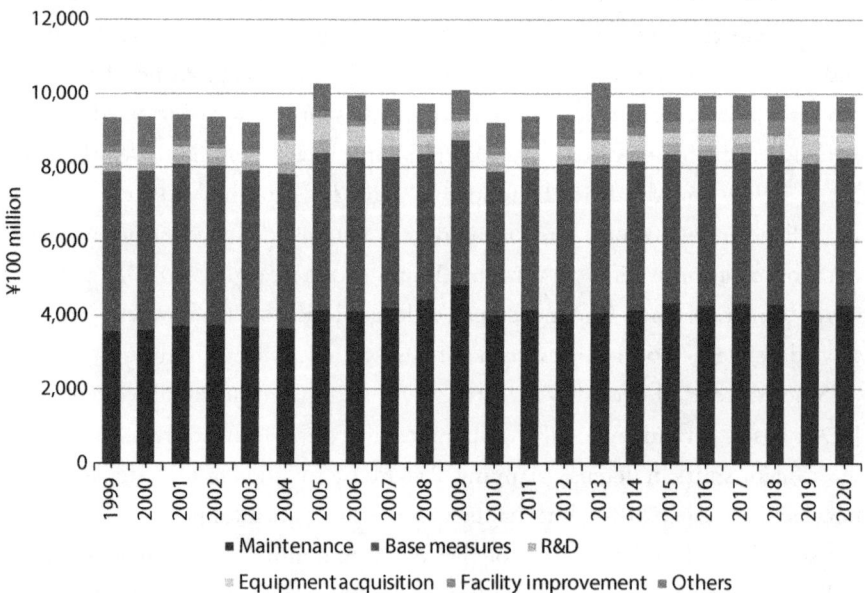

FIGURE 4.1   General material (activity) expenses, 1999–2020.
Source: Defense Programs and Budget of Japan, various years.

27 percent the following year. Over the eleven-year period, facility improvements comprised only 2 to 4 percent of total general material expenses.

The funds the MOD allocates for base measures (community grants, host nation support, and rent and compensation costs), which do not permanently improve the conditions of JSDF bases, are on average ten times greater than facility improvement funds. In the 2020 defense budget, the MOD spent six times more on host nation support (not including Special Action Committee on Okinawa-related expenses) than it did for domestic facility improvements.[16] Relatedly, many of the facilities improvement measures did not increase the capacity of the JSDF but were intended to decrease the impact of the bases on local communities, such as residential soundproofing and public works projects (¥114.7 billion) and compensation for the loss of income due to training exercises (¥152.7 billion). Of the ¥992.6 billion general materials budget in 2020, 43.2 percent was spent on basic maintenance, such as oil, repair, education and training, medical care, and utilities. The lack of direct investment in bases constrain the JSDF's ability to expand quickly and take full advantage of new arms procurements.

Much of the facility improvement resources go toward addressing the recruitment problem, specifically, building female-only facilities.[17] In 2015—the first time the word "female" even appears in a defense budget—¥600 million was allocated for female-only facilities and an additional ¥100 million for daycare facilities (ASDF Iruma Air Base). In 2016, ¥900 million was used for improving conditions for female personnel, which included building accommodation sections and related facilities on Aegis-equipped destroyers, refurbishing buildings for training units, and providing mentorship and counseling. An additional ¥200 million was set aside for the establishment of childcare facilities (ASDF Fuchū Air Base, ASDF Hamamatsu Air Base, and Ichigaya District), three of which were newly established in 2016. In 2017, ¥1.4 billion was budgeted for developing spaces for women on bases, residential spaces for students at the National Defense Academy, and personal support. Seventy million yen was dedicated to child-care facilities, which included a new center at the National Defense Medical College and renovation of the Komaki Base and Iruma Air Base. In 2018, ¥1.8 billion was allocated for development facilities for female personnel and ¥100 million for renovating workplace nurseries, including a new space in Ichigaya for pregnant women. In the 2019 Defense Budget Request, the MOD requested

¥3.3 billion to "install female-only sections in barracks and ships, improve living and working conditions, and development education and training foundations for female personnel in order to recruit, retain and promote female personnel," but the final figure was 20 percent less at ¥2.6 billion.[18] The 2020 budget allocated an additional ¥400 million for female-only facilities and support for work-life balance. Thus, over the past half-decade, the MOD has made a concerted effort to improve the conditions of female personnel, however, the more substantial infrastructure, such as female-only barracks and training facilities, will take years to complete. Uncertainty over the strength of the economy due to demographics and unforeseen environmental disasters makes the long-term viability of these projects questionable. Until the base infrastructure is fully modernized, the full incorporation of women in the JSDF will be limited.

Infrastructure-related defense spending has overwhelmingly been allocated to the maintenance of current bases, the improvement of facilities for women to increase recruitment, and the construction of surveillance stations. Moreover, the GOJ's focus on acquiring technologically advanced—and expensive—capital equipment has further limited the resources available for critical infrastructure. Concerning the state of affairs, one GSDF base commander lamented, "Money is everything when you judge what an organization values most. With the rising cost of weapons and maintenance, base facilities have not enjoyed enough finance to improve themselves."[19] A robust base infrastructure is critical for the rapid movement of forces to counter threats, training to mount new and large exercises, improving the standard of living to increase recruitment and retention, testing new defense equipment and technologies, and increasing equipment operating rates. The infrastructural constraint limits the strength of the JSDF until time, financial resources, and political capital become available to construct new bases.

One development of note is the construction of Japan's only postwar overseas base in Djibouti, which on average bases two hundred JSDF personnel. Established in July 2011, the ¥4.7 billion base allows the MSDF to conduct patrols in the Indian Ocean and augment its antipiracy capabilities. Its establishment crosses a significant normative bright line in that there is now a permanent presence of Japanese troops outside the mainland. However, the base's impact on the overall strength of the JSDF is minimal. The JSDF is hamstrung by strict rules of engagement, and the troops in Djibouti amount to less than one-thousandth of a percent of the authorized JSDF force size. The base, therefore, fulfills its stated purpose—to allow Japan to contribute to international antipiracy efforts—and does little to balance against rivals in East Asia or increase the capabilities of the overall force.

MISSING REPS: THE JSDF AND COMBAT EXPERIENCE

The underdeveloped base infrastructure is caused by a lack of economic and political resources, but it is also a symptom of an additional technical constraint—the JSDF's lack of combat experience. Here, the computer analogy again proves useful. One can conceptualize combat experience as "firmware," which is "a software program or set of instructions programmed on a hardware device. It provides the necessary instructions for how the device communicates with the other computer hardware."[20] Combat experience, analogous to firmware, provides the necessary instructions for how JSDF personnel mobilize, operate equipment, and conduct warfare. This experience is critical for a symbiotic relationship between the soldier and the tools they use to protect the nation, and it greatly influences the overall strength of the military. Combat experience can be gained as firmware can be upgraded; however, it is unlikely the JSDF will do so in the near future.[21] It was not until the early 1990s—sixty years after the end of World War II—that the JSDF engaged in limited international PKOs. Time-limited PKOs have provided few opportunities to gain valuable combat experience or the impetus to significantly invest in the base infrastructure.

East Asia has enjoyed relative peace in the past few decades. This was not the case, however, in the early postwar period where most countries in the region participated in a myriad of conflicts. Chinese troops experienced combat in the invasion of Xinjiang (1949), the invasion of Tibet (1950–1951), the Korean War (1950–1952), the Chola incident (1967), the Zhenbao Island incident (1969), the Vietnam War (1969–1975), the Battle of the Paracel Islands (1974), and the Sino-Vietnamese War (1979). Although the superpowers did not engage in direct warfare during the Cold War, both states were on a permanent war footing and participated in proxy wars around the world. The USSR was involved in fourteen conflicts between 1945 and 1991, the most notable being the Soviet-Afghan War that lasted over nine years. Following the dissolution of the USSR, Russia has fought in twelve conflicts nears its borders and in the Middle East, such as the First and Second Chechen Wars (1994–1996 and 1999–2009), as well as interventions in the Ukraine (2004–present) and Syria (2015–present). Both China and Russia are engaged in a war on terror that primarily consists of counterterrorism and counterinsurgency operations. North Korea and South Korea signed an armistice in 1953 but remain on a permanent war footing. Over the last six decades, North Korea and South Korea have engaged in almost yearly small-scale skirmishes, the most significant in the 2010 with the bombardment of Yeonpyeong Island. All states in East Asia are involved in multistate international conflicts and participate in PKOs (except North Korea). Unlike the JSDF, other militaries are not bound by strict legal prohibitions on the use of force during PKOs, and thus they are more likely to be placed in combat scenarios that accurately reflect conventional warfare. Japan, therefore, is particularly exceptional in its lack of combat experience. JSDF personnel have not fired a live round in combat in seventy-five years.

Of course, one cannot definitively conclude the JSDF is ill-prepared for the defense of the homeland solely due to the lack of combat experience. The JSDF is well-regarded for its professionalism and high-quality training. Moreover, the JSDF participates in joint training and combined exercises with the United States and like-minded countries with increased frequency. These exercises simulate actual warfare and create opportunities to identify technical and logistical weaknesses.

The limits of simulations and exercises, nevertheless, suggest that Japan's militarization is unlikely to have a tangible impact on power projection and the regional power balance. For one, simulations have differing impacts on each branch of the JSDF. The MSDF can rely on computer simulations because they closely mimic live combat scenarios. On the other hand, the GSDF—the largest branch of the JSDF—requires outdoor training exercises to simulate the battlefield. Pilots in the ASDF can replicate some operations from simulations, but actual flight time prepares them for the extreme stresses of jet fighter operation. Regardless of the type of training, simulations cannot replicate the pressure and high stakes of live combat. Concerning the significance of combined exercises, one U.S. Navy captain reminds us that although Japan and the United States participate in annual combined exercises, usually lasting three to fourteen days per exercise, there are not significant day-to-day interactions that help build familiarity between the two sides.[22] The captain concludes, "The connection, although not superficial, is not deep," and the combined operations are a "parabola, where if Japan were engaged in real warfare, they would be neck-and-neck with the U.S., or if there were absolute peace, they would spend more time with Americans." As long as both forces are preoccupied with external threats, but not engaged in actual warfare, the nature of the defense-oriented alliance will remain.

Combat experience is essential for developing leadership and command skills that are necessary for a high-functioning military force. Currently, there are no senior ranked officers in the JSDF that have participated in an active combat theatre. The lack of combat experience also prevents the JSDF from developing nonoffensive but critical tactics, such as the extraction of hostages abroad. In the past two decades, several Japanese civilians have been kidnapped in the Middle East, but the JSDF lacked the legal codes and tactical know-how to save them. The value of combat experience lies in removing some of the uncertainty that comes with warfare so that a state can make more effective decisions. Ultimately, best practices are developed when *practiced*. When realists contend that Japan has increased its power projection, they neglect *how* the power would be projected. In providing a cautiously optimistic assessment of the JSDF's readiness, one ASDF staff officer observes, "We cannot conclude that the JSDF sees it [the lack of combat experience] as a problem for its readiness. Of course, we would never know the real capability unless we actually engage in combat. At the same time, it is needless to say that experience is always better than just learning from a book."[23]

Some scholars contend the JSDF has gained valuable overseas operational experience through PKOs and HA/DR missions.[24] Ishizuka Katsumi, for example, concludes that the operational experience, opportunities to develop and evaluate the leadership of the JSDF, training and team development, among other benefits gained from PKOs "would be especially significant for the SDF, which has not experienced conventional warfare since its establishment."[25] Others are more ambitious, arguing that "Japan is back" because the JSDF has "demonstrated its ability to project military power in the region [South China Sea] in 2013 when over a thousand soldiers and three vessels were sent to the Philippines for relief operations following the Haiyan cyclone disaster."[26] PKOs are valuable experiences for JSDF personnel. However, a closer examination of the JSDF's experience abroad reveal a much more restricted experience than suggested.

The JSDF participated in its first PKO in 1991, over thirty years after its establishment. Since then, over twelve thousand JSDF personnel have been dispatched to fourteen UN peacekeeping and humanitarian support operations. JSDF duties included election monitoring, human resource development, engineering, construction, and other noncombat activities. These activities facilitate the improvement of logistics, organization, command and control, and Japan's image abroad, but their combat applicability is less evident.

According to the Act of Cooperation with United Nations Peacekeeping Operations and Other Operations, Japanese peacekeeping troops must follow five principles to ensure their participation is in accordance with Article 9 of the Constitution. The five principles are as follows: (1) Agreement on a ceasefire shall have been reached among the parties to the armed conflict. (2) Consent for the conduct of UN peacekeeping operations as well as Japan's participation in such operations shall have been obtained from the host country as well as from the parties to the armed conflict. (3) The operations shall strictly maintain impartiality and not favor any of the parties to the armed conflict. (4) Should any of the requirements in the above-mentioned guidelines cease to be satisfied, the International Peace Cooperation Corps may suspend International Peace Cooperation Assignments. Unless the requirements are satisfied again quickly, the GOJ may terminate the dispatch of the personnel engaged in International Peace Cooperation Assignments. (5) The use of weapons shall be within the limits judged reasonably necessary according to the circumstances.[27] The strict conditions deprive the JSDF of experiences that closely mimic warfare; it is not allowed to participate in operations that have not been pacified or without the protection of other militaries. Even under these strict conditions, the GOJ has faced intense public opposition for missions that endanger the lives of JSDF personnel. In 2017, for example, Minister of Defense Inada Tomomi and General Okabe Toshiya were forced to resign due to poor recordkeeping that concealed the dangers of the UN mission in the Republic of South Sudan. As a direct response to the public outcry over the mismanagement of records in Sudan and Iraq, the Ministerial Council on the Management of Administrative Documents and Related Matters adopted the Measures for Ensuring Appropriate Management of Public Records the following year. The new measures stipulated that records of daily reports would be retained for ten years, and reports on JSDF overseas activities be retained for three years, among other transparency measures. Moreover, the GOJ adopted

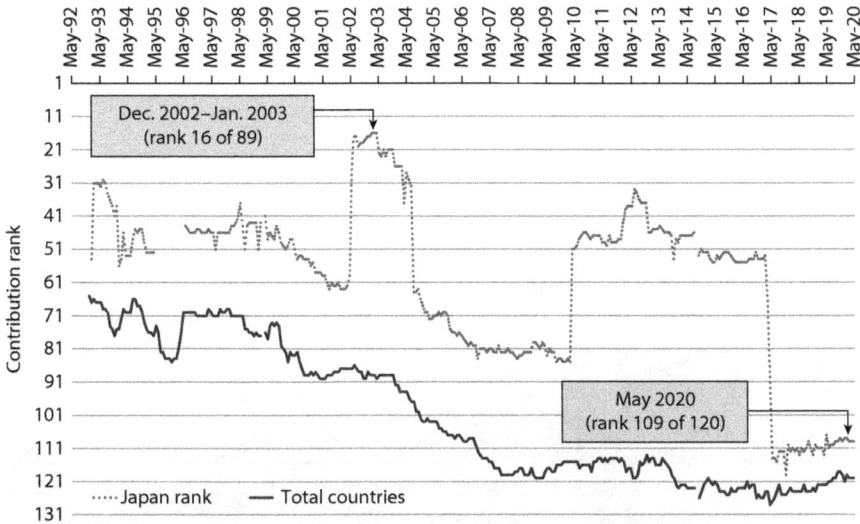

FIGURE 4.2 Country rankings: UN PKO contributions, May 1992–May 2020.

Source: United Nations Peacekeeping, "Troop and Police Contributors," accessed November 30, 2020, https://peacekeeping.un.org/en/troop-and-police-contributors.

measures to digitalize public records as well as impose severe penalties for manipulating or hiding public records.

The strong aversion to troop deployment has more to do with principle than scale because Japan has contributed very few JSDF personnel to UN missions, typically around thirty troops per year over the past three decades.

As illustrated in figure 4.2, Japan's contributions are historically ranked in the bottom half among contributors to UN missions. At its peak, Japan ranked 16 out of 89 countries between December 2002 and February 2003, when it contributed 680 JSDF personnel. Japan's contribution has since declined and as of November 2020, is ranked 109 out of 120 countries. The limited participation of JSDF troops is consistent with the trend of declining Japanese participation in politically controversial PKOs. Since January 2013, the JSDF has participated in one mission out of the possible sixteen to twenty-three missions.

Over the last three decades, the UN has authorized between eleven and twenty-three missions each year (including special operations). Of those missions, Japan participated in at most five missions at once (see figure 4.3). The

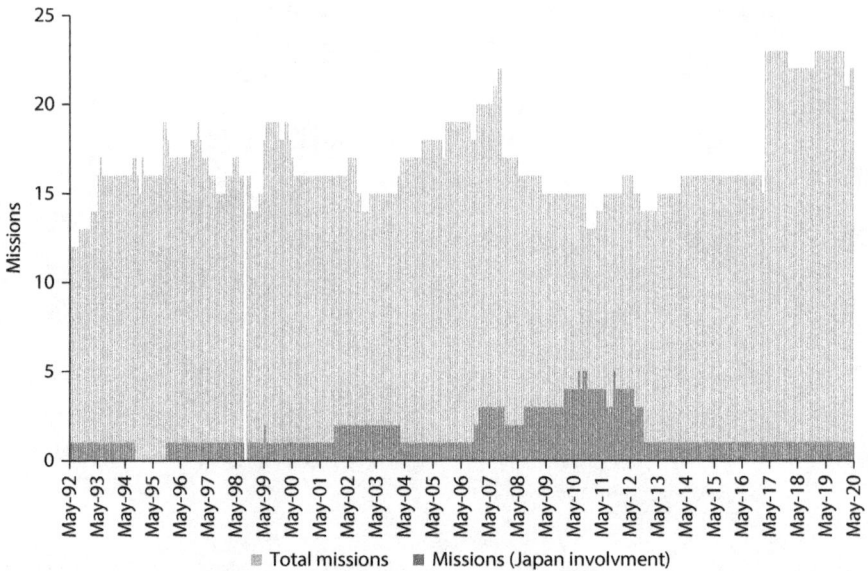

FIGURE 4.3   UN and Japan PKO missions, May 1992–May 2020.
Source: United Nations Peacekeeping, "Troop and Police Contributors."

participation in five simultaneous missions, however, lasted for a total of four months over the last twenty-six years. Japan rarely participates in more than two missions at once, and when it does, it makes a modest troop contribution. Its most substantial contribution was in May 1993, when Japan provided 729 of the 77,310 total peacekeepers. Japan's contribution dropped to fifty-three within half a year. The average number of JSDF personnel per month has hovered around 101 out of an average of 69,670 UN peacekeepers. China regularly ranked among the top ten contributors to UN missions, with over 2400 troops sent to nine missions as of December 2020. South Korea (546 troops) and Russia (55 troops) do not have as large a footprint as China abroad but participate in most UN missions.

For all attention given to Abe's proactive contribution to peace doctrine, Japan has not significantly increased its participation in PKOs. During Abe's first term (September 2006 to September 2007), Japan contributed between thirty-five and thirty-eight personnel split between two and three missions (out of twenty-two UN missions). In Abe's second term beginning December 2012, Japan contributed between 4 and 322 personnel to one mission, the United Nations mission in

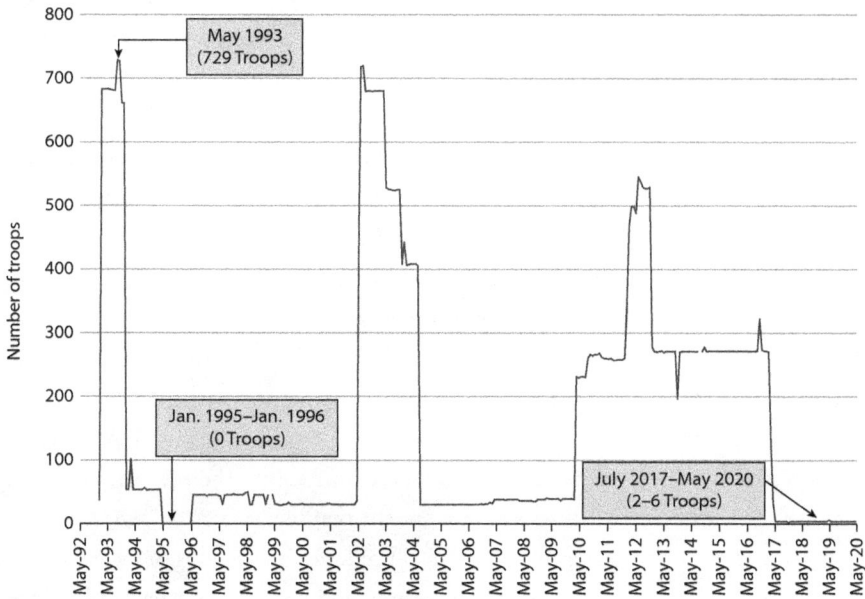

FIGURE 4.4 JSDF Personnel contributions to UN missions, May 1992–May 2020.
Source: United Nations Peacekeeping, "Troop and Police Contributors."

the Republic of South Sudan. According to the director of the Space and Maritime Security Policy Division at MOFA, Yamaji Hideki, there were few lessons
learned from the South Sudan mission because "there were few opportunities
to perform armed guard missions."[28] Yamaji concludes it was fortunate that the
JSDF could just focus on reconstruction activities, but opportunities for growth
depend on the global situation. Since June 2017, only four JSDF staff officers have
been dispatched to South Sudan per month, the fewest since January 1996. Japan
withdrew the majority of personnel because conditions on the ground deteriorated and public support evaporated from the recordkeeping scandal.

The decision to withdraw troops was made before Abe came into office, but
upon return, Abe was unsuccessful at leveraging PKOs to increase the JSDF's
activities abroad, and indirectly, experience in the field. Regardless of Abe's
ability to overcome the antimilitarist attitudes of the public, PKO deployments
are not an effective method for increasing the combat experience of the JSDF
because, under the current legal prohibitions, PKOs do not accurately simulate

warfare. Moreover, the JSDF's participation in such missions is beyond the control of the GOJ. If there are no new conflicts, or current conflicts have not been pacified, or public support for current missions diminishes, then the JSDF does not have missions that it can join.

The JSDF has been much more active in HA/DR operations (discussed further in chapter 7). Between 2004 and 2013, over 120 teams of civilian medical experts from the Fire and Disaster Management Agency, National Police Agency, Japan Coast Guard, JSDF, and Japan International Cooperation Agency (JICA), among other organizations, were dispatched up to 892 times per year (not including the 2011 Tōhoku earthquake and tsunami). Although HA/DR operations provide opportunities to improve logistics and improve the reputation of the JSDF, their impact on combat experience is minimal due to the lack of opposition forces or the necessity to use weapons. If this is Japanese militarism, then it is not the sort that would deter external threats or disrupt the regional power balance.

In sum, the militarization of the JSDF is hindered by decades of peace. Material constraints, such as aging infrastructure and lack of combat experience require significant economic and political investment to overcome, which is unlikely to occur given the public's resistance to dramatic changes to the military (discussed further in the next two chapters). The longer the JSDF avoids live combat theatres, the more politically costly it would be to engage in warfare. A single combat death could be a deathblow to normalization efforts because the public has been primed to believe the JSDF should only be deployed for nontraditional security operations.

THE DEFENSIVE JAPANESE MILITARY-INDUSTRIAL COMPLEX

Due to underwhelming recruitment and clear indicators that this will be a trend going forward, the MOD has sought to make up the human resources deficit with technology. The reliance on technology is not specific to Japan, as the American-led Revolution in Military Affairs (RMA), military transformation, and the third offset strategies have influenced how nations engage in warfare. Yet, states do not acquire and develop defense technologies uniformly. Japan's arms procurement is shaped by a combination of factors, such as strategic location, domestic politics and norms, economic realities, and the demographic crises.

The principle of *senshu bōei* (exclusively defense-oriented defense) permeates Japanese security strategy. The repetitively worded concept holds that Japan will not employ force unless attacked and only with the minimum force necessary to defend itself. This constitutionally-informed position functions as a commitment-rule and is institutionalized in guidelines, laws, practices, and even the design of defense equipment. Furthermore, this position forbids participation in conflict abroad and questions the need to develop an arms industry. The GOJ is hesitant to embrace the domestic arms industry because "providing weapons into conflict areas might draw Japan into military conflict," and it would undermine "any principled pacifist stance held by Japanese."[29] The aversion to international disputes has stunted growth in the defense industry, which poses several obstacles to the militarization of the JSDF, namely: (1) Japanese arms are defense-oriented, (2) the defense sector lacks innovation, (3) the MOD is overly reliant on imported and expensive defense equipment, and (4) the defense sector lacks experience and technical knowledge to grow out of its weaknesses. Taken together, Japan lacks a military-industrial complex that is common among superpowers and critical for rapid militarization.

Growing Pains

Following the end of World War II, much of Japan's arms manufacturing base was destroyed, and the defense industry never recovered. Not only were factories lost, but the culture necessary for a vibrant arms industry faded as major companies shifted their resources toward the consumer goods sector. As a result, critical practices, such as research and development (R&D), prestige, and know-how were lost. In recent years, particularly under the Abe administration, the MOD became increasingly aware of the consequences of a weak indigenous defense industry. A 2014 MOD report examining the importance of arms production on the proactive contribution to peace doctrine concluded that once lost, the "specialized and advanced skills, technology and facilities" required for defense R&D would require a long time and great cost to recover.[30]

The Japanese military-industrial complex is defined by a tight-knit relationship between the government and corporations and has developed several characteristics: (1) Japan does not possess state-owned armament production facilities, (2) small- to medium-size companies comprise a significant portion of the defense sector, (3) domestic demand drives arms sales because of the lack of access to foreign markets, (4) defense comprises a small portion of company revenue, and (5) the defense industry is insulated from conventional market forces.

The defense sector primarily produces vehicles, ships, explosives, clothing, and fuel. Japanese defense contractors are mostly dual-use consumer goods companies that are subsidiaries of a small group of corporations whose revenue is not dependent on the defense sector. As illustrated in table 4.1, in 2017, the

TABLE 4.1 Top Twenty Defense Contractors Percentage of Revenue from MOD Contracts, 2017

Company	Percent	Company	Percent
1 Mitsubishi Heavy Industries, Ltd.	4.74	11 Cosmo Oil Marketing Co., Ltd.	0.56
2 Kawasaki Heavy Industries	9.74	12 The Japan Steel Works, Ltd.	6.28
3 Mitsubishi Electric	2.63	13 GS Yuasa Corporation	3.14
4 NEC	2.57	14 Itochu Enex Co., Ltd.	1.10
5 Fujitsu	1.39	15 IHI AEROSPACE Co., Ltd.	0.80
6 Komatsu Limited	1.09	16 Nakagawa Bussan Co., Ltd.	6.59
7 Toshiba Infrastructure Systems & Solutions Corporation (TISS)	0.67	17 Idemitsu Kosan Co., Ltd.	0.29
8 JXTG Nippon Oil & Energy	0.23	18 Isuzu Motors Ltd.	0.43
9 Hitachi	0.21	19 Itochu Aviation Co., Ltd.	0.18
10 Daikin Industries, Ltd.	0.75	20 Oki Electric Industry Co., Ltd.	1.73

Source: Acquisition, Technology & Logistics Agency, "Chūō Chōtatsu no Gaikyō" (Central Procurement Overview), July 19, 2019, https://www.mod.go.jp/atla/souhon/ousho/index.html; and company financial reports.

three largest military contractors, Mitsubishi Heavy Industries (MHI), Kawasaki Heavy Industries, and Mitsubishi Electric generated between 2.6 percent and 9.7 percent of their revenue from MOD contracts. Seventeen of the top twenty contractors generated less than 5 percent of their revenue from MOD contracts, nine of which generated less than 1 percent.

Among the world's top arms manufacturers, Japanese manufactures are a rarity. In the last fifteen years, only eight Japanese companies appeared among the top one hundred (see figure 4.5).

Based on 2019 revenue, only MHI (21) was among the top one hundred manufacturers. MHI generated 17 percent of its total sales from arms sales.

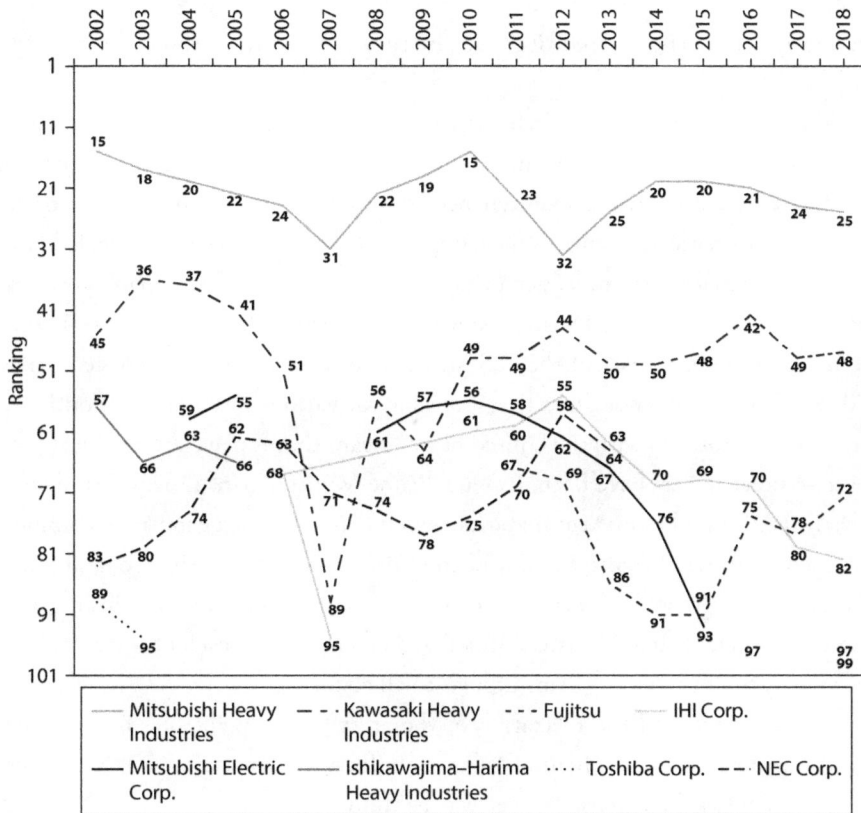

FIGURE 4.5 Top Japanese defense manufacturers global rankings, 2002–2018.

Source: Stockholm International Peace Research Institute, "SIPRI Arms Industry Database," accessed November 30, 2020. https://www.sipri.org/databases/armsindustry.

Chinese companies, on the other hand, have quickly climbed the ranks, with eight companies among the top one hundred.[31] Among the top one hundred, only seventeen companies generated less than 20 percent of their total sales from arms sales—the top five Japanese companies in recent years were within that group. According to some estimates, the entire defense industry is approximately ¥1.8 trillion, or approximately 3.5 percent of the auto industry.[32] Japan also lacks a substantial aviation industry, which is essential for crossover technologies. In the United States, the UK, and France, aviation companies possess sizable defense divisions. In total, the defense industry currently makes up less than half of 1 percent of the GDP and is not vital to the Japanese economy. Watanabe Tsuneo, a senior fellow at the Sasakawa Peace Foundation, concludes Japanese defense contractors are a "part-time military industry" that does "not seriously want to be competitive" because they can survive without the military industry.[33]

There are several reasons why Japanese companies generate little revenue from the defense sector. For one, the Peace Constitution committed Japan to defensive-defense and the maintenance of only the absolute minimum power necessary for national security. The Constitution, as a commitment rule, led Japanese policymakers to introduce principles that further affirm Japan's position as a peace-loving nation. During the Korean War, Japan produced various non-lethal equipment as part of the U.S. strategy to reignite the Japanese economy. Although Japan was not directly responsible for various international conflicts, its close relationship with the United States meant that it played some role, however indirect it may have been. In 1967, Prime Minister Satō Eisaku introduced the Three Principles on Arms Exports, which banned armed exports to communist bloc countries, countries subject to United Nations Security Council arms exports embargo, and countries involved in or likely to be involved in international conflicts. Prime Minister Miki Takeo extended the reach of the arms ban in 1976 by further limiting arms exports to all countries.

Between 1976 and the relaxation of the arms export principles in 2014, the GOJ was the only major client of Japan-manufactured arms. The GOJ is a rather frugal client, as the defense budget was held under 1 percent of the GDP since 1961. As illustrated in figure 4.6, over the last decade, close to 45 percent of the defense budget has been allocated for personnel and provision expenses, such as salary, retirement allowances, meals, and boarding.

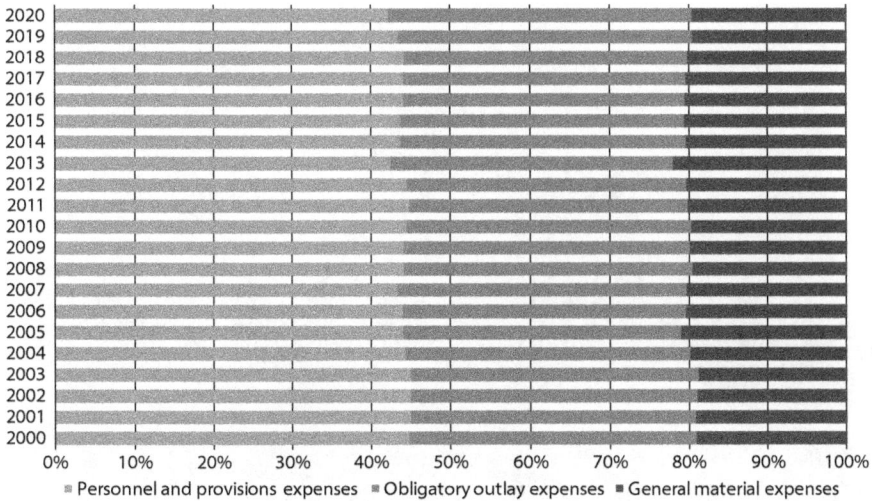

FIGURE 4.6   Defense budget of Japan allocation, 2000–2020.
Source: Ministry of Defense, "Defense Programs and Budget of Japan."

Although Japan routinely has one of the largest defense budgets in the world, 80 percent is budgeted for mandatory nonequipment and obligatory outlay spending, which leaves little room for year-to-year adjustments and new big-ticket item purchases. Within obligatory outlay expenses—expenses paid for contracts concluded in previous years—aircraft acquisition, shipbuilding, R&D, and equipment acquisitions are directed toward the defense sector.

As illustrated in figure 4.7, although overall obligatory outlay expenses increased in recent years, from ¥1.63 billion in 2012 to ¥1.93 billion in 2020, much of the funds went toward maintenance costs. Since the GOJ rarely makes bulk domestic defense equipment purchases, Japanese defense contractors take an initial loss hoping that they will eventually recoup development costs; the GOJ may not be a big spender, but it is a dependable one given that it consistently spends between .08 percent and 1 percent of the GDP on defense. This arrangement has been maintained for decades, and thus the JSDF has slowly and steadily increased its capabilities. However, these expenditures are less remarkable when taking into account fluctuations in the value of the yen, inflation, and Japan's uniquely high cost of procurement due to the uncompetitive domestic market and reliance on FMS.

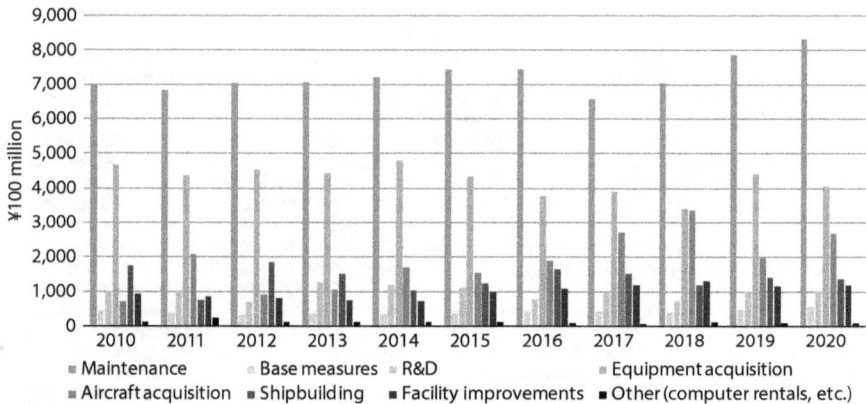

FIGURE 4.7   Obligatory outlay expenses, 2010–2020.
Source: Ministry of Defense, "Defense Programs and Budget of Japan."

The small domestic arms market has taken a toll on Japanese defense contractors. Between 2003 and 2010, roughly twenty companies left the defense sector altogether.[34] The high costs and limited growth prospects led Sumitomo Electric to conclude that allocation toward civilian purposes would be a better use of its limited human resources and production facilities.[35] In December 2009, Fuji Heavy Industries filed a civil case against the government because the MOD canceled a contract for sixty-two AH-64D attack helicopters after just ten units due to high costs.[36] In 2011, the MOD canceled a contract with Toshiba to remodel jet fighters due to production delays that were caused by Toshiba's inability to procure parts from abroad. Toshiba sued the MOD for damages, only to be hit with a countersuit for breach of contract.[37] The weak economic prospects of the arms market create a vicious cycle where Japanese defense contractors are reluctant to dedicate precious resources to defense R&D, and therefore they do not develop the production capabilities and innovation to attract government contracts or international buyers. Minister of Defense Morimoto Satoshi concludes, "The defense industry is reluctant to invest the high costs because the payoff is so unclear."[38]

Stagnation within the defense sector can also be attributed to a lack of a promilitary culture within defense contractors themselves and greater Japanese society. According to Tokuchi Hideshi, "Growth in the Japanese industry is dependent on the civilian sector. If they can get enough profit from the civilian sectors, then they can do military business."[39] Yet, such a conversion would be difficult. Since arms sales comprise only a small portion of revenue, companies do not place their most talented engineers on defense projects. Top engineers are often assigned to larger and less politically fraught divisions. Companies do not want to jeopardize their core businesses for an industry that carries the merchant-of-death stigma. Concerning the stigma, Masuda Masayuki, a senior fellow at NIDS, argues, "The Japanese people do not want to make Japan a death merchant country. It is very strict. It is not the current policy, but we have such a background, the history, that the Japanese people do not like our weapons used in war, like in the Middle East or in foreign countries."[40] Kotani Tetsuo, a senior research fellow at the Japan Institute of International Affairs, concludes the "defense industry is not ready" because "company culture is still very reluctant" to commit to the industry.[41]

This antimilitarism culture is cultivated by the academic community, which has severed the pipeline of new talent that is vital for jumpstarting the stagnant industry. Following the establishment of the Acquisition, Technology, and Logistics Agency (ATLA) in 2015, the GOJ sought to reinvigorate weapons research and development, particularly through dual-use technologies such as robotics, stealth, and aerodynamics. To achieve this objective, the GOJ offered grants to scholars and universities to conduct research with implications for defense. It should go without saying, but academic researchers *rarely* turn down grant money. Japanese scholars, however, were skeptical of the government's intentions. Hamada Junichi, the president of the University of Tokyo, reasoned that "the ban on any military-related research is one of the most important principles of education."[42] Hamada Morihisa, a geochemist at the Japan Agency for Marine-Earth Science and Technology, concluded that the GOJ was "enlisting the cutting-edge technology of universities and research institutes to produce military arms more cheaply and then sell them abroad" as part of Prime Minister Abe's growth strategy.[43] The aversion to this use of academic research led the Science Council of Japan (SCJ), an advisory body to the cabinet, representing over 850,000 Japanese scientists, to release a statement calling on scientists to boycott military research and for universities and research organizations to evaluate the threats posed by such work. The statement read, "SCJ adopted a statement on its commitment to never become engaged in scientific research for war purposes, and in 1967, issued again a statement on its commitment to never become engaged in scientific research for military purposes, which included the same wording used in the 1950 statement. Behind these statements there existed remorse for the scientist community's past cooperation with war efforts and a deep concern for a possible resurgence of similar situations."[44] The purpose of such speech acts is to "have an effect on some state of affairs."[45] The SCJ's statement was intended to not only prevent the militarization of research but also to commit the academic community to antimilitarism principles. One does not find similar antimilitarism rules operating in the rest of East Asia where Chinese and South Korean universities play an active role in defense R&D.[46] What university-military collaboration that does occur in Japan is limited to strictly defense-oriented research.

The academic community's guilt over its role in the colonial era and its deep skepticism of the government's intentions has slowed the advancement of the JSDF capabilities and cultivated an antimilitarism culture that permeates security debates. Over a dozen Japanese universities, including top-tier institutions such as the University of Tokyo, Nagoya University, and Waseda University, have charters, guidelines, or presidential decrees that forbid or dissuade researchers from accepting dual-use grants. Other universities adopted similar policies because they feared the Abe administration's goals were more militaristic than economic.

Not only are scholars unwilling to support defense research themselves, but they also have not promoted the industry among their students. According to one anonymous MOD official, Japanese scholars "have some ethical constraints" that lead them not only to forbid researching defense-related technology but also studying security altogether.[47] Compared to other states, Japan does not *practice* militarism—conventionally understood—to the same degree. Tokuchi Hideshi surmises that "young boys and girls do not have a clear sense that the military is one of their possible future professions because they do not have much experience exposed to military life. . . . If you live in a very urban area, you have very few opportunities to see any military."[48] One anonymous Japanese international relations professor specializing in security policy arrives to the same conclusion, finding "little interest among students to enter the defense sector, or even cyber security, because with such coveted skills, they can just join an information technology company and make much more money."[49] As discussed in chapter 3, the declining population creates opportunities for young Japanese in the private sector. Market forces simply do not favor the defense sector. Even for graduates of the National Defense Academy (NDA) and retired JSDF personnel, the defense sector is not an attractive option. Upon the completion of service, opportunities for JSDF personnel are few and far between because the industry is so small; even high-ranking officers struggle to find jobs as consultants in the defense sector and security think tanks.[50] In recent years, fresh graduates of the NDA have refused their commissions in order to join the private nonmilitary economy. This is not to say that there not highly trained security experts in the public and private sectors, for there are many. There are simply fewer of the same opportunities that are found in countries that lack Japan's unique postwar history. This context prevents Japan's security experts from transforming the defense sector and hence leveraging technology to address the JSDF's human resource deficit.

Not a Game-Changer: Softening the Arms Exports Ban

As discussed earlier in this chapter, the GOJ softened the self-imposed arms exports ban in 2014 to reinvigorate the defense sector and increase its ability to jointly develop and procure weapons.[51] According to one Liberal Democratic Party parliamentarian who served in the Abe cabinet, the easing of the three principles is a small but meaningful change that can lead to growth in Japan's defense industry.[52] Here, it is important to note that although the three principles limited growth in the defense industry, the arms export ban was not as absolute as the nomenclature suggested. For example, even prior to the introduction of the Three Principles on Transfer of Defense Equipment and Technology in 2014, Japan engaged in limited joint-development projects with the United States.

The intent of the 2014 principles was to clarify the original three principles with the consideration of the new security environment. This new security environment not only included the rise of traditional and nontraditional security threats but also the understanding that addressing those threats required multinational cooperation on increasingly sophisticated defense hardware. The 1976 principles allowed for exceptions to the arms export ban but were overly strict and haphazardly applied. Historically, the three principles were the functional equivalent of a blanket ban, with a few exceptions. Each arms sale required vetting by the Ministry of Economy, Trade, and Industry. However, the 2014 principles allowed Japan to export arms as long as it met the following conditions, or commitment-rules: (1) defense of the nation, (2) development of a domestic defense industry, and (3) contributing to world peace. In essence, the 2014 principles *reversed* the guidance as to allow exports, barring exceptions. Hence, it can be argued that the 2014 principles were the most significant change to Japanese security policy since the 1992 PKO Law because it crossed a normative bright line: Japan could now indirectly influence the military dimension of international conflicts.

The loosening of the arms export ban was met with measured optimism. Colonel Craig Agena believes Japan will benefit most from data exchange agreements made easier to achieve by the new principles.[53] Nishida Jun contends that the new principles increase Japanese security because the MOD will no longer be as hamstrung by "illogical" complexity in the legal code and rules that prevented exports in the past, notably "clearly defensive technologies such as helmets and bullet-proof vests."[54] Ambassador Fujisaki Ichirō surmises that the easing of the three principles is not a game-changer, but it can be beneficial if Japan develops some improved capabilities.[55] Fujisaki is nevertheless hesitant to conclude that Japan can significantly improve its domestic arms industry because the process of modernizing is very costly. Unlike the consumer electronics industry where manufacturing can be outsourced, defense R&D and manufacturing are highly sensitive undertakings, and the entire purpose of the 2014 principles was to develop an indigenous industry.

The most notable development following the introduction of the 2014 principles was the establishment of the ATLA. Agena surmises that the intent of the ATLA was to "create better synergy, eliminate duplication of effort, save money, and streamline acquisition."[56] The immediate impact, however, is unclear because as Agena concludes, "This is difficult and new so it will most likely take them time to figure out how to make the new organization as effective as possible. Up until now everything has been purchased in a piecemeal fashion. It made systematic upgrades very difficult to manage."

Following the initial announcement, defense contractors expressed some optimism for the industry. The 2015 MHI financial report, for example, stated that the new principles would open up joint-development opportunities with the United States, which were necessary to overcome the weakness of the single market. The 2018 MHI financial report was also cautiously bullish and identified the use of space for national defense as a growth opportunity, whereas NEC found opportunities in cybersecurity. The cyber domain may be the area with the most growth in the next ten years, as the 2019 NDPG placed particular emphasis on cybersecurity, and recent budgets have dedicated more resources in that direction as well.

Whether the relaxation of the arms export ban will have tangible impacts remains to be seen, but early indicators suggest that material constraints and ideational restraints will prevent significant growth. According to Satake Tomohiko, a research fellow at NIDS, the three principles reforms were not necessarily major because they were, to an extent, simply codifying what Japan has done previously regarding exports.[57] Ueda Isamu (Kōmeitō) concludes there will not be "substantial change" because "Japan, like most of the other developed countries, has strict control of the trade of arms" and is "much more strict than international treaties."[58]

The objectives of the new principles—growth and innovation in the arms industry—are unlikely to be achieved because of deeply embedded institutions and practices. For one, the Japanese defense industry is entering a crowded international arms market, which is dominated by dedicated defense contractors who possess a wealth of experience, resources, and data. In 2019, of the top one hundred arms producers, fifty generated at least 50 percent of their total sales from arms sales. To crack any market, a company needs a comparative advantage, such as innovation, price competitiveness, and effective marketing.

Unlike their counterparts who innovated because of the importance of arms sales and ability to test weapons in live combat theatres, Japanese companies lack tactical experience because Japan-made weapons have not been tested in combat. MHI, for example, noted "limited experience in pursuing leading overseas opportunities" and "inadequate cost competitiveness in global markets" as its two weaknesses in defense and space in company financial reports. Such weaknesses lead Colonel Jonathan C. Goff to conclude that the quality of Japanese equipment is high, but it is not designed with the live battlefield in mind.[59] In one notable case highlighted by Goff, tanks designed by Mitsubishi possessed "amazing tread and were built to last" but lacked space for wounded soldiers because the engineers had not considered the possibility of battlefield injuries. Goff believes that the Japanese defense sector lacks the crucial understanding that "it is inevitable" for weapons to fail in live combat. Instead, Japanese companies possess the logic of *jasuto* (just enough), that is, equipment is designed to work as intended and not much more. Masuda Masayuki prefers the term "Galapagos-style" because it "fits Japan's environment, but not others."[60] This peculiar design philosophy may be acceptable for consumer goods, but in warfare this weakness can be the difference between victory and defeat. Goff concludes "militaries need arms overkill because equipment will fail, and lives depend on having more than just enough."

As discussed earlier, Japan's top-tier researchers are unlikely to provide the innovation the industry needs because defense is beyond the popular imagination of an antimilitaristic public. In its current state, parliamentarian Haraguchi Kazuhiro (Democratic Party of Japan) concludes that Japanese R&D "just is not competitive."[61] Watanabe Tsuneo adds, "change will be gradual and will need a complete rethinking of the industry."[62] This "complete rethinking of the industry" has yet to reveal itself among companies and Japanese defense specialists. Among the top twenty defense contractors, only half have mentioned the defense sector in annual company financial reports since the new principles came into place. When defense is mentioned, it is limited to only a few sentences. The absent defense discourse can be attributed to the lack of rules that guide behavior. Tsuruoka Michito, former NIDS researcher and current professor at Keio University, for example, argues "companies are still wondering what is okay and what is not" and the "government has yet to come up with a clear defense industry policy."[63]

In discussing the need for "a fundamental reorganization" of the Japanese defense industry, one anonymous executive at a major American defense contractor suggests it may be necessary to break off defense divisions in major companies into independent entities.[64] The creation of specialized defense contractors would circumvent the impact of the antimilitarism restraints on major companies and force the new entities to innovate or fail. This strategy, however, exacerbates another constraint on the Japanese defense industry: its poor economies of scale. Since the defense sector is so immature, major contractors have not developed the infrastructure to produce arms at a level that would be cost effective. New and small companies would lose the negotiating power and access to the well-developed civilian sector supply chains of their former parent companies. Japanese shareholders are unlikely to force innovation either because traditionally they do not hold as much influence as American shareholders. Yashiro Naohiro contends that Japanese companies are risk-averse and prefer stable profits over costly pursuits of innovation and cutting-edge capabilities, even to the detriment of shareholders.[65]

Despite the new principles, the Japanese defense industry will struggle because the GOJ is still its only dependable customer. The countries that are able to purchase expensive Japanese defense equipment are the Western powers that possess robust and well-protected indigenous defense industries of their own. ATLA has aggressively pursued opportunities in Southeast Asia, India, and Australia, but negotiations have stalled or failed, partly due to the high costs of procurement.

The difficulty also lies with fundamental traits of the defense sector, the lack of experience negotiating international deals, the lack of understanding of client needs, and rigid domestic cultural practices. The most revealing example of these obstacles was the failure to secure a submarine deal with Australia in 2016. Japan possesses the world's most advanced diesel-powered submarines and enjoys positive relations with Australia. However, despite Prime Minister Abe's full-court press to secure Japan's first major international arms deal, Australia opted to go with France because of Japan's inability to produce more than one submarine per year and the high costs of production. The inability to produce more than one submarine a year is due to a weak industrial defense infrastructure, which lacks shipyards, skilled technicians, and a well-developed supply chain. Companies are reluctant to invest in this infrastructure because defense is not a profitable or high-growth industry. The failed deal was a significant blow, and Japanese security experts are divided over the cause. According to one ASDF staff officer, Japanese companies tend to be "supply side" and not "demand side" producers and have been unable to adjust the specs of their products to meet the demands of the market.[66] The staff officer continues, stating that "China, and other countries may sell weapons cheap, but they lack care, operations, and long-term support. *Yasukarou, warukarou* [the cheaper something is, the worse it is, or you get what you pay for]." Not all countries have the luxury of paying for the best. Take for example Japan's struggles with exporting trains and *shinkansen* (high-speed bullet train, or literally "new truck line"). Although the shinkansen is the gold standard of public rail—possessing an impeccable safety record—countries such as India and Singapore have signed contracts with Chinese manufacturers or purchased used Japanese trains. These price-cutting concerns are the very reason why MHI identified new U.S. companies as threats to its competitiveness in another defense sector, space systems and launch services. Foreign policymakers are willing to sacrifice some quality to save on costs, and Japanese manufacturers are never going to be able to compete on costs. This disconnect between supply and demand will continue because, as Tsukamoto Katsuya concludes, Japan's struggles are due to the lack of experience in the international arms market and Japan has not developed strong relations with foreign customers or effective negotiation strategies.[67]

Defense industry proponents have considered two unconventional ideas to generate growth in the defense sector; Japanese contractors should become licensed producers or develop a niche as high-spec producers. However, the first option would not allow Japan to develop a robust and independent arms industry, and the second option would reduce economies of scale, thus driving up the costs of defense equipment. In short, when one considers the international market, there is not a space for Japan. Major Western democracies have their own industries, Southeast Asia cannot afford Japan's capital equipment, and the rest of the world is likely to violate the 2014 principles. Decades of sluggish sales have reinforced poor practices that make it difficult for the defense industry to course correct. Moreover, Japanese companies do not believe there needs to be a course correction because they have flourished selling high-quality—and expensive—consumer goods to domestic and international audiences not interested a militarized Japan.

The GOJ has settled with the reality of the high costs of an underdeveloped defense industrial base. In the last decade, Japan has become increasingly dependent on U.S. deliveries and leases of defense equipment. Between 2007 and 2016, FMS increased by 5.5 times to a total of ¥485.8 billion. In 2018, over half of the Japan's defense procurement came from the United States, which tends to push high-spec but expensive equipment. The GOJ solidified this dependency for the immediate future by increasing its order of F-35 joint strike fighters by one hundred, becoming the second-largest owner of the fifth-generation fighter in the world (behind the United States). The GOJ's purchase of U.S. weapons at uncompetitive prices starves the Japanese industry of its one reliable client. Morimoto Satoshi laments this dependency, stating that "the problem is almost 30 percent of the total budget for procurement is exclusive for FMS, foreign military sales of the U.S.. We purchase F-35, Osprey, Aegis ships, and standard missiles, almost all major equipment from the U.S. It is very expensive. . . . We cannot allocate budget for the defense industry, some of the defense industry is bankrupt, or some technicians who used to work on defense equipment, are allocated to other sections, such as cars, or communication systems, or some normal equipment. Not the defense industry."[68] Japanese companies are sensitive to the "lower domestic budget for front-line combat equipment expenses due to increased overseas procurement,"[69] which only reinforces their reluctance to commit to the defense industry.

It is a testament to the strength of the alliance how Japan's security is so interconnected with the United States, but such dependency goes against a central tenet held by many security experts—self-help. Buck-passing proponents will argue that Japan has no choice and must rely on the United States. However, the lack of choice created by this material constraint is heavily shaped by the many decisions Japanese companies, policymakers, and the public have made due to the guiding power of antimilitarism rules.

IDEAS AND THE SHAPING OF THE MATERIAL WORLD

Stephen Biddle contends that "skill interacts with technology and numerical preponderance in a powerful, non-linear way."[70] Thus, weak infrastructure, defense-oriented technology, lack of combat experience, and an underdeveloped military-industrial complex are not isolated factors that limit the militarization of the JSDF. Hardware, software, and firmware need to be optimized to work properly—and Japan is lacking in all three.

Technology is not a silver bullet because it is a force multiplier more so than a force replacement. The GOJ's inability to leverage technology to make up for the JSDF's human resource deficit is emblematic of how the interaction between ideas and the material world form an antimilitarism ecosystem that binds efforts to quickly militarize and adopt more offensive capabilities. The antimilitarism norms that exacerbate the demographic crises by way of deterring JSDF enlistment are the same rules that shape the defense sector, from the classroom to the battlefield.

During an interview with a U.S. Navy captain who worked closely with the JSDF, I asked why the U.S. military is so redundant, as there seems to be multiple people who can do the same job. The captain answered, "It is always said that a ship could get underway and be highly effective without needing any single person, including the captain. It is inefficient, but that's the name of the game in the military."[71] This military culture, or type of militarism, is foreign to Japan. Unlike the United States, it is not a country of excess, especially concerning the JSDF. The logics of "minimal manning" and "just enough" are embedded in the MOD's approach to addressing its power deficiencies. This approach is logical, and more importantly, *appropriate* given the antimilitarism ecosystem and the limited prospects of having more.

This need not be seen as a weakness. Japan has not developed an arms culture that is profit-motivated and conflict-blind. According to one senior MOD official, this culture has more to do with "national character" than the Constitution. The official states, "Of course our Constitution really reflects national character. It is also true the Constitution sometimes shapes national character. But I think there is an obvious consensus that we do not seek prosperity by selling weapons to whoever wants weapons, respective of their characters."[72]

The official's sentiment reveals the incredible power of ideational restraints on the JSDF. These commitment-rules—whether expressed as character, identity, or culture—regulate Japanese security policy in ways that seek to assure domestic and international audiences that Japan is a nation transformed and uninterested in power projection. The following chapter will explore the first half of the ideational forces that form the antimilitarism ecosystem, political restraints.

CHAPTER FIVE

Antimilitarism and the Politics of Restraint

The previous two chapters investigated the material constraints on the content and direction of Japanese security policy. In both body and machine, the JSDF is limited in power projection and growth potential. Material constraints, however, take on their character and are reinforced by ideational restraints, namely antimilitarism rules. Whereas material factors operate as constraints because government policies cannot change how biology and physics shape force size and defense technology, ideational factors operate as restraints because they constitute self-regulating behavior among policymakers and the general public. This chapter introduces Japanese antimilitarism and explains how it shapes the politics that restrain the GOJ from pursuing more aggressive security policies.

Ideational restraints function as instruction-rules, directive-rules, and commitment-rules in that they (1) provide context for how security is understood, (2) influence how the GOJ and the public calculate threat, and (3) provide guidance for how Japan presents itself to the regional and international community. Specifically, Japan's peace identity influences security debates, which ultimately lead to policy decisions that reflect the antimilitarism ecosystem.

This chapter proceeds as follows. First, it outlines six defining characteristics of Japanese antimilitarism. Second, this chapter analyzes how antimilitarism forms political restraints, namely Japan's reassurance policy, reliance on the U.S.-Japan alliance, neutrality in international disputes, and sensitivity to international condemnation. In examining political restraints, this chapter demonstrates how antimilitarism has evolved and strengthened over time.

KEY CHARACTERISTICS OF JAPANESE ANTIMILITARISM

For many Japanese, antimilitarism, informed by a self-interested avoidance of conflict or ethical distain of violence, is commonsensical. This attitude has become so ingrained in the public that it serves as the starting point for policy-makers when they discuss security policy, including those who have not internalized the antimilitarism norm themselves. The logic of consequences and the logic of appropriateness are not wholly separate motivations. When the government pursues security, its motivation is survival of the state because it has the *responsibility* to protect its constituents. Responsibility has power over politicians not only due to conceptions of right and wrong but also because internal and external sanctions compel leaders to act in accordance to societal expectations. In other words, normativity links means and ends.

Antimilitarism governs security debates and leads the government and public to conclude that militarization risks Japan's security, squanders its wealth, and harms its international standing. Moreover, antimilitarism increases the costs of pursuing militarization in that politicians must expend considerable resources to manage expectations and inform the Japanese public and the East Asian community about potential policy changes for what is often limited gain. Hence, antimilitarism norms or rules are "not simply passive conduits of the contents of an environment. They perform constitutive and regulative tasks, as revealed in the speech acts they employ."[1] These constitutive and regulative tasks are not static, and over the last seven decades Japanese antimilitarism evolved and took on six unique characteristics.

Japanese Antimilitarism Is Not Pacifism

Pacifism is the deontological rejection of violence as a means of settling disputes. Most commonly associated with Nelson Mandela, Martin Luther King Jr., and Thích Nhất Hạnh in popular culture, this philosophy requires profound commitment from its practitioners—a commitment many find too difficult to bear. The avoidance of violence has both ethical and utilitarian underpinnings. Pacifists believe that violence is morally objectionable and ineffective for settling disputes. In lieu of violence, pacifists rely on tools such as dialogue, peaceful protests, civil disobedience, and even surrender.

Pacifism was influential in Japan during the early postwar period, informing key antinuclear activists such as Moritaki Ichirō and Toda Jōsei. Yamaji Hideki contends that "utopian pacifists took advantage of GHQ's [government headquarters'] policy of a demilitarized Japan and influenced the Japanese people through labor union activities and expanded [their] influence not only in the education sector, but also through the mass media and some state-owned companies and organizations."[2] For many, the rejection of violence ensured Japan would not be subjected to another catastrophic war. Pacifist discourse allowed survivors to downplay the nation's shameful colonial history and defeat while honoring the millions lost in World War II. During the Cold War, pacifism served as a useful tool for deflecting U.S. pressure to adopt a more militarized role in balancing against the Soviet Union. To full-bodied pacifists, the mobilization of the JSDF to defend Japan, even from invasion, would be unacceptable. Such a position, however, was not held by the majority of the Japanese public, who accepted the right to self-defense outlined in Article 51 of the UN Charter and the need of a sizable defense force in alliance with the United States. Despite the differences between the two groups of pacifists, Yamaji concludes "The sentiment of the Japanese people is always looking towards pacifism, which means peace."[3]

Pacifism provides the foundational tenets of Japanese antimilitarism, especially in terms of the consequentialist rejection of the use of force. Article 9 of the Constitution of Japan states:

> Aspiring sincerely to an international peace based on justice and order, the Japanese people forever renounce war as a sovereign right of the nation and the threat or use of force as means of settling international disputes.
>
> In order to accomplish the aim of the preceding paragraph, land, sea, and air forces, as well as other war potential, will never be maintained. The right of belligerency of the state will not be recognized. (Constitution of Japan)

Article 9 can be read as two independent clauses. The first clause renounces war as a means of settling international disputes. At first glance, it is the most ambitious. However, this is rather uncontroversial because it is a generally accepted norm that states should not start wars. The second clause, which denies Japan the right to maintain war potential, is truly novel because it severely hinders its ability to carry out self-defense. The strictest interpretation of the second clause would also suggest the very existence of the JSDF constitutes war potential. However, since the right to self-defense is universally recognized, the international community, including former colonies, never held Japan to this standard.

Since the end of World War II, Japan willfully imposed and maintained limits on its capabilities to the bare minimum necessary for self-defense. Skillful and pragmatic politicians capitalized on the early Cold War security environment and took control of the nation's security agenda by appeasing pacifists domestically, making limited concessions to the United States, and signaling to the international community that Japan was an interdependent trading state—what American political scientists refer to as the Yoshida Doctrine.

The Yoshida Doctrine prioritized economic development over remilitarization as the source of Japan's strength, and thus necessitated only a small military footprint. Japan's lack of military power was lamented as a bug of the new constitution by hawks, but over time, it became a feature of Japanese stability and soft power. The antimilitarist characteristics of Japanese foreign policy took shape under the Fukuda Doctrine in the late 1970s, which emphasized ODA (Official Development Assistance), democracy, and a peace-loving nature as hallmarks of a reformed nation. The various administrations that followed routinely passed new policies that gave further clarity to Japanese antimilitarism, such as the Three Principles on Arm Exports, antinuclear principles, and PKO laws. Thus, while the language of pacifism was enshrined in the Constitution, what it meant for the Japanese and how it was practiced evolved. This practice, however, should not be conflated with absolute pacifism because even if Japanese considered the use of force a last resort option, the U.S.-Japan alliance implicated the Japanese whenever Americans used force on their behalf and in defense of Japan.

Scholars misread Japan's acceptance of the use of force under prescribed circumstances and routinely conflate pacifism and antimilitarism. Specifically, they call attention to increases in defense spending and the acquisition of dual-use technologies as evidence of the erosion of pacifism. This misreading obscures the justifications policymakers make when policy change is enacted, which is critical to understanding the intent and scope of a policy, as well as the character of modern-day Japanese militarism (discussed further in chapter 7). Recognition of threat such as international terrorism or the rise of China is not inherently a rejection of antimilitarism or indicators of aggressive forms of militarism.

Although any use of force would violate pacifistic principles, the limited use of force is consistent with antimilitarism. According to one SAGE poll, 78.1 percent of Japanese believe going to war when attacked is legitimate, and 50.7 percent believe going to war to prevent genocide in another country is legitimate.[4] The Japanese also support the limited use of force in PKOs. While undertaking UN-sanctioned missions, JSDF personnel follow strict guidelines—so strict that they are often escorted by other militaries while conducting operations. PKOs demonstrate that the Japanese support the mobilization of the JSDF for values associated with pacifism, namely human rights and democracy, but they are less willing to authorize the use of force during missions wholeheartedly.

Uncritical Antimilitarism

Following the end of World War II, survivors constructed a victim's discourse to cope with the devasting losses of the war and to deflect attention from their roles, whether directly or indirectly, in the atrocities committed by the military. The Japanese highlighted the suffering caused by two nuclear bombs, which served as an impetus for an antinuclear movement and provided legitimacy for a universal peace movement.[5] Moreover, peace discourse shielded the modern citizen by obfuscating the nation's shameful past and attributing excessive militarism to rogue militarists. No longer shackled by an undemocratic government, the Japanese public highlighted their resiliency and liberal ethics, exemplified by a miraculous postwar recovery and significant contributions to development around the world. The simple peace narrative of "no war, no armaments and neutrality" left little room for differing interpretations of the Constitution.[6]

It should come as no surprise that to former colonial victims, Japanese antimilitarism appears to be platitudes that extol the values of peace while lacking critical examination of Japan's colonial history and underappreciating the difficulties of creating world peace. Skeptics of Japanese peace culture believe the lack of reflection created a space for revisionists to stretch the Constitution thin. The generic peace message, however, also allowed antimilitarism culture to branch out into different antiwar attitudes, all of which reinforce the nation's aversion to the use of force.

The Hiroshima Peace Memorial Museum is the prime example of an antinuclear institution that utilizes generic messaging to promote the values of peace.

Although some exhibits discuss Japan's imperial history, the chief focus of the museum is to call attention to the suffering of Hiroshima residents and caution visitors of the destructiveness of war. The museum is careful not to be critical of Americans, hoping a sanitized account of U.S.-Japan history prevents the politicization of the atomic bomb. Displays advocating nuclear disarmament are limited to one floor, roughly one-tenth of the museum's exhibits. The absence of an overt political agenda allows visitors to contemplate the meaning of peace in a nonthreatening and nonpartisan space. Despite the lack of critical examination of Japan's motivations in the war, patrons leave the museum with antiwar and antinuclear sentiments, best exemplified by statements written in journals stationed near the exit such as "No war! No nukes!" and "War is a curse on all mankind."

The emphasis on victimhood allows the Japanese to grapple with antimilitarism on their terms, which includes repentance. Since the end of World War II, government leaders have issued over fifty formal apologies for Japan's wartime aggression, including two funds designated for comfort women. One can question the sincerity of the apologies, which undoubtedly has been done in the academic literature on war memory and reconciliation in East Asia, but revisionism is difficult to sustain when a nation apologizes every couple of years. Ultimately, not all strains of Japanese antimilitarism attitudes are contingent on an awareness of the atrocities committed during World War II; some are built on consequentialist beliefs that peace is valuable and desirable.

The generic peace message travels far and wide, but it has also atomized the peace movement, making it difficult for peace activists to propose clear policy recommendations and gain hegemonic control of security policy. For the average Japanese citizen, antimilitarism is more a way of life than a political orientation.

Consequentialist Antimilitarism

The most well-known image of the atomic bomb is the mushroom cloud covering Hiroshima on August 6, 1945, taken by the crew of Enola Gay as they flew away from the unbridled destruction. From a distance, the sheer size and force of the blast could be interpreted as a testimony of brilliant human engineering and the awesome power of nature unveiled. For the 255,000 residents in Hiroshima and 195,000 residents in Nagasaki, who suffered a similar attack on August

9, 1945, no description can capture the sound, fury, heat, pain, and fear during and after the atomic bomb. *Hibakusha* could not see the mushroom cloud; they were engulfed by it. Survivors have referred to the moment as *pikadon*—*pika* for the blinding flash and *don* for the thunderous noise that immediately followed. There are lengthier terms for describing seared flesh, cancerous sores, and cavernous hunger that survivors endured. The transmission of hibakusha experiences through their testimonials is central to Japanese antiwar attitudes. According to Kawasaki Akira, executive committee member of the Tokyo-based NGO Peace Boat, the Japanese gained a general feeling that war is terrible through storytelling, which was routine in his youth. Although people do not know the basic facts of the war today, they draw on the same general lessons and develop a dislike of conflict.[7]

Hibakusha became parents, teachers, activists, and leaders who dedicated their lives to educating those who did not experience the atomic bomb firsthand. However, it was not just hibakusha who suffered greatly during and after World War II. Between 1941 and 1945, over 3.2 million died and hundreds of cities were leveled by firebombing. According to some estimates, U.S. air raids destroyed 20 percent of all houses, 30 percent of industrial capacity, and 80 percent of shipping capacity.[8] Nine million Japanese were left homeless.[9] For every casualty of combat, Soviet detention camps, disease, and starvation, there existed many more who lived through and learned from the painful and humiliating reconstruction. Survivors suffered from a shortage of supplies, and recovery was slow because vital infrastructure was neglected during the war or was utterly destroyed. The Japanese were convinced they were fighting a holy war against a demonic enemy, only to lose and discover that the Americans were nothing like what militarists had warned. This profound sense of betrayal and loss are reflected in the early writings of survivors who lamented the destructiveness of war and the tragic waste of life.[10]

Equally powerful lessons of the benefits of avoiding conflict were drawn from the nation's miraculous recovery and decades of peaceful existence. Under the Yoshida Doctrine, the standard of living increased significantly, and Japan reclaimed its world power status through economic might. By 1955, the economy returned to prewar levels. Instead of sacrificing comfort at home to send the young to die abroad, Japanese enjoyed the fruits of interdependence and free trade. Even after the economic bubble burst in the late 1980s, the international community still held Japan in high regard for its soft power, democracy, and social welfare system. The centrality of antimilitarism within the Yoshida Doctrine may be debated among security specialists, but the immense prosperity and prestige that came with avoiding conflict were clear to the Japanese public.

Decades of peace, especially in a liberal world order, led the Japanese to believe that the use of force is not an effective tool of statecraft. Japanese aversion to the offensive use of power stems from the "disastrous use of offensive military power to promote foreign policy goals in China and elsewhere in East Asia in the 1930s and 1940s."[11] The Japanese can legitimize the use of force if a certain utility threshold is met, but force is often relegated to defensive purposes.[12] Recent government efforts to expand the international role of the JSDF have been met with trepidation because the utility is unclear. In 2015, shortly after Prime Minister Abe announced Japan's nonmilitary commitment to fighting terrorism, the Japanese public received a violent preview of what may await if Japan becomes involved in international conflicts. ISIL terrorists kidnapped and beheaded two Japanese civilians, Gotō Kenji and Yukawa Haruna, for Japan's involvement in the war on terror. The GOJ had no means of saving the hostages and proposed no credible way of avoiding a similar crisis in the future. The dangers that Japanese face abroad became the dominant narrative in the media, which further solidified skepticism of a Japanese military presence outside of the homeland. Debates over collective defense revealed similar public anxiety over being pulled into foreign conflicts. These concerns are not entirely tied to utility, however, because the costs and benefits of a more assertive foreign policy are readily apparent. The shadow of the future is as instinctive as it is intellectual.

Consequentialism is not entirely divorced from ethics and norms. Legitimacy is normative and can exist without utility. Japanese citizens do not see the value of more assertive military policies not only because of the suffering it brings but also because the noncritical remembrance of the war led many to believe that militarists committed an injustice in inviting conflict. The outrage over this injustice and empathy for those who suffered shades the cost-benefit calculation. Japan's monumental defeat and its imprint on the nation's psyche have not faded and continue to shape Japanese security policy. Antimilitarism can come from a logic of consequences and logic of appropriateness when burnt bodies, crying orphans, and beheaded civilians are the lasting images of war.

Antimilitary (of a Certain Type) Antimilitarism

In explaining the deep hatred of the military following the war, historian John Dower argues, "The militarists and super patriotic ideologues were now portrayed—by the Japanese civilian elites and their American conquerors alike—as corrupt influences who had distorted the pure essence of the Imperial Way. They were outsiders who had somehow muscled their way into close proximity to the throne."[13] This mix of guilt and deflection is common in Japanese reflections of the war. Tanaka Terumi, general secretary of Nihon Hidankyō (Japan Confederation of A- and H-Bomb Sufferers Organization), for example, expressed that Japan never apologized for the war, and many Japanese were angry that those responsible for the war came back to power.[14] This anger could not be voiced openly because of the U.S. occupation, but it quietly shaped and sustained peace movements in the early postwar period. In 1946, Nanbara Shigeru, a Christian educator and professor at Tokyo Imperial University, led a memorial service that sought "to evoke the memory of dead countrymen—and the problems of guilt, repentance, and atonement."[15] Nanbara conveyed to the dead "bluntly that Japan had been led into war by ignorant, reckless militarists and ultranationalists."[16] This narrative, of course, was overly simplistic because the majority of the public supported the government's expansion into East Asia.[17] By placing blame solely on the military, the Japanese public minimized their complicit and explicit militarism and created the intellectual space for their national innocence.

Japan's colonial victims strongly object to this narrative. Nevertheless, the self-serving interpretation of the war cultivated Japanese antimilitarism, as it could not be denied that the military committed shameful acts of violence that led to suffering throughout the empire. According to Ambassador Fujisaki Ichirō, after the war, people were dismayed with the military because they had been led to believe they were "the best and brightest, especially the navy."[18] Specifically, Fujisaki calls attention to the army fleeing its colonial possessions at the end of the war, leaving civilians to fend for themselves. Such actions were "burned into the Japanese psyche" and entrenched a deep mistrust in the military.[19] The militarists could easily be accused of subverting Japan's "true" intentions because they "took over through a far more insidious and protracted process of political assassinations, attempted *coup d'état*, and engineered military emergencies abroad. The independent position of the army under the Meiji Constitution allowed it to evade civilian control and stage military incidents abroad to expand Japanese control over North China."[20]

The public also had Class A war criminals to blame. Many Japanese regarded them as "hateful persons who had given heavy pains to ordinary people by sending them to the fronts, or making them suffer terrible air raids."[21] After monumental defeats in Iwo Jima and Okinawa, the militarists continued to push for the continuation of the war. Hiroshima and Nagasaki paid the ultimate price for their zealotry by suffering the only use of nuclear weapons on a human population in history. Emperor Hirohito, against the wishes of military advisors, ended the war because "he could no longer allow his people to suffer death and destruction" and asked his officers to "endure the endurable" and accept the Allies's terms.[22] Even the emperor's decision could not convince the most hardcore ultranationalists, who attempted a coup d'état upon hearing news of the imminent surrender.

The bloodlust of the military and destructiveness of the atomic bombs were symptomatic of a war entirely out of control. Much of the postwar anger was directed at the government for its inability to control the militarists and utilize force effectively and legitimately.[23] This anger was converted to a strong ethos of civilian control of the military. The Japanese public is "extraordinarily reluctant to allow their armed forces to engage in military planning for fear that, as in the 1930s, the military might try to engineer an international incident that could drag Japan into a war in Asia."[24] Thus, until 2007, the military arm of Japan was relegated to a defense agency. After the JDA was upgraded to ministry status, civilian control remained a defining characteristic of the Constitution and military-civilian relations. Within Japan's chain of command, no military officer has direct access to the prime minister and bureaucrats maintain significant control over how security policies are implemented.

Reinvigorated and Diverse Antimilitarism

The lifeblood of Japanese antimilitarism is the peace activists who pressure the government on issues, such as preserving Article 9, promoting antiproliferation, ending reliance on nuclear power, and moving the U.S. bases in Okinawa. These groups seek to educate the general public on Japan's militaristic past and contemporary security issues.

Although the end of the war motivated many to join peace movements, it was not the only event that activated the antiwar ethic. Before World War II, young intellectuals challenged the nation's militarization, but lack of public support and authoritarian laws, such as the 1925 Maintenance of the Public Order Act, limited the impact of peace movements on foreign policy. Peace movements remained constrained immediately after the war due to the American occupation. When the occupation ended on April 28, 1952, pent-up antiwar feelings could finally be expressed, resulting in an outpouring of peace literature.[25] On March 1, 1954, the Japanese were reminded of the destructiveness of nuclear weapons when the twenty-three-member crew of the *Daigo Fukuryū Maru* (*Lucky Dragon No. 5*) was exposed to the contaminated fallout from the U.S. Castle Bravo nuclear test on the Bikini Atoll. The *Lucky Dragon*'s chief radio operator, Kuboyama Aikichi, died six months after the incident. This event jumpstarted a global antinuclear movement that continues to shape Japanese nuclear policy. The *Lucky Dragon No. 5* incident inspired the creation of *Gojira*, a pop culture phenomenon that signified the "travesty of nature brought on by the atomic blasts of the Americans" and provided "a vehicle for reliving the terrors of the war relieved of any guilt or responsibility."[26] The Godzilla franchise would expand to thirty-six films (four produced by Hollywood), multiple television series, and countless novels, comic books, video games, and memorabilia. The reimagining of the atomic bomb through popular discourses, such as *Gojira* and Tezuka Osamu's *Astro Boy*, brought antimilitarism to the mainstream consciousness not just for the Japanese, but the world.

The public's sensitivity to the costs of war tested the U.S.-Japan relationship throughout the postwar period, most dramatically in 1960 when thousands of Japanese surrounded the National Diet Building to protest the Treaty of Mutual Cooperation and Security between the United States and Japan (Anpo Jōyaku). The Japanese "still had vivid memories of World War II, which had ended only fifteen years (earlier), and believed the treaty would lead to another war."[27] However, the anti-*anpo* movement could not prevent a ratification of the treaty, which resulted in the quick end of the "overall-peace" movements of the early 1950s.[28] Many veterans of these protests continued their peace activism, albeit with a reluctant recognition that the U.S.-Japan alliance and the use of force for self-defense were necessary.

Japanese peace movements were reinvigorated when activists' concerns of American adventurism were confirmed during the Vietnam War. The public objected to the use of Okinawa for staging U.S. missions and Japan's complicit role in the war. The status of Okinawa was already a sore point in U.S.-Japan relations because it previously served as a U.S. base during the Korean War—the United States stockpiled chemical weapons and nuclear warheads on the island in the 1950s and 1960s,[29] and the territory remained under American jurisdiction until 1972. For activists such as Nakashima Takeshi, the fact that Japan was hosting U.S. planes and soldiers that "went to Vietnam to kill" was offensive and necessitated activism.[30] Although Nakashima was the son of an A-bomb survivor, it was the Vietnam War that sparked his antimilitarism streak and motivated him to join student-led peace movements. The American bases in Okinawa are still significant issues for peace activists today, and antibase mobilization has gained momentum over the last ten years. In 2014, Inamine Susumu won the Nago mayoral election and Onaga Takeshi won the gubernatorial election on staunchly antibase platforms. In 2018, Tamaki Denny succeeded Onaga after his abrupt passing with the promise to resolve the base issue.

In the 1970s, antinuclear activism continued to diversify while becoming increasingly institutionalized. The Joint World Conference Against Atomic and Hydrogen Bombs held in 1977 spawned grassroots peace movements that "brought together housewives, students, retired individuals, and workers who had no affiliations with either the socialist or communist groups in the country."[31] These groups believed nuclear weapons were "absolute evils" and insisted on total abolition of nuclear weapons.

Nontraditional security events have also reinvigorated Japanese antimilitarism. After the Tōhoku 3.11 triple disaster, antinuclear energy, anticollective defense, and pro-Article 9 groups formed deep and international coalitions (to be discussed further in chapter 6). The poor handling of the crises by the government and apparent corruption of the Tokyo Electric Power Company led thousands to protest Abe's efforts to restart the nuclear reactors, resulting in a new trajectory for national energy policy and the decommissioning over half of Japan's fifty-four nuclear reactors.

Since the end of World War II, Japan's antimilitarism attitudes have evolved and acquired several new missions. These missions reflect diverse actors who are informed, networked, and active. The impact of peace activism in Japan has been marginalized by some scholars, who usually cite political apathy among Japanese youths, activists' historical connection to the far left, and the aging population as reasons for its decline. Antimilitarism skeptics also believe that the further contemporary Japanese are from war, the weaker antiwar feelings become. These characterizations of peace movements are deficient for several reasons. For one, peace activists come from diverse backgrounds, and the majority of college-aged activists have no connection to the socialist-communist split that weakened the antinuclear movement in the 1960s and 1970s. Many Japanese peace movements are connected to international movements that promote a broader conception of peace and security, which include environmentalism, economic equality, gender equality, as well as more traditional security issues. Second, although Japanese and American civil societies differ, the Japanese public is no less politically active. The Japanese tend not to publicize their political views, which have hurt the fundraising of peace groups, but they vote in high numbers. Since World War II, every national election has witnessed greater than 50 percent voter turnout. According to Paul Midford, public attitudes empower more defensive-minded politicians in the government to "delay, curtail, and block altogether desired missions by hawks."[32] These policymakers draw on, and are influenced by, public opinion that is shaped by activists that participate in letter-writing campaigns, meetings, and protests.

Political engagement and activism continued long after World War II for reasons unrelated to personal suffering. While some strands of antimilitarism weakened over time, new ones emerged and drew the attention of the next generation. Peace movements are a fundamental part of the political environment that government leaders navigate.

Commonsensical Antimilitarism

When asked a question concerning security policy, one high-ranking LDP parliamentarian answered flatly, "peace culture is always deep in our mind, no doubt about that."[33] Although expressed in different ways, this sentiment is prevalent among nonelected civil servants, elected officials, and defense officials.[34] When the Japanese people perform the speech act of "peace culture," they strengthen its impact on security policy because "culture provides support for rules."[35] Antiwar attitudes and restricted foreign policy have simply always been that way because the vast majority of the public has never experienced conflict, and those who fought in World War II advocated for a more peaceful approach to international relations. The war generation, particularly teachers, were "filled with grief over the deaths of their young charges, often overwhelmed with guilt for having encouraged them onto a path of destruction. Many embraced the ideals of peace and democracy with fervor."[36] Many of the lessons passed on from the war generation often go uncontested. According to one RENGO (Japanese Trade Union Confederation) officer working on the trade union's peace programs, their grandparents often recalled the suffering caused by the war and warned of the dangers of conflict.[37] Similarly, Kawai Kimiaki, director of peace and human rights for Sōka Gakkai International, became interested in peace activism from listening to his parents, war survivors, and teachers talk about their war experiences. His father put it simply, "war is terrible."[38] Millions grew up with this simple yet powerful idea.

Chalmers Johnson once observed, "Most Japanese equate Article 9 of the Constitution with democracy itself; to alter one is to alter the other."[39] Antimilitarism is a package deal that comes with stability, prosperity, status, democracy, and human rights. The Constitution introduced "pacifism as the means by which Japan, as well as other countries, could best promote civilization and become a cultured nation."[40] A poll conducted by the Cabinet Office of Japan in 2004, found that 51.9 percent of respondents believed Japan should contribute to maintaining world peace (including physical support), 16.1 percent believed Japan should protect universal values (freedom, democracy, human rights), and 25 percent believed Japan should provide humanitarian support to refugees.[41] These figures increased to 58.8 percent, 34 percent, and 31.6 percent in the 2018 poll.[42]

Beyond advocating a peace culture approach, Japanese practice what they preach at home. Japan has some of the strictest gun laws and enjoys one of the lowest violent crime rates in the world. Japan's reputation as a peace nation, epitomized by the Peace Constitution and domestic stability is a source of pride and is promoted by the GOJ as a uniquely *Japanese* contribution to the world.

This peace culture is so commonsensical that activists hope to expand antimilitarism beyond Japan's borders and deconstruct a global security order that seems irrationally conflict prone. Steve Leeper, former chairman of the Hiroshima Peace Culture Foundation, conveys his frustrations with contemporary international relations, arguing, "Humans can no longer resolve conflicts through disruptive power. . . . Humans need to graduate to a civilization of love, influenced by Gandhi and MLK, or people will not survive war, which is becoming controllably violent."[43] Leeper's successor and secretary general of Mayors for Peace, Ambassador Komizō Yasuyoshi, echoes these sentiments, stating that "the current security framework does not work, and leaders need another credible security framework not built on nukes. . . . Article 9 has worked, and its useful for Asian countries as well."[44] Komizō elaborates on his skepticism of the current security framework and ideas for possible alternatives arguing:

> Security frameworks may need military elements for back up, but if security merely depends on military means, it is likely to create an arms race that could enhance rather than reduce risks of military confrontations. A security arrangement that promotes wider exchange in culture, economy, youth, and professional areas to keep and promote trust, broader channels of communication, and mutual dependence can provide a better basis for peaceful solution of disputes. Security frameworks need to look into a much wider perspective than mere military readiness. There is growing awareness that if security is meant to protect people, nuclear weapons that kill millions of people indiscriminately and even continue to torture survivors for many decades with serious health and other gravely adverse consequences, it has no place in the security architecture to protect people.[45]

The hope that the world will eventually align with Japan and accept antimilitarism as the only sustainable approach to international relations is what motivates peace activists in a conflict-prone world. When rules become commonsensical, they are automatic and unquestioned. Behavior that violates commonsensical rules appears absurd. In a sense, the Japanese in the present day are reflections of the survivors of World War II and hope that their values are reflected by future generations. They are a part of, shaped by, and contribute to the antimilitarism ecosystem.

UNDER THE MICROSCOPE: POLITICS OF RESTRAINT IN THE POSTWAR ERA

Antimilitarism serves as a powerful tool for Japan to not only contribute to world peace but also for maintaining regional stability. Due to the atrocities Japan committed during World War II, its history is a useful starting and end point for analyzing contemporary Japanese security policy and identity. For many East Asians, the perceived lack of remorse among Japanese government leaders over the past two decades indicates that Japan is on a path toward normalization, and even aggressive militarization. However, as problematized in chapter 2, the concepts of normalization and militarism as conventionally understood reveal little about contemporary Japanese security policy. If nationalism is indeed growing, its links to JSDF PKO activities and Japan's reliance on the U.S.-Japan alliance are not readily apparent. Moreover, nationalism appears unable to motivate the Japanese public to make the personal sacrifices to overcome the recruitment and demographic crises that weaken the JSDF. Politics restrain far more than they initiate policies that increase Japan's military strength.

Since normalizing relations with former colonies, the GOJ routinely invokes peace culture to signify that postwar Japan is a transformed nation dedicated to peace, democracy, and human rights. Each time Japan self-identifies as a peace-loving nation, it commits to restrained future conduct. The Japanese public serves as the guarantor of this international commitment because, as Kusunoki Ayako writes, Japan's renunciation of war "did not merely serve as an outward promise that Japan would never again challenge the peace and stability on international society. . . . It was its significance as an internal promise that came to have a strong normative function. For the many citizens who lost family, friends, and neighbors in 'that war,' the constitution's pacifism was not merely a lofty goal but an actual policy goal to be pursued."[46] Such promises are quite restraining because even if free agents have the "right" to make promises freely, "they are not so freely broken."[47] These promises, or political restraints, are expressed in four ways: (1) reassurance policy, (2) reliance on the U.S.-Japan alliance, (3) neutrality, and (4) sensitivity to international stigma.

Friends You Keep and Hope to Make: Japan's Reassurance Strategies

The classic puzzle in international relations is the security dilemma, where the actions one takes to increase security may lead to the opposite outcome. Because states can never fully know the intentions of others, they misread positive signals or ignore them altogether. For former colonial powers such as Japan, the trust deficit appears insurmountable. However, since states respond to probable, not possible, threats, reassurance has become a defining characteristic of Japanese foreign policy since the end of World War II. The GOJ's promise that Japan will never pursue militarism again is not pacifistic—or at least not solely motivated by an deontological denial of violence—but a calculated decision to reduce the intensity of the security dilemma in Northeast Asia.[48] Paul Midford, for example, concludes, "Japan has recognized that 'normal' great power behavior could fan a spiral of suspicion by its neighbors, producing counterbalancing and an arms race. Japan has engaged in an iterated series of unilateral and noncontingent conciliatory measures that significantly limit Japan's offensive capabilities, entail risk for Japanese security, and benefit others."[49] Japanese reassurance requires possessing just enough capabilities for defense, while also preventing a power vacuum or engaging in an arms race. Maintaining this delicate equilibrium not only ensures Japanese security but also protects Japan's livelihood that is heavily contingent on the stability of its neighbors.[50] Good relations among East Asian states are critical for the region's security for the foreseeable future, as transnational threats, such as energy insecurity, food scarcity, environmental disasters, nuclear proliferation, cybercrime, and terrorism, increase. Ambassador Komizō Yasuyoshi commits to this broad conception of security, contending that Japan must work closely with its neighbors or its security cannot increase.[51] Komizō's argument is not uncommon within policy and military circles in East Asia, where one is likely to find more cooperation and understanding than disagreement concerning regional and global insecurity.

The MOD has gone to great lengths to ensure its defense policies do not unduly alarm Japan's neighbors. Based on the Basic Policy for National Defense passed in 1957, the MOD has adopted several basic policies over the years that include the exclusively defense-oriented policy, commitment to not possess and maintain a military capability strong enough to pose a threat to other countries, three nonnuclear principles, and maintaining civilian control of the military. To facilitate understanding of Japan's intentions among its neighbors, MOD defense papers and policies are readily available in print and digital formats, and they are often translated into English and Chinese.

Gaining the trust of former colonies is difficult and requires consistent positive signaling from the GOJ. When pursuing policy change, Nishida Jun reiterates that it is "important to the Japanese government to explain its position and provide justifications to countries abroad."[52] Following the establishment of the National Security Council (NSC), and similarly significant developments, Japan held high-level bilateral meetings with representatives from the United States, China, and South Korea, among other countries, to reassure that the new policies did not disrupt the status quo. During an interview for this book, Nishida called attention to the first page of an information packet Prime Minister Abe personally handed to his counterparts concerning the NSC, which articulated Japan's intentions and was designed to "help readers understand Japan's defense policy, promote relationships of mutual trust and improve the transparency" in the Asia-Pacific region.[53] The Ministry of Foreign Affairs supplements these high-level documents by producing and disseminating dozens of easy-to-digest documents that clearly outline changes in Japanese security policy to elites abroad and at home. In the last few decades, reassurance strategies have diversified to include formal apologies, promotion of trade, cultural exchanges, regular Track Two and Track Three meetings, ODA, and other confidence-building measures (CBM). Each reassurance speech act begets further commitments to antimilitarism, which reinforces Japanese peace culture.

Japan's engagement with its neighbors goes beyond strategic necessity, however, as there is a normative dimension to owing another state an explanation for what is a universally recognized right to self-defense. Consider, for example, that reassurance is only a viable strategy if potential rivals positively respond to reassurance signals and respond in kind. Despite Japan's efforts, China continues to augment its military capabilities and Japan-South Korea relations remain frosty. According to a 2013 Pew Research Center survey, 89 percent of Koreans and 78 percent of Chinese believe Japan has insufficiently apologized for its military actions in the 1930s and 1940s.[54] The same survey found that only 12 percent of Koreans and 9 percent of Chinese have a favorable view of Prime Minister Abe. The lack of trust in Japanese leaders has held constant. In a 2014 Pew Global Attitudes survey, of twelve Pacific nations, South Korea and China expressed the least confidence in Abe, at 5 percent and 15 percent respectively.[55] Genron NPO polls between 2014 and 2019 found that over half of Chinese respondents believed military conflict between Japan and China would occur in the future, with approximately 10 percent answering within the next few years. The same polls found that over a quarter of Chinese respondents believed Japan was "militaristic," or about 10 percent higher than Japanese respondents on the same question concerning perceptions of the other country.[56]

Reassurance has not seemed to comfort the Japanese public either. In the afore-mentioned 2014 Pew Global Attitudes survey, 68 percent of Japanese respondents believed China was the "greatest threat."[57] Genron NPO surveys consistently find well over 70 percent of Japanese respondents holding a negative impression of China and over 40 percent holding a negative impression of South Korea, mostly attributed to the history issue and related conflicts.[58] Given that reassurance does not guarantee the security dilemma can be avoided, why does Japan continue to appeal to the better angels of its rivals and itself? Japan reassures and restrains because antimilitarism rules dictate that it *should*. Reassurance, like apologies, is much more of a one-way street than the conventional wisdom would suggest. Positive gestures can be accepted or ignored regardless of the guarantees behind the gestures. According to parliamentarian Nagashima Akihisa, the GOJ's efforts to communicate its security intentions work with all countries except three—China, North Korea, and South Korea. Nagashima concludes, "They have their own intentions, their own fears, and their own things to say. So, we understand their reactions. But again, we have to try to communicate."[59]

Japan's reliance on ideational and identity discourse reflects norms not cap-tured in realist theory. Japan can simply limit its arms, increase transparency, and pursue more direct CBMs if it wants to reassure. For any other country, the creation of a national security strategy and amendments to arms exports policies would be considered solely sovereign domestic matters beyond the purview of other states as long as they do not violate international law. Nishida Jun high-lights the fact that Japan is not required to explain its position but does so partly due to its colonial history.[60]

Japan uses specific language when it engages with its neighbors. The GOJ emphasizes Japan's peace culture, support of democracy, and remorse for its past actions. These discursive strategies reveal a normative dimension to reassurance and policymaking. Even the oft-criticized Prime Minister Abe made a concerted effort to alleviate concerns about Japanese remilitarization. During a 2013 trip to Southeast Asia, Abe stated, "I will explain Japan's position carefully to avoid misunderstandings in other countries in the region. Throughout this trip, I have explained these matters to the leaders of the countries I visited."[61] Furthermore, Abe declared, "As for revising the Constitution, we are currently deepening the discussions on what a Constitution suitable for modern Japan should be, naturally premised on pacifism, popular sovereignty, and fundamental human rights."[62] In response to a question posed by a *Tokyo Shimbun* reporter during a press conference regarding constitutional reinterpretation less than a year later, Abe affirmed the new interpretation would not lead to more conventional security operations. Specifically, Abe stated, "On no account will we participate in the future in conflicts like the Iraq War or the Gulf War, which had the exercise of force as their objective. We will continue to fully uphold the pacifism advanced in the Constitution. Since the end of World War II, Japan has consistently followed the path of a peace-loving nation. There will be no change in this path in the future."[63] Concerning collective defense, Abe stated that Japan "will continue to fully uphold the pacifism set forth in the Constitution. The course Japan has taken as a peace-loving nation since the end of World War II will remain entirely unchanged."[64]

Reassurance language is not unique to the Abe administration. Since the Koizumi era of the early 2000s, every prime minister has reiterated either antimilitarism or pacifism as central components of Japanese foreign policy. Most prime minister speeches and press statements are translated into English and Chinese and made readily available on the prime minister's website.

Realists would contend the GOJ's peace identity discourse does not reflect a genuine pacifistic attitude, and reassurance is fundamentally a strategy to avoid conflict—a diplomatic way of saying politicians lie. While the true intentions of government leaders are difficult to decipher, backtracking comes with costs—promises are freely given but not so freely abandoned. Even if reassurance is a nongenuine performance, its practice is the functional equivalent of a normative restraint. When politicians reassure and apologize, they put ideas out there. Antimilitarism statements are then codified as principles and laws, and restraints become constraints. This process of internalization and externalization of these ideas can be understood as "two phases of the same process."[65] The public, in and out of Japan, pressures politicians to follow through on their statements, which embeds peace discourse in security discussions. Constant polling on constitutional revision and security legislation demonstrates that politicians are sensitive to public opinion. Prime Minister Koizumi openly acknowledged the government's sensitivity, stating, "the Constitution cannot be revised without the support of a majority of the people under an initiative taken by two-thirds of the Diet members. Faced with the reality, I believe that this issue cannot be resolved unless public debate is thoroughly initiated nor without the cooperation of political parties."[66] Four years earlier, during his first press conference as prime minister, Koizumi inferred that the aftereffects of the war were still felt strongly by the public, which made it difficult to even put Article 9 on his political agenda.[67]

The constraining power of public opinion on government leaders in democratic countries should not come as a surprise. As long as the public is sufficiently engaged, which spikes when antimilitarism norms are threatened (to be discussed in chapter 6), politicians will adjust their strategies to avoid the political fallout. Across governments, "Japanese cabinets tailor policies that avoid provoking the emergence of stable opposing opinion majorities."[68] Reassurance is primarily a *preemptive* strategy that forces government leaders to start from the position that they must *justify* policies that could be interpreted as militarization.

Reassurance has also bound Japan to the U.S.-Japan alliance for its security. As discussed in chapter 4, material constraints compel the GOJ to increase its FMS to make up for human resource and technological deficits. However, the alliance is not just a stopgap, it is a powerful signal to the peoples of East Asia who hold painful memories of unbridled Japanese militarism that Japanese security policy is bounded. The U.S. presence in Japan maintains the "cork in the bottle,"[69] while also driving future security policy decisions. Following the 9/11 terrorist attacks, Japan became an important member of the coalition of the willing and provided support for U.S. missions in the Middle East (discussed further in chapter 7). Under the Abe administration, Japan adopted collective self-defense, increased U.S.-Japan joint operations, and updated the Guidelines for Japan-U.S. Defense Cooperation. Under the 2015 guidelines, the alliance introduced new coordination mechanisms, enhanced operational coordination, increased bilateral planning, and clarified policies on noncombat evacuation operations and use of facilities, among other issues.

Changes to Japanese security policy, therefore, must be understood within the framework of alliance needs, which creates problems of abandonment and entrapment for Japanese policymakers. Strengthening the links between the U.S. Armed Forces and the JSDF addresses concerns of abandonment, but Japan is cautious in its approach because it seeks to avoid being drawn into U.S.-led international conflicts, alarming China and South Korea, and jeopardizing Japanese neutrality around the world.

Self-imposed political restraints on the JSDF make Japan particularly vulnerable to international criticism. When Japan adopts policies that could be interpreted as aggressive, former colonized states routinely call attention to past leadership statements to pressure the GOJ to explain its rationale and ensure the status quo remains. For example, following debates within Japan over dispatching troops to support coalition forces in the Gulf War, China warned historical issues would force it to observe Japan's actions closely.[70]

Japan is regularly pressured to reaffirm previous apologies, that is, play by the rules of antimilitarism. Prior to Prime Minister Abe's speech before the U.S. Congress in 2015, South Korea's Foreign Ministry spokesperson cautioned that Japan "should reflect carefully, looking squarely at history how the international community and its neighboring countries will react if it takes key parts from statements by Murayama on the 50th anniversary and Koizumi on the 60th."[71] Japanese politicians also call upon previous apology statements to censure the government. As Abe prepared his seventieth anniversary statement, former Chief Cabinet Kōnō Yōhei and former Prime Minister Murayama Tomiichi urged the Abe administration to uphold previous statements, withdraw security-related bills from the Diet, and avoid the constant efforts to diminish the value of previous apologies.[72] After some resistance, Abe conceded and prefaced the speech with statements concerning Japanese colonization.

The Abe administration spent significant political resources to rectify Japan's colonial history, most notably with the 2015 comfort women agreement that included a formal apology from the prime minister and $8.3 million to establish a foundation under the control of the Korean government to support victims. Although the agreement was controversial in South Korea, over half of the comfort women accepted payouts from the foundation, and Japan did not withdraw despite no settlement over the placement of the comfort women statues in front of the Japanese embassy in Seoul. More importantly, the agreement was a remarkable reversal from Abe, who in the past had called into question the veracity of the comfort women issue and sought to reexamine previous apology statements. Settling the comfort women issue could strengthen a U.S.-Japan-South trilateral response to a rising China, but Japan-China relations are not contingent on Japan-South Korea relations. The 2015 agreement was a costly endeavor without obvious political or security payoffs. Abe's engagement with this issue demonstrates that his foreign policy was influenced by the desire to project Japan as a peaceful and reformed nation, or at the very least necessary for achieving his other foreign policy objectives.

East Asian states have leveraged Japan's sensitivity to its international reputation to bind it to its antimilitarist commitments, often comparing Japan's
apology record to Germany's. International shaming campaigns, such as erecting
comfort women statues around the world and lobbying international governance
bodies, create a reverberation effect that restrains aggressive Japanese security
policy. A Chinese Foreign Ministry spokesperson, for example, warned, "Will it
[Japan] play down the history of aggression and continue to carry that negative
asset? Or will it show profound and sincere remorse over its history of invasions
and travel lightly forward? The international community waits and sees."[73] Concerning a potential amendment to Japan's Constitution, another Chinese Foreign
Ministry official commented, "people can't help questioning, whether the path
of peaceful development which Japan has upheld for a long time after the war
will not change."[74] On the same issue, China's ambassador to Japan, Cheng Yon-
ghua, argued that Japan should "take the correct attitude, stick to its previous
correct positions and statements, including the Murayama Statement, we also
expect Japan will remain on the pathway of peace."[75] China's official news agency
referred to a possible amendment as a "brutal violation" of the spirit of Japan's
Peace Constitution.[76] If China does not believe Japan's Peace Constitution to be
genuine, it surely hopes it would be.

Although these strategies can backfire, leading to apology fatigue and countermovements in Japan, the constant international pressure makes it difficult
for government leaders to act without incredible scrutiny and the need to justify
their actions. Nagashima Akihisa, for example, demonstrates the constraining
effect of international pressure, stating, "If you revise Article 9 of the Constitution, I think other countries will feel that Japan has finally dropped the idea of
international peaceful nation. I like reinterpretation. We would like to maintain
Article 9 as a long-term objective. At the same time, we must adjust ourselves to
the reality to the real strategic environment."[77]

Peace culture discourse, produced by the GOJ and foreign governments, is a
fundamental component of the antimilitarism ecosystem. This discourse is a useful
tool for journalists and academics looking to increase the political costs of normalization policies. The GOJ and private sector therefore expend significant resources
to promote Japanese soft power and protect its image in East Asia and beyond.

Japan enjoys its reputation around the world as an industrious, democratic,
free, safe, and helpful nation. As one of the largest donors of ODA, influential

leaders in the most impactful financial and political global institutions, and apolitical contributors to PKOs, Japan has positive relations with most countries. Japan's lack of overt religiosity and avoidance of conflict over the last seventy-five years also provide it a valuable neutral position in foreign affairs, especially in conflict-prone areas that seem to trap the world's superpowers in unending conflicts. Ambassador Komizō, for example, contends that Japan has a good reputation in the Middle East, and its missions in Iraq are seen favorably.[78] Unhindered by historical baggage, Japan enjoys a "free hand" in Middle East diplomacy.[79] Parliamentarian Konō Tarō argues that if Japan were to begin to take actions that lead others to question its neutrality, its diplomacy and security would be negatively impacted.[80] Peace activists share this sentiment. Under the Global Article 9 Campaign, Japanese peace activists have pushed for Article 9 to be adopted in constitutions worldwide and for it to be selected for the Nobel Peace Prize. Its proponents contend the peace identity and neutrality are advantageous to the Japanese public. To change paths would lead the nation down an unknown and likely dangerous road. This reputation is valuable, and needless militarization would squander decades of hard-earned goodwill.

THE LANDMARKS OF ANTIMILITARISM

Government leaders possess the unenviable responsibility of having to maintain state security, garner support of domestic constituents, and build positive relations with the global community. These responsibilities, often opposed to each other, may explain why they are a cautious lot who often look for policy guidance from others, whether through polls, protests, consultation, or sanction. Antimilitarism produces the rules that govern how Japan conceptualizes, debates, and pursues security in international relations. The GOJ and the public reinforce antimilitarism norms by expressing, and therefore reaffirming, commitment-rules. These rules provide the context in which Japan calculates the costs of acquiring security, wealth, and standing. In practice, the ideational restraints strengthen the material constraints discussed in previous chapters. Policies such as reassurance increase the costs or remove policy options altogether. To overcome the demographic crises or the technological deficits of the JSDF, Japan could consider conscription, acquiring nuclear weapons, or increasing defense expenditures like every other country in East Asia. Yet such actions would erase its hard-earned reputation as a peace-loving nation and global leader of antimilitarism norms. The politics that restrain the JSDF, such as reassurance and reliance on the U.S. Armed Forces, are intersubjective—that is to say they are ultimately about *relationships*. Relationships regulate and constitute behavior. The following chapter will continue this examination of Japanese antimilitarism and the relationships among the people of Japan, their government, and the international community. An examination of peace discourses from material expressions, such as peace museums and monuments, to speech acts, such as principles and laws, demonstrate that antimilitarism has only strengthened over time.

CHAPTER SIX

Peace Culture and Normative Restraints

The antimilitarism ecosystem provides rules that govern how the GOJ and the Japanese public perceive security and how it *should* be pursued. Material constraints, such as demographics, create policy objectives for the government, while ideational restraints determine the character and limits of remilitarization policies. For the Japanese public, the aging and declining population and antimilitarism norms provide few reasons to support the militarization of the state.

This chapter provides further insight on antimilitarism by examining Japanese peace culture and how activists and peace discourses imbue normativity into security policy debates. Antimilitarism—expressed *by* activists and *as* education in its many forms—has been cultivated for over seventy-five years and serves as a normative restraint on Japanese security policy. In this examination, I provide up-to-date analysis of peace actors—from grassroots groups to government organizations—which have been discussed in peace studies literature but are increasingly dismissed as inconsequential. Although many activists do not hold a seat at the table, they are surely heard.

This chapter proceeds as follows. The chapter begins with an analysis of how the regulative and constitutive dimensions of norms are oversimplified in the academic literature. The pacifism-militarism dichotomy that informs much of the scholarship fails to properly account for how antimilitarism norms allow, and at times promote, the use of force under circumscribed conditions and for specific needs. The chapter proceeds to explain how the epicenters of peace discourse, Hiroshima and Nagasaki, generate peace-oriented speech acts that have come to define the antimilitarism ecosystem. Peace museums, exhibitions, and ceremonies represent lasting expressions of peace that occupy material and ideational spaces in the lives of the Japanese public. The chapter concludes with a broad overview of the Japan-based peace groups that cultivate the antimilitarism norm and explains how they have direct and indirect influences on Japanese security policy.

NORMS IN INTERNATIONAL RELATIONS

Skeptics of antimilitarism norms argue that they are contingent on regional security, have eroded over time, or do not exist.[1] Christopher Hughes, who has been one of the most reliable critics of norm-based arguments, contends that the consistently positive support of the JSDF, a weakening taboo on the pursuit of nuclear weapons, and moves toward reinterpreting Article 9 demonstrate a weakening of the antimilitarism norm.[2] Others give particular credence to the U.S.-Japan alliance for restrained Japanese security policy.[3]

These arguments are compelling because contemporary international relations conflicts are tied to the most destructive period in human history. The injustices committed in the late-nineteenth and early-twentieth centuries were never fully prosecuted, and frequent disputes over territories and the legacy of colonialism remind states that peace is contingent on the successful operation of alliances and institutions. Over time, Japanese antiwar feelings may fade, as direct experience of the suffering caused by World War II morph into historical memory, and thus create opportunities for conflict.

Despite the intuitiveness of a converse relationship between stability and antimilitarism norms, the academic literature in the realist tradition mischaracterizes how norms operate. To begin, the claims that norms erode and norms do not exist are mutually exclusive. If remilitarization occurs when norms erode, then one must concede that norms are impactful when there is no erosion. Norms are neither static nor concrete and, most importantly, do not exist *because* of the external environment. If norms do not exist (or are not impactful), then they are not actually contingent on alliances, public opinion, or nationalism. Moreover, although norms can be strengthened when there is regional stability, the absence of stability does not necessarily mean they go away; they can take on new meaning and sometimes be reinforced. Lastly, when realists attribute capability changes to balancing behavior, they bypass norms altogether because capabilities and norms are not linked in this formulation.

The discussion of norms among East Asia experts is overly reliant on unidirectional causal language—for instance, peace *causes* pacifism or pacifism *causes* peace. Peace activists, through speech acts, generate antimilitarism rules that govern security policy. Specifically, material discourses, legal codes, commemorations, protests, and cultural practices cultivate the popular attitude that aggressive militarism led to Japan's monumental defeat in World War II. For seventy-five years, this narrative has been tethered to Japanese experiences and identity and, as a result, became the most popular game in town. Here, some sports analogies seem appropriate. Although American football is the most popular sport in the United States, Los Angeles is considered a basketball town—Lakers Nation to be exact. Like sports teams, multiple norms can exist simultaneously and have varying degrees of strength and popularity depending on the context. The mutual constitution between actors and their context is obvious in sports. Rule number 7 in basketball, for example, limits each possession to twenty-four seconds. This rule influences how players play the game because a time limit determines the parameters of playmaking and when to shoot the ball. Over time, players have developed tactics to exploit the rule, such as "walking the dog," or allowing the ball to roll down the court without touching it during an inbound play. Teams could move down the court to gain more playmaking opportunities by not triggering the twenty-four-second clock rule. The rules (or structures) influence player behavior, and players (agents) alter the impact of rules through their interpretations.[4] In other words, "people make rules, rules make society, and society's rules make people conduct themselves in specified ways."[5]

Japanese peace culture is not "merely a lofty ideal but an actual policy goal to be pursued."[6] Peace museums and monuments hold privileged positions in the physical spaces that occupy important city centers. Antimilitarism discourses shape public opinion, inform policy debates, and apprise the international community as to what Japan represents. Without popular support, and thus legitimacy, the JSDF is significantly constrained in its ability to function.[7] Since the Constitution does not clearly articulate the legality of the JSDF, public opinion is critical to its legitimacy. That is to say, *rule* does not cause peace. Rule can make peace more likely.

Norms and regional security are not distinct spheres; norms traverse domestic and international boundaries because they are imbued within security practices. Take, for example, Japanese reassurance policy as discussed in chapter 5. The GOJ's peace culture rhetoric directed toward China and South Korea, as well as the restrained operations and arms procurement, are a part of the regional security environment. In other words, norms are an inherent characteristic of the regional power balance. Moreover, Japan's desire to fulfill its *role* as a credible ally of the United States significantly impacts the regional power balance. Contrary to the popular perception of free-riding, Japan has consistently paid high financial and social costs, providing host nation support, implementing the Special Action Committee on Okinawa (SACO), and allowing U.S. bases on its territory.[8] Some may argue that several benefits emerged from the U.S. presence in Japan, such as stronger alliance coordination and development of local economies, but the net social costs have been incalculable and absorbed unequally among the Japanese public.

Solely linking antimilitarism norms to regional security also neglects how they govern JSDF operations, in content and scope, outside of East Asia. Norms, which are rules by another name, not only prevent actions through sanctioning or shaming, but they also allow and compel new practices because rules are both constitutive and regulative. Antimilitarism norms have led to an expansion of the concept of security and have therefore increased the responsibilities of the JSDF. Beyond the defense of Japan from conventional threats, the JSDF has engaged in thousands of PKO and HA/DR missions at home and abroad.

The antimilitarism ecosystem thus provides rules for a society to interpret, act upon, and pursue security. Realists correctly attribute the acquisition of new capabilities to external threats; it would not be security policy otherwise. However, realists do not have a monopoly over determining what qualifies as the legitimate use of force. The fact that external threats influence security policy does not disprove the existence of antimilitarism nor its influence on the content and direction of security policy. As an illustration, consider Paul Midford's defensive realist argument that Japan's restrained security policy is due to fear of entrapment and concern for its inability to control the military.[9] Midford convincingly demonstrates through careful analysis of polling data that the public's belief that the offensive use of force lacks utility and force is only useful for territorial defense is primarily self-interested, which has been mischaracterized as pacifism in the academic literature. As discussed in chapter 5, consequentialism is a fundamental characteristic of Japanese antimilitarism. Yet a purely consequentialist analysis of Japanese security policy ignores the regulative and constitutive dimensions of norms. According to one Japanese government official, the "Japanese public's perception is almost the same as people in Europe. Basic values such as human rights, liberalism, and democracy are very rooted and established in society. So, people do not seek to expand, annex, or conquer other countries. Basically, war is brutal, and no one wants to die. People are very, very cautious about the use of force or war. This is not because Japanese are too pacifist, it is partly true, but more because of the establishment of basic values in Japanese society."[10] To the government official, the lines between ethics and rational-choice decision making are completely blurred and internalized as basic Japanese values. As Onuf argues, "rules are persuasive to the extent they provide instrumental guidance and reflect moral considerations."[11] The belief that militarization threatens Japan's security is compelling because of antimilitarism norms. There are innumerable cases of states weaker than Japan choosing the use of force to achieve security. Furthermore, it is that same antimilitarism norm that values human security that has led the public to support the deployment of the JSDF for PKOs and HA/DR missions. In other words, arguments in the realist tradition discount what makes norms powerful; they are *normative*.

Here, it is worth noting how the logic of consequences and logic of appropriateness concepts that demarcate realism and constructivism are problematic. Animosity toward the military following World War II is not only due to the pain it caused the Japanese public but also because it was wrong of the government to pursue militaristic foreign policies. Governments are responsible to the people and responsibilities are enforceable by external (shaming) and internal (shame) sanctions.[12] Some scholars may find the restraining power of shame and shaming insufficient in the Japanese context because it has been argued Japanese culture is consequentialist and pragmatic. Kim Mikyoung, for example, argues that Japan's poor relations with its East Asian neighbors over the history issue is a consequence of a Japanese "hollow center" that leads Japan to respond according to situations instead of concrete moral principles.[13] Yet public opinion data expressing frustration over Chinese and Korean criticisms,[14] and the GOJ's efforts to remove comfort women statues and discussion of Japanese colonialism in international forums suggest shame is meaningful in Japanese culture. Moreover, Japanese leaders demonstrated the power of shaming when they responded to criticisms that Japan did not make a meaningful contribution in the First Gulf War.[15] The desire for prestige and attention to hierarchy are compelled by material considerations as well as ideational conceptions of oneself. It is difficult to determine the degree to which any abstract concept such as shame shapes foreign policy, but it is clear that the logic of appropriateness and the logic of consequences are intrinsically linked.

The lack of attention to what makes norms normative is due in no small part to the literature's focus on elites, especially in the early postwar period. Unquestionably the successes and failures of government leaders from the 1950s and 1970s significantly influenced security policy and the content of antimilitarism norms. Prime ministers Yoshida Shigeru, Satō Eisaku, and Miki Takeo adopted nonpacifistic doctrines and policies that nevertheless limited militarization and preserved the peace. The political failures of the Left also contributed greatly to the more consequentialist logic of Japanese foreign policy. However, antimilitarism and pacifism did not originate in Japan on August 15, 1945, nor were they the exclusive domain of political elites. Students, teachers, religious leaders, and activists fought for democracy and against aggressive expansionism before, during, and after the war. The sense of guilt among survivors, particularly educators and parents, imbued normativity into security debates.[16] The museums, monuments, commemorations, and peace education that has been passed down for three-quarters of a century are the material and ideational evidence of the impacts of antimilitarism norms.

HIBAKUSHA AND THE PACIFISM OF TWO CITIES

Central to Japanese antimilitarism are the antinuclear ethics of Hiroshima and Nagasaki. As the only two cities to suffer direct nuclear attacks on a human population, antiproliferation and advocacy for the end of armed conflict have become defining characteristics of their identities. *Hibakusha* (survivors of the bomb attacks) remain a powerful voice in Japanese security debates, despite their decreasing numbers.

Nihon Hidankyō is the largest organization representing hibakusha.[17] Hidankyō was originally established to assist survivors in finding missing family members, to gain recognition from the national government as a special class of victims, and to secure medical benefits, but it has expanded its core missions to include nuclear disarmament, preservation of Article 9, and opposing nuclear power. Hidankyō leads many antinuclear activities, such as sending delegates to anniversaries and international events, leading speaking tours to build support for the abolition of nuclear weapons, speaking with government leaders, and setting up photo exhibitions at the NPT Review Conference. Members also join protests and serve on conference panels with other peace groups. Tanaka Terumi, an A-bomb survivor and secretary general of Hidankyō, links antinuclearism with antimilitarism more broadly, arguing the abolishment of nuclear weapons is impossible if war is still acceptable.[18]

According to the Ministry of Health, Labour, and Welfare, as of March 2020, the average age of the remaining 136,682 hibakusha was 83.31.[19] The population has declined since 1982, which was the last year the issuance of new A-bomb certificates outpaced deaths.[20] Over the past decade, approximately eight thousand hibakusha died from old age or illness per year, or 6 percent of the total population. To mitigate the consequences of the demographic crises on the peace movement, Hiroshima and Nagasaki have shifted their short-term objectives to lay the foundation of peace campaigns that can exist without hibakusha.

The transition to a world without their voices has been underway for some time, as the role of hibakusha already shifted due to retirements and population decline. Consider, for example, a hibakusha who is eighty-four years old in 2020 would have been nine years old when the bombs dropped on Hiroshima and Nagasaki, which is likely as young as an individual can be and still remember the event with clarity. Trauma and dominant historical narratives can warp how survivors remember and share their testimonials. Younger hibakusha tend to recall the atomic bombing in a detailed, scientific, and contextualized manner, which suggests their testimonials have been influenced by data that was acquired after the initial event; survivors would not know about the exact temperature generated by the atomic bomb or its strategic significance as they experienced it, for example. Going forward, hibakusha testimonials will likely be historical accounts more than visceral expressions of experiences.

To address this development, the Hiroshima City and Nagasaki City governments established programs to record testimonials and train a new generation of official storytellers to convey the experiences of hibakusha. In 2013, MOFA, under the direction of Minister of Foreign Affairs Kishida Fumio—who also represents Hiroshima-1st District—launched the "Youth Communicator for a World without Nuclear Weapons" program to train young Japanese how to "pass on the realities of the use of nuclear weapons in the international community as well as to future generations through attending various international events."[21] Kanazaki Yumi, a reporter for the *Chugoku Shimbun*, explains a new sense of urgency, stating "we say there will be no 80th anniversary, or 100th anniversary because there will be no *hibakusha* to tell their story. The A-bomb will be history."[22]

Upon reflection of the declining hibakusha population, Taue Tomihisa, mayor of Nagasaki, laments, "without a doubt, the voices of atomic bomb survivors have the persuasive power on how nuclear weapons are inhumane. However, there is not much time left for us to be able to listen to their voices."[23] Taue and Matsui Kazumi, mayor of Hiroshima, like their predecessors, hold responsibilities uncommon of local-level political offices. The citizens of Hiroshima and Nagasaki expect their leaders to be committed peace advocates. Their duties include inviting dignitaries to the peace museums to learn about the atomic bombings, attending national and international events to promote the abolition of nuclear weapons, and building city-level antinuclear coalitions, most notably through Mayors for Peace. Within the last five years, Taue and Matsui have increased the spotlight on nuclear issues through high-profile and global events. Notable examples include attending the Third NPT PrepCom in New York in 2014, hosting Secretary of State John Kerry and President Barack Obama in Hiroshima in 2016, and hosting the U.S. ambassador to Japan during the peace memorial ceremonies in Hiroshima and Nagasaki. At the 2014 PrepCom, Taue and Matsui submitted letters of requests and signatures collected by Mayors for Peace calling for the early conclusion of the nuclear weapons convention.[24]

The mayors of Hiroshima and Nagasaki are also each responsible for writing and delivering a peace declaration to an international audience during the annual peace memorial ceremonies. These speech acts convey the suffering of hibakusha, call on the international community to abolish nuclear weapons, pressure the GOJ on security issues, and at times, establish an action plan. For example, in response to the GOJ's refusal to sign the Treaty on the Prohibition of Nuclear Weapons during the 2018 Nagasaki Peace Declaration, Taue declared, "In response to this, more than three hundred local assemblies have voiced their desire to see this treaty signed and ratified. I hereby ask that the Government of Japan, the only country to have suffered from the wartime use of nuclear weapons, support the Treaty on the Prohibition of Nuclear Weapons and fulfill its moral obligation to lead the world towards denuclearization."[25] Matsui made a less direct appeal in the 2018 Hiroshima Peace Declaration, asking the government "to manifest the magnificent pacifism of the Japanese Constitution in the movement toward the entry into force of the Treaty on the Prohibition of Nuclear Weapons by playing its proper role, leading the international community toward dialogue and cooperation for a world without nuclear weapons."[26] Matsui's approach was met with criticism by some in the hibakusha community.[27] It is important to recognize, however, that Matsui makes a call to action based on the *role* given to Japan by the Peace Constitution. The differences between how the cities interpret their roles as peace advocates reveal how antimilitarism can take different paths and still arrive at the same destination.

The peace declarations share similar objectives but differ in tone and content. Taue's declarations routinely deploy more forceful language and mention hibakusha by name. Matsui's declarations, on the other hand, focus on international antiproliferation efforts and general needs of hibakusha, such as expanding "black rain areas" so more victims can receive benefits. According to Ambassador Komizō Yasuyoshi, Hiroshima tends to be more interested in advising than criticizing the central government.[28] Nagasaki's more critical approach makes national headlines. In 1990, Mayor Motoshima Hitoshi was shot by a member of the right-wing group Seikijuku for saying that the emperor bore some responsibility for World War II. In 2007, Taue's official letter of protest against Minister of Defense Kyūma Fumio for insensitive remarks relating to the atomic bomb capped a broad national backlash and helped lead to the defense minister's resignation.

Hiroshima and Nagasaki are regularly treated as a single peace movement, but the peace statements are reflective of divergent approaches toward peace and the complexity of Japanese antimilitarism more generally. Their distinct histories and geographies allow for peace discourse to expand in scope and content. It is said, "*ikari no Hiroshima, inori no Nagasaki*" (Hiroshima rages, Nagasaki prays).[29] Most assuredly, both cities rage and pray, but according to Tanaka Terumi, the peace movements of the two cities are quite different, with Hiroshima being more "logical" whereas Nagasaki being more "emotional."[30] The differences may not be noticeable day-to-day because the cities cooperate on many initiatives.

During the First Sino-Japanese War, the Meiji government temporarily moved the Imperial General Headquarters to Hiroshima to directly command the war effort, establishing it as a hub of military activity. Hiroshima served as a major supply and logistics base for the military up until the atomic bomb destroyed the city. Following the war, Hiroshima, under the leadership of Mayor Hamai Shinso, lobbied the national government for financial support to establish a "peace city," with the Peace Memorial Park and A-Bomb Dome serving as "a lasting stronghold for world peace."[31] Spanning approximately ninety thousand square meters in downtown Hiroshima, Peace Memorial Park holds a prominent place in the city's physical landscape and residents' psyche. Tourists and locals have easy access to the park via hondōri (main street), where hundreds of people pass through daily for work, leisure, or peaceful contemplation. The park's wide and flat terrain is home to seventy-six peace monuments, the most notable examples include the Atomic Bomb Dome and the Children's Peace Monument. The park is a popular destination for major cultural events, such as cherry blossom viewing, concerts, protests, and the annual Flower Festival. The Flower Festival originated as a championship parade for the Hiroshima Carp baseball team, which itself was established by Hiroshima Prefecture as part of the postwar reconstruction effort. The Carp became a symbol of recovery, and after being sponsored by Toyo Kogyo (Mazda Motor Corporation) in 1968, it served as an example of the private sector playing a role in the peace movement. Since 2005, the Hiroshima Carp host the *pīsunaitā* (peace night) baseball game in August to commemorate the end of the war. Fans receive a gift and join in a moment of silence before the game begins. Peace-themed decorations and various peace-related activities surround the stadium on the day of the big game. According to Hiroshima Carp representative Morishita Yusuke, the Carp's main message is for people not to forget "that day" and to think about the successful postwar reconstruction of the city.[32] The soccer teams Sanfrecce Hiroshima and V Varen Nagasaki also host peace matches to honor the victims of the atomic bomb. Peace Memorial Park—and the activities that connect to it—are deeply intertwined with the daily life and provide an essential component of Hiroshima residents' identity.

The peace city identity is equally strong in Nagasaki, albeit manifested differently. During the Meiji period, Nagasaki was a major industrial center, particularly for shipbuilding, which made it a target of American war planners. In 1949, the Diet unanimously passed the Nagasaki International Culture City Reconstruction Law, which provided the resources to rebuild Nagasaki as an international culture city. City planners replaced the old war industries and promoted the revival of foreign trade, shipbuilding, and fishing industries. Due to Nagasaki's history as a hub of Christianity and one of the few trade ports opened to Western, Chinese, and Southeast Asian traders in Japan, the city developed a distinct international identity, expressed in its architecture, food, and politics. Following the construction of Peace Park in 1951, the Peace Statue (1955), Nagasaki International Culture Hall (1955), Peace Foundation (1969), World Peace Symbol Zone (1980-1992), Nagasaki Atomic Bomb Museum (1996), and Nagasaki National Peace Memorial Hall for the Atomic Bomb Victims (2003) were added. However, as a smaller and more isolated city on the southwestern end of Kyūshū that lacks a *shinkansen* line connecting it to Tokyo, Nagasaki is less accessible to tourists than Hiroshima and is, at times, outside the international popular imagination.[33]

The Nagasaki geography does not lend itself to the same types of events one finds in Hiroshima and reveals how the material world can shape the expression of antimilitarism discourses. Although Nagasaki Peace Park is approximately 25 percent larger than Peace Memorial Park, it is divided into three areas, each at a different elevation. This layout and narrow walkways make it more difficult to navigate the park and hold large demonstrations. Moreover, Nagasaki's major social centers are distributed across the city, making it less necessary for residents and tourists to walk through the park daily.

Nagasaki's relative seclusion and international history have led to an outspoken and critical peace message. Hiroshima adopts a less confrontational insider strategy that promotes a general peace message to attract foreign dignitaries and to influence the national government. Nagasaki, on the other hand, adopts an outsider strategy that works toward building strong bilateral relations with sister cities and states. In 1978, Nagasaki established the Peace Symbols Zone and invited countries around the world to donate peace monuments. There are thirty peace monuments in the zone and approximately fifty monuments throughout the city; the two most recent additions being the Tree of Life: Gift of Peace donated by Australia and the Monument to Commemorate Chinese Victims of the Atomic Bombing.

The differences between the cities' peace discourses are apparent in the ideational landscape. The most significant peace events in Hiroshima and Nagasaki are the annual Peace Memorial Ceremonies held on August 6 and August 9, respectively. Hiroshima's ceremony is a large and expensive event that is attended by tens of thousands of locals and international visitors, including leaders from around the world. The highly structured forty-five-minute program begins with a dedication of the register of names of atomic bomb victims who passed away over the previous year and is followed by an address by the chairperson of the Hiroshima City Council and dedication of flowers. At 8:15 a.m., the city goes silent for a one-minute prayer to honor the victims of the atomic bomb. I have experienced this moment while watching the ceremony, riding the light rail, and walking through a department store. At all locations everyone stops without commotion, pay their respects, and continues their business without skipping a beat. The moment of peace is as natural as breathing. The program concludes with the mayor's peace declaration, releasing of doves, a commitment to peace given by two elementary school children, addresses by distinguished guests, and the Hiroshima peace song. Hibakusha do not give a speech but take part in the submission of names to the registry and flower dedication. Park visitors experience a mix of solemn and festive events hosted by the city government, NPOs, local activists, and students for the remainder of the day. Visitors usually conclude the day by writing peace-oriented messages on lanterns that are released in the river adjacent to the Atomic Bomb Dome.

The Nagasaki Peace Ceremony adopts a more forceful and personal approach to educate visitors on the ugliness of war. Visitors must walk past panels that display graphic images of atomic bomb victims before they can access the main ceremony site. The fifty-two-minute ceremony includes a hibakusha-led chorus, dedication of the list of victims who died in the past year, opening address, water offering, flower offering, one-minute silent prayer at 11:02 A.M., mayor's peace declaration, pledge for peace, children's chorus, addresses by dignitaries, chorus of "A Thousand Paper Cranes," and closing words. Following the ceremony, visitors take part in events hosted by public and private groups across the city. The mayor's peace statement is often critical of the national government's failed efforts to abolish nuclear weapons. The following speech is less tame. Hibakusha have a much more prominent presence in the ceremony and in recent years, give a speech that is a fiery in its criticism of Prime Minister Abe, who sits just a few feet away. In 2014, Jodai Miyako, an A-bomb survivor representative, stated in the pledge for peace:

> Japan, the only country to have suffered a nuclear bombing, has a duty to be a world leader and to stand at the forefront of this abolition movement. However, is the government of Japan fulfilling that role? Doesn't the approval of collective self-defense say that the use of military force will create peace for Japanese nationals? Please stop exporting weapons. War begets war. History proves that. Please do not threaten our young people and children who will shoulder Japan's future. Please do not forget the suffering of the *hibakusha* and pretend that the atomic bomb never happened.[34]

Jodai also used the opportunity to comment on the Fukushima nuclear disaster, stating, "Is it really acceptable that we restart nuclear operations? After all, we still do not know how to dispose of nuclear waste. Instead, we should be looking into decommissioning the nuclear reactors as quickly as possible. As survivors, we *hibakusha* are using what remaining time we have left to desperately pass on our experiences of exposure to nuclear weapons."[35] Jodai's speech connects Japan's militaristic past with broader security concerns of the present and demands that Japan fulfill its role as a world leader in peace. At the peace memorial ceremonies, Prime Minister Abe sought to appease detractors by echoing the sentiments of Hiroshima and Nagasaki. In his 2017 speech, Abe stated, "Here in Hiroshima, which has developed admirably as an International City of Peace and Culture, I now pledge once again that Japan will make its utmost efforts for the realization of 'a world free of nuclear weapons' and eternal peace."[36] Abe made similar remarks in his Nagasaki speech. Abe's statement performs the speech act of giving a pledge, or promise, to promote peace and therefore reenacts Article 9, where the Japanese people forever renounce war as a sovereign right. Despite the effort, Abe's speech was received with jeers, although it is unclear where they came from in the audience.

Abe's speeches can restrain future security policy decision making because "principles are legal when they are enunciated by dignitaries of sufficiently high station and on occasions of such solemnity that their principled content cannot be impugned without also impugning the source and circumstance of their enunciation."[37] In the context of Hiroshima and Nagasaki, Abe is bound by commitment rules and cannot venture beyond pacifistic overtures, such as reaffirmation of the nonnuclear principles and assurance of Japan's antiproliferation efforts. The audience's demands of the Abe administration to match words with deeds demonstrate that the antimilitarism norm can be strengthened when not followed by elites. Words *are* deeds, but the public often demands more than words from their representatives. Hiroshima and Nagasaki have shaped Japanese security policy "by example, appeal and, if necessary, discrimination."[38]

The contrasts of Hiroshima and Nagasaki's differing approaches shed light on two branches of Japanese antimilitarism, each appealing to different peace ethics in the general population. Moreover, the cities demonstrate that there are different peace-oriented environments *within* the antimilitarism ecosystem, hence making it difficult to conclude that peace culture is dead because there is not one peace culture. Hiroshima cultivates a peace culture through positive messaging and an appeal to pacifism, which is symbolized by the paper cranes of Sasaki Sadako, a twelve-year-old girl who died from black rain–related illness. Nagasaki Peace Park leverages the water motif, which is made available throughout the Nagasaki Peace Museum and Peace Park to remind visitors of the great pain suffered by atomic bomb victims. Nagasaki cultivates a peace culture through emotional reminders of the consequences of war and benefits of antimilitarism. Through collaboration and intense internal debate, peace groups adapt and expand their missions to meet the needs of the current context.

Despite these different approaches toward peace, both cities advocate for the abolition of nuclear weapons, pacifism, and the rejection of militarism and therefore establish strong instruction rules that "promote general conformity of behavior by reference to shared values."[39] The residents of Hiroshima and Nagasaki are aware that the peace parks that occupy the central material and ideational city landscapes are also the gravesites for thousands of fellow Japanese, and thus they possess a responsibility to the past and future generations to never repeat those fateful days.

PEACE MUSEUMS: PHYSICAL ANTIMILITARISM DISCOURSES

Despite efforts by scholars to illustrate the complexity of war memory across schools of thought,[40] there is a persistent narrative that the Japanese public lacks remorse for the actions of Imperial Japan. Media stories on revisionist textbooks and lack of critical discussion of colonial history in school further perpetuate the belief that nationalism is on the rise in Japan, and aggressive militarism may follow. Sociologist Saito Hiro summarizes the politics of war commemoration, writing:

> The "history problem" is a complex phenomenon and hard to pin down because it consists of multiple controversies dealing with diverse issues, ranging from the Yasukuni Shrine to history textbooks, that have political dynamics and historical trajectories of their own. In this sense, it may be more appropriate to translate *rekishi ninshiki mondai* as "history problems" in the plural. Nevertheless, these multiple controversies are historically homologous—tracing back to Japan's actions during the Asia-Pacific War—and inextricably entangled to form a more or less bounded domain of public debates and policy problems.[41]

The attention paid to rising nationalism overshadows how antimilitarism endures and even flourishes in the postwar era through peace education that has critically examined Japan's colonial history.[42] In Hiroshima and Nagasaki, for example, peace education is included in elementary and junior high school, and over fifty colleges and universities use education materials provided by the city governments.[43]

Peace education extends beyond the classroom and uniquely manifests as museums throughout Japan, which has the most peace museums in the world. Peace museums can "bring to life, as school textbooks cannot, the ideas and subjects under consideration."[44] According to Roy Tamashiro and Ellen Furnari, "museums' exhibits, narratives, and programs reflect a wide range of definitions of peace including some which conflict and contradict each other" and from these contradictions, "museums for peace can play a significant role in peace education by raising awareness about multiple definitions of peace and by enabling audiences to reflect on, discuss and participate in deliberated paths toward personal peace and cultures of peace."[45] Peace museums provide extensive literature, archives, artifacts, and exhibitions that cultivate antimilitarism that is simultaneously broad in scope and specific to a visitor's personal interests. As physical, verbal, and written expressions, peace museums provide powerful instruction rules and commitment rules for visitors who passively observe exhibitions and scholars who actively use museum resources to disseminate peace discourses. Museums thus possess immense authority, or rule, from their privileged position in public education.

Peace museums and monuments require significant financial and political resources to construct and maintain, and therefore, signify what society considers important and unacceptable. One can look at the contested politics around the placement of comfort women statues around the world, public unrest concerning confederate monuments in the United States, public criticism of individuals who behave disrespectfully at Holocaust memorial sites, and millions of lobbying dollars seeking to influence the content of textbooks and museums to understand the significance of how the past is commemorated. Since "museums' objects and artifacts are infused with meaning and woven together as a plot that claims legitimacy as historical truth,"[46] the material world and ideational world are intrinsically connected in generating meaning. Museums are not only influential for the intellectual space they occupy but also for their physical presence in the environments where the public socializes. Many peace museums are located near popular tourist destinations—if not the destinations themselves—and within large parks. They provide spaces for people to congregate for focused engagement with peace and war, draw lessons, protest, and enact change. In short, physical discourses guide people on how to behave inside and outside their premises.

With approximately seventy-six museums, Japan is home to the most peace museums in the world. Peace museums are located in thirty-two of Japan's forty-seven prefectures and are spread evenly across the country (see figure 6.1). To illustrate the proximity of peace museums to every person in Japan, consider that the average size of a prefecture is approximately equal to a county in California. As such, the distance between a museum and any point in Japan is no more than a two-hour train ride (no museum is located more than two prefectures away from another museum).

Grassroots movements have maintained antimilitarism through the consistent support and construction of peace museums for over six decades. The first peace museums, the Hiroshima Peace Memorial Museum and the Nagasaki International Culture Hall, were not built until 1955 due to U.S. censorship of the atomic bomb. Peace museums are temporally spread apart, as many peace museums were established by local governments with the support of grassroots movements in the 1990s (twenty-eight museums) and 2000s (twenty-three museums).

FIGURE 6.1 Peace museums and war history museums in Japan. Prefectures with a peace museum are highlighted in light gray; prefectures with a war history museum and no peace museum are highlighted in dark gray; and prefectures with both types of museums are striped. The number in parentheses represents the total number of museums in each prefecture. The museums, by date of establishment, from oldest to newest, are located in the following prefectures: Hiroshima (7), Nagasaki (6), Saitama (3), Okinawa (5), Tokyo (8), Osaka (6), Hokkaidō (2), Kagoshima (1), Shizuoka (2), Kyoto (3), Kochi (2), Wakayama (2), Aomori (1), Kanagawa (3), Tokushima (1), Kagawa (1), Iwate (2), Hyōgo (5), Miyagi (1), Fukuoka (3), Nagano (1), Oita (1), Gifu (2), Fukushima (1), Fukui (2), Niigata (1), Okayama (1), Aichi (1), Yamanashi (1), Ibaraki (1), Tochigi (1), and Akita (1).

Source: Figure created with information from Anzai Science & Peace Office (2017) and independent research. Map created using freevectormaps. The original list is edited by Yamane Kazuyo, Katsura Ryotaro, and Anzai Ikuro.

The content of exhibitions evolved over time because "each museum's particular definition of peace satisfied the political and social needs of the time when the museum was constructed."[47] Many of these peace museums, however, are united by a peace education mission and are part of the Network of Peace Museums, which has hosted conferences, published educational materials, and supported scholars who promote peace discourses.[48]

The most visited peace museums in Japan are the Hiroshima Peace Memorial Museum and the Nagasaki Atomic Bomb Museum. Both museums offer low admission prices and are staffed with visitor guides whose tours are offered in several languages.[49] The primary missions of the museums are to convey the history of the atomic bombs, the suffering of the Japanese during and after the war, the success of postwar reconstruction, and contemporary antinuclear and peace movements.

Prior to the 2013-2019 renovations, visitors of the Hiroshima Peace Memorial Museum were greeted by a one-minute video narration of a brief history of the atomic bomb. The video proceeds as follows:

> On August 6, 1945, the first atomic bomb in the world was dropped on Hiroshima, and a vast number of her citizens perished. (*Image of a woman praying.*)
>
> It is now about half a century since the curtain was lifted on the Nuclear Age. (*Image of Atomic Dome in rubble.*)
>
> And still today we are living through that age. (*Image of four nuclear tests.*)
>
> This is the Hiroshima Peace Memorial Museum, an expression of our desire for world peace and the total abolition of nuclear weapons. (*Image of the museum.*)

The video ends with the sounds of chirping birds, hopeful music, and still images of the Hiroshima Peace Memorial Ceremony. Many of the museum's exhibits utilize passive language when discussing Japan's actions during World War II. Exhibit signage suggests Japan was hijacked by militaristic forces and a corrupt government that "insisted on 'spiritual mitigation,' denying even freedom of thought." Of the over one hundred information panels in the museum, less than ten discuss Japanese militarism. In lieu of a critical view of the war are exhibits that seek to educate visitors about nuclear-free zones, the work of Mayors for Peace, postwar reconstruction, and the harms caused by nuclear weapons. Shiga

Kenji, the museum's director, contends curators adopted a "facts-based" approach in the most recent renovation,[50] choosing to replace the museum's iconic mannequins of a woman and her two children walking through the charred remains of the city with additional artifacts. Museum content, and hence character of antimilitarism continues to be debated well after the war. The decision to remove the mannequins was met with protests because activists believed the museum needed to provide emotional weight behind education concerning the destructiveness of nuclear weapons. The new exhibitions feature interactive displays that allow patrons to navigate multilevel menus and access more information than the previous iterations. This layout lends itself to invested students and researchers more so than to casual observers and tourists.

The Nagasaki Atomic Bomb Museum, on the other hand, utilizes graphic imagery to appeal to the emotions of visitors and convince them of the humanitarian consequences of war. After descending the long museum stairwell entrance, visitors enter a full-scale replica of Nagasaki's Urakami Cathedral, which was destroyed by the atomic bomb. LED lighting projects images of flames and speakers pump the sound of howling wind throughout the exhibition. The room hosts few artifacts. The Nagasaki Atomic Bomb Museum also displays many images of charred bodies to educate visitors about the physiological consequences of the atomic bomb. The museum once hosted a notorious exhibit of an infant preserved in formaldehyde that was especially impactful to young visitors. The exhibit ended in the mid-1980s when peace movements sought to construct a wider tent.

The Nagasaki Atomic Bomb Museum directly addresses Japanese imperialism. Halfway through the museum are several monitors looping videos about comfort women, forced labor, cultural genocide, and the suffering endured by Japan's colonies. In one video, titled *The Greater East Asia Co-Prosperity Sphere*, the narrator states, "Japan said it wanted to free Asia from Western control and create a sphere of co-prosperity, but in fact it was simply an invasion by Japan." The final exhibition discusses the impact of nuclear weapons on communities around the world, such as Ronneburg, Hanford, Nevada, and New Mexico.

A close examination of visitor data (see figure 6.2) suggests museums are a wide-reaching resource for the education of the public and promotion of antimilitarism norms.

As of April 2020, 74,033,621 people have visited the Hiroshima Peace Memorial Museum. Annual attendance first peaked at 1,554,897 in 1991 following a

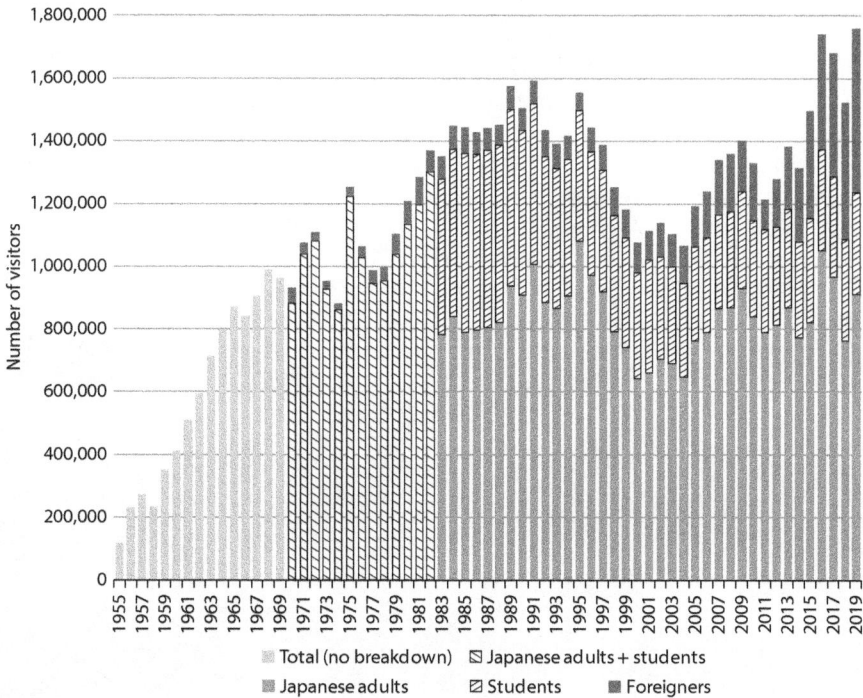

FIGURE 6.2 Hiroshima Peace Memorial Museum annual visitors, 1955–2019.

Source: City of Hiroshima, "Nendo Betsu Sō Nyūkanshasū Oyobi Gaikokujin Nyūkanshasū-tō" (Total Number of Visitors and Foreign Visitors by Fiscal Year and Such). April 7, 2020, https://www.city.hiroshima.lg.jp/uploaded/attachment/112311.pdf.

major renovation project and proceeded to decline over the next fourteen years, yet has never fallen below one million visitors since 1979. Museum visits began to significantly rise in 2015, the seventieth anniversary of the end of the war. The city government's efforts to internationalize the peace message and transform Hiroshima into a major tourist destination have sustained museums visits, which reached an all-time high of 1,758,746 in 2019.

Visitor data of the Nagasaki Atomic Bomb Museum is less granular, but it still provides insight on some noteworthy trends. Since opening in 1955, 56,734,449 people have visited the museum. Visitors peaked at 1,248,836 in 1975 and moderately declined over the next twenty-one years. The museum experienced a 16.5 percent visitor bump in 1996 when its current iteration replaced the Nagasaki International Culture Hall. The Hiroshima Peace Memorial Museum

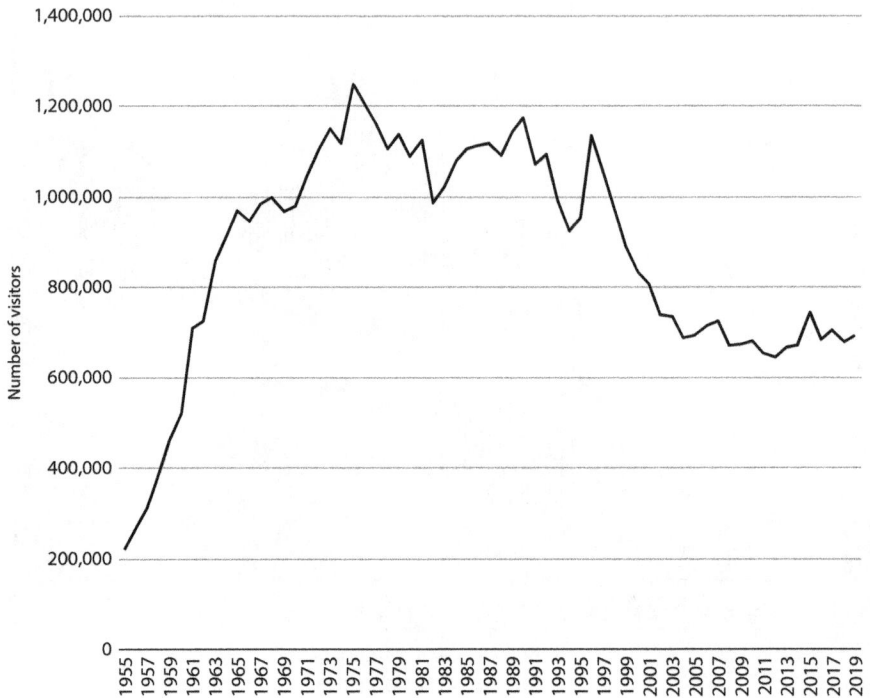

FIGURE 6.3   Nagasaki Atomic Bomb Museum annual visitors, 1955–2019.

Source: Nagasaki Atomic Bomb Museum, "Genbaku Shiryōkan Nendo Betsu Nyūkanshasū (FY1955–)" (Number of Visitors to the Atomic Bomb Museum from FY1955–). N.d.

experienced similar increases after renovation projects were completed, in 1991, 1994, and 2019. Japanese visitors have remained stable since the mid-1990s in both museums, but the Hiroshima Peace Memorial Museum experienced a significant increase in international visitors, which rose from 5.1 percent of total visitors in 1970 to 29.7 percent in 2019. International visitors increased by 240 percent in the last two decades alone.

Both museums play a vital role in sustaining antimilitarism among youth. At first glance, recent trends suggest peace museums are becoming a less important element of primary school and secondary school education. Figure 6.4 shows that attendance peaked at 535,101 student visitors in 1985 and reached a nadir of 297,643 student visitors in 2007. Middle school and high school students are less likely to take organized museum trips than elementary school students, who have held

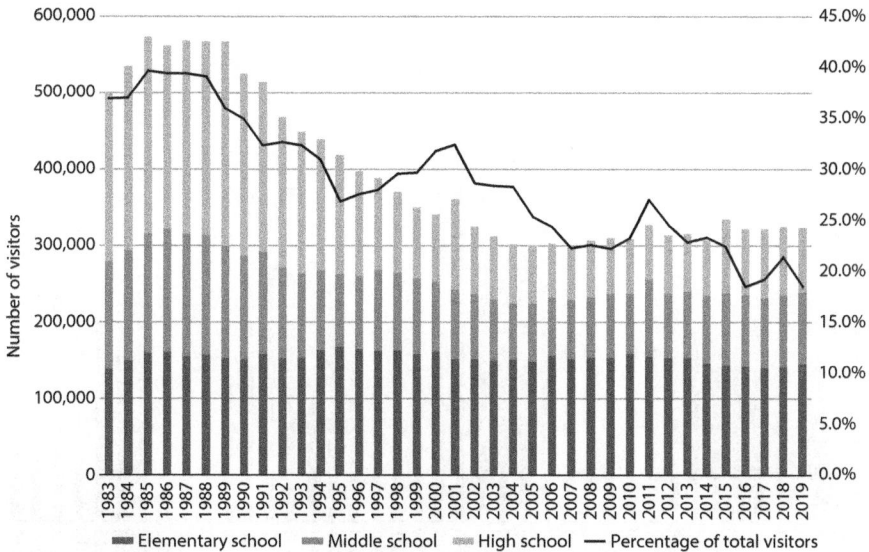

FIGURE 6.4 Hiroshima Peace Memorial Museum annual student visitors, 1983–2019.

Source: City of Hiroshima, "Sō Nyūkanshasū Oyobi Shūgakuryokō-tō Dantai Nyūkanshasū-to" (Total Number of Visitors and Number of Student Group Excursions and Such), accessed November 30, 2020. https://www.city.hiroshima.lg.jp/uploaded/attachment/112310.pdf.

steady at approximately 150,000 students per year. What accounts for this change? Similar to the broader impacts on the economy and JSDF, the aging and declining population may have contributed to declining attendance rates. Between 1985 and 2019, the student population decreased by 44.6 percent, while student visits to the Hiroshima Peace Memorial Museum decreased by 43.3 percent. The impact of demographics on museum attendance is not equally distributed among the three age groups. In the same period, Japan's elementary school population fell by 42.6 percent (11.09 million to 6.36 million), the middle school population fell by 46.4 percent (5.99 million to 3.21 million), and the high school population fell by 38.8 percent (5.18 million to 3.17 million), whereas museum visits fell by 8.99 percent, 39.9 percent, and 66.9 percent respectively.[51] The figures suggest that museum visits play a greater role in primary education because population decline far outpaced attendance rates. An examination of total class trips supports this hypothesis.

The total number of class trips to the Hiroshima Peace Memorial Museum has remained steady, despite the decline in the student population (see figure 6.5).

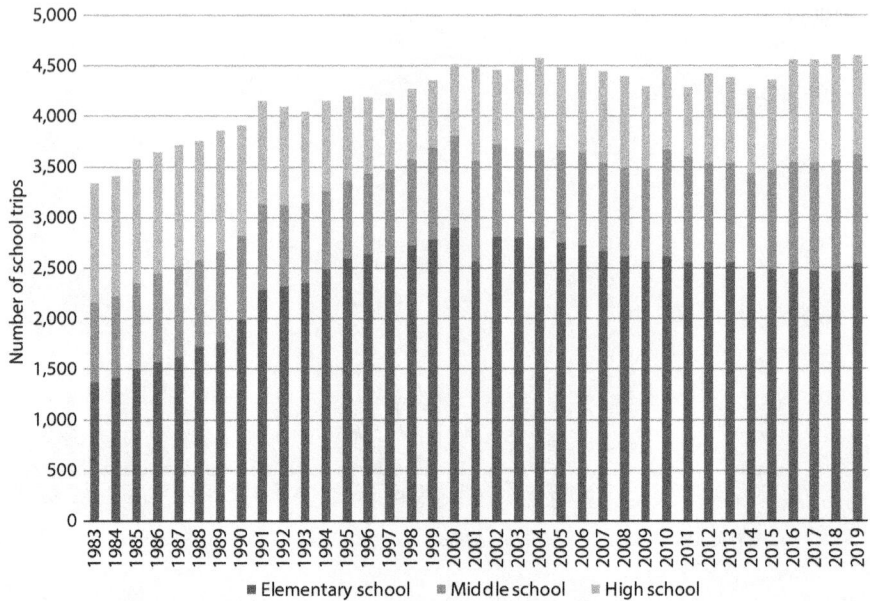

FIGURE 6.5   Hiroshima Peace Memorial Museum annual school trips, 1983–2019.

Source: City of Hiroshima, "Sō Nyūkanshasū Oyobi Shūgakuryokō-tō Dantai Nyūkanshasū-to" (Total Number of Visitors and Such and Number of Student Group Excursions and Such), accessed November 30, 2020. https://www.city.hiroshima.lg.jp/uploaded/attachment/112310.pdf.

Between 1983 and 2019, annual class trips increased almost every year, peaking at 4,606 trips in 2018. Since the overall student population declined, but total trips increased, the size of each group became smaller, which offers students a more intimate education experience. Elementary school and middle school trips increased over time, whereas high school trips decreased. The overall drop in high school attendance and organized school trips may be linked to the declining cost of commercial aviation over the past thirty years. Since 1985, domestic air travel doubled, and international air travel tripled.[52] Secondary school students are more likely to be able to travel to farther destinations than elementary school students for their school trips and therefore may not be visiting local museums as often. In 2019, the departing destination for elementary school trips were overwhelmingly from the Kansai (81,151) and Chūgoku (44,059) regions. Middle school and high school students travel farther distances and are 1.5 times and 7.5 times more likely to be coming from the Kansai and Chūbu regions, respectively.[53]

There is a high likelihood that the average Japanese student will visit a peace museum within their academic career. Each year, approximately one million children enter and leave elementary school. In the average six-year period (the average time it takes to complete elementary school in Japan), over 900,000 students visit the Hiroshima Peace Memorial Museum. If a student does not visit the museum during this period, there is a chance they will do so over the next six years of their secondary education. When taking into account the other seventy-five peace museums in Japan—at least seven of which average over 100,000 visitors a year—it is likely that the typical student has visited a peace museum (see appendix B for list of peace museums and war history museums and corresponding visitor data). In short, antimilitarism plays a prominent role in the formative years of many Japanese.

ANTIMILITARISMS ALL THE WAY DOWN: THE PEACE MUSEUM NETWORK

The subject matter covered in each museum has grown beyond the antinuclear narratives of Hiroshima and Nagasaki. Many of these private and grass-roots museums were established to complement the antiwar narratives of larger institutions or challenge them altogether. Due in no small part to their private status, grass-roots museums enjoy greater freedom of speech compared to the well-funded city museums. This freedom expands antimilitarism instruction rules and commitment rules because as one "moves away from the center—in terms of museums' discourses—the expressions of peace and of war responsibility become more critical, even radical."[54] The Japanese peace museum network then caters to different parts of Japanese society; the general public is taught an easy-to-digest antimilitarism at the most famous institutions and the vanguard of peace movements receive their marching orders from the more issue-oriented institutions.

Tucked away in a small apartment building near Waseda University's Nishi-Waseda Campus, the Women's Active War Museum on War and Peace (WAM) in Tokyo, for example, educates visitors on comfort women and human trafficking. WAM's main objectives expand the definitions of peace and security and include: (1) focusing on wartime violence with the objective of upholding that justice is free from any gender bias, (2) gathering and exhibiting data on victims and clarifying who is to take responsibility for their victimization, (3) establishing a people's network to rid the world of violence, (4) creating a network not dependent on state power, and (5) taking action to enable cross-border solidarity.[55] Careful readers may notice that WAM seeks to address many of the insecurities and inequalities that stem from, and are not solved by, a state-centered security policy that was discussed in chapter 3. WAM hosts several special exhibitions related to women's rights each year, such as seminars on the Sunflower Student Movement and the impact of foreign U.S. military bases. As a private entity, WAM provides a critical examination of issues that are inadequately covered or entirely ignored in textbooks and public education.[56]

The *Lucky Dragon No. 5* Exhibition Hall, established on June 10, 1976 by the Tokyo metropolitan government, seeks to raise awareness of disasters caused by nuclear weapons. The free-admission exhibit allows the approximately 100,000 annual visitors to view the *Lucky Dragon No. 5* vessel and to read approximately twenty panels outlining the history of nuclear testing on Bikini Atoll, the impact on the *Lucky Dragon No. 5* crew, and the dangers of nuclear fallout, or death ash. Half of the exhibition hall provides information on contemporary antinuclear and peace movements. In 2014, the hall hosted a special exhibit on Godzilla and displayed drawings by Japanese elementary school students.

Established in 2002, the Center of the Tokyo Raids and War Damage educates visitors the history of the Tokyo air raids. Visitors can view artifacts, such as debris, letters, documents, pictures, and other war-related materials. General history museums also promote antimilitarism though war-related exhibitions, such as the Edo-Tokyo Museum's air raid exhibition. In 2006, the Yamagata Museum hosted the *War and Children—School and Life* exhibition. This is particularly notable because Yamagata is one of the few prefectures that does not have a peace museum. In 2015, the Kyūshū Medical History Museum opened in Fukuoka and discusses formerly taboo subjects, such as medical experiments conducted on U.S. prisoners of war by the Japanese military.

The pervasiveness of antimilitarism is apparent when examining how military history museums discuss World War II.[57] The Chiran Peace Museum for Kamikaze Pilots, Bansei Tokko Peace Museum, and Tachiarai Peace Museum are among a network of military history museums that frame World War II, and specifically kamikaze missions, in terms of peace. Philip Seaton, for example, has found that kamikaze museums began as individual initiatives but expanded into tourist sites, which further complicates their narratives.[58] Beyond including the term "peace" in their names, these museums seek to educate visitors about the consequences of war while commemorating pilots by sharing letters, photos, and artifacts. According to its website, the Chiran Peace Museum seeks to "expose the tragic loss of their lives so that we may understand the need for everlasting peace and ensure such incidents are never repeated."[59] Similarly, the Tachiarai Peace Museum has served "more as a local history museum" and has collaborated in "peace education projects for school children with non-kamikaze facilities, including the Nagasaki Atomic Bomb Museum."[60]

The Kure Maritime Museum, also known as the Yamato Museum, depicts the history of Japan's greatest warship, the *Yamato*. For casual observers, the museum is a prideful exhibition of Japan's former military might, especially when viewing the dozens of model ships and fighter planes prominently displayed throughout the museum grounds. But according to Todaka Kazushige, director of the Yamato Museum, the exhibits are designed to teach young people about the history of the city, advances in technology, and the possible dangers of war.[61] Todaka contends, "it took seventy years for Japan to become a strong country, and due to the war, Japanese lost everything in four years. Yet, it took ten years for Japan to recover, so there is hope for Japan."[62] According to Tamashiro and Furnari, "The narratives and messages presented in museums are not objective or historical truths, but rather products of the museum designers' constructed interpretations of the chronicle of events, the people or the places they memorialize. Knowledge of the social world is a matter of human and social construction, rather than objectively knowable."[63] Todaka's interpretation of the war aligns with the popular antimilitarism attitudes that Japan was overtaken by corrupt forces, in this case, technology run amok. Without objective truth, one can conclude the Japanese public is free to interpret World War II as it wishes. However, Todaka's account demonstrates even military history museums are bound to the dominant rules outlined by Japanese peace culture, which contextualizes Japanese suffering as the product of war.

The Yamato Museum is part of a network of museums that shares exhibits, artifacts, and information. Although the Yamato Museum depicts Japan's naval history, it rarely collaborates with the Maritime Self-Defense Force (MSDF), and interactions are limited to lending uniformed personnel for special events. The MSDF manages the MSDF Kure Museum. This museum has no exhibits on the

Imperial Japanese Navy and focuses solely on the history of the JSDF. With so few missions since its inception, the majority of exhibits cover the JSDF's recent history with underwater minesweeping missions, PKOs, and humanitarian missions. Shōwakan, the official museum of emperor Hirohito and managed by the Ministry of Health, Labour, and Welfare, downplays the emperor's role in colonialism and emphasizes the suffering of people during the war, the difficulty of recovery, and Japan's rise as a global power.[64] Japanese colonialism is referenced, but never critically engaged. For history museums, war is decontextualized and simplified. In doing so, Japan deflects blame from itself and cultivates an easy-to-digest and popular antimilitarism that closely resembles pacifism. These museums therefore propagate appealing rules concerning how the government and public should think about peace and security.

When war history museums break with antimilitarism norms, the stronger commitment rules apply. An illustrative example of antimilitarism *rule* is the troubled development of a war museum in Nishiki, Kumamoto. City planners planned to build a war museum on the site of a former navy base to serve as a hub for education and tourism. However, the museum was met with protests from residents who believed the museum would downplay its peaceful purposes.[65] The town's mayor was forced to clarify that the intent of the museum is to provide peace education.

The controversy surrounding Yūshūkan, the military history museum located on the grounds of the Yasukuni Shrine, may be the most illustrative example of how antimilitarism norms shape Japanese conceptions of security. At its peak during World War II, the Yūshūkan averaged more than 1.9 million annual visitors.[66] The popularity of the Yasukuni Shrine is tied to its historical significance, central location in Tokyo, and controversial reputation. Critics often call attention to the long lines in front of the shrine during war anniversaries and Japanese New Year (at times ten persons wide and the length of the entire main street of the Yasukuni Shrine grounds), problematic historical accounts in the Yūshūkan, and Prime Minister Abe's unofficial visits as evidence of rising nationalism and historical revisionism. This assessment ignores that museum visitors have significantly decreased despite efforts to attract younger patrons, averaging between 200,000 to 300,000 in recent years. The shrine's priests are concerned that the Yasukuni Shrine is losing prominence, mainly because "new generations of Japanese are bewildered by the concept of Japan being at war with the US, given that much of society is increasingly influenced by global (and American) culture."[67] The dismissal of the shrine's head priest in 2018 for characterizing the emperor's absence as "trying to crush Yasukuni Shrine" is indicative of its precarious status.[68]

More informatively, antimilitarism constrains even the Yūshūkan's admittedly whitewashed historical accounts of Japanese colonialism because its curators are careful to frame exhibits within peace discourse. Exhibits in the museum portray warfare as an honorable and tragic sacrifice of soldiers who gave their lives for the homeland. Implicit in this narrative is that the Japanese must learn from the past and appreciate the efforts of fallen soldiers to ensure peace in the present day, which "effectively sees the rehabilitation of the past through the rhetoric of peace in the present."[69] Matthew Allen and Rumi Sakamoto describe further how Japanese learn from war history, writing "peace is used to frame events of the Pacific War, allowing people's roles in these events to be acknowledged publicly and enabling these experiences to be rehabilitated in the public domain. Such approaches that emphasize the importance of learning from our 'suffering' (*rouku*) simultaneously emphasize the importance of peace in the world."[70]

As discussed in chapter 5, Japanese antimilitarism rebuffs specific strands of militarism, but it does not entirely reject the use of force. The use of force must be justified—that is, conform with the rules. Museums, like the Yūshūkan, are locations where the parameters of the rules are determined and enforced. Consider, for example, the negotiation of language surrounding Prime Minister Abe's 2013 visit to the Yasukuni Shrine. Abe sought to preempt criticism and released a statement titled, "Pledge for Everlasting Peace." Abe stated, "Japan must never wage a war again. This is my conviction based on the severe remorse for the past. I have renewed my determination before the souls of the war dead to firmly uphold the pledge never to wage a war again."[71] Abe also sought to pacify regional criticisms, stating "It is not my intention at all to hurt the feelings of the Chinese and Korean people. It is my wish to respect each other's character, protect freedom and democracy, and build friendship with China and Korea with respect, as did all the previous Prime Ministers who visited Yasukuni Shrine," and "for 68 years after the war, Japan created a free and democratic country, and consistently walked the path of peace. There is no doubt whatsoever that we will continue to pursue this path." In the eighteen-sentence statement, the word "peace" appears six times, and the promise to "never wage a war" is made three times.

Three sentences ask for China and Korea's understanding, and the remaining seven sentences are comprised of transition clauses and expressions of respect for fallen soldiers. Friedrich Kratochwil explains the duty-imposing nature of promises, writing "moral facts expressed in rules of conduct are valid not because of threatened deprivations but because of their duty-imposing character, which is in turn the precondition for the legitimacy of physical sanctions."[72] In the "Pledge for Everlasting Peace," and similar reassurance acts, Abe commits himself and the Japanese people to carry out the role of a peace-loving nation. This pledge is not just to the Chinese and the Koreans, but to the Japanese as well.

Skeptics may conclude that Abe did not mean what he said. But at best, Abe's visits to the shrine were a wink and a nod to hardcore conservatives and not the rallying cry for a powerful Japan that East Asians feared. Rules shape the parameters of acceptable speech. Since the Yasukuni Shrine represents a violation of Japanese antimilitarism, the "Pledge for Everlasting Peace" reaffirms the commitment to peace in stronger terms than Abe's Hiroshima and Nagasaki peace memorial ceremony speeches. Japanese peace culture generates instruction rules that regulate how government leaders are allowed to justify the use of force. Instruction rules tell society what actions to take to arrive at the desired outcome and, in doing so, generate commitment rules that guide behavior. This commitment is expressed as "a pledge that we must build an age which is free from the sufferings by the devastation of war; Japan must be a country which joins hands with friends in Asia and friends around the world to realize peace of the entire world."[73]

Allen and Sakamoto contend, "Japan's ability to represent its war experiences is blunted by its defeat," hence "Japan's public war memories are framed within the discourse of 'peace,' regardless of the political persuasion of the institution."[74] Museums play a significant role in how contemporary Japanese engage with their memories, represent the war, and draw lessons from the past. As summarized by Peter van den Dungen and Yamane Kazuyo, museums inform the public of the "dark side" of Japanese history, give a voice to victims, allow visitors to learn from the past and work toward protecting human rights in the future, and promote understanding and reconciliation.[75] Museums are multiform speech acts that also mutually constitute Japanese peace culture in that they operate within boundaries, define boundaries, and on occasion, expand boundaries. Their physical presence in the Japanese landscape perpetually reinforces instruction rules and generates commitment rules. Hibakusha and comfort women gain a voice through these rules, and this voice is a material resource that is leveraged for recognition (status and standing), apologies (commitment and security), and compensation (wealth).[76]

PURVEYORS OF PEACE: RECENT ACTIVISM IN JAPAN

Peace museum discourse is only one dimension of the antimilitarism ecosystem that shapes the content and direction of Japanese security policy. Peace culture is promoted by diverse actors that include grassroots activists, city governments, private corporations, and parliamentarians. Peace groups' membership and missions differ in size and scope—some are locally based single-issue NPOs, while others are transnational networks advocating a broad conception of peace. Regardless, civil society is a powerful restraint on government efforts to normalize security policy.

The Japanese Trade Union Confederation, or RENGO, may represent the largest footprint in the antimilitarism environment. With a membership of over 6.86 million members across several economic sectors, RENGO possesses the resources and reach to influence the government and the general public. As a workers' union, RENGO's primary objectives are to create jobs and protect workers' rights. However, RENGO advocates for an all-encompassing definition of rights and includes "overcoming all injustice in society" in its core mission statement. RENGO financially supports peace movements that one would normally not associate with workers' rights, such as hosting four annual peace rallies—the Okinawa Peace Rally, the Hiroshima Peace Rally, the Nagasaki Peace Rally, and the Nemuro Peace Rally. These rallies draw thousands of attendees and help connect the national membership to local and international peace movements.

RENGO also produces literature, provides information tours, and hosts international events that aim to influence the public on antimilitarism issues, such as the reduction of U.S. military bases in Japan, reexamination of the U.S.-Japan Status of Forces Agreement, abolition of nuclear weapons, and a resolution of the Northern Territories dispute. Notable actions over the last twenty-five years include hosting the first overseas showing of the *Hiroshima-Nagasaki Atomic Bomb exhibition* in Paris, assisting with a signature-collection campaign aimed at the

2005 Review Conference of NPT, participating in the NPT Review Conference in New York, and leading a ten-million-signature campaign to advocate for the abolition of nuclear weapons at the 2015 NPT Review Conference.

RENGO is also critical to the cultivation of small, locally based NPOs. For example, in 2014, RENGO distributed approximately $800,000 in membership fees to support 123 NPOs.[77] Beyond its private activities, RENGO holds important links to the Japanese government, particularly opposition parties. Every two years, RENGO produces a policy issues information packet and presents it to members of the government. More formally, the Ministry of Health, Labour, and Welfare has a special council that regularly meets with RENGO to discuss the trade union's demands.

Another influential organization in the peace movement is Sōka Gakkai International (SGI), an international lay Buddhist association with over twelve million members in 192 countries and territories. According to Kawai Kimiaki, program director of peace affairs at SGI, Japan's peace culture after World War II can be viewed from three dimensions: religion, war history, and geography.[78] Kawai contends that Japan's religious ethic and a sense of remorse stemming from World War II cultivated a distinct Japanese peace culture. Japan's island geography, according to Kawai, lead the Japanese to be inherently introverted and thus preferring to focus on domestic issues over international issues, such as war. SGI's objectives seem to reflect this mindset, and they are mainly focused on nuclear disarmament, sustainable development, peace education, and human rights. SGI peace-related activities include holding antinuclear exhibitions, networking with other faith-based groups, and lobbying governments at international conferences, such as the NPT Review Conference and the Non-Proliferation and Disarmament Initiative. In 2007, SGI launched the People's Decade of Action for Nuclear Abolition initiative. As part of this initiative, and in collaboration with the International Campaign to Abolish Nuclear Weapons (ICAN), SGI hosted the antinuclear exhibition titled *Everything You Treasure—For a World Free from Nuclear Weapons*, which coincided with the twentieth anniversary of the International Physicians for the Prevention of Nuclear War (IPPNW) World Congress in Hiroshima. The forty-panel exhibition has been translated into five languages and has been viewed in over thirty-eight cities across thirteen countries. In 2014, SGI hosted an interfaith symposium on nuclear weapons in Washington DC. At the symposium, participating organizations pledged increased activism and prepared a statement on the humanitarian consequences of nuclear weapons that was later presented at the NPT PrepCom. SGI also lobbies the government on disarmament issues and maintains regular contact with the arms control section in MOFA.[79] Although officially separate entities, SGI is also closely connected to Kōmeitō, which in recent years has served as a pacifistic check on Liberal Democratic Party (LDP) attempts to change long-standing antimilitaristic laws and policies. Ikeda Daisaku, president of Sōka Gakkai, founded Kōmeitō in 1964, and the two groups continue to meet regularly to discuss peace issues.[80]

Some peace groups have as large a presence internationally as they do in Japan. Located in the trendy Shinjuku ward in Tokyo, Peace Boat was first established in 1983 by Tatsuya Yoshioka and Tsujimoto Kiyomi.[81] The Peace Boat headquarters is staffed by over fifty young Japanese and non-Japanese who work on a myriad of peace issues. Peace Boat utilizes an innovative model of chartering peace voyages that provide peace education to generate revenue. Since its founding, Peace Boat has completed 103 voyages and has visited more than 250 ports in over eighty countries (as of December 2020).[82] The approximately one thousand passengers, mostly comprised of students and retirees, on each of the four annual voyages receive a peace education comprised of group dialogues, speaker series, tours, and related programming at each of the docking sites. Peace Boat is divided into different sections that tackle various causes of instability, such as disaster relief, peace education, conflict prevention and peacebuilding, disarmament, and sustainability. One such project that seeks to promote peace through person-to-person relationship building is Peace Ball, a series of friendly soccer matches between Peace Boat participants and teams from local communities. According to Peace Boat International Coordinator (Disaster Relief) Robin Lewis, Peace Boat's many projects are "very different but ultimately are aiming to achieve similar things—a most resilient and peaceful world."[83]

Peace Boat operates as a focal point for many NPOs focused on issues such as nuclear disarmament, environmental protection, preservation of Article 9, phase-out of nuclear power, and U.S. bases in Okinawa.[84] Large NPOs possess the resources to launch transnational campaigns, such as the Global Article 9 Campaign to Abolish War initiative jointly managed by the Japanese Lawyers International Solidarity Association and Peace Boat in 2005. The initiative seeks "not only to locally protect Article 9 but also to educate people around the world about existing international peace mechanisms such as Japan's Constitution and encourage governments to work towards disarmament, demilitarization and a culture of peace."[85] In 2008, the three-day Global Article 9 Conference to Abolish War hosted Nobel Peace Prize laureates and leaders from NPOs from over forty countries. The conference drew over 33,000 participants to discuss the role of citizens in realizing the principles of Article 9. Peace Boat hosted two international follow-up events the next year. In 2012, Peace Boat worked with several groups and held the Nuclear Free Now event series in Tokyo and Fukushima, drawing thousands of attendees.[86] Organizations such as Peace Boat pressure the government directly or through issue reverberation by promoting initiatives at international venues where Japan has sought to increase its global clout. Beyond mobilizing the public and influencing public opinion, Peace Boat communicates with parliamentarians in all major parties and works closely with local governments to block undesirable nuclear weapons and nuclear energy policies.[87]

Local governments are an important tether between civil society and national governments. Mayors for Peace, founded in Hiroshima and Nagasaki in 1982, works toward the abolition of nuclear weapons by networking city-level governments to influence national nuclear policies. As of December 2020, Mayors for Peace has a membership of 7,974 cities in 165 countries and regions. Mayors for Peace's primary objectives are to: (1) raise public consciousness through petitions and other activities, (2) influence Japanese and other nationals, (3) commence negotiations for a nuclear weapons convention, (4) sign a nuclear weapons convention, and (5) achieve "a peaceful world free from nuclear weapons."[88] Its most significant initiative in recent years is 2020 Vision, which aims to lobby national governments and international organizations, expand local government participation in antinuclear activities, and increase peace education among youth through exchanges and exhibitions. Lobbying by Mayors for Peace has led to resolutions in support of the 2020 Vision by the EU Parliament, Council of European Municipalities and Regions, United Cities and Local Governments, National Conference of Black Mayors, Japan Association of City Mayors, National Council of Japan Nuclear-Free Local Authorities, and IPPNW. Moreover, Mayors for Peace produces annual progress reports, collects signatures, and assists in good faith negotiations. The Cities Are Not Targets (CANT) campaign, for example, collected over two million signatures calling for the abolition of nuclear weapons.

National and transnational peace movements would not be as successful if not for small and locally based NPOs that provide local expertise and vital services such as translation, networking, and event management. Founded in 1989 by Watanabe Tomoko, ANT-Hiroshima engages in peace building activities, peace education programming, and hosting international visitors in Hiroshima while participating in information dissemination, letter writing campaigns, lobbying at embassies, humanitarian aid and disaster relief, and other peace activities abroad. ANT-Hiroshima cultivates a peace culture that includes "human dignity and rights, water, food, and shelter, education, bonding, and free expression."[89] This all-encompassing human security conception of peace is consistent with the development of peace culture in Japan following World War II, which began as antinuclear and antiwar attitudes and evolved into active promotion of human security (discussed further in chapter 7). One of ANT-Hiroshima's primary objectives is to ensure that peace education continues after the first generation of activists is gone and therefore has worked toward educating youth about the consequences of war to create a new generation of peacebuilders.

Ogura Keiko, a first-generation hibakusha, founded Hiroshima Interpreters for Peace (HIP) in 1984. Ogura was eight years old and 1.2 kilometers away from the epicenter of the atomic blast, and therefore she is part of the last generation of survivors who can remember the event with clarity. Like many hibakusha who hid their status due to fear of discrimination, Ogura was not active in peace activism until much later in life and currently serves as one of the Hiroshima Peace Memorial Museum's "official storytellers."[90] Consisting of approximately eighty volunteer members, HIP provides translation services and information tours on nuclear weapons. Like many small Japanese NPOs, HIP did not originate as a peace organization and began as an informal collection of tour guides interested in producing a peace education pamphlet for visitors of Hiroshima. Due to the passing of hibakusha, Ogura and other members took on more activist roles and now regularly work with the local city government in peace promotion activities and give talks in Japan and around the world.

The Japanese antimilitarism landscape is also comprised of individuals who are not connected to official government channels or formal NPOs. These grassroots movements are no less vital to the enduringness of peace culture, and they actively challenge the dominant antimilitarism narratives. Mito Kosei, an in-utero A-bomb survivor, started Free and Informative Guides (FIG) in 2006. Like many activists, Mito's activism was ignited later in life. After fifteen years of teaching high school and volunteering at the Hiroshima Peace Memorial

Museum, Mito became disenchanted with the sanitized version of World War II and decided to give free tours to visitors at Peace Memorial Park. Over the years, Mito's solo project grew to include approximately fifteen semiregular members, who include students, hibakusha, and like-minded individuals. Since its founding, Mito estimates that FIG has given tours to over 280,000 Japanese and 73,000 tourists from over 177 countries. During FIG tours of Hiroshima Peace Park, visitors are encouraged to touch *haka* (tombs) damaged by the atomic bomb to gain a tactile connection with the victims. Mito credits FIG's informal status for allowing it to express strong anti-Abe and anti-U.S. foreign policy attitudes as well as candid criticisms of the Hiroshima Peace Memorial Museum for "not adequately displaying the tragic nature of war and Japan's wartime atrocities."[91]

Although FIG has a critical stance of the Abe administration and is not formally supported by the city government, it is allowed to station its tables, chairs, signs, A-bomb articles, artifacts, and information packets (translated into seven languages) in front of the Atomic Bomb Dome. FIG's loitering, interaction with tourists, and storage of its supplies in one of the most valuable locations in Hiroshima is made possible by a tacit understanding with the city government. The city government is aware of FIG's criticisms and personal use of public property but allows it to continue its activities. In exchange, FIG contacts city officials to inform them of broken fixtures, pollution, and vandalism. According to Yokoyama Motonobu, director of peace programs of Hiroshima City, the city does not reject any independent peace activity because private groups can spread their message as they please since all peace activists are fighting for the same goals—abolishing nuclear weapons and world peace.[92] Although Mito prefers FIG to maintain its unofficial status because he believes registering as a formal NPO may lead to censorship, not all members agree, and many have splintered off to join other movements. Yamaoka Michiko, a second-generation hibakusha, splits the difference and spends time with FIG while also working for the city as an official tour guide. Yamaoka gained her knowledge of the atomic bomb through testimonials of first-generation survivors, such as her mother's. Yamaoka's father is also an A-bomb survivor but never spoke of his experience because of the immense trauma, as is common among survivors.[93] The complex relationships among members within groups, and between activists and the state, reveal an antimilitarism that is never static enough to be dismissed as gone. Tensions among activists can not only weaken their collective power but also create spaces for new antimilitarism discourses.

Lastly, Japanese peace culture is promoted by citizens who do not regularly engage in peace activities. Following the introduction of new security bills in 2015, students throughout Japan joined antiwar protests, many of which were led by Students Emergency Action for Liberal Democracy (SEALDs). As discussed in chapter 4, scholars have historically promoted antiwar education and, in recent years, actively challenged the Abe administrations foreign policies.[94] Tokuchi Hideshi articulates the general character of the antimilitarism environment frankly, stating, "If you look at the academic world, some people adamantly say that Japan should not be involved in military study. It is also true if you look at the media and newspapers. Some newspapers are quite anti-military."[95] The less tempered critiques of the government are rarer, yet they punctuate the continued passion among activists. When the Abe government pursued changes to Japanese security laws, some activists self-immolated to protest possible amendments to the Constitution.[96]The individuals of the peace movement are both the material and ideational components of the antimilitarism ecosystem; their bodies vote and obstruct while their voices condemn, educate, and instruct.

ANTIMILITARISM: PERVASIVE AND ENDURING, BUT NOT HEGEMONIC

The Japanese antimilitarism ecosystem is comprised of peace movements small and large, young and old. The rules that constitute the ecosystem are articulated not only in principles and laws but also in the physical landscape as monuments and museums. Antimilitarism is strengthened by the diversity of peace groups whose contrasting views challenge the public and government to pursue a deeper understanding of war and peace.

That very diversity, however, has made cross-group cooperation difficult over the years. Without a clear action plan, peace movements can seem more aspirational than practical. Small NPOs pursue different agendas, and although members often join other groups during protests, there is less enthusiasm for combining missions or resources. Instruction rules provide guidance, but activists regularly differ over how to commit. Strong egos have atomized peace groups, most notably in the split of the Hiroshima chapter of Hidankyō in the 1960s that has remained to the present day.

Despite the splintering of peace groups, antimilitarism attitudes endure because peace discourses appeal to the basic emotions of ordinary citizens. Peace groups cultivate a visceral response to the suffering caused by World War II, which draws the public's attention while not demanding active participation. This easy-to-digest and nonconfrontational approach allows peace groups to educate the public, thus transferring antimilitarism sentiment from one generation to another. Yet, since antinuclear attitudes are so commonsensical, the public can become complacent. Pacifism is no longer vigorously discussed at the national level unless threatened or during anniversary events. Large-scale protests erupted following Prime Minister Abe's announcement that debates would commence on passing new security legislation, and significant media coverage followed the seventieth anniversary of the A-bomb in 2015 and President Obama's visit to Hiroshima in 2016. Obama's visit was a particularly significant event for Hiroshima residents. I remember quite vividly how residents would look toward the sky whenever they heard a loud noise because the rumor was that the president would be arriving via helicopter. Although I was supposed to attend the ceremony, my press pass was not cleared due to overbooking, and I rushed to the Sogo department store to find a television. Dozens of people crowded around every screen and intently watched Obama and Abe give their speeches, and many cried when the president hugged Mori Shigeaki, an atomic-bomb survivor. I attended several NGO-hosted events and observed activists vigorously debate the appropriate actions going forward. The day ended at a small café where a friendly, if a little tipsy, man told me that he loved the U.S., and me, because "America is OK!"

Nonetheless, the public does not follow security topics closely day-to-day. In recent years, the Peace Memorial Ceremony has not been aired in its entirety by commercial broadcasters, not even in Hiroshima, and peace editorials have less traction than in the past.[97] NHK continues to broadcast the ceremony, and short clips are played by other stations on the night of the event. I also returned to Hiroshima on the first anniversary of President Obama's visit and discovered that there was not any additional media coverage of the previous year's event. The only noticeable change was that a few small paper cranes that Obama had folded were now on display at the Peace Memorial Museum.

Declining national coverage, however, has not eroded the importance of peace discourse in education. Many activists believe the education they received immediately following the war helped keep Japan on a peaceful path. Japanese educators are notoriously liberal, and young Japanese learn about the consequences of World War II, albeit without a critical view of who was responsible. Extensive media coverage of waning pacifism and rising nationalism keeps civil society and policymakers aware of the potential threat. According to one LDP parliamentarian, it is the government's job to "prevent unhealthy nationalism" because it "jeopardizes the security of the region."[98]

This vigilance goes hand-in-hand with the long-term view of peace held by activists. Steve Leeper contends "true peace" may seem like a "goal really far off," and would require "huge systemic change," but it is possible because there is "progress every day."[99] Few activists believe absolute peace can be achieved within their lifetimes and therefore establish short-term goals such as educating youth, lobbying the government to abide by disarmament agreements, and enhancing dialogue. The long-term view of peace may not completely change the government's security agenda, but it ensures the peace discourses remain in the zeitgeist.

Antimilitarism's greatest obstacle toward policy hegemony may be cultural. Many peace groups suffer from poor fundraising, and therefore they lack resources to utilize modern mobilization tools, such as well-run websites and social media. The lack of resources also makes it difficult to hire and keep young talent. Hidankyō, for example, operates out of a small office in Tokyo and generates most of its budget from membership fees, approximately ¥40 million annually. Hidankyō executive officers are unpaid, and employees either volunteer or are paid low salaries. Hidankyō lacks a grant writer, which is not uncommon among Japanese NPOs. This lack of fundraising limits the scope of activities. In one of its most important campaigns, Hidankyō reached less than a quarter of its fundraising target to send A-bomb survivors to the NPT Review meeting.[100] Hidankyō also chooses not to invest in a modern website because it does not want to convey to its supporters that they are using their funds "extravagantly."[101] The lack of use of free platforms, such as Facebook and Twitter, suggests a fundamental human resource problem. Robin Lewis posits, "Nonprofits in Japan are a bit more shy in some ways. There are groups doing incredible work who do not get the message out effectively."[102] Demographics play a role in the stagnation found here. Hidankyō is still dominated by older activists who are unequipped for modern activism. Change will be hard to come by because, as Steve Leeper argues, the peace movement suffers "serious problems of horizontal communication because Japan is a very vertical society."[103]

Smaller groups are more dependent on leadership and possess fewer resources. FIG, for example, is an entirely unpaid voluntary group of retirees and students. HIP collects ¥300 per meeting and ¥1,000 from people who take their tour, which is not enough to even cover their bus fares. Neither of these groups own professional and easy-to-navigate websites, both of which are plagued with outdated scripts and dead links.

The lack of fundraising is due to a culture that is not comfortable asking for donations for private political causes. The Hiroshima Peace Memorial Museum, for example, only has a single unmarked donation box, which is located in front of the Memorial Cenotaph. The museum does not solicit donations from patrons. Large corporations must independently contact the museum to offer donations and only for maintenance of the Atomic Bomb Dome or general peace activities.[104] Watarida Masahiro, a second-generation hibakusha and founder of Global Watch Hiroshima, contends that peace groups are reluctant to fundraise due to a stigma of pushing one's politics onto others, and therefore they rely on small membership fees to support their activities.[105] Watarida concludes Japanese peace groups are "not concerned about growth" and instead focus all their energies on the most current project. Consequently, it is difficult for peace groups to retain young activists, who eventually quit to pursue more stable career paths and to plan for the long-term.[106] Similar to how gender roles limit the GOJ's ability to transform the economy and strengthen the JSDF, rigid age-based hierarchies prevent rapid innovation among peace groups.

The strength of Japanese peace culture does not ebb and flow in accordance with shifts in regional power balance. The peace movement has aged, literally and figuratively, allowing it to evolve and take on new missions and abandon some old ones. Its elastic nature, due to demographics and historical developments, prevents antimilitarism from taking over the security agenda but keeps it persistently relevant and influential. Peace culture is strengthened through repeated practices and expressed in law and principles. Although at times taken for granted, antimilitarism rules govern security debates and are diffused and formalized in Japanese security policy. In short, antimilitarism is pervasive and enduring but not hegemonic.

THE CONSTITUTION AND ANTIMILITARISM PRINCIPLES

According to Onuf, "The formal statement of principles gives them weight—the more formal the weightier. This property enables people to rank and choose among large numbers of sometimes incompatible rules."[107] The weightiest of Japanese antimilitarism principles is the Peace Constitution, which provides the normative and legal framework for restraining aggressive militarization. The Constitution is particularly powerful because its clear instruction rules, direction rules, and commitment rules guide how the Japanese public think of themselves and their place in the world. Within Japanese security policy debates, Article 9 serves as a byword for the Peace Constitution, but this shorthand underappreciates that the Constitution is a democratic and antimilitaristic document through and through.

The Constitution's American and Japanese architects designed the document to completely demilitarize Japan. If one considers the order of the Constitution as indicative of importance, then the spirit of the document is made starkly evident by the nine-sentence preamble, where the word "peace" appears five times. The preamble is followed by chapter 1, which in eight articles ended the emperor system that was central to Japanese expansionism since the Meiji period.

Article 9, which states, "Aspiring sincerely to an international peace based on justice and order, the Japanese people forever renounce war as a sovereign right of the nation and the threat or use of force as means of settling international disputes. In order to accomplish the aim of the preceding paragraph, land, sea, and air forces, as well as other war potential, will never be maintained. The right of belligerency of the state will not be recognized," comprises the entirety of chapter 2.[108] No other chapter in the Constitution so emphatically and directly articulates Japan's commitment to peace, which may explain why the renunciation of war clause has such an outsized impact on Japanese identity. According to one LDP parliamentarian, Article 9 "influences discussion of defense all the time, and it will continue to influence all discussions."[109]

Conservatives have sought to amend the Constitution to help facilitate change in Japanese security policy but have been met with resistance from centrist and liberal politicians and angry protests from the public.[110] Article 96, which mandates the approval of two-thirds of both houses in the Diet and a simple majority in a national referendum, ensures an amendment is difficult to achieve. This procedural obstacle alone, however, does not explain the enduringness of Article 9 because an amendment is possible as long as there is enough political and public support. In other words, the lack of support for amending Article 9 is not *due to* Article 96 but because antimilitarism norms provide the public guidance on which policies to support. Rules do not determine human conduct but give it social meaning.[111] Here, it bears repeating that society writes the rules.

Some scholars contend that changing public attitudes would eventually lead to constitutional revision, specifically citing a 2006 *Mainichi Shimbun* poll that showed 65 percent of respondents in favor of constitutional revision.[112] The reading of polls often ignores how antimilitarism manifests in public opinion surveys and has contributed to the misconception that the public supports constitutional revision to strengthen the military.

Often neglected in discussions of polling data is that the majority of the Japanese public has never supported a constitutional revision to empower the armed forces. In the aforementioned *Mainichi Shimbun* poll, 53 percent of respondents who supported change did so because they felt the "Constitution did not fit the times" and 13 percent because there is a "gap between the activities of the Self-Defense Forces and Article 9."[113] A revision to the Constitution would clearly outline the authority of JSDF, which became an Abe talking point in later debates. An April 2005 *Nikkei Shimbun* poll showed that 29 percent of respondents did not support constitutional revision, and of this group, 47 percent answered that revision could change pacifism.[114] Of the 53 percent who supported revision, respondents were divided over the problems that needed to be fixed (civil rights issues, security, clauses concerning the Diet, and local autonomy concerns). Of the 53 percent of respondents who supported an amendment in a 2009 *Asahi Shimbun* poll, 74 percent did so to "include a new system of rights."[115] Of the 33 percent opposed, 44 percent answered "the revisions of the constitution may trigger a change on pacifism." An April 2010 *Asahi Shimbun* poll showed only 24 percent of respondents supported an Article 9 amendment.[116] Moreover, 67 percent of respondents wanted to retain the renunciation of war clause, 70 percent of whom answered that Article 9 was "somewhat useful" or "useful" for the peace of Japan and stability of East Asia. The utility of the Constitution was overwhelmingly supported in a 2017 *Mainichi Shimbun* poll, which found less than half of respondents supporting an amendment. Concerning the Constitution's "effectiveness in maintaining peace and improving people's lives in Japan after World War II,"

29 percent answered, "very effective," and 47 percent answered, "effective to a certain extent."[117]

The public is also not receptive to reinterpretation of the Constitution, a strategy Prime Minister Abe adopted to bypass the amendment process and introduce collective self-defense. The right to collective self-defense would allow Japan to protect an ally, such as the United States, and can only be exercised only when the ally is defending Japan and requires assistance. Even under such narrow conditions, the Japanese public is concerned with being drawn into unnecessary and protracted conflicts. According to an April 2014 *Asahi Shimbun* poll, of those surveyed, 27 percent supported reinterpretation, while 56 percent opposed reinterpretation.[118] A May 2014 *Asahi Shimbun* poll found 50 percent of respondents answered that Abe's security bills would likely increase conflict, and 75 percent answered that Japan would be pulled into conflict.[119] The following year, an *Asahi Shimbun* poll showed that although 45 percent of respondents supported the Abe cabinet (32 percent opposed), only 33 percent supported Abe's bills permitting the use of collective self-defense (43 percent opposed). Respondents were skeptical of Abe's claims that Japan would not be pulled in a U.S.-led war, with 19 percent agreeing and 68 percent disagreeing.[120]

Consistent in polling data is that respondents oppose revision because they believe the Constitution has brought peace, and they support revision out of a desire to better articulate rights and the legality of national defense. In polls conducted by the *Yomiuri Shimbun*, *Asahi Shimbun*, and NHK between 1995 and 2017, the most popular reasons for revision were, "Japan confronts new issues that cannot be addressed under the current constitution, such as contribution to international cooperation," "new rights and rules need to be included,"[121] and "explicitly articulate the right to self-defense."[122] In the NHK poll, of the 43 percent who supported constitutional revision, 54 percent of respondents cited the need to respond to changes in the security environment. In other words, less than a quarter of respondents supported revision for traditional security reasons.

Even if one were to concede that the postwar Constitution is a wholly American creation, the Japanese people are still the ones who adopted and maintain it. Okudaira Yasuhiro, a professor of law at the University of Tokyo, contends that although "the founders were fanatical about insisting that preservation of the *tennō* system [emperor system]," it is arguable that the tennō system still occupies "a real, pivotal position in the constitutional regime, and whether the people still regard that system as one of the most important institutions of government."[123] MacArthur preserved the emperor system in a severely weakened form, to the chagrin of conservatives. Polling data shows far-right groups remain at the fringe, and support for constitutional amendment on the grounds that it was written by Americans rarely rises above 30 percent.[124] What the Constitution represented to political elites in 1945 differs from what it represents to the Japanese public today. The origins of the Constitution need not to be known to Japanese for it to effectuate rule because "although social rules necessarily have authors and histories, neither need to be known for rules to work as such."[125]

The role of Article 9 in Japanese politics evolved from a strategy of curtailing Japanese militarism to serving as a shield for economic growth and providing a guide for Japanese foreign policy. The Constitution also serves as a symbol of peace identity and an exemplar of Japan's modernity and lasting contribution to the international community. Mayor Taue links antimilitarism to Japan's international role via the Constitution, stating, "The origin of the principle of peace in the Japanese Constitution that was established after the war is based on the experience of the atomic bomb that caused devastation and claiming the lives of many citizens. I believe that this principle enabled us to gain trust as a pacifist country in the international society."[126] In several interviews conducted for this book, respondents referred to the Constitution as a national treasure. This national treasure is more than a convenient excuse to avoid conflict and is a standard for democracy, human rights, and pacifism. A 2008 *Yomiuri Shimbun* poll showed of the 43 percent of respondents who opposed amending the renunciation of belligerency clause, 42.7 percent believed it was entrenched among the people, and 52.5 percent answered that the Peace Constitution could be "boasted to the world."[127]

The Constitution's constraining power is effectuated by way of Japan's strong democratic principles and institutions. Chapters 3 and 4 of the Constitution outline the rights and duties of the people, which include civilian control of the Diet, the cabinet, and the judiciary. The rights protected in chapter 3 stall policies that aim to increase the capabilities of the JSDF. For example, Article 21 states, "Freedom of assembly and association as well as speech, press and all other forms of expression are guaranteed. No censorship shall be maintained, nor shall the secrecy of any means of communication be violated." This article is a response to the invasive policies of the imperial government that were vital to the maintenance of a militarized state in the prewar era. According to Tsuchiya Motohiro, Article 21 is a major impediment to GOJ efforts in relaxing privacy laws. With strict privacy laws in place, the MOD cannot augment its cybersecurity capabilities and participate in more robust international cyber intelligence.[128] Specifically, Tsuchiya calls attention to the inability to tap into landlines, which prevents the MOD from engaging in counter-cyberattacks critical to modern-day defense. Although Japan possesses the technical capabilities to tap into wired digital communications, the courts and the Ministry of Internal Affairs and Communications have fiercely guarded privacy rights. Polling data suggests that public attitudes align with court decisions. In a 2017 NHK poll, the protection of privacy rights was the second-most popular response by supporters of constitutional revision.[129]

The Constitution demilitarizes Japan not only in terms of war-making potential but also by restructuring the power relationship between the government and the people. The codification of rights provides the Constitution normative power because "institutionalization expedites the assignment of value to and through rules offering instruction."[130] Article 43 states, "Both Houses shall consist of elected members, representatives of all the people." Article 66 dictates all ministers "must be civilians." And Article 78 maintains the independence of the judiciary, where judges can only be removed by public impeachment. The JSDF personnel themselves are civilians.[131] In other words, well-defined democratic rules allow the people to decide the direction of the country. Poor JSDF recruitment, consistent polling data, and the oldest unamended constitution in the world make clear the direction that the Japanese people have chosen.[132]

Purchasing Security on a Tight Budget

The renunciation of the war clause generated formal and informal rules that restrain the GOJ's ability to strengthen the JSDF. The 1 percent of GDP soft cap on defense spending may be one of the most debated data points among Japanese security experts and policymakers. I use the term "soft cap" because when including the *hosei yosan* (supplementary budget) in recent years, the defense budget rises above 1 percent. Returning to a sports analogy once more, in the NBA, each additional dollar above the cap becomes prohibitively expensive over time. The NBA Collective Bargaining Agreement stipulates that teams pay three additional dollars for every dollar above the cap. Once the cap is reached, teams begin to second-guess player acquisitions because they will be paying a 300 percent premium. The Japanese government, like NBA teams, is legally allowed to go above the spending cap but not without significant costs and, eventually, diminishing returns. The GOJ invites criticism from the media, the Japanese public, and regional rivals when it crosses the 1 percent threshold, which lengthens policy debates and increases the need for reassurance. Hence, the cap creates rules that influence actor calculations and guide their behavior.

According to Onuf, "Human agents author rules and deploy resources in accordance with those rules as to secure and ensconce advantages over other agents."[133] The mobilization of human and financial resources to construct and maintain peace museums, hold demonstrations, and lobby the government demonstrate how antimilitarism influences public attitudes and security debates. The control of resources, ultimately, is a method of *rule*. This rule has prevented the GOJ from providing the JSDF the financial resources necessary for significant growth.

Within East Asia, the Japanese defense budget takes up the smallest share of the national GDP (see figure 6.6). Defense expenditures reached a nadir in 2008 and slowly increased over the next decade. The overall budget increased by about 4.3 percent between 2008 and 2019. The defense budget was informally capped at 1 percent of the GNP by the Miki cabinet in 1976 and was repealed by the Nakasone cabinet in 1987. The fact that the spending cap is neither law nor a clearly outlined principle but has remained for over thirty years provides insight on the internalization of antimilitarism rules. Ueda Isamu (Kōmeitō) frames defense debates in terms of fiscal constraints and concludes that an increase in the defense budget "would be difficult to tolerate."[134] Sado Akihiro finds a general reluctance to increase defense spending, arguing that, "The biggest problem is the mindset of officials that financial considerations take precedence over anything else."[135] The Ministry of Finance, in particular, maintains incredible influence over the defense budget. The defense budget is informally linked to the size of the economy and not changes in regional power balance. Japan's regional rivals are not bound by the same self-imposed restraints. In the last thirty years, China and Taiwan allocated approximately 2 percent of GDP to defense. Following a decline in defense expenditures in the immediate aftermath of the Cold War, Russia's defense spending increased to over 4 percent of the GDP. South Korean defense spending similarly reversed course in recent years, increasing to 2.7 percent of the GDP in 2019.

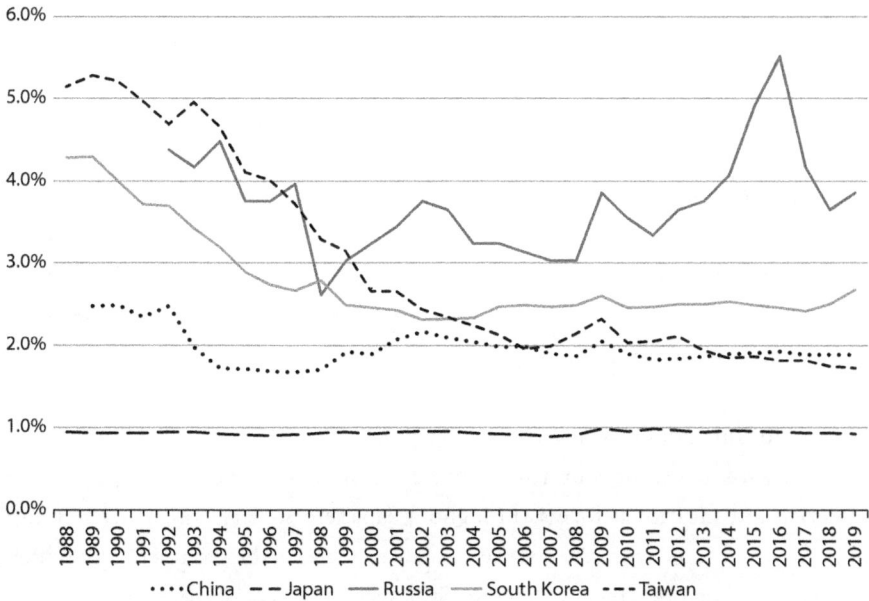

FIGURE 6.6   East Asia defense expenditures by share of GDP, 1988–2019.
Source: Stockholm International Peace Research Institute, "SIPRI Military Expenditure Database."

Despite Prime Minister Abe's announcement that the 1 percent cap would no longer be followed, policymakers have had difficulty overcoming the restraint. According to Morimoto Satoshi, Japan has not seriously discussed by *how much* the defense budget could be increased because the percent cap is not a political problem but a tacit understanding in the government.[136] Since 2017, a 2 percent cap has been floated among officials, academics, and media pundits. The figure, originating from the 2014 NATO Wales Summit and gaining new life from President Donald Trump's pressure on U.S. allies to increase alliance burden sharing, was met with tepid interest by government elites. Minister of Defense Iwaya Takeshi dismissed the 2 percent target during a press conference, stating, "I do not believe 2 percent of the GDP is a realistic figure."[137] In a follow-up interview, Iwaya clarified that spending targets are not optimal to address Japan's security needs, and the government would need to "obtain the understanding of the people for moving towards a numerical target from the start."[138] Among policymakers, there is little confidence that such public understanding for doubling the defense budget is likely. One senior government official contends,

> the Abe government is very cautious. We need to increase defense spending, but we need public support for defense policy. Our immediate question is the rising social welfare costs. It is the most serious question. It is very hard to pursue both objectives...Increasing defense spending is not an easy task for any Japanese politician. Prime Minister Abe has been making serious efforts to address this question. But at the same time, all of us have to be very cautious and take a step-by-step approach.[139]

Morimoto concludes it is "impossible in a political sense."[140]

As discussed throughout this book, antimilitarism rules are expressed in material and ideational forms throughout Japanese society. The 1 percent cap does not need to be formally codified in law to provide the parameters in which the government operates. When the GOJ seeks to increase defense spending, scholars, policymakers, and to a lesser extent, the public engages in impassioned debates about its necessity and what it could mean for Japanese antimilitarism. At the prospect of raising defense spending above 1 percent, Captain Kitagawa Keizō (MSDF) explains, "It depends on the international situation. Japan is a very pacifist country. We [Japanese] do not want to spend on defense. Actually, if it is smaller, that is better."[141] Unlike U.S. policymakers who traditionally advocate for higher defense spending to signal to their constituents they are serious about defense, Japanese policymakers do not gain cheap political points with higher defense spending. According to Tsuruoka Michito, "The bleak reality here is that the government has been trying to make the defense budget look small for domestic political reasons."[142] For this reason, defense-related expenditures, such as the Japan Coast Guard budget and supplementary budgets, are not often counted toward the defense budget estimates by the GOJ.[143]

Kitagawa's framing also illustrates defense expenditures are not directly tied to specific needs, such as equipment and infrastructure. The MOD has specific requests, but its ability to fund them are dependent on the size of the economy and its effect on the 1 percent baseline. The discussion of the 1 percent cap leads Morimoto to conclude that Japanese debates on defense spending are "quite strange" because so much time is spent on arbitrary figures and not on the specific needs of the JSDF.[144] Unless the GOJ can break free from the rules that govern the budget debates, defense expenditures will gravitate toward the 1 percent cap and the MOD will continue to lack the resources to quickly and significantly increase the power projection capabilities of the JSDF. With limited resources, the GOJ can only increase defense expenditures at the expense of other budget expenses. In other words, the defense hawks within the government must replace the dominant rules that have guided defense spending for decades if they ever hope to effectuate significant change. However, the GOJ and public have shown little interest in making defense spending a priority.

I should note here that all defense expenditures discussed in this section are denominated in U.S. dollars to allow for comparative analysis. Thus, exchange rate fluctuations can account for some variance over the years; the yen averaged a 0.22 percent positive exchange rate against the dollar over the last thirty-two years (–18.73 percent to +21.48 percent range). Consequently, Japanese defense spending decreased in dollars but increased in absolute yen terms in some years, 2019 being the most notable example where the percentage increase in budget was smaller than the exchange rate.

Since 1993, Japanese defense expenditures remained below 3 percent (up to 5.3 percent in yen terms) of overall government spending (see figure 6.7). The lack of

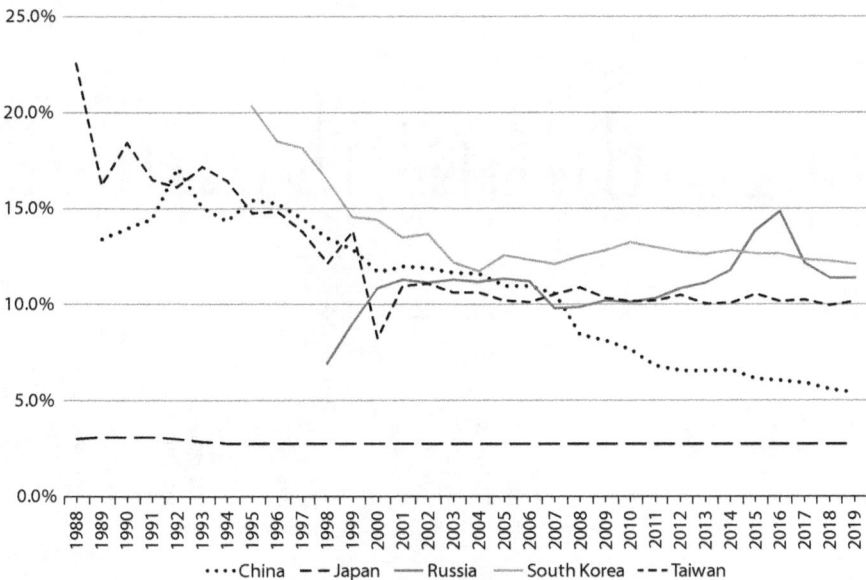

FIGURE 6.7 Defense expenditures as share of government spending, 1988–2019.
Source: Stockholm International Peace Research Institute, "SIPRI Military Expenditure Database."

primacy of defense for the Japanese is made more apparent when compared to other East Asia states. For smaller economies, such as South Korea and Taiwan, defense expenditures as a share of government spending remained above 10 percent over the last three decades. China, which has an economy twice the size of Japan's economy, allocated 5.4 percent of the overall budget to defense in 2019. China has continued to maintain stable defense spending over the last decade despite economic growth diminishing by approximately 40 percent. Unlike Japan, which has experienced economic stagnation for the last quarter century, China can decrease the ratio of defense spending while continuing to increase the absolute value of the defense budget.

Year-to-year changes to defense spending provide further context on the significance of the GOJ's efforts to balance regional threats and alleged record-breaking defense budgets. Over the last twenty-seven years, defense expenditures have increased nine times, decreased eight times, and increased/decreased by less than half a percentage point ten times (see figure 6.8). Japanese defense spending remained remarkably stable despite the radically changing environment; the band

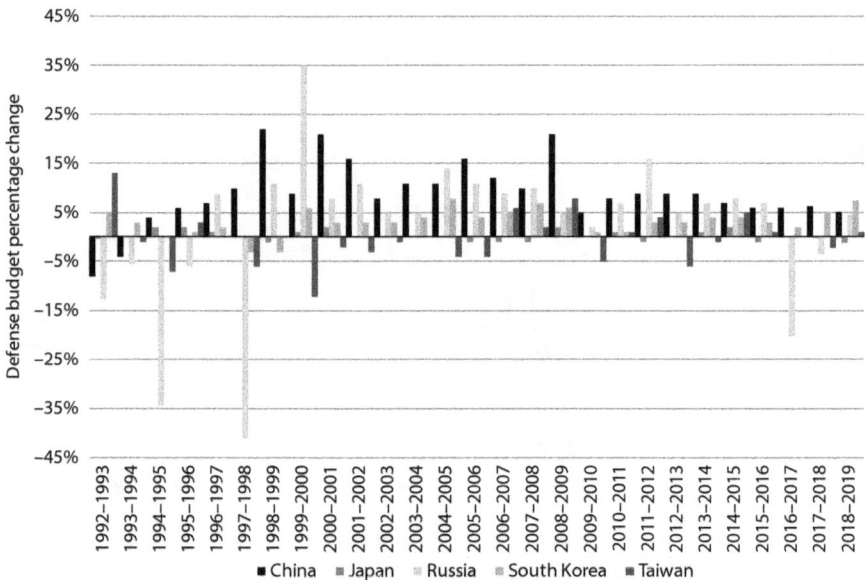

FIGURE 6.8 Year-to-year growth and decline of defense expenditures, 1992–2019.
Source: Stockholm International Peace Research Institute, "SIPRI Military Expenditure Database."

of growth is between minus 1 percent and plus 2 percent (up to 4.5 percent in yen terms). Russian defense spending underwent the most fluctuation due to political instability following the end of the Cold War and oil price volatility. Nevertheless, the defense budget increased in twenty-one of the last twenty-seven years. China has not decreased the defense budget in the last twenty-five years. South Korea shares the most similar characteristics with Japan but has only decreased defense spending twice over the same period. Under the current Moon Jae-in administration, defense expenditures increased by 12.9 percent despite its dovish reputation and full commitment to reconciliation with North Korea. In short, unlike its neighbors, Japan has not sustained meaningful defense expenditure growth over the last three decades.

Realists have dismissed the significance of the 1 percent cap by calling attention to absolute defense expenditures. Japan has a rather large defense budget that has ranged between $41.9 billion and $46.7 billion over the last thirty years (see figure 6.9). These figures are less impressive when taking into account that overall government expenditures increased from $583 billion to $963 billion over

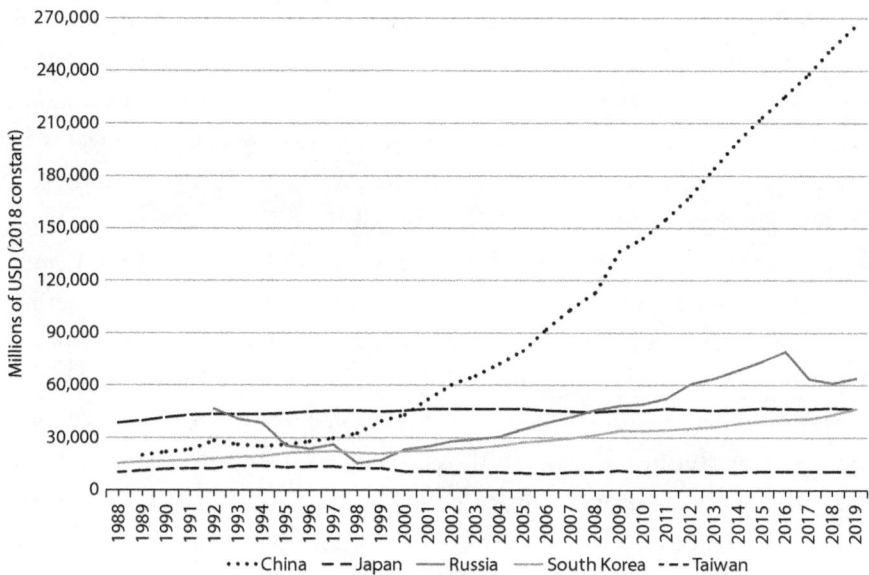

FIGURE 6.9 Defense expenditures in East Asia, 1988–2019.

Source: Stockholm International Peace Research Institute, "SIPRI Military Expenditure Database."

the same period.[145] Contextualizing Japanese defense spending, especially in comparison to countries in East Asia, provides further insight on how Japan views regional threats. After overtaking Japan in 2001, it only took five years before China's defense budget was two times greater than Japan's. As of 2019, the Chinese defense budget is $220 billion, or 5.7 times greater than the Japanese defense budget. Russia overtook Japan in 2011. South Korea's defense budget increased year-over-year since 1999 and reached parity in 2019. Detractors of the defense budget metric cannot ignore that Japan has remained still while China has exponentially become stronger, and South Korea has caught up despite an economy a third the size of Japan's.

Of all the countries in East Asia, Japan receives the least bang for its yen. Japanese defense expenditures have not kept pace with inflation or mitigated the impact of fluctuations in the value of yen, which has become increasingly important due to Japan's reliance on FMS. Japan's dependence on the U.S.-Japan alliance further chips away at the defense budget and financial commitment to HNS and SACO draw resources away from its autonomous defense capabilities. Absolute defense expenditures are misleading when not taking into account how ideational restraints exacerbate the material constraints on the JSDF. The JSDF suffers from high labor costs because it is an all-voluntary force. As discussed in chapter 3, over a third of the defense budget is allocated to personnel expenditures. When considering the high costs of arms procurement due to the immature defense sector, as discussed in chapter 5, the Japanese defense budget is far less impressive than the raw numbers suggest.

Antimilitarism rules have been codified in more legalized terms than the 1 percent cap, such as the Three Principles on Arms Exports and the nonnuclear principles. I have discussed arms exports at length, so further examination is not warranted here. Given the material constraints on the size of the JSDF and defense budget, acquiring nuclear weapons capabilities would be the most direct and consequential way for Japan to address its conventional security concerns. Ratified in 1971, the Three Nonnuclear Principles state that Japan shall never possess, manufacture, or permit the introduction of nuclear weapons in its territories. Scholars have attributed Japan's rejection of the nuclear option to economic interests, norms, and elite agenda setting,[146] to name just a few factors. Occasionally, right-wing politicians look to ignite discussions on acquiring indigenous nuclear capabilities but have never come close to having the support to introduce debate or legislation. Debate over nuclear weapons in Japan instead center on the U.S. nuclear umbrella and Japan's stance on a no first use policy.[147] Discussion of acquiring nuclear weapons remains a non-starter. When rumblings of nuclear weapons made the rounds on national television because former defense minister and self-described *gunji otaku* (military geek) Ishiba Shigeru remarked it was strange that Japan was under the nuclear umbrella but forbid the presence of nuclear weapons within its borders, Foreign Minister Kōnō Tarō shot the idea down, stating that the government "has not reviewed the three non-nuclear principles so far and has no plan to discuss a review of them."[148] Yamaguchi Natsuo, leader of Kōmeitō, reiterated the principles "are a national policy and must not be changed" in response to Ishiba's remark. Nuclear disarmament remains a cornerstone of Japanese foreign policy, and Kōnō highlighted Japan's leading role in the NPT and Group of Eminent Persons for Substantive Advancement of Nuclear Disarmament in a foreign policy speech to the national Diet in 2019.[149]

Ishiba's comment, however, brought to light that Japanese antimilitarism was far more complex than popularly understood and is not the equivalent to pacifism. Nevertheless, momentum is on the side of nonproliferation, as there have been several major successes in recent years. In 2013, activists successfully lobbied the GOJ to sign the New Zealand Joint Statement on the humanitarian impact of nuclear weapons after it refused to sign the past three statements and had only signed the Australia drafted statement that supported the nuclear umbrella.[150] In 2017, the Nobel Peace Prize was awarded to ICAN for its work to draw attention to the humanitarian consequences of nuclear weapons and efforts to achieve a nuclear weapons prohibition treaty.[151] Although seventy-five years removed from the atomic bombings of Hiroshima and Nagasaki, antinuclear activism, and antimilitarism more generally, continue to guide the direction of Japanese security policy.

PAYING PEACE FORWARD

According to the TripAdvisor's annual rankings, the Hiroshima Peace Museum consistently ranks among the top two most popular travel destinations in Japan, occasionally trading honors with the famed Fushimi Inari Shrine in Kyoto.[152] The

Nagasaki Atomic Bomb Museum has ranked among the top twenty, despite its inconvenient location and the abundance of other tourist destinations throughout the country. Japan has successfully cultivated the idea that visiting its peace memorials is as important to understanding the nation as visiting trendy shopping districts and ancient shrines. This peace culture may have started with the trauma of defeat but could only have been sustained by a concerted effort by the Japanese people to hold onto the lessons of war. This was not a linear process, and the traditional pacifism-militarism framework fails to capture how internal debates complicated the trajectories of antimilitarism.

The aging of peace movements, and the members that constitute them, have reinvigorated efforts to influence the content and direction of Japanese security policy. The passage of time has also provided activists with the space to reconsider dominant antimilitarism narratives, and in recent years, antimilitarism expanded to include critical self-reflection of the atrocities committed by Imperial Japan.

Peace movements vary in resources and mission, some transnational, others local, but all are essential to the safeguarding of Japanese peace culture. The fruits of activism, whether in material or ideational discourses, restrain the aggressive militarization of Japan. Whereas militarization involves the "encroaching of military forms, personnel and practices upon civilian institutions or social orders,"[153] antimilitarism is the resistance of such intrusions and the promotion of the nonuse of force in society and government. Resistance, of course, implies the existence of countervailing militaristic forces. Yet the longest-serving prime minister in Japanese history did not significantly increase the defense budget to the degree that notably strengthened the capabilities of the JSDF. Contrary to the popular belief that defense expenditures have increased every year under Abe, the defense budget *decreased* in 2016 in line with a contraction of the overall budget. The antimilitaristic 1 percent soft cap remains quite firm.

Antimilitarism restrains the GOJ directly as laws and principles and indirectly through public opinion informed by peace education and peace movements. As discussed in previous chapters, the material constraints on the JSDF are exacerbated by the public's lack of a militaristic impulse. The demographic crises and poor military infrastructure are aggravated when the public does not see them as problems to solve.

When rules become so internalized, the boundary between the government and the public in security policy decision making becomes less absolute. Government officials *are* members of the public, are influenced by public opinion, and act according to their personal standards of honorable conduct. This honorable conduct has evolved beyond self-restraint and has generated commitments to antiproliferation and creating a peaceful and secure world. The next chapter will explore how Japan became an active contributor to global security through PKOs, HA/DR missions, and ODA.

CHAPTER SEVEN

Crafting Peace Among Militarisms

S ince the end of the isolationist policies of the Tokugawa period, Japan has sought its rightful place within the international hierarchy. Japan adopted a "rich army, strong country" doctrine in the following Meiji period, during which it utilized military power to secure its sovereignty and extend its power across East Asia. Militant nationalism and the failure to be treated as an equal power by the West led Japan on a destructive mission to place itself on top of a Greater East Asia Co-Prosperity Sphere. Following its total defeat in World War II, Japan was rebuilt as a full-fledged democracy and achieved economic growth that was the envy of the world. However, the many atrocities committed by Imperial Japan during the early twentieth century continued to shape Japanese identity and strain relations in East Asia. For the majority of the postwar period, Japan became reliant on economic statecraft, in part due to its reluctance to mobilize the JSDF beyond self-defense for the preservation of international stability. In the post-Cold War era, Japan again found itself searching for its proper place in the world—a world that placed a normative premium on military contributions for tackling transnational causes of insecurity, such as terrorism, state collapse, and environmental catastrophe. The means to occupying an honored place in an international society changes with the rules of a given period. In each era, Japan sought a balance between preserving its unique character, adapting to international norms, countering security threats, and making a meaningful contribution to the international community.

Thus far, this book has focused on the material constraints and ideational restraints that limit the GOJ's ability to quickly augment the power projection capabilities and change the character of the JSDF. The material constraints, such as the aging and declining population and the underdeveloped defense sector, ensure that the JSDF is only capable of defending the Japanese mainland and is not fit for disrupting the power balance in East Asia. Ideational restraints, such as a policy of reassurance and antimilitarism, reinforce these constraints. These rules—reified through speech acts—include peace education, peace museums, laws, and institutions. The material constraints and ideational restraints comprise an antimilitarism ecosystem that influences the public's perception of security and pull its willingness away from supporting the use of force in international affairs. Antimilitarism suppressed JSDF recruitment, limited investment in the defense industry, and made it difficult for the GOJ to pursue more aggressive forms of militarization. This is rule.

Rules also inform actors how to make sense of the material world and social interactions, which leads to the regulation of conduct. Concerning the content and direction of Japanese security policy, Japan rejects militarisms that require personal and economic sacrifices of the public for reasons beyond self-defense. Rules, however, are both regulative and constitutive. To regulate conduct is also to allow one to conduct. Japanese peace culture is comprised of numerous commitment rules that confer voluntarily assumed roles. To realize a role through action is also to construct an identity, because identity is "what a state is and what it aspires to be."[1] Rules constitute agency, and agents "act in and on the world, but always within the limits specified by roles."[2]

This chapter analyzes how Japan acted upon roles conferred by its peace identity and how it responded to an emerging international humanitarian norm. Aging is not just a biological process that can weaken an individual; it is also an experience that brings wisdom and a sense of purpose. Aging allowed Japan to repurpose the armed forces to commit to international security. In the process of committing, Japan created new rules that push the content and direction of security policy, which has come to accept the deployment of the JSDF for the protection of human security beyond the Japanese mainland.

Japan has been immensely successful in this arena, despite the material constraints on the JSDF. To return to a sports analogy a final time, athletes often desire regaining the physical prowess of their mid-twenties, while holding onto knowledge gained over the years. Regardless of the medical science that has improved strength and conditioning, physicality cannot replace knowhow, nor does experience replace the raw power of youth. It is rare for any person, or state, to have it all.

Michael Jordan's final three NBA championships were more physically demanding compared to his first three, but because he knew when to pick his spots, fans were rewarded with some of the most iconic moments in sports history. Some may argue that the victories were sweeter because they were hard-earned. Japan may have found its sweet spot by making peace with the reality of aging and has found novel ways to contribute to international stability without the use of force.

This chapter is organized as follows. First, it examines Japan's contributions to the global humanitarian intervention norm, specifically human security. Second, this chapter analyzes the JSDF's participation in humanitarian assistance/disaster relief (HA/DR) missions. In the spirit of the Constitution, Japan aspires to be a peace-loving nation and commits to the roles that come with this identity. HA/DR missions bring this identity into practice, and in practice, increases the responsibilities of the JSDF beyond traditional domestic security. Third, this chapter discusses how Japanese Official Development Assistance (ODA) has changed in recent years. The chapter concludes with an examination of how the GOJ utilizes the U.S.-Japan alliance and its efforts to rebalance alliance obligations.

LOCALIZING GLOBAL NORMS: HUMAN SECURITY AND THE RESPONSIBILITY TO PROTECT

Following the end of the Cold War, interaction among states was no longer solely defined by trade and war. International relations became increasingly characterized by bilateral and multilateral cooperation to address nonstate and transnational threats such as terrorism, disease, poverty, and environmental disasters. In 1994, the UN introduced the concept of human security in the *Human Development Report*, which is comprised of two primary components—freedom from fear and freedom from want. To achieve these objectives, seven essential security needs must be met: (1) economic, (2) health, (3) personal, (4) political, (5) food, (6) environmental, and (7) community. This concept expanded the responsibilities of the state, whose survival was no longer limited to power balancing, and required effective problem solving. States preoccupied with traditional notions of state sovereignty at the expense of global stability and human security risked international condemnation and isolation, such as North Korea and, at times, even superpowers like the United States and China.

Japan was an early advocate of the human security concept and helped create and propagate the norm abroad. Simultaneously, it implemented human security via specific policy guidelines at home.[3] The emerging international norm encouraged Japan to act because "states are subject of a great many standards, which provide state agents reasons for their conduct."[4] The human security concept naturally complemented Japanese peace culture, as it allowed Japan to contribute to international peace and stability without an overreliance on the use of force. Moreover, the mobilization of the JSDF for human security upheld central tenets of the Constitution, such as articles 11, 12, 14, 18, 19, 20, 21, and 25.

Nevertheless, any mobilization of the JSDF outside of Japan is fraught with controversy. The GOJ has regularly committed to the antimilitarism norm when it seeks to increase the JSDF's responsibilities or capabilities to manage public disapproval. For example, following a cabinet decision to introduce legislation—referred to as "seamless security legislation to ensure Japan's survival and protect its people"—aimed at increasing the ability of the JSDF to respond to security threats and carry out additional roles in UN PKOs, the GOJ prefaced the decision with the following:

> Since the end of World War II, Japan has consistently followed the path of a peace-loving nation under the Constitution of Japan. While adhering to a basic policy of maintaining an exclusively national defense-oriented policy, not becoming a military power that poses a threat to other countries, and observing the Three Non-Nuclear Principles, Japan has flourished as an economic power through continuous efforts of its people and built a stable and affluent livelihood. Japan, as a peace-loving nation, has also been cooperating with the international community and international organizations including the United Nations, and has proactively contributed to their activities, adhering to the Charter of the United Nations. The course that Japan has taken as a peace-loving nation has garnered significant praise and respect from the international community, and Japan must continue these steps to further fortify such a position.[5]

The statement is informative of how rules determine the content and direction of Japanese security policy. There is a myriad of rationales that the GOJ can employ to justify changes to the JSDF, such as external threat or its legal authority. However, "rules are persuasive to the extent they provide instrumental guidance and reflect moral considerations."[6] The GOJ can only overcome public resistance if it can persuade the public that the new duties of the JSDF commit to antimilitarism and do not threaten domestic and regional security. As Onuf makes clear, "legality is a property bestowed on rules through rhetoric, or practical reasoning, by people who are professionally trained in putting specific, principled rules to persuasive use. Drawing analogies, invoking precedents, justifying claims, and weighing alternatives are among the familiar ways they do so. That persuasion works is what we mean when we say the law works."[7] In the statement, the GOJ reaffirms its core antimilitarist policies and the Constitution as the guiding principles of this new security decision. The decision seeks to balance between addressing external threats and maintaining the peace and stability gained not by the use of force but by the economy and diplomacy. Antimilitarism regulates the use of force by determining its appropriateness and the parameters in which it is implemented. In short, rules tell agents "what to do and, simply and succinctly, how to do it."[8]

The human security concept and related legislation were permissible because they helped cultivate the postwar narrative that Japan was a reformed democratic and peaceful nation. Japan's willingness to act in international affairs also called attention to its work ethic, miraculous recovery, and honored standing in the international community. The mobilization of the JSDF for humanitarian purposes, however, did not come naturally for a peace nation that evolved slower than the international context. Immediately following the war, the greatest concern for Japanese and American leaders was the eradication of Japanese militarism, not for an aid recipient nation to play a major role in international affairs. Once Japan recovered, it naturally gravitated toward economic and institution-building tools, such as trade agreements, participation in IOs, and ODA. Japan's early postwar foreign policy was comprised of three pillars: (1) centering its foreign policy around the UN, (2) cooperation with the free and democratic nations of the Western alliance, and (3) identifying closely with Asian nations.[9]

However, according to historian Akira Iriye, Japan's foreign policy had failed to articulate clearly "how it proposes to behave in the world, beyond pursuing its own security goals and economic interests. The nation has not made a notable contribution to the international order. Its foreign affairs have tended to be devoid of a sense of purpose going beyond self-interest."[10] This lack of purpose materialized into tangible problems when Japan faced intense criticism from the international community during the first Gulf War. In particular, Japanese foreign policy and its strategic use of ODA were increasingly viewed as "checkbook" diplomacy.[11] Although Japan imposed economic sanctions on Iraq and contributed $13 billion to the war effort, the largest among the allies, many argued it was too little and too late.[12] Here it is worth noting that the U.S.-led coalition did not make a consequentialist calculation in their criticisms of Japan; the war was easily won. Japan was criticized for not meeting norms of honorable conduct. To buy off the responsibility of putting one's life on the line while others risk their lives is beyond the pale. This was especially so during the Gulf War because it was a UN-sanctioned campaign. Norms of reciprocity lead states to perceive multilateral operations as more legitimate than unilateral operations. The lack of recognition of Japan's contribution was made embarrassingly clear to the GOJ in a Kuwait-commissioned advertisement depicting national flags in the *Washington Post* that thanked the Allied forces but omitted the Japanese flag. Whereas nationalistic militarism failed Japan during World War II, Japan's reluctance to use military force failed it in the immediate aftermath of the Cold War.

Japan's inability to quickly adapt to the evolving norms on the legitimate use of force should not have been so unexpected. Operation Desert Storm was revolutionary. The Cold War made multilateral interventions almost impossible. The norms concerning the use of force outside of the Cold War context was as unclear to the newly minted unipolar power, the United States, and the international community as it was for Japan. The United States' failure to intervene in Rwanda in 1994 after its disastrous intervention in Somalia the previous year is a testament to the infancy of the human security intervention norm at the time.

The lack of a clear mandate ensured that a Japanese military contribution was unlikely. As discussed in chapters 5 and 6, Japan's predisposition to avoiding the use of force beyond self-defense was the result of ideational restraints such as a reassurance policy and antimilitarism norms. However, the criticisms for not making a military contribution to Operation Desert Storm signaled to Japanese leaders that the most prized international currency was not yen or dollars but blood. Criticisms of Japan continued after the war ended, even though there were minimal coalition forces casualties. The participation of the JSDF had little to do with winning the conflict but with meeting the expectation that like-minded states should equally share the risks. Japan had financed over 20 percent of the total costs of the Gulf War, but the normative expectations that states must act as responsible stakeholders, contribute their fair share, and accept appropriate risks necessitated debate in Japan on the use of force.

Japan was not a fully accepted and embraced member of the international community because the "general complaint about Japan concern[ed] the insularity of its outlook—an outlook that tend[ed] to confine itself to narrow national concerns without taking into account the broader international perspective."[13] The Gulf War was not an American expansionist campaign that required the commitment of an ally; it was a UN-sanctioned mission to stop a belligerent spoiler that would benefit from the assistance of a member. To many in the international community, the peace that came with pacifism was a privilege that Japan had no right to enjoy. The Persian Gulf crisis suggested to Japanese government leaders that "any expansion of Japan's international contribution beyond its minimalist economic strategy will come in the area of military-strategic affairs, especially in terms of military manpower contribution to international efforts."[14] It should be noted, however, that criticisms of Japan's one-nation pacifism underplayed how its restrained security policy contributed to international security. Moreover, as discussed in chapters 5 and 6, Japanese peace culture was sustained by the vigilance of actors throughout Japan. It was less of a privilege than a hard-earned right. Nonetheless, the antimilitarism rules that were refined through decades of practice did not travel beyond the borders of Japan.

Immediately following the Gulf crisis, the GOJ sidestepped significant legal and political hurdles and passed the UN Peace Cooperation Bill, which allowed the JSDF to participate in UN-sanctioned PKOs, albeit with limitations on the use of force. The PKO law outlined five strict conditions under which the JSDF could be dispatched. In addition to the UN's three PKO principles of the existence of a ceasefire agreement, consent of the parties for deployment, and impartiality, Japan added the conditions that if the above conditions could not be met, the GOJ would withdraw its contingent and the use of weapons would be "limited to the minimum necessary to protect the lives of personnel."[15] Since its establishment, the JSDF sought to "convince ordinary Japanese that they do not pose a threat to democracy or the wellbeing of citizens, and second, that they could instead assume a role beneficial to society."[16] These conditions were adopted to appease a public suspicious of the use of force abroad and to ensure that the JSDF would not violate the Constitution. The JSDF's international operations following the passage of the PKO law have strictly followed these underlying principles of Japanese antimilitarism, and the majority of Japan's human resource contributions have been limited to noncombat personnel such engineers, election monitors, educators, and medics.

From September 1992 to November 2020, Japan dispatched on average 159 personnel to one to five UN PKO missions at a time (however, most missions received approximately thirty personnel). The JSDF participated in at least thirty-four missions as of December 2020, including minesweeping missions, activities based on the Anti-Terrorism Special Measures Law, activities based on the Special Measures Law for Humanitarian and Reconstruction Assistance in Iraq, and antipiracy activities.[17] Such missions included humanitarian relief operations in Rwanda and Indonesia, transport of supplies in Iran, disaster relief in Haiti and New Zealand, and supplying engineers to maintain roads in Sudan.[18] Japan can only dispatch the JSDF when an area is secured and with the permission of the host nation. As a result of these strict conditions, the JSDF often relies on protection from other military forces when in the field, such as the Australian Forces protection of the JSDF Iraq Reconstruction and Support Group. Once on the ground, the JSDF may have more freedom to act. Kitagawa Keizō contends that restrictions have loosened on the JSDF in the last few years. In the past, the JSDF operated with a positive list that details what actions *can* be taken. In contrast, a negative list details what actions *cannot* be taken. Kitagawa states, "It is very difficult [to operate with a positive list] in war, you never know what is going to happen. At least when I went in 2003 [to Syria], things have changed. Gradually changing, so eventually, I think we can do many things now. I do not think we are handcuffed."[19]

PKOs have been popular with the public. According to public opinion polls conducted by the Cabinet Office, between 1994 and 2019, respondents who answered, "should maintain current engagement level" and "should make more efforts in engaging proactively" regarding PKOs increased from 58.9 percent to 78.3 percent.[20] Nevertheless, the passage of the PKO law required legal gymnastics because a strict interpretation of the Constitution prohibits the deployment of troops abroad under any conditions. The PKO law crossed a clear, bright-line distinction and was a concession to the international community that loosened a forty-year restraint on the JSDF. The Gulf crisis sparked the process of Japan transitioning from a "peace state" to an "international state."[21] This transition was not prompted by a rebalance in regional power or the emergence of a new threat but by the admonishment from the international community for not being a team player. The content and direction of Japanese security policy during this transition were as much defined by international norms as they were by domestic political and normative restraints.

The international humanitarian intervention norm introduced new rules and roles for Japan to follow, but the domestic Japanese antimilitarism environment shaped how those rules and the content of those roles were interpreted, debated, accepted, and implemented. Government leaders continued to dwell on Japan's failure long after the Gulf War crisis and debated the appropriate security policies for a state of Japan's stature. In a speech presented at the 42nd Munich Conference on Security Policy, Senior Vice-Minister of Foreign Affairs Shiozaki Yasuhisa confessed that Japan's omission from the Kuwait mural was a "painful experience."[22] This painful experience prompted Ozawa Ichirō, one of the most powerful parliamentarians in the postwar era, to raise the concern that Japan was an "abnormal country" because of its inability to act when called upon by the international community. Ozawa argued that a "normal country" must be willing to shoulder the responsibilities of the international community and cooperate fully with other nations to "build prosperous stable lives for their people."[23] Ozawa maintained that domestic politics were no excuse for Japan to recuse itself from these responsibilities, and the Japanese should be eager to contribute to the international community without the need for international pressure.[24] Ozawa's conclusion was of course a normative statement. Standards of honorable conduct, or rules, can compel leaders to adopt more proactive security policies given that the alternative would be abnormal behavior.

This sentiment was prevalent among some of Japan's most influential prime ministers. Prime Minister Nakasone, for example, proposed an independent constitution (*jishu kempo*) that was anti-Article 9 and written by the Japanese.[25] Prime Minister Koizumi argued that Japan "must fulfill a constructive role as a member of the global community."[26] Koizumi utilized the Constitution to justify this role in the "Policy Speech to the 164th Session of the Diet" stating, "In keeping close to the heart this spirit of the Preamble of our Constitution, Japan has upheld freedom and democracy and achieved a peaceful and prosperous society in the postwar period. We will continue to contribute to the peace and stability of the world, resolutely maintaining our principle of resolving all matters not by force, with the Japan-U.S. alliance and international cooperation as the basic principles of our foreign policy."[27]

Koizumi was one of the earliest and most ardent supporters of the U.S.-led war on terror. According to Ashizawa Kuniko, Japan assumed the "lead country" role in the DDR program designed to "disarm, demobilize, and reintegrate former combatants into Afghan society."[28] Due to constitutional and domestic political constraints, Japan could not contribute militarily to combat operations but did deploy the MSDF to the Indian Ocean to refuel ships engaged in Operation Enduring Freedom. In a press release on the adoption of UNSC Resolution 1776, which extended the International Security Assistance Force deployment in Afghanistan, Minister of Foreign Affairs Machimura Nobutaka, who served under Koizumi and later Abe, stated that the GOJ "believes that it is essential to maintain the supply activities provided by the Japanese Maritime Self-Defense Force for the OEF—MIO [Operation Enduring Freedom—Maritime Interception Operations] in order for Japan to be considered a responsible member of the international community."[29] Machimura's successor, Kōmura Masahiko reiterated that Japan "must play a responsible role in the international community as a 'peace fostering nation' " and "demonstrate leadership in building peace in the world."[30] In the same month, Prime Minister Fukuda Yasuo promised to "carry forward a diplomacy which contributes to world peace, so that Japan will realize its responsibilities commensurate with its national strength in the international community, and become a country which is relied upon internationally."[31] Following the withdrawal of the MSDF after more than nine years, Japan provided further financial contributions to Afghanistan to the sum of $8 billion.[32] This tailored contribution to the war effort makes evident the constitutive and regulative dimensions of norms. The GOJ acted upon the idea that Japan was a peace-loving nation of the international community, which entailed the deployment of the JSDF for nonmilitary purposes while not abandoning its traditional reliance on financial tools in promoting security.

In the last three decades, Japan developed, refined, and redefined its security policy in relation to the emerging humanitarian intervention norm. This norm allowed Japan to adopt the role as a responsible member of the international community, but the limits on the use of force within that role were subject to debate internationally and domestically. Although Japan accepted greater responsibilities, the domestic antimilitarism environment prevented wholesale adoption of the use of force for the promotion of human security, especially since the norm of military intervention to protect vulnerable communities remained unsettled in the international community. The humanitarian intervention norm became clearer when Ban Ki-Moon, secretary-general of the UN, outlined the responsibilities of humanitarian intervention in the report, *Implementing the Responsibility to Protect*. Although the Responsibility to Protect (R2P) concept existed since the 1990s, it was not until 2009 that the UN issued a clear mandate.

In a general sense, Japan is a supporter of the R2P concept. According to Alex J. Bellamy and Sara E. Davies, in the Asia-Pacific, Japan, Australia, New Zealand, the Philippines, and South Korea are R2P advocates, whereas others in the region are either R2P engaged, fence-sitters, or opponents.[33] R2P advocates are a group of states that are determined to "help translate the principle from words to deeds."[34] As I have sought to illustrate throughout this book, words are also deeds and Japan was one of the leaders in crafting both.

R2P consists of three main pillars. The first pillar states that, "Each individual state has the responsibility to protect its populations from genocide, war crimes, ethnic cleansing and crimes against humanity. This responsibility entails the prevention of such crimes, including their incitement, through appropriate and necessary means."[35] The second pillar states the international community must be committed to assisting states in meeting their responsibilities of pillar one. Specifically, these provisions suggest that assistance could take one of four forms: (1) encouraging states to meet their responsibilities under pillar one, (2) helping states exercise this responsibility, (3) helping states to build their capacity to protect, and (4) assisting states under stress before crises and conflicts break out.[36] The third pillar states that the international community, through the United Nations, has the responsibility to respond in a "timely and decisive manner, using Chapters VI (Pacific Settlement of Disputes), VII (Action with Respect to Threats to the Peace) and VIII (Regional Arrangements) of the UN Charter as appropriate, when national authorities are manifestly failing to protect their populations from genocide, war crimes, ethnic cleansing and crimes against humanity."[37]

R2P is inconsistently implemented because the erosion of traditional state sovereignty is a fluid process and often met with resistance, especially by authoritarian governments. Moreover, the military dimension of R2P alarms states hoping to avoid the political use of force, being pulled into international disputes, and exacerbating local conflicts. Due to these concerns, Japan also remains a cautious supporter of R2P. Jun Honna argues that the divisions in Japan regarding R2P can be clustered in four main groups. Conservatives, epitomized by figures such as Prime Minister Yasuo Fukuda, contend the use of force is not compatible with Japan's view of security. Revisionists, on the other hand, believe that R2P provides the window of opportunity for military growth.[38] Revisionists do not have much support within the government or among the public due to fears that they are stretching the limits of the Constitution. Liberals embrace a view that "reverberates in Japan's vibrant security discourse," and they "wish to preserve the Peace Constitution, and rollback defense guidelines that appear to flout the letter and spirit of Article 9."[39] Honna contends that liberals are wary of Japan's implementation of R2P due to its "uncertain status under international law and the potential for politically 'instrumentalizing' the doctrine to legitimize interventions not strictly within its ostensible remit. However, these concerns are presented as 'practical' problems that should be overcome, rather than as critical reasons for rejecting R2P."[40] Lastly, peace activists, reflecting the voice of the global anti-neoliberal network, are most resistant to the idea. They argue the principle of R2P emphasizes an individual state's failure to protect its population and obscures international causes of state failure and the consequent violent conflicts in the Global South.[41]

The absence of a universal concept of peacebuilding allowed Japan to create its own concept, one that is not solely reliant on the use of force.[42] Japan has not fully committed to the military dimensions of R2P because its conceptions of security are more holistic, focusing on freedom from want as much, if not even more, than on the freedom from fear. In December 1998, Prime Minister Obuchi Keizō outlined Japan's broad interpretation of human security that embraced "both freedom from fear (in such manifestations as conflict, terrorism, landmines, small arms, and human trafficking) and freedom from want (including currency crises, natural disasters, environmental degradation, infectious diseases, and poverty)."[43] This approach targets the underlying causes of insecurity, such as environmental degradation, inequality, and lack of development to achieve long-term human security. Thus, the "responsible member of the international community" role allows the GOJ to deploy the JSDF for HA/DR operations to address these causes of insecurity.

DEFINING RULES AND ROLES: HUMANITARIAN
ASSISTANCE AND DISASTER RELIEF

Several scholars contend that the GOJ mobilizes the JSDF for domestic disaster relief operations to gain respect from the public and to instill a sense of pride and purpose for those serving in the JSDF.[44] Polling data does suggest that public opinion of the JSDF has increased markedly over the years; however, the utilitarian explanation overly politicizes this activity. From the beginning, the JSDF has been intended for the "benefit citizens at the local level."[45]

To put into practice is also to practice. Since Japan is a country prone to earthquakes and typhoons, the JSDF and the Japanese public have accumulated valuable disaster relief and recovery experience. Over time, the JSDF developed expertise in disaster relief operations, and the very expertise in these kinds of operations contributed to the Japanese peace identity. Similar to how a painful recovery and lingering postwar trauma of the Japanese following World War II led to the emergence of a universalist antiwar ethic, the experience of natural disasters allowed Japanese people to develop empathy for victims of environmental catastrophes throughout the world.

Universal empathy can be a powerful force because, as Onuf argues, "Rules are general and impersonal within their reach and they provide general and impersonal reasons for conduct sufficient for most occasions."[46] Here, I diverge from Onuf and contend that since rules are always interpersonal, they are personal. Rules work because the subjects of rules share common experience, language, or norms that allow them to make sense of said rules. Some may call this culture. Even greater levels of abstraction, such as Benedict Anderson's "nation" or Jean-Jacques Rousseau's "pity" require subjects to have a shared understanding of their interactions and the world with which they engage. Thus, universal empathy is not detached but grounded in shared experiences that are as concrete as they are conceptional. The Japanese antimilitarism ecosystem provides the space and justifications for new JSDF roles that enable Japan to contribute to world peace and protect human security while adhering to the spirit of the Constitution and avoiding criticism from formers colonies. Moreover, the demilitarized nature of HA/DR missions, which are safer than PKOs, increases public confidence in deploying the military abroad.

Since the Japan Disaster Relief Team Law (JDR Law) was enacted in 1987, a total of 151 JDR teams have been dispatched to forty-five countries and regions (as of April 2019).[47] The JDR Law was amended in 1992 to allow the JSDF to participate in international HA/DR operations and, since its first deployment in 1998, the JSDF has conducted over a dozen overseas missions. In total, the JSDF has been dispatched for disaster relief missions more than thirty thousand times in Japan and abroad.[48]

Japan's extensive experience with HA/DR operations allowed it to take on a leadership role within multilateral security frameworks such as the Association of Southeast Asian Nations (ASEAN) and spearhead peacebuilding initiatives. Since 2011 Japan has provided capacity building assistance to countries throughout Asia in nontraditional security areas, such as HA/DR, noncombatant evacuation operations, training of coast guards for piracy control, training in peacekeeping operations focusing on infrastructure, and defense medicine.[49] These activities build up the domestic capacity of trade partners and strengthens links between Japan and the region. Some may read into Japan's efforts as a way to balance against China, but regional resilience against environmental disaster benefits everyone.

Japan is also a significant financer and norm driver of disaster risk reduction. In 1998, Japan helped establish the Asian Disaster Reduction Center in Kobe, whose mission is to enhance disaster resilience, build safe communities, and support sustainable development. Between 2001 and 2011, Japan provided approximately $55 billion in overseas development assistance toward international disaster-related projects, "including technical assistance, grant-based and loan-based aid, and emergency relief projects."[50] In 2011, Japan "provided funds and dispatched experts to the ASEAN Coordinating Center for Humanitarian Assistance on Disaster Management," which was launched in Jakarta, Indonesia.[51]

Japan also hosted all three United Nations World Conferences on Disaster Reduction in Yokohama (1994), Kobe (2005), and Sendai (2015), respectively. Japan chaired the Kobe conference, which resulted in the Hyōgo Framework for Action. The Hyōgo framework sought to make disaster relief reduction a priority, improve risk information and early warning, educate the public on safety and resilience, reduce underlying risk factors, and strengthen disaster preparedness for effective response at all levels.[52] The 2015 conference in Sendai, the region that was most impacted by the 2011 Tōhoku earthquake and tsunami, produced the Sendai Framework for Disaster Relief Reduction. The Sendai framework adopted the Build Back Better philosophy of making postdisaster communities more resilient and targeting underlying disaster risk, such as the consequences of poverty and inequality, climate change and variability, unplanned and rapid urbanization, demographic change, weak institutional arrangements, limited availability of technology, declining ecosystems, pandemics and epidemics, among others.[53] Soon after the conference, Japan was one of the first responders to the April 2015 Nepal earthquake. The Japan International Cooperation Agency (JICA) held seminars to share Japan's experience and knowledge of postearthquake reconstruction, and the MOD dispatched over one hundred JSDF personnel to the recovery efforts.[54] JICA activities in Nepal continued into 2020.

The GOJ's mobilization of the JSDF for the protection of human security is complemented by increased government-civil society collaborations. In 2007, MOFA created the Hiroshima Peacebuilders Center (HPC) to build stronger links between Japanese and international peacekeepers as well as strengthen civilian capacity for peacebuilding. In 2014, the HPC, in collaboration with the United Nations Volunteers, established the Program for Human Resource Development for Peacebuilding. In the six-week course, thirty participants (fifteen Japanese and fifteen from other countries) receive training in peacebuilding and develop skills for a career in the field.[55] Many alumni in the program moved on to work for the UN.

Following the end of Operation Tomodachi, the most significant combined and joint mission of the JSDF, the U.S.-Japan Council and U.S. embassy in Tokyo established the TOMODACHI Initiative to continue the spirit of the collaboration. While Operation Tomodachi lasted approximately two months and ended soon after the 2011 Tōhoku earthquake and tsunami, the TOMODACHI Initiative has been going strong for over the eight years and has grown in scope and reach. With the support of the GOJ, the initiative connects local governments, private actors, businesses, and donors to create peace programs, education exchanges, and disaster relief, among many other programs. From its inception, the initiative has experienced year-to-year growth and has sponsored 293 programs in the United States and Japan. In total, the initiative has impacted over 41,800 event and program participants.[56]

The mobilization of the JSDF and increased public-private partnerships for HA/DR missions further developed Japanese antimilitarism norms by introducing a peace-oriented military to the Japanese physical and ideational landscape. For decades, civilian-military interactions were traditionally limited to tense community-base relations. The JSDF personnel's close work with on-the-ground NGO workers and face-to-face interactions with regular citizens humanized the military more so than any anime-inspired advertisement ever could. In previous disasters, the GOJ was criticized for not acting promptly, such as during the 1994 Great Hanshin earthquake when its failure to immediately mobilize the JSDF led to unnecessary casualties. The Japanese public has slowly come to realize that the JSDF can be a force for good if it is *allowed* to act. According to retired Lieutenant General Yamaguchi Noboru, the JSDF is uniquely qualified for HA/DR missions because it comes with its own infrastructure. Unlike other disaster relief first responders, such as firefighters and police, JSDF personnel do not rely on the regular economy (local infrastructures) for logistics such as meals, lodging, and healthcare—the JSDF generate and provide many of their own supplies.[57] Moreover, unlike international conflicts and PKOs where diplomacy and ODA are reasonable alternatives to the deployment of the military, natural disasters require immediate action. As one of the few actors that has the legal authority and capabilities to act when basic infrastructure collapses, the JSDF has accomplished significant societal good. In the 2011 Tōhoku earthquake and tsunami, the JSDF rescued 19,286 people, or approximately 70 percent of the total number rescued.[58] Surveys conducted by the Cabinet Office before the 2011 Tōhoku relief efforts found that a combined 75.6 percent of respondents held a "neutral," "negative," or "relatively negative" image of the JSDF.[59] After the disaster, a Cabinet Office survey found that "positive" impressions of the JSDF increased from 19.5 percent to 37.5 percent while "neutral," "negative" and "relatively negative" decreased to 59.5 percent.[60] In the Tōhoku region, a Yomiuri Online survey found that 82 percent of respondents rated the JSDF as "positive." Survey results from the three most affected areas (Iwate, Miyagi, and Fukushima prefectures) show that 72.4 percent described the activities of the JSDF as their "major source of post-disaster encouragement," compared to 27.2 percent that stated the central and/or local government as such.[61] More generally, according to the World Values Survey, public confidence in the armed forces significantly increased between 1995 and 2019. For Japanese who have "quite a lot" of confidence in the JSDF, there was a substantial increase from 29.3 percent in 1981 to 56.5 percent in 2019.[62] Moreover, during the same period, the number of respondents who had "a great deal" of confidence in the JSDF increased from 5.8 percent to 21.1 percent.

A consequence of the GOJ's success in cultivating public support through HA/DR missions, however, is that the public's perception of the JSDF's primary responsibilities has narrowed to nonmilitary activities, sometimes to the chagrin of JSDF personnel and security experts. The JSDF's primary responsibility is the defense of Japan. Yet, according to a 2017 Cabinet Office survey, 79.2 percent of respondents believed the primary objective of the JSDF should be disaster relief activities, surpassing even national defense (60.9 percent).[63] In an NHK poll conducted in the same year about the Constitution, 90 percent of respondents answered that saving lives after natural disasters was the JSDF's primary responsibility, followed by stopping terrorism before it occurs (63 percent), defending the nation against other states (62 percent), participating in PKOs (47 percent), and supporting alliances (33 percent).[64] Yezi Yeo contends, "Large-scale disasters are not anticipated or premeditated publicity stunts," so they may provide "public relations opportunities for militaries if carried out successfully. This is because humanitarian/disaster relief missions are (usually) not depicted/perceived as military or militarist in nature."[65] The GOJ's emphasis on the peaceful dimensions of the "responsible member of the international community" role facilitates the expansion of JSDF responsibilities, but the strategy of utilizing "affirmative essentialisms" typecasts the JSDF in highly constrained roles.[66] This typecasting is especially strong because the postwar narrative placed all the blame for Japan's defeat on the military elite and the government's inability to control the armed forces. In other words, the rules of the antimilitarism ecosystem lend credence to the GOJ's contention that HA/DR missions are conducive to Japan playing a meaningful international role and protecting human security. Nevertheless, the public remains suspicious of any militarism creep.

Singh contends that, "The international-state security identity has become a permanent feature of Japan's security discourse, and it is also increasingly accepted by the larger Japanese society. This process of change is irreversible, and it will gradually gain greater momentum as a result of Japan's domestic and external environment."[67] The international environment has been conducive to change in Japanese security policy—and not just in terms of power balancing. The international human security norm allows the Japanese to commit to the postwar narrative that Japan is a first-tier, modern, democratic, and peaceful nation. In a 2004 poll conducted by the Cabinet Office about "the role that Japan should fulfill," 51.9 percent of respondents answered, "contribute to world peace through efforts to stabilize the region and resolve conflicts peacefully, including the contribution to human resources."[68] Only 16.1 percent answered that Japan should protect universal values, and 25 percent answered Japan should provide humanitarian support for refugees. In the same poll, 22.2 percent believed Japan should participate more in PKOs, 68 percent supported current or increased participation in the Cambodia, Golan Heights, East Timor, Afghanistan, Iraq, and Rwanda UN missions, and only 22.1 percent answered Japan should have minimal or no involvement at all.[69] In the 2018 poll, the figures increased to 58.8 percent, 34 percent, 31.6 percent, and 80.2 percent for the corresponding questions. Only 2.2 percent answered Japan should not participate in PKOs.[70]

Not all dimensions of Japanese antimilitarism norms are equally negotiable. Kōsai Yutaka contends, "When wars become holy wars, when their objectives are sanctified to an extreme degree, the war ceases to be a game played according to rules—it becomes total war in which all means are to be employed, even the total destruction of the enemy."[71] As discussed in the previous chapters, Japan's ability and willingness to remilitarize is constrained by material and ideational forces. Total war militarism is beyond the scope of Japanese security policy or common sense. Yoshimura Shinsuke reminds us that, "The end of the Pacific War has left a deep imprint on the Japanese consciousness, and one constituent of that imprint is an acute skepticism about sacrificing one's light for lofty objectives."[72] Many Japanese believe that even with just interventions, "Japan's commitment to international peacekeeping should stop short of using military force."[73] Furthermore, Yoshimura argues that the public's reluctance to use force lies in "a deep visceral distrust of the state and particularly, a hatred of that most stark expression of state sovereignty, namely war and the deployment of military force."[74] For activists such as Watanabe Tomoko, the JSDF should be able to be dispatched to address piracy and natural disasters, but combating "terrorism is tricky because one cannot know who a real terrorist is."[75] Watanabe's skepticism about the neutrality of intervention is echoed by many in Japan's peace community. Kawasaki Akira warns that piracy and PKOs are too similar to military endeavors and can be used as a "steppingstone" for further militarism.[76] Watarida Masahiro concludes that the moment the JSDF leaves Japanese territories, even for PKOs, it would no longer be a self-defense force.[77]

Yoshimura concludes that after decades of postwar pacifism, the Japanese people have "become genuinely 'peaceful,' " and "even if they recognize in principle there can be just wars, they no longer 'have the courage' to take up the sword of justice against those who start wars that are unjust."[78] Hence, for endeavors such as the promotion of democracy through the use of force or preventive attack against North Korea, many Japanese would find it beyond the pale. Over seventy years of peace provides little room for hawkish politicians to persuade the public to go off to far-off lands to fight unknown enemies with the only certainty being the possibility of death. To the Japanese public, that is not commonsensical at all.

PAYING FOR HUMAN SECURITY: OFFICIAL DEVELOPMENT ASSISTANCE

Although the Gulf War crisis compelled Japan to make a human contribution to international security efforts, it did not replace the strategic importance of financial resources and diplomacy in protecting human security. Comprehensive security requires a holistic approach.

Japan has regularly ranked within the top five donors among OECD countries, and the highest in Asia, since 1955 (see figure 7.1). Between 1990 and 2000, Japan was the world's top ODA donor and, as of December 2019, Japan has provided $379.77 billion in assistance packages to 190 countries/regions.[79] One notable ODA contribution for the promotion of human security is to the United Nations Trust Fund for Human Security, which has totaled $450.9 million as of December 2018. Initially the sole donor, Japan persuaded other UN member states such as Thailand, Greece, and Mexico to contribute to the fund—thus taking on a leadership role in ODA.[80] Japan has also contributed $361 million to the United Nations Development Group Iraq Trust Fund, ranked second behind the European Union's $594.2 million contribution. Japan's contribution is approximately 3.5 times that of the next single state donor; Spain ranked third at $93.1 million.[81] Among other programs in the fund, Japan provided $50 million for the Peace Building Fund (ranked seventh), $17.1 million for the Iraq UNDAF Trust Fund (ranked first), $9.5 million for the UN Action Against Sexual Violence (ranked second), $5.9 million for the Ebola Response MPTF (ranked twelfth), $3 million for the UN REDD Program Fund (ranked fifth), $2 million for the Yemen NDCF Trust Fund (ranked fourth), $1.6 million for the Counter Piracy Trust Fund (ranked third), and $1 million for the UN

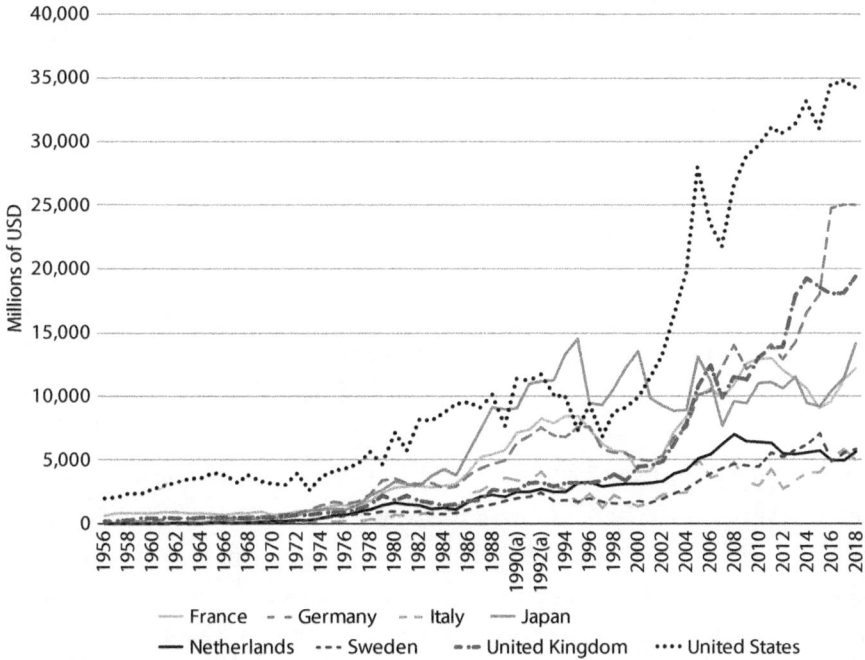

FIGURE 7.1 Top eight ODA donors in OCED, 1956–2018.

Source: OECD, "Official Development Assistance 2018–Preliminary Data," accessed November 27, 2020. https://www1.compareyourcountry.org/en. (a) includes loan forgiveness.

Haiti Cholera Response MPTF (ranked fourth). In addition to financial assistance, Japan promoted human resource development and technology transfers, accepted 560,000 trainees, and dispatched over 190,000 experts and volunteers since 1955.[82]

The MOD considers "humanitarian contribution led by the SDF and the Government's Official Development Aid [ODA]" as "two wheels of the same shaft" in its international reconstruction activities, such as the Iraq War.[83] ODA serves several security-related functions, such as creating reliable trade partners with ODA recipient countries, (2) providing reparations to former colonies, (3) providing humanitarian relief, and (4) addressing human security threats before they become unmanageable.

In recent years, the GOJ has sought to make ODA more cost-effective in protecting human security. In 2015, the ODA Charter was renamed the Development

Cooperation Charter to emphasize a new strategic logic, one that also relies on the characterization of Japan as a "responsible member of the international community." The Development Cooperation Charter states that "as a peace-loving nation," Japan must "contribute to the world through cooperation for non-military purposes" with a focus on human security, equal partnership with developing countries, and public-private partnerships with local governments and NGOs.[84] In line with Japan's human security goals, the Development Cooperation Charter promotes "universal values" in order to achieve rule of law, good governance, human rights, democratization, peace building, capacity building of law enforcement, antiterrorism, and promotion of women's rights.[85] The new charter drew criticism from the media, notably from the *Japan Times*, which ran an editorial titled "Aid That Could Foment Conflict." MOFA responded directly to the editorial and clarified that the new aid charter allows Japan to provide aid to a recipient country's military forces as long as it is not for military purposes. To ensure that this condition is met, the government considers aid on a case-by-case basis by "assessing the objectives, recipients, activities and possible impact, as well as the development needs of the country or region."[86]

The changes to the ODA Charter reflect the GOJ's attempt to support international military human security efforts without violating the Constitution and raising concerns among the public. According to Jochen Prantl and Nakano Ryoko:

> Human security policies played an important role for successive Japanese governments to establish a distinct identity in international relations. Japan has adopted an extremely broad view of human security that "comprehensively covers all menaces that threaten the survival, daily life and dignity of human beings and strengthens the efforts to confront these threats." In essence, the two components of the concept, "freedom from fear" and "freedom from want," have become separated in the Japanese policy discourse, with a very clear preference for implementing aspects related to "the freedom from want" rather than "the freedom from fear" which is underlying R2P.[87]

The GOJ and the Japanese public are mainly in agreement on playing a more significant role in the international community. Although the Japanese economy has been stagnant for over three decades, support for ODA remains high. According to an October 2018 Cabinet Office public opinion survey, 33.2 percent of respondents answered, "Japan should more actively promote development cooperation," and 48.2 percent answered, "the current level of development of cooperation is appropriate." In contrast, 12.5 percent answered, "Japan should minimize the level of development cooperation," and 2.3 percent answered, "Japan should stop development cooperation." For those who supported development cooperation, 46.7 percent answered, "because there is a need to increase the international community's confidence in Japan."[88] These figures have held steady for over a decade.

ODA will continue to be an essential tool for security policy because Japan is far from ready to engage in more direct uses of force. The Japanese public remains uncertain regarding the necessity of the military dimensions of R2P—it does not want to contribute to military conflict. According to Honna, "Japan's concern about R2P focuses on how it meshes with human security, the country's core diplomatic policy. As the second largest contributor to the UN budget, Japan is expected to play a role in implementing R2P and thus it is crucial to understand the prospects for synchronizing R2P with human security doctrine and practice."[89] Seeking to synchronize R2P and human security in practice, Japan modified its ODA charter to better assist foreign military forces as long as their missions are humanitarian. In a sense, Japan is militarizing through the financial support of other militaries and the deployment of the JSDF to PKOs. However, ODA is a convenient tool for limiting the deployment of the JSDF because it can provide stability before there is a need for a military solution.

Paul Midford has discussed in detail the JSDF's efforts to improve its reputation through disaster relief, referring to such efforts as confidence-building measures (CBM) where "an actor can build trust in its intentions in the eyes of others through repeated unilateral acts benefiting the observer that are not tied to reciprocity or to its social norms of obligation."[90] However, through the interaction with other states, agents cannot escape social norms of obligation. CBMs are only comprehensible if there are rules that lead the initiator to believe in positive gestures, rules that lead the recipient to make sense of the action, and rules for both countries to understand that the actions are worthy of trust. The international norm of intervention, whether military or economic, has to make sense to the Japanese public and the GOJ in order for JSDF disaster relief activities to instill confidence.

Global norms are better received when they are localized to match the local norms.[91] International pressure forced Japan to reconsider when and how it deploys the JSDF, and that when and how is shaped by the domestic material constraints and ideational restraints. The antimilitarism environment has thus far limited Japan's PKO, HA/DR missions, and ODA to the promotion of "universal values" while upholding the Constitution. However, international human security missions will become increasingly risky as states further commit to the R2P concept. Many of the "freedom from want" issues that Japan prioritizes, such as climate change, disease, poverty, and refugee assistance are increasingly linked to postconflict peacebuilding. Prantl and Nakano conclude that Japan may not fall to that pressure of leveraging its military for such purposes, writing, "Japan's human security policies created the political space for gaining global influence without revising the 1947 peace constitution. Tokyo has fully embraced human security as a policy it can develop independently and as an alternative means to humanitarian intervention for cultivating influence."[92]

RECALIBRATING RULES AND ROLES: THE U.S.-JAPAN ALLIANCE

The deployment of the JSDF for PKOs and HA/DR missions has not replaced ODA as a tool for protecting human security, nor has ODA replaced the JSDF and the U.S.-Japan alliance as tools for the defense of the nation. Following the election of Donald Trump for the U.S. presidency in 2016, scholars and security experts believed Japan would develop a more independent security policy. This prediction was the latest version of the entrapment-abandonment debate. Contrary to expectations, the GOJ strengthened its commitments to the U.S.-Japan alliance, which it regularly refers to as "the cornerstone of Japan's national security."[93] The alliance not only protects the Japanese mainland, but it also allows Japan to fulfill its role as a responsible ally and member of the international community. Prime Minister Abe's "Proactive Contribution to Peace," carried out by the Indo-Pacific strategy, is the most realized vision of these objectives (to be discussed in chapter 8).

On April 29, 2015, Prime Minister Abe became the first Japanese head of state to address a joint meeting of Congress. For approximately forty-five minutes, Abe spoke in English about an "Alliance of Hope" and working together to make the world a better place. Abe promised that Japan's support for the

U.S. "rebalancing" in East Asia would be "first, last, and throughout," and offered concrete actions such as providing up to $2.8 billion in assistance to help improve the bases in Guam and passing new security legislation in the upcoming summer.[94] In concluding the speech, Abe proclaimed that Japan has a "new self-identity," one that will ensure that "human security will be preserved in addition to national security" and allow Japan to proactively engage the problems of terrorism, infectious diseases, natural disasters, and climate change.[95] It seemed that after decades of pressure, Japan was finally meeting the expectations set by the U.S. "reverse course" decades ago and was willing to play a greater part in the U.S.-Japan alliance. The previous day, Abe and President Barack Obama extolled the virtues of the upgraded alliance. Obama proudly stated, "Together, our forces will be more flexible and better prepared to cooperate on a range of challenges, from maritime security to disaster response. Our forces will plan, train and operate even more closely. We'll expand our cooperation, including cyber threats and in space. And Japan will take on greater roles and responsibilities in the Asia Pacific and around the world."[96] Abe added, "Japan and the United States are partners who share basic values, such as freedom, democracy, and basic human rights and the rule of law" and "now, Japan wants to be a country that can respond to such calls.[97]

Prime Minister Koizumi once stated, "The US is the only nation in the world which says that an attack or aggression against Japan is an aggression or attack against their own country. There is no other nation that perceives an attack or aggression against Japan as an attack against itself. If you think about this and judge for yourself, I think you will understand how important Japan-US relations are."[98] Certainly, the alliance has never been so important. The U.S. rebalance to Asia was equal parts defensive, political, and economic. It needed more than Japan's support; it necessitated a recalibration of the alliance. Japan's upgraded role in the alliance served three main functions: (1) it addressed changes in the regional security environment; (2) it addressed changes in the global security environment, such as the rise in terrorism, natural disasters, and cybercrime; and (3) it created a more equitable partnership. Recalibrating the responsibilities, and therefore the status, of the United States and Japan within the alliance shaped both the content and direction of Japanese security policy for the foreseeable future. However, as the previous six chapters sought to make clear, despite the rhetoric, none of these objectives are new or beyond the scope of the antimilitarism rules that govern Japanese security policy.

In a joint statement issued by Minister of Foreign Affairs Kishida Fumio, Defense Minister Onodera Itsunori, Secretary of State John Kerry, and Secretary of Defense Chuck Hagel, several broad references to the changing security environment and the need to manage China are made, but the bulk of the statement concerned modernizing the alliance. Specifically, the ministers "affirmed that the alliance should remain well positioned to deal with a range of persistent and emerging threats to peace and security, as well as challenges to international norms. Among these are: North Korea's nuclear and missile programs and humanitarian concerns; coercive and destabilizing behaviors in the maritime domain; disruptive activities in space and cyberspace; proliferation of weapons of mass destruction; and man-made and natural disasters."[99] The statement laid the groundwork for Japan to play a greater role in the region through cooperation with the United States in order "to effectively promote peace, security, stability, and economic prosperity in the Asia-Pacific region." In regard to bilateral relations, the ministers cited the need for further cooperation in ballistic missile defense, cyberspace, space, joint ISR activities, joint/shared used of facilities, bilateral planning, defense equipment and technology, extended deterrence dialogue, information security, joint training exercises, and host nation support. The alliance is expected to increase regional security through regional capacity building, maritime security, HA/DR, trilateral cooperation, and multilateral cooperation. The contemporary alliance is a far cry from the defense-of-Japan-only arrangement of the previous half-century but remains decidedly defensive in nature.

The Underpinnings of an Alliance

The centrality of the United States to Japanese security policy dates back to the very beginning of the postwar period. Immediately after World War II, the United States sought to make Japan "armless and harmless" and played an authoritative role in getting Japan to enact the Peace Constitution, which the vast majority of Japanese people welcomed.[100] In doing so, the United States adopted the role of guarantor of Japanese security, most clearly articulated in Article VI of the Japan-U.S. Security Treaty. The ten-article treaty ensured that the United

States would have a base of power in East Asia, and Japan would be protected by the United States. This initial arrangement basically entailed Japan paying for the United States' military strength. Since the Treaty of Mutual Cooperation and Security between the United States and Japan was signed on January 19, 1960, the alliance has gradually shifted from a purely defense-oriented arrangement to a security management arrangement.

Underwriting any change to the U.S.-Japan alliance are alliance norms. At the most basic level, allies are expected to fulfill their commitments and not betray each other.[101] This expectation can be further enhanced by a formal treaty, which itself has power from legal rules. Upholding commitments need not be understood as purely a consequentialist calculation. There is something particularly taboo about an ally attacking an ally in comparison to an enemy attacking an enemy, despite both actions inviting retribution. After all, the final circle of Dante's Hell is reserved for treachery. Regardless of the security context, alliances only work if each member is willing to fulfill its role. The U.S.-Japan alliance endures and is adaptable to change because the United States and Japan share common values as democratic countries, leaders work to strengthen ties, and both publics value the relationship.

Take, for example, the high-level connections between the United States and Japan. Between 1952 and 2020, Japanese heads of state visited the United States for official business eighty-four times, third only to the United Kingdom and Germany, and ahead of France (see figure 7.2). Visits by heads of states have different degrees of significance and formality. "State visits" are the highest honor given by one leader to another, and they symbolize the strength of the relationship. This is followed by "official visits," "official working visits," and so forth. "Other visits" include official working visits, informal visits, private visits, and side meetings at conferences. Japanese leaders enjoy an honored place in U.S. diplomacy and have the highest combined state visits and official visits in the world.

When taking into consideration that the first visit by a head of state from the United Kingdom predates Prime Minister Yoshida's attendance at the Japanese Peace Conference in San Francisco in 1951 by twenty years, it is clear the U.S.-Japan alliance is a cornerstone of American and Japanese foreign policy in the post–World War II era. Since 1945, Japan is the most visited East Asian country by U.S. presidents. Beginning with President Gerald Ford, U.S. presidents visited Japan first before embarking on to the rest of Asia. The affinity between leaders

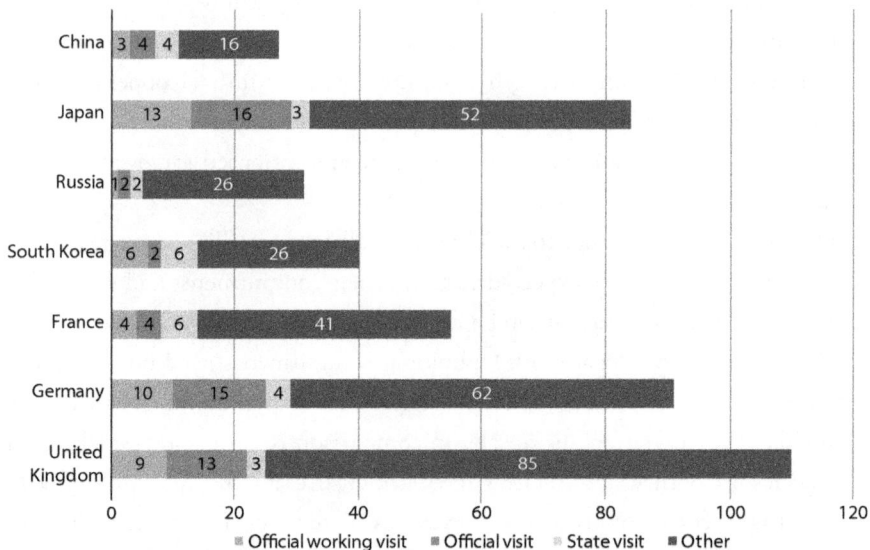

FIGURE 7.2 Visits by foreign leaders to the United States, 1921–2020.

Source: Department of State, "Visits by Foreign Leaders," Office of the Historian, accessed November 30, 2020. https://history.state.gov/departmenthistory/visits. France, Germany, and the United Kingdom are included in this figure because they are traditional U.S. allies.

is seen in the public as well. According to a November 2016 Cabinet Office public opinion poll, 84.1 percent of respondents "feel affinity" toward the United States, 88 percent of respondents believe current relations are "good," and 95 percent of respondents consider the future development of relations "important" for the two countries and for Asia and the Pacific region.[102] Affinity toward the United States dropped to 78.4 percent, and view of relations fell to 84.4 percent in the first year of the Trump presidency but remained significantly above the low of 67.5 percent in October 1986.[103] The uncertainty brought upon by the Trump presidency, however, reinforced the belief that future development of relations is important for the two countries and the rest of Asia, which *increased* to 95.2 percent. Despite continued criticism from Trump throughout his presidency, the 2018 poll showed similar results.[104] A 2018 Pew survey showed that Japanese views of the U.S. president fell to a record low of 24 percent and the belief that the United States does not consider Japan's interest reached a record high of 71 percent.[105] Despite such negative views of the what the Trump administration had done to American politics and foreign policy, when given a choice, 81 percent of respondents preferred the United States as the world's leading power, the highest among twenty-five countries surveyed.

On the other side of the Pacific, polls show similar favorability ratings. A 2015 Pew survey showed that 68 percent of Americans have a "great deal" or "fair amount" of trust in Japan. The survey also showed that the 2011 earthquake and tsunami was tied with World War II for "the most important events in US-Japan relations" for Americans. "US-Japan military alliance since World War II" and the 2011 earthquake and tsunami were the top two answers given by Japanese respondents. Following the 3/11 triple disaster, the term *kizuna* (bond) was used not only to describe the collective Japanese recovery effort but also the relationship between the United States and Japan following Operation Tomodachi. Operation Tomodachi or "friend" in Japanese, symbolized the special relationship and greatly improved public opinion on already high figures. A 2012 Pew survey found Japanese views of the United States increased 19 percent just weeks after the tsunami. The 85 percent positive rating was the highest among nations who received disaster relief from the United States. In the United States, there was wall-to-wall media coverage of the disaster and many stories praising Japanese "social order," acts of kindness, and morality. According to the aforementioned 2015 Pew survey, 94 percent of respondents answered that Japanese are "hardworking," 75 percent answered "inventive," and 71 percent answered "honest." A 2016 survey conducted by the Chicago Council on Global Affairs showed that Americans hold the highest recorded favorable feeling toward Japan in nearly forty years, and 60 percent of respondents support long-term military bases.[106]

Old Rules, New Guidelines, and Borrowed Risks

Positive relations and alliance commitments allow the United States and Japan to adapt to the changing security environment, check U.S. security overreach, and absorb the high social costs of hosting U.S. bases. As a responsible ally and contributor to global security, broadly defined, the GOJ implemented changes to its security policy, which are most clearly articulated in the 1978, the 1997, and the 2015 Guidelines for Japan-U.S. Defense Cooperation. The guidelines are informative because they are aspirational. Since the guidelines do not create legal obligations of either government to take legislative, budgetary, or administrative measures, their effectiveness is entirely dependent on each side's willingness to *commit*. Japan and the United States commit by engaging in the recurrent practice of updating the guidelines with increased responsibilities while maintaining core principles, such as the U.S.-Japan Security Treaty and Japan's adherence to its exclusively national defense–oriented policy and Three Nonnuclear Principles.

The 1978 guidelines are relatively vague and focus primarily on defending Japan from a potential Russian invasion. However, through the alliance, Japan played an important role in maintaining international security during the Cold War era because, by guarding its own coastal waters and airspace, Japan ensured that the Soviets were blocked from entering important strategic routes in the Asia-Pacific theater.[107] The U.S.-Japan alliance also ensured that Japan was "a bastion of anti-communism in Asia."[108] The 1997 guidelines were developed after the Gulf War crisis and destabilization of the Korean Peninsula. International condemnation for Japan's alleged passiveness during the Gulf War forced Japanese leaders to consider the necessity of dispatching the JSDF beyond the defense of the mainland to ensure the viability of the alliance and the nation's security to gain recognition as a contributor to global stability. The most significant change between the two guidelines is that "the 1997 revision expanded the focus of the alliance from Article V of the U.S.-Japan security treaty, which is focused on the defense of Japan, to Article VI, which is focused on the maintenance of peace and stability in the Asia-Pacific region, where the greatest challenges to the post-Cold War order were evolving."[109] The 1997 guidelines also outline several items of cooperation in situations in areas surrounding Japan, such as relief activities, search and rescue, rear area support, and minesweeping. Thus, the key bright line crossed was the introduction of maintaining regional stability as an important objective of the alliance.

Much has changed in the world since 1997. In the post-Cold War era, the United States waged a global war on terror, China emerged as a rising superpower, North Korea acquired nuclear weapons, new battlefields emerged in space and cyberspace, and even problems of antiquity such as piracy resurfaced. Again, the GOJ faced pressure to adapt to new challenges to Japanese security.

However, it would be an oversimplification to conclude that the changing security environment directly leads to changes in security policy. China has been rising since the 1980s, and it overtook Japan in defense spending in 2005. North Korea has been a threat to Japan for most of its existence, having kidnapped dozens of Japanese civilians, conducted several missile tests, and acquired nuclear weapons. The U.S. war on terror began just four years after the 1997 guidelines were established, and it was not until fourteen years later that Japanese leaders could credibly claim that they were implementing meaningful changes to the security doctrine in the form of the 2015 guidelines. Between 1997 and 2015, Japan's economy became stagnant, Japan's status declined, and the Okinawan base issue worsened. Moreover, Japan enjoyed another eighteen years of peace, and the world became increasingly interconnected. These developments, along with the international security environment, shaped the U.S.-Japan alliance.

Appendix A summarizes the major points of the guidelines. The 1978 guidelines are by far the shortest and most general. It consists of five main parts: (1) aim of the guidelines, (2) basic premises and principles, (3) cooperation under normal circumstances, (4) actions in response to an armed attack against Japan, and (5) cooperation in situations in areas surrounding Japan that have an important influence on the peace and security of Japan. The 1978 guidelines did not outline specific threats and were primarily focused on establishing the responsibilities of each side. The 1997 guidelines expanded on the 1978 guidelines significantly and added two sections: (1) bilateral programs for effective defense cooperation under the guidelines, and (2) timely and appropriate review of the guidelines. The 1997 guidelines are twice the length of the previous version and emphasized closer cooperation across all aspects of the alliance. The 2015 guidelines called for increased cooperation in the space and cyberspace domains. The 2015 guidelines were much more direct and clearly defined the proactive and seamless nature of the alliance, emphasizing defense, cooperation, and interoperability. The length of the 2015 guidelines is more than three times the previous version. The added length is due to the specificity of the issues that the United States and Japan planned to engage.

Unlike the 1978 guidelines that focused on Japan's security and the 1997 guidelines that increase attention to regional security, the 2015 guidelines proposed a whole-of-government approach with a particular emphasis on interoperability at multiple levels. The 2015 guidelines maintained Japan's defense-oriented security policy but expanded the idea of what Japan's security entails. Japan's security became linked to global threats such as cybersecurity, maritime security, terrorism, space, and maintaining a healthy alliance by working together in PKOs and HA/DR missions. Moreover, the 2015 guidelines sought to end the cumbersome approach to tackling international threats. After 9/11, at the behest of President George W. Bush, Prime Minister Koizumi dispatched the JSDF to support the U.S. Armed Forces in the Middle East. To allow participation in missions such as Operation Enduring Freedom and Operation Iraqi Freedom, Japan passed highly controversial special measures (short-term laws with sunset provisions). Each time Japan participated in these international operations, it stretched the limits of the Constitution, and leaders paid high political costs for what would likely be regular occurrences. The 2015 guidelines ended the need to rely on awkward interpretations of the Constitution and clarified precisely what Japanese security policy entailed.

However, when analyzing the U.S.-Japan alliance and Japanese security policy, it is important to consider what Japan can accomplish. As discussed in previous chapters, the JSDF is highly constrained by material and ideational forces, constraints that will not go away regardless of the necessity for change. Although commitment rules shape the content and direction of Japanese security policy, the material resources available to meet those commitments are equally significant.

Japan will unlikely be able to contribute more personnel and equipment to U.S.-led missions due to the small size of the JSDF, the limited defense budget, and the public's unwillingness to join the armed forces. Moreover, concerning the collective defense security bills, Abe emphasized that Japan would not be drawn into U.S. conflicts and the appropriate "brakes" would remain in place. Although Abe had enough support in the Diet to pass the bills, opposition forces, the media, and the public made it hard to force the bills through.[110] Abe was thus compelled to reassure the public that the bills were not a threat to Japan's peace and security. Similarly, Japan's contributions to fighting terrorists are also likely to be limited, as Abe has also promised that the JSDF would not be able to aid nations fighting ISIS in a logistics capacity, and instead would offer nonmilitary aid, such as goods and medical support, to refugees.[111]

Japan is also not likely to increase host nation support as it already pays most of the costs for maintaining the U.S. bases, and the Okinawan base issue remains a significant obstacle to hawkish security aspirations. Unresolved for decades, the troubled relocation of the U.S. base on Okinawa increased scrutiny of Abe's overall security agenda. Due to pollution, crime, and incidents of rape related to the base, the Okinawans have moved further away from working with the government.

Collective self-defense, the linchpin of the new security arrangement between the United States and Japan, is also likely to be carefully watched by the public. Representative Nagashima Akihisa argues that Japan needs to play a greater role through collective self-defense—but with clear limits. Nagashima clarifies that Japan should be banned from entering the territorial space of other countries but should be able to provide logistical support.[112] In Abe's first term, the Advisory Panel on Reconstruction of the Legal Basis for Security was established to determine those limits. The panel examined the JSDF's right to defend U.S. vessels on the high seas, to intercept ballistic missiles that might be headed toward the United States, the use of weapons in UN PKOs, and to provide logistical support for the operations of other countries participating in UN PKOs and other activities. Abe resigned before the report was submitted in June 2008, but in February 2013, Abe resumed the meetings of the advisory panel. In addition to the four original cases, the panel examined what concrete actions Japan could take to maintain peace and security, what ideas underline the government's interpretation of the Constitution, and how the domestic legal system should be structured. The panel argued that to ensure the right to life, liberty, and happiness (Article 13) of the people, Japan needed to exercise the appropriate use of force to repel attacks, protect its sovereignty, and pro-actively participate in international operations related to peace and security. Moreover, the panel introduced a novel interpretation of pacifism, concluding that, "Pacifism in the Constitution should be interpreted from an international perspective and not from a self-centered view and thus is beyond the passive form of pledging not to disturb peace, and demands proactive actions to real-ize peace."[113]

The panel offered some concrete examples of actions the JSDF can take. For example, under the new reinterpretation of the Constitution, Japan can protect U.S. forces when they are under attack (if the U.S. forces are protecting Japan), conduct minesweeping operations in maritime areas where Japanese ships are significantly affected, participate in UN PKOs to maintain international order, use weapons in UN PKOs, and protect Japanese civilians and vessels from armed attack. Moreover, Japan can exercise the right to collective self-defense if the following conditions are met: (1) when a foreign country in a close relationship with Japan is under attack and if "such situation has the potential to significantly affect the security of Japan"; and (2) Japan can use limited force to the minimum extent necessary, having obtained an explicit request or consent from the country under attack.

Following the recommendations of the report, Abe pushed for a package of security bills concerning collective self-defense and the bills passed in the lower house in July 2015. However, there was much resistance from the public, political opposition, and members of the LDP before the upper house voted on the package of bills. The new security bills were also met with strong criticism from the Japanese academic community, and daily protests greeted parliamentarians outside of the Diet building. On August 30, 2015, over three hundred protests against the security bills were staged across Japan, the largest drawing a crowd of over 120,000 in front of the National Diet building. Abe sought to appease critics and extended the Diet session, which was the longest extension in postwar history, to give himself more time to win over public opinion. Abe promised in Diet sessions that collective self-defense would not lead to involvement in foreign wars. Such promises create benchmarks that constrain future behavior inconsistent with the pledge. According to one senior government official, "some may say Prime Minister Abe is hawkish, but the Abe government is also working within the limits of Japanese public opinion."[114]

Nevertheless, collective self-defense critics claimed that the bills violated the Peace Constitution because it would allow Japan to use force in certain scenarios.[115] The media also adopted this narrative and were critical of collective self-defense. The *Asahi Shimbun* conducted a poll of over one hundred constitutional scholars and found near unanimous agreement that the bills were unconstitutional.[116] A 2014 Asahi Shimbun poll showed that 63 percent of respondents opposed lifting the self-imposed ban on collective self-defense.[117] A July 2015 Asahi Shimbun poll found that only 39 percent of respondents supported the Abe cabinet, compared to the 42 percent that opposed. The same polled revealed that 56 percent of respondents opposed the security bills (26 percent supported) and 31 percent believed the security bills would "contribute positively to peace, and to Japan's safety." Lastly, 42 percent of respondents answered the bill would not contribute to Japan's safety and 48 percent answered the security bills violate the Japanese Constitution (24 percent answered the bills do not violate the constitution).[118] These results reflect a steady decline in support for the bills and increased opposition of the Abe cabinet when the government tries to force through security bills that do not conform with the antimilitarism rules that shaped security debates over the last few decades.

The constraints and restraints on Japan's contributions to the alliance and international community will be less severe in the areas of the JSDF's force structure, professionalization, interoperability, and combined operations with the United States. Although Japan cannot contribute more, it can contribute better. One of the primary goals of the 2015 guidelines and security bills was to develop the JSDF into a seamless force. In the 2014 NDPG, Japan adopted the Dynamic Joint Defense Force, which emphasized readiness, mobility, flexibility, sustainability, versatility, and advanced technology. The 2014 NDPG also added mobile deployment capabilities and a wide range of logistical support systems to the JSDF. Another key development was the introduction of the Amphibious Rapid Deployment Brigade. This was not simply a modernizing of the JSDF but the adoption of new amphibious tactics to improve the flexibility of the GSDF. The Amphibious Rapid Deployment Brigade was formally established in March 2018 but has operated with nine hundred personnel short of its original three-thousand-person target. The 2014 NPDG established the goal of allocating "limited resources in a focused and flexible way to prioritize the functions and capabilities from a comprehensive perspective, identified through joint operation-based capability assessments of the Self-Defense Force's (SDF's) total functions and capabilities in various situations."[119] The MOD had also set up a Joint Staff Office in order to increase interoperability between the different branches of the JSDF.

The 2014 NPDG also sought to "strengthen and expand the Japan-U.S. cooperative relationship over a broad range of fields, including efforts for intelligence cooperation and information security, and cooperation in the field of defense equipment and technology, to build a firmer and effective alliance."[120] Since 2005, the GSDF has conducted combined training operations with U.S. Marines, which should allow for easier transition into a new phase of operations that include amphibious defense of remote islands. Interoperability is emphasized throughout Defense of Japan white papers, NSS, and NDPG. The United States and Japan have conducted joint exercises since 1985, but under the 2015 guidelines, the MOD looked to increase the seamlessness between the two forces and "strengthen the Japan-US alliance in all its aspects, including political, economic, and security areas."[121] The Abe cabinet also proposed legislation that would allow the JSDF to carry out "very passive and limited 'use of weapons' to the minimum extent necessary to protect weapons and other equipment of the units of the United States Armed Forces, if they are, in cooperation with the JSDF, currently engaged in activities which contribute to the defense of Japan (including joint exercises)."[122] Nagashima Akihisa sums up what the recalibration of the alliance aims to achieve best, stating, "The United States is taking the risks during wartime, while Japan is taking up the costs in peace time. This kind of balance is asymmetrical. We would like to rebalance, to correct the balance, by Japan taking more risks and the US taking more costs."[123]

RULES, RULE, AND A SENSE OF MISSION

Paul Midford and Robert Eldridge conclude the JSDF successfully replaced the "negative images" of the prewar with positive images, and in doing so built legitimacy and acceptance among the public.[124] For this strategy to be effective, however, it had to fall within the rules outlined by Japanese conceptions of security and the use of force, which are informed by antimilitarism. Legitimacy is given, not taken.[125]

Government justifications for the mobilization of the JSDF, and the actual deployments, are reiterated Japanese antimilitarism practices. Reiteration reifies rules and roles but also allow agents to craft new identities and reformulate old ones. According to Colonel Craig Agena, a lot of progress in the U.S.-Japan alliance has occurred over the last twenty-five years, and it has finally developed a "sense of mission."[126] This sense of mission has always been made possible by commitments to critical and complementary roles in the alliance. The U.S.-Japan alliance evolved not only due to U.S. pressure but also due to Japan's recalibration of its responsibilities to the international community and expanded domestic norms on the legitimate use of force.

The following chapter will conclude this book with a contextualization of Prime Minister Abe's Proactive Peace doctrine. In doing so, the chapter will demonstrate that despite the new rhetoric, enduring material constraints and ideational restraints form the content and direction of security policy. Lastly, the book with conclude with some final thoughts on the significance of Japan's security policy in international relations.

CHAPTER EIGHT

Aging Gracefully

Having served longer than any Japanese prime minister in the post-World War II era, Abe Shinzō was one to take stock of the past when formulating a vision of Japan's future. Abe's security policies were grounded in Japan's colonial history, antimilitarism, and material resources as much as they were by external threats. Introduced in Japan's first national security strategy in 2013, Abe's Proactive Contribution to Peace doctrine is the latest iteration of the nation's century-long search for security, wealth, and standing.[1] Aging provides the experience necessary to successfully pursue such ambitious goals.

Longevity is an anomaly in Japanese politics. Abe is the only prime minister to serve two nonconsecutive terms in the postoccupation era and one of only six postwar prime ministers to serve over one thousand days in office. Prior to ending his term on September 16, 2020, Abe was the second most senior member of the G7, behind German chancellor Angela Merkel. During his tenure, Abe provided much-desired stability to the office of the prime minister after the lost political decade of the 2000s. To his supporters, Abe led with a clear foreign policy for the twenty-first century, one that could instill pride in the nation. However, his detractors routinely criticized Abe for policies that they believed weakened democratic institutions and would unleash the JSDF, inviting instability in the process.

Abe's conservative vision of a *utsukushii kuni* (beautiful country) make for a convenient shorthand for what scholars argue are the normalization and militarization of Japanese security policy over the last decade. Christopher Hughes, for example, writes, "The impact of the 'Abe Doctrine' can best be comprehended through its underpinning revisionist ideology. Abe's ideology derives from a tradition of pre-war colonial and wartime attempts to assert for Japan a position as a first-rank nation and leader within Asia and a postwar ambition as an autonomous state, US equal partner and liberal-capitalist power facing down authoritarianism. Abe's pursuit of this role demands the casting off of international and domestic constraints imposed by defeat and the negative burden of history."[2]

As this book has argued, those constraints are much more difficult to cast off than purported. More importantly, the antimilitarism ecosystem demands more than coming to terms with defeat and the "negative burden of history" but a foreign policy consistent with the democratic spirit of the Constitution. There is more than one way to fulfill the role of a first-rank nation. Hence, Abe's justifications for ending one-nation pacifism warrant further examination, as they provide insight on how the use of force is legitimized in contemporary security debates. Justifications are fundamentally normative actions because, "The reasons that people offer for their conduct must refer to the kind of standards that people always start with—the personally relevant, highly specific, recurrently inconsistent standards that make their worlds inescapably their own. The most important of these . . . are standards of honorable conduct."[3] Whether or not the Abe doctrine achieves Japanese security or makes a meaningful contribution to the international community, it must conform to standards of honorable conduct—that is to say, antimilitarism rules. This concluding chapter explores the content and direction of the Proactive Contribution to Peace and situates its justifications and policy components within the antimilitarism ecosystem outlined in the previous seven chapters.

Here, it is worth noting that although "Proactive Contribution to Peace" is used in official government translations, the direct translation of the Japanese term "*sekkyokuteki heiwashugi*" is "proactive pacifism."[4] The doctrine, if one may call it that, speaks to two audiences, or conforms to two sets of rules. Since the early 1990s, the GOJ signaled to the international community that Japan is supportive of human security norms and is willing to mobilize the JSDF for PKOs and HA/DR operations. Nevertheless, antimilitarism remains the dominant ethic in Japan, and the GOJ must reassure the Japanese public that the nation is committed to peace. Proactive pacifism is specifically tailored to conform with international and domestic human security norms.

The main contributions of proactive pacifism are the introduction of the National Security Strategy (NSS), the establishment of the National Security

Council (NSC), relaxation of the arms exports principles, and adoption of collective defense. Beginning in late 2016, Abe laid the groundwork for a more specific vision of proactive pacifism called the Indo-Pacific Strategy. In the opening address at the opening session of the Sixth Tokyo International Conference on African Development, Abe stated, "Japan bears the responsibility of fostering the confluence of the Pacific and Indian Oceans and of Asia and Africa into a place that values freedom, the rule of law, and the market economy, free from force or coercion, and making it prosperous."[5] The Indo-Pacific Strategy seeks to establish Japan's global presence by linking the rapid growth of Asia to the high potential growth of Africa through military, diplomatic, and economic means. It was formally adopted by MOFA in the 2017 Policy Priorities for Development Cooperation white paper and the 2017 Diplomatic Bluebook.

In the Abe doctrine, scholars again see a turning point in Japanese security policy.[6] Lionel Fatton, for example, argues, "The recent evolution of Japan's security policy is remarkable in that it breaks with past practices."[7] Similarly, Hugo Dobson sees the "shackles" of the postwar regime broken and an abandonment of traditional middle-power internationalism out of Abe's desire to secure "Japan's great power status, promote a more proactive and robust Japanese security role, engage in historical revisionism to challenge post-war taboos and constraints, and promote Abenomics as a solution to rebuilding an economically strong Japan."[8] Abe's emphatic proclamation that "Japan is back" in a 2013 policy speech to an American audience at the Center for Strategic and International Studies only reinforced these popular assessments.[9] Yet, if concern for status and economic security is foreign policy, then Japan is not back; it never left. Japan's coherent and proactive approach to tackling international causes of instability, however, is a break from the past. Over the last five years, Abe secured a landmark treaty with South Korea concerning comfort woman, engaged in bilateral negotiations with North Korea over abductees, repaired relations with China, and recommitted Japan to the U.S.-Japan alliance.

Japan's assertiveness, specifically the adoption of collective security by way of the U.S.-Japan alliance, also led commentators to conclude it is the thin end of a wedge. Hughes argues the Abe doctrine is a "sharp break with the antimilitarism principles," and "Japan's move toward the exercise of collective self-defense indeed opens pathways to radical shifts rather than maintaining continuity with the past security trajectory."[10] Notwithstanding a brief reference to public opinion, Hughes does not provide polling data or define antimilitarism to establish a reference point for what exactly Japan is breaking from. As argued in this book, Japanese antimilitarism allows for the use of force under limited circumstances. Hughes is correct that the new collective defense guidelines can be loosely interpreted and thus create the opportunities for more "normalized" security behavior.[11] However, this is true of all guidelines, including the Constitution. What determines if and how policies are broken, reinterpreted, and upheld are the rules that provide justifications and the availability of material resources to effectuate change.

Antimilitarism rules determine the scope of proactive pacifism and provide the justifications for its existence. For all the new rhetoric, the content of proactive pacifism is consistent with Japanese security policy since the end of World War II. "Proactive pacifism" is the *term* for Japanese security policy of the past half-decade, but how policy is practiced and implemented will continue to be governed by material constraints and ideational restraints. What makes the Abe doctrine unique, however, is a level of sophistication of security policy discussions and the coherent linkage of the military, diplomatic, and economic tools for achieving Japanese security. To return to the computer analogy a final time, proactive pacifism seeks to troubleshoot many of the bugs found in the legal code and optimize Japanese security policy in accordance with the parameters of the antimilitarism ecosystem.

This concluding chapter is organized as follows. First, the chapter analyzes the different components of proactive pacifism and explains how the policy conforms to the antimilitarism ecosystem. Second, the chapter discusses the political and security implications of Japanese security policy. Last, I offer some final thoughts on the relationship between scholarship and international relations.

WHAT'S IN A DOCTRINE? JAPAN'S PROACTIVE CONTRIBUTION TO PEACE

Contrary to popular opinion, defense expenditures, JSDF operations abroad, and procurement of regional power-balance-disrupting technologies did not increase under the Abe administration. The widening gap between Japan and China and the narrowing gap between Japan and other states in the region demonstrate that relative Japanese power has declined. Proactive pacifism, however, has provided a more coherent approach to the many security initiatives that Japan has undertaken since the end of World War II.

According to the official MOFA website, proactive pacifism is a response to the increase and diversification of international causes of instability. Japan is compelled to act because it "cannot protect its day-to-day peace and security unless it actively contributes to regional and global security in cooperation with the international community." How Japan will contribute to regional and global security is most clearly outlined in the NSS. Up until the introduction of the NSS in December 2013, Japanese security policy was based on the 1957 Basic Policy on National Defense. The four-sentence document specified that the "objective of national defense is to prevent direct and indirect aggression, but once invaded, to repel such aggression, and thereby to safeguard the independence and peace of Japan based on democracy." To achieve this objective, four policies were outlined:

1. Supporting the activities of the United Nations, promoting international collaboration, and thereby, making a commitment to the realization of world peace.
2. Stabilizing the livelihood of the people, fostering patriotism, and thereby, establishing the necessary basis for national security.
3. Building up rational defense capabilities by steps within the limit necessary for self-defense in accordance with national strength and situation.
4. Dealing with external aggression based on the security arrangements with the U.S. until the United Nations will be able to fulfill its function in stopping such aggression effectively in the future.[12]

Over time, the GOJ introduced additional policies based on the Basic Policy on National Defense, the most notable being the commitment to an exclusively defense-oriented policy, not possessing or maintaining the capability to pose a threat to other countries, the Three Nonnuclear Principles, and civilian control of the military.

As the world became increasingly interconnected and threats more complex, the Basic Policy on National Defense provided insufficient instruction and necessitated a whole-of-government and transnational approach to security. Nontraditional security threats such as cybercrime, piracy, and climate change cross borders and lines of jurisdiction, thus requiring a multilateral response involving public and private actors. No nation is an island, not even Japan. The debates over increasing the role of the JSDF internationally were not a rejection of anti-militarism but a further development of what the rules and norms allowed in a new context.

Since the NSS did not replace many of the laws and institutions that grew out of the Basic Policy on National Defense and maintained its core antimilitarism principles, a more accurate description of the introduction of the NSS is that it was an update of the previous policy. The NSS outlined six broad strategic approaches to national security: (1) strengthening and expanding Japan's capabilities and roles, (2) strengthening the U.S.-Japan alliance, (3) strengthening diplomacy and security cooperation with Japan's partners, (4) proactive contribution to international efforts for peace and stability of the international community, (5) strengthening cooperation based on universal values to resolve global issues, and (6) strengthening the domestic foundation that supports national security and promoting domestic and global understanding.[13]

Each of the six pillars of the NSS had military, diplomatic, and economic dimensions. The first two strategies, increasing Japan's capabilities and roles, and strengthening the U.S.-Japan alliance were the most militaristic. Concerning the former, the NSS proposed developing a "highly effective and joint defense force" to ensure operational readiness in the context of a changing international security environment. To achieve this objective, Japan would increase cybersecurity capabilities, enhance intelligence capabilities, and strengthen technological capabilities, all of which would be expedited through the relaxation of the arms exports ban. Strengthening the U.S.-Japan alliance was more evolutionary than revolutionary. The NSS reaffirmed Japan's commitment to the alliance while acknowledging the need to decrease the alliance's burden on local communities. As discussed in chapter 7, Japan sought to clarify its role in the alliance and adopt more responsibilities to calibrate a more balanced relationship.

The other four pillars of the NSS are decidedly diplomatic and economic strategies. The third and fourth pillars emphasize cooperation with regional and international partners to enhance relationships and increase stability in troubled regions around the world, strengthen the rule of law, and counter terrorism. The primary tools under these strategies are Official Development Assistance (ODA), PKOs, and enhanced bilateral and multilateral communication. The fifth pillar, strengthening cooperation based on universal values to resolve global issues, was the most aspirational and focused primarily on achieving "freedom from want." The professionalization of Japanese security policy is most apparent in the sixth pillar, which is designed to reassure the international and domestic audiences of Japan's intentions through the promotion of security education and the development of professional security networks. During Abe's tenure, he held over two hundred summit meetings and introduced new initiatives that connected policy, security, and trade, such as the Mount Fuji Dialogue. In sum, the NSS is designed more so to address Japan's capabilities deficits than augment power projection capabilities.

Proactive pacifism is interpreted as normal and pragmatic by scholars because it mimics several U.S. security institutions. In 2013, the Abe administration established the NSC to create a centralized, cohesive, and efficient security planning mechanism among defense-related agencies. According to Adam Liff, the NSC was a long time in development and was made possible because "a critical mass of leaders in both parties held that Japan's institutions were ill equipped to handle its rapidly changing security environment."[14] Beyond creating new security-related positions such as national security advisor, the NSC introduced the 4-Minister Meetings, which aimed to "sharpen the focus of discussions at the NSC and allow the prime minister and his top advisors to more efficiently direct foreign and defense policies regarding national security" as well as increase coordination with Japan's allies.[15] For seventy-five years, Japan operated without a permanent apparatus to deal with "gray zone" scenarios and security crises, which the NSC sought to rectify.[16] Whereas the NSS provided a clear vision of Japanese security policy, the NSC streamlined the decision-making process to see that vision through.

The Indo-Pacific Strategy is the most realized implementation of proactive pacifism and is a case where Japan has shown uncharacteristic leadership. This leadership includes salvaging the Trans-Pacific Partnership after the U.S. withdrawal by taking on outsized responsibilities in the Comprehensive and Progressive Agreement for Trans-Pacific Partnership.

Abe first introduced the idea of a free and open Indo-Pacific (FOIP) in 2007. In a speech to the Indian Parliament, Abe stated, "The Pacific and the Indian Oceans are now bringing about a dynamic coupling as seas of freedom and prosperity. A 'broader Asia' that broke away geographical boundaries is now beginning to take on a distinct form. Our two countries have the ability—and the responsibility—to ensure that it broadens yet further and nurture and enrich these seas to become seas of clearest transparence."[17] Similar to previous doctrines, the Abe doctrine sought to achieve Japanese security through international cooperation, democracy, promotion of institutions, promotion of economic development, and support for a "rules-based order." This "value-oriented diplomacy" also drew inspiration from the Arc of Freedom and Prosperity that Aso Tarō briefly promoted as foreign minister in late-2006.[18]

Scholars and the media have focused primarily on the military dimensions of proactive peace, but the diplomatic and economic dimensions are equally important. Specifically, Japan would continue to provide ODA to developing countries and deploy the JSDF for PKOs and HA/DR missions as it had over the past quarter-century. ODA and the deployment of the JSDF for nontraditional security purposes are essential components of proactive pacifism because they assuage the lingering negative memories of World War II, especially in Southeast Asia and East Asia. All three dimensions of proactive peace are designed to preempt causes of insecurity by addressing causes of instability.

The commitment rules that emerged from Japan's post-World War II experience are foundational to the construction of the proactive peace doctrine. In a speech to the 73rd session of the United Nations General Assembly linking Japan's future to a rules-based, free, and open international economic system, Abe asked, "Should Japan, the country that reaped the greatest benefits of all under this system, ever fail to support the maintaining and strengthening that system who, else should we wait for to rise to support it? Japan's responsibility is tremendous indeed."[19] Abe continued, "In order to expand free and fair economic rules befitting to the twenty-first century into the vast region extending from Asia and the Pacific to the Indian Ocean, the countries that have created the system and reaped the greatest benefits from that system—that is to say, countries like Japan—must lead the effort." The FOIP derives from Japan's "desire to preserve the blessings of open seas, together with these very countries, as well as the United States, Australia, India, and others, and indeed, all countries and peoples who share the same intent."[20]

The main components of proactive pacifism are neither new nor aggressively militaristic. Abe justifies the FOIP by claiming that Japan holds a responsibility to the international system that made its security and prosperity possible. Unlike the revisionism of the pre-World War II era, Japan's security is contingent on preserving the status quo. To break from the last seventy years is to reject modern Japan.

Cooperation with the states that share the universal values of freedom, democracy, respect for basic human rights, and the rule of law is essential to upholding the current system. Furthermore, the GOJ has remained cautiously hopeful that China can be a part of this system. Unlike the Quadrilateral Security Dialogue, which can be more easily militarized, the FOIP provides the space for the inclusion of China. Within a year of introducing the FOIP, Abe incorporated nonconfrontational language in speeches to reassure China and ASEAN that it was not a containment strategy. For example, in the opening statement at the APEC Economic Leaders' Meeting, Abe stated, "We will make this region, extending from the Pacific Ocean to the Indian Ocean, one which is free and open to all. It is imperative that Japan and China deepen their cooperation to help foster peace and stability in this region. During this trip I held talks with President Xi Jinping and also with Premier Li Keqiang. President Xi stated our meeting was 'a new start for Japan-China relations' and I am of the very same mind."[21] In Abe's policy speech to the 198th session of the Diet, Abe continued to use the more welcoming language, stating, "We will make the vast seas and skies from the Indian Ocean to the Pacific Ocean the foundation of peace and prosperity from which every country, whether large or small, can benefit. Japan will create a 'free and open Indo-Pacific,' working together with all the countries that share this vision.[22] As long as China follows a rules-based order, it would be included in any Japanese foreign policy vision. Hence, Japan's initial opposition to the China-led Asia Infrastructure Investment Bank (AIIB) and the Belt and Road Initiative (BRI) quickly eased after they were introduced. Abe has stated that Japan would work with the BRI when objectives align and would consider joining the AIIB if transparency concerns are addressed.[23] Since Abe's remarks, Japan-China economic ties were significantly strengthened when both states signed the Regional Comprehensive Economic Partnership (RCEP) free trade agreement in November 2020.

Japanese antimilitarism allows for the use of force under narrow conditions but seeks to avoid it whenever possible because it is fundamentally at odds with the protection of human security. In promoting proactive pacifism at home and abroad, Abe maintained that the "path as a peace-loving nation that Japan has followed over sixty years since World War II will never, ever change," and the "principle of a peace-loving nation set forth in the Constitution of Japan is something we should be proud of within the international community."[24] By following the logic that Japan's peace is connected to the world community, Abe concludes that Japan's "inward-focused 'one-country pacifism'" cannot be regarded as "truly pursuing peace."[25] As Dower concludes, "The ruin the militarists brought upon Japan made clear that 'autonomy' was a pipe dream."[26]

One can gain further insight into how Japan's colonial history significantly shaped proactive pacifism from Abe's 70th Anniversary of the End of the Second World War statement. Before issuing the statement, Abe established a *kondankai* (advisory group) to discuss five key questions concerning Japan's past and future. Each of the following questions was addressed in separate sessions, which were attended by Abe or the chief cabinet secretary:

1. How should we view the path the world and Japan took during the twentieth century? What are the lessons that we should draw from the experiences of the twentieth century?

2. What is the path Japan has taken in the seventy years since the war's end in light of the lessons learned from the twentieth century? In particular, how should the commitment to peace, economic development, and international contributions by postwar Japan be evaluated?

3. How did Japan pursue reconciliation with the United States, Australia, and European countries in the seventy years since the war ended? How did Japan pursue reconciliation with China, the Republic of Korea and other Asian countries in the seventy years since the war?

4. What is our vision of Asia and the world in the twenty-first century, drawing on the lessons of learned from the twentieth century? What are the contributions Japan should make?

5. What are the specific measures that Japan should take on the occasion of the seventieth anniversary of the end of World War II?

The five questions proposed by Abe demonstrate that proactive pacifism is intrinsically linked to Japan's colonial past, specifically with remorse and repentance. During the session concerning question one, a lengthy debate ensued on how to contextualize Japan's actions in the colonial era, specifically whether the word "aggression" should be used in the seventieth anniversary statement. Despite some members arguing that it would be unfair to apply the standards of the present day to the past, the majority of the advisory group argued that Japan was indeed aggressive and needed to show remorse. One member remarked, "Since the prime minister is going to release a statement, it will become the assertion of the Japanese government," and therefore, the statement should be constructed carefully.[27] Speech is an action in and of itself. In the final statement, Abe used the term *shinryaku* (aggression), stating, "Incident, aggression, war—we shall never again resort to any form of the threat or use of force as a means of settling international disputes."[28]

The debates within the advisory panel also demonstrated the constitutive dimension of the Japanese antimilitarism ecosystem. During the session concerning question two, one member stated, "There is a broad national consensus regarding the fact that, as a peace-loving nation, Japan is not seeking hegemony over Asia and that it is contributing to the development of a free, open, and stable international order through the Japan-US alliance and the principle of international cooperation. Reconfirming this provides an important lesson for us."[29] The seventieth anniversary statement and proactive pacifism are very much commitments, or promissory notes, for Japan to fulfill according to its identity as a peace-loving nation. Commitment rules lead agents to consider future actions. One individual remarked, "What is the objective of releasing the upcoming statement by the prime minister in the first place? If the statement is to be released in accordance with values of the past, then it seems to me that there is no need to release it on the seventieth anniversary of the war's end to begin with."[30] The individual further argued that if the statement is to reflect how Japan regards the values of the twenty-first century, then it is "extremely important for Japan to indicate to the world how it regards the things it did in the past."[31] In the final statement, Abe linked the past and future behavior, stating, "With deep repentance for the war, Japan made that pledge. Upon it we have created a free and democratic country, abided by the rule of law, and consistently upheld that pledge to never wage war again. While taking silent pride in the path we have walked as a peace-loving nation for as long as seventy years, we remain determined never to deviate from this steadfast course."[32] Abe ends the speech that is simultaneously an apology to Japan's colonial victims, a reminder to the Japanese of the suffering caused by war, and a pledge to the international community, announcing:

> We will engrave in our hearts the past, when Japan ended up being a challenger to the international order. Upon this reflection, Japan will firmly uphold basic values such as freedom, democracy, and human rights as

unyielding values and, by working hand in hand with countries that share such values, hoist the flag of 'Proactive Contribution to Peace,' and contribute to the peace and prosperity of the world more than ever before.

Repentance can effectively demonstrate remorse when it is a repeated practice. Abe demonstrated Japan's commitment to peace and remorse by concluding his New Year's address with the following:

> Over these seventy years, Japan has earnestly built up a free and democratic nation while feeling deep remorse regarding World War II. We have also made our greatest possible contributions in order to bring about the peace and development of our friends in Asia and around the world. Taking pride in this, as we head towards the 80th, 90th, and 100th anniversaries to come, Japan must make still greater contributions towards world peace and stability under the flag of "Proactive Contribution to Peace." In this milestone anniversary year, I intend to send out to the world the message of our clear resolve regarding this.[33]

It is impossible to know Abe's true feelings about the war, but by repeatedly affirming apologies and pledging to keep Japan on the path toward peace, he creates boundaries on the acceptable use of force moving forward. Proactive pacifism, specifically through FOIP, is Japan's most coherent and strategic approach to achieving comprehensive human security in the last three decades. However, the implementation of security policy is a nonlinear process because antimilitarism is not an absolutist ethic. Like all rules, it is continuously negotiated in the context of material and ideational conditions. According to Satake Tomohiko, security reform under the Abe government, including the approval for the right to collective self-defense, is partly to ratify what the government has already done before. In other words, "Reality comes first, then policies adjust."[34] Antimilitarism allows for this elasticity concerning the use of force because it is not a deontological rejection of violence. Antimilitarism is a *type* of militarism, and militarism is a collection of rules that inform a society how to value the lives of its members, its enemies, and everyone in between. Militarism rules also govern how societies determine how much financial and social costs they are willing to pay to protect lives, or end them. Over time, recurrent practices shape identity, and identity leads to practices. As a peace-loving nation, Japan places a high value on life. Therefore, the Japanese public is supportive of deploying the JSDF for PKOs and HA/DR missions to protect the vulnerable but not to the degree that would unnecessarily risk Japanese lives. The GOJ's reluctance to deploy the JSDF to higher-risk scenarios lead some scholars to conclude Japan is practicing passive pacifism.[35] The use of force is indeed passive, and it works in conjunction with the diplomatic and economic tools of proactive pacifism. Proactive pacifism is consistent with the Japanese concept of peacebuilding, which is the long-term commitment to creating stability in troubled regions through "promoting peace processes, providing humanitarian and reconstruction assistance and restoring domestic stability."[36] Not all roads toward peace and stability go through the military. Aging forced Japan to accept earlier than most states in the global community that unrestrained militarism is seldom rewarding.

CONSIDER THE IMPLICATIONS OF JAPANESE SECURITY POLICY

Researchers are motivated by infinite justifications and topics, but two basic questions rule contemporary international relations scholarship: (1) Are the findings generalizable, and (2) Are the findings policy relevant?

This book introduced the multiple militarisms concept to broaden discussions of security policy. By providing the space, comparative analysis is no longer bound by a dichotomous view of the use of force. Each type of militarism is shaped by the material conditions and the rules of a given context. Japanese security policy is distinct in that it is the product of an antimilitarism ecosystem unlike any other. No other country has suffered the devastation of nuclear weapons or enjoyed such a miraculous postwar recovery. In this sense, the Japan case is not generalizable.

However, the multiple militarisms concept should make researchers more aware of the conditions that lead to specific security policies and allow for further study on the similarities and differences among militarisms. John Dower, again, provides the most apt analysis of how the war changed Japan, writing, "What survived was a strong bedrock of skilled human resources that had expanded greatly under the mobilization of war, and a collective devotion to starting over in a society that directed these resources to peaceful civilian pursuits."[37] There are numerous cases of postwar antimilitarisms that warrant comparative research, such as Irish neutrality, Swiss neutrality, and Finnish neutrality. Conversely, aggressive militarisms have only grown stronger in many parts of the world, where conscription, weapons proliferation, and unchecked military heads of state are commonplace. A comparison of divergent cases may reveal how material and ideational conditions shape security policy outcomes.

Some may find the multiple militarisms concept too broad and the cases too unmanageable because, according to this book's definition of "militarism," the majority of states, and certainly major powers that scholars find so interesting, are militaristic. What is apparent since the end of the Cold War, however, is that militaries serve diplomatic, policing, peacebuilding, and disaster relief roles in addition to their traditional security responsibilities. International relations have long been militaristic, but sharper analytical differentiation is needed to make sense of how the use of force has evolved. The broadness of the multiple militarisms concept is necessary for shifting debates from measuring degree of change to *how* and *why* change is possible.

The findings of this book also provide important insights for policymakers and individuals invested in the U.S.-Japan alliance and regional security. As discussed in chapter 3, the chronic recruitment problem should caution defense planners on expanding the responsibilities of the JSDF, particularly within the U.S.-Japan alliance and UN PKOs. The JSDF will likely be increasingly burdened with disaster relief missions, and personnel will find their duties more taxing. Careful attention to the mental and physical health of JSDF personnel will be necessary, especially since the suicide ratio is higher in the JSDF than in the general public. Here, one finds the professionalization of Japanese security policy paying dividends. The MOD is increasingly sensitive to personnel health, demonstrated by the increased frequency of mental health discussions in Defense of Japan white papers. According to Lieutenant General Yamaguchi Noboru, Japan conducted extensive research before the Iraq deployment and "learned from the US Armed Forces how to respond to PTSD issues, and we [Japan] have developed a very good system to detect problems through allocating questionnaires to those who might have been affected."[38] Since human security is a core concept within Japanese security policy, further discussion over the tradeoffs between maintaining state security and individual security is warranted. JSDF personnel are Japan's most valuable security asset, and the limited force size should influence how the

MOD allocates its resources and prioritizes its missions. The GOJ would do well to avoid the allure of unbridled aspirations.

The recruitment issue is a symptom of more existential problems—specifically, the dual demographic crisis. It's two things, aging population and declining population will continue to limit economic growth and make it increasingly difficult to divert resources to the military. How Japan balances between freedom from want and freedom from fear in the years to come should be followed closely by countries whose population crisis are just beyond the horizon. Japan's pension system is already stressed, and the procurement of capital equipment, such as the F-35s listed in the 2019 National Defense Program Guidelines, will most assuredly be paid for with further deficit spending. Japan currently has the highest debt of all OECD countries, at 200 percent of the GDP, with some projections reaching as high as 600 percent.[39] This situation is not sustainable, and the cultural consequences of the aging and declining population are equally alarming. Increased cases of debilitating diseases, such as Alzheimer's disease and lack of elderly care, demand the attention and sound policymaking of government leaders.[40] Moreover, the traditional Japanese family has been disrupted by population decline, and the GOJ will have to take into account changing cultural norms when implementing policies designed to alleviate the demographic crises.

Poor demographics are fundamentally a problem of gender equality in the workplace and greater society. Despite claims that Japan has never been a more equal society, gender equality manifests more in policy than in practice. Not including paid time off, the average number of working days per year in Japan is 249 days.[41] According to the OECD, in 2019, women made 23.5 percent less than men, which means women have to work 58.5 extra days to earn the same amount as men.[42] The World Economic Forum estimates that when including unpaid work such as caregiving and household chores, Japanese women actually work more hours per day than men. Japanese men spend a total of one hour and twenty-minutes a day on housework and childcare, the lowest in the world. That figure is likely inflated as studies show men tend to exaggerate their contribution. Women will also be disproportionately burdened with eldercare in the world's first hyper-aged society. Japan's economic and demographic woes comes down to a matter of physics. Women are not an untapped resource ready to be mobilized for the state because they are not working enough hours; they do not have more hours to give.

Womenomics has failed to take off not for the lack of vision by the Abe government but due to deeply embedded cultural practices that make it difficult for women to have the same opportunities and enjoy the same societal benefits as men. In 2019, 1,293,095 women attended university, or 44.3 percent, the highest on record.[43] According to the Japan Student Services Organization, in 2019, 59.7 percent of Japanese students who studied abroad were women.[44] Women are a source of untapped temerity and innovation, which are precisely what Japan requires. Yet, between 2010 and 2014, 46.9 percent of women cease employment upon becoming pregnant. It should be of no surprise that only 14.9 percent of Japanese women hold managerial positions, a rate only higher than South Korea. Policies, therefore, should be designed to increase rights and equity, not merely to address the state's economic and security concerns. Correspondingly, men not only have to do their part, they have to fulfil their roles as supportive partners and invested members of the household, workplace, and society. According to the Ministry of Health, Labour, and Welfare, in 2018 only 7.48 percent of Japanese men took childcare leave, the highest on record; 83 percent of women took time off to care for the child; 69.7 percent of women took at least ten months of paternity leave, while only 2.7 percent of men did the same; and 36.3 percent of men took less than five days (0.5 percent of women took less than five days). Although these figures show some improvement on the low end, 17.3 percent more men took up to two weeks off for paternity leave compared to 2015, 0.6 percent *fewer* men were willing to take ten months or more. In fact, 4.4 percent *more* women opted for ten months or more of paternity leave compared to three years prior.[45] The Japanese government should consider steeper penalties for companies that do not enforce parental leave rules, vacation time, and other cases in which the benefits and costs of work are not equally distributed. Increased work-life balance, more flexible work hours, and generous leave would benefit men and women and provide the space for genuine reflection of how the current economic system is not conducive toward healthy family planning.

Immigration policy also is long overdue. The declining population will mean that Japan will become a greener and less expensive place to live. Its strong education system, alluring soft power,[46] and pacifist reputation also make Japan a desirable immigration destination. Japan can quickly meet its labor needs if it can rid itself of the *gaijin arerugī* (foreigner allergy). Japan appears to be on the right track, as tourism has significantly risen in the last three years. The Abe administration prudently increased the acceptance of medium-skilled workers, especially from Southeast Asia. The current Suga Yoshihide administration has not given any signs of an abrupt change in direction from the previous administration. Going forward, a deeper reflection on who is considered Japanese is necessary, which may even open the possibility of immigrants joining the JSDF. Japan watchers should also not be distracted by the difficulties and high costs of addressing the population crises because Japan's robust welfare system, low mortality rates, and high life expectancy are evidence of a successful postwar democratic transition. Sustaining Japan's democracy requires it to be more open, not isolationist and less generous.

The findings in this book can provide insights for policymakers seeking to decrease Japan's reliance on foreign military sales (FMS). As discussed in chapter 3, there are deeply embedded market inefficiencies in the defense industry. Here, the GOJ has a tough decision to make. Does it rely on FMS to ensure security in the short term, or does it invest in the domestic industry to achieve long-term autonomy? The significant financial and technological burden of an underdeveloped domestic arms industry and reliance on FMS came to a head in June 2020, when Japan was forced to suspend the Aegis Ashore ballistic missile system that was supposed to be a linchpin of the nation's security. A smooth transition from FMS to self-sufficiency is difficult to achieve because opportunity costs push Japanese companies to pursue other growth opportunities. Unless the GOJ fully commits to the domestic industry in the near future, it will find that engineering talent will age out of the defense industry—a problem that has already arisen in the nuclear power industry.

How Japan addresses its myriad of problems provides valuable lessons for the international community. Other East Asia states addressed their military recruitment problems with conscription, but finding enough bodies in uniforms is the least of their problems. South Korea (1.29), Singapore (0.87), Hong Kong (1.21), China (1.6), Russia (1.6), and Taiwan (1.14) all have low fertility rates and, unlike Japan, have not had decades to develop robust safety nets or democratic institutions to ensure peace in times of weak economic growth.[47] The transition will be less graceful in the rest of East Asia, which could lead to instability and conflict. East Asia will need to reconsider reversing course on significant investment in the military and pour those resources in strengthening the immigration system and improving the position of women in society.

Most importantly, gender inequality *must* be addressed. Here, East Asia remains stubbornly behind much of the world. According to the World Economic Forum, Japan, South Korea, and China rank below the global average in the 2020 gender gap index. China is ranked 106 out of 153 countries, with a particular weakness in health and survival (ranked last). Japan is ranked 121, with economic participation and opportunity ranking higher than only four of the thirty-seven OECD countries. South Korea is sandwiched between Ghana and Kenya, with a global gender gap index ranking of 108.[48] Like their Japanese counterparts, South Korean women lack economic opportunities.

The material constraints and ideational restraints on security policy and its commitment to global human security should put an end to the myth that Japan is remilitarizing. Japan's economic future will lie in exports, mostly to China. While acknowledging the rise of China, white papers, government speeches, and polling data routinely show that the Japanese believe peaceful coexistence is essential for regional prosperity. As discussed in chapter 5, Japan has sought to reassure its neighbors that it is looking to maintain the peace and not disrupt the regional power balance. Japan turned away from isolationism and aggressive militarism for over seventy-five years, and it embraced the rules-based order of the international system. China and South Korea must recognize this transformation, as their security depends on regional cooperation. Misjudging Japan's military threat pulls vital resources from the preservation of other forms of human security.[49]

Here, the findings in chapter 5 and chapter 6 may prove useful. Antimilitarism and positive signaling between Japan and its neighbors are made possible by activism at the grassroots level. These movements, however, fall short of their potential due to poor fundraising strategies and the aging population. Actors across East Asia will need to act quickly to preserve the lessons of World War II. If justice is ever to be achieved for the comfort women, forced laborers, and all the individuals who directly suffered during the colonial era, then reconciliation must be honestly pursued by all sides in the immediate future.

On Rules, Roles, and Scholarship

The issue of policy relevance is of greater consequence and warrants further reflection. There is no shortage of articles that call upon academics to get out of their ivory towers and take upon themselves a more substantial role in the policymaking process.[50] Scholars have a lot to offer. They are highly trained, possess immense knowledge, and are incredibly passionate about their subjects of interest. Unlike politicians, they are not sensitive to short-term gains and have the luxury, in resources and time, to explore complex phenomena in depth. The ivory tower provides a vital vantage point for understanding long-term developments. Scholars should indeed write some of the rules that govern policy.

And they are. Every day, scholars are contributing to a better understanding of peace and conflict by teaching undergraduates, training graduate students, giving public talks, providing consultation, working in think tanks, publishing peer-reviewed articles and books, commenting in opinion editorials, and participating in government. Academia has a profound impact not only on policy but also in how society thinks about the significant issues of our time, especially through the education of the next generation of leaders. The borders between the academy, private sector, and public sector are quite porous.

It is with this appreciation for the impact of scholarship that I propose two additional questions to consider: How does generalizable and policy-relevant scholarship shape the world? Is it justified? Academics are agents, and all agents utter speech acts that construct—and justify—the world in which they operate. Producing scholarship of consequence entails consequences, and it has not always been for the greater good. The Kyoto School of Philosophy, for example, constructed the *Shu no Ronri* (Logic of Species) philosophical argument, which served as the "metaphysical foundation for the idea of the Greater East Asia Co-prosperity Sphere."[51] Jeffrey Sachs's promotion of "shock therapy" resulted in long-term and devastating consequences throughout Latin America and the former Soviet states. The Chicago School of Economics advocacy of free markets and little government intervention may be responsible for the extreme inequality and instability of the modern global economy.[52] Political science has played a role as well. Prime Minister Tony Blair, for example, infamously espoused the merits of the democratic peace theory in justifying the Iraq War to millions of viewers during an interview on *The Daily Show with Jon Stewart*. Deterrence theory raised the stakes of the Cold War to a degree that threatened the existence of all living beings on earth, an existential threat that continues to the present day.[53]

American academia produced many of the core theories and concepts in the field of international relations, and therefore it secured many of the privileges of being the first mover. That is to say, Americans wrote the rules of the discipline, and hence rule. And "rule is exploitive."[54] The largest political science conferences and top journals originate from the United States, while leaders from all over the world come to American universities to obtain an education.[55] Some of Japan's most passionate advocates of more normal security policy were trained in the top U.S. political science programs. Prime Minister Nakasone, for example, was a member of the Harvard International Seminar in the 1950s, which was run by Henry Kissinger and under the direction of William Y. Elliot, dean of the Harvard Summer School. Both political scientists, Kissinger and Elliot served in prominent roles in the U.S. government. In the late 1970s, Prime Minister Abe studied three semesters at USC and took courses in political science and international relations. Prime Minister Miki also studied at USC in the 1930s. Minister of Defense Kōno Tarō and former Minister of State for Okinawa and Northern Territories Affairs Yamamoto Ichita earned degrees in foreign service at Georgetown University. Koizumi Shinjirō, a son of a prime minister, received a master's degree in political science at Columbia University. Koizumi's high approval ratings and pedigree lead many in the media and academia to predict an eventual prime ministership.

Realism, in particular, has enjoyed intellectual hegemony in the study of international relations. By staking the claim of reality, liberalism was construed as pacifistic idealism in the first great debate of the discipline. This, of course, was a *normative* claim. Responsible leaders cannot afford to be idealistic, and therefore they should follow realist prescriptions. All prescriptions begin with ideas. Ideas may be right or may be wrong, but they are not to be trifled with. International relations theories and concepts have a profound impact on the world to which they construct. In describing asymmetries of control and privilege, Onuf writes of a system of heteronomy, where agents are bound by rules that lack a formal enforcement mechanism.[56] In security studies, concerning East Asia in particular, the logic of realism permeates most security discussions and is rarely challenged in elite circles, and therefore privileges those who perform it best. This performance expends a disproportionate amount of time and financial resources toward the study of nuclear weapons and great power rivalries while underappreciating topics such as demographics, the environment, immigration, class, race, and gender. It should come as no surprise that conference panels, think tanks, government policy groups, and Track Two meetings sorely lack diversity, with a glaring absence of women and people of color.[57] Efforts to increase diversity have been more performative than consequential. Young scholars and practitioners, especially women and people of color, are rarely given significant time to speak at conferences and workshops, let alone have a seat at the main table. If one wants innovation and well-researched analysis, speak with and *listen* to the young fellows in the back row; you will be impressed. Security studies is falling behind other fields in terms of acknowledging new voices that are researching issues outside of the realist lens because it stubbornly continues to provide reasons for why states should militarize when the data has demonstrated that conflict and battlefield casualties have been on the decline for over half a century.

Here, I return to the book's subject of inquiry. In determining how Japan navigates the material and ideational forces that govern its security policy, this book investigates how state-sanctioned violence is justified and delegitimized. Academics have played a role in the construction of militarisms through their scholarship. The term "normalizing" is a *normative* statement because it implies that Japanese antimilitarism is abnormal. This book makes the case that normal is determined by its context, or the rules that society constructs and abides. Militarism has been too broad a concept and has encouraged wild imaginings of the dangers of contemporary Japanese security policy by the media, security specialists, pundits, publics, and governments in the United States and East Asia. The academic literature, of course, is much more nuanced. However, increasingly dense literature reviews have oversimplified counterarguments, and selective reading among the general public has diluted well-argued cases. Thus, this book is a cry for specificity. Militaries now serve police, disaster relief, and diplomatic roles in addition to their security duties. A simple adjective, such as "minimal-use," can reframe how Japanese security policy is interpreted. If the term is unclear to readers, then it invites conversation.

I will end this book with a normative claim because it cannot be avoided. Antimilitarism brought stability and prosperity not only for Japan but also for the international community. It is within living memory that zealous militarism led to immense suffering throughout Asia and unleashed nuclear weapons that have cast a shadow over humanity since. Over the last seventy-five years, however, the judicious deployment of the JSDF has saved hundreds of thousands of lives in and outside of Japan. Alarmist claims of Japanese remilitarization and normalization ignore the lessons that were learned following the end of World

War II. Japan utilized the sword in the name of security and paid for its violence dearly. The postwar period is never truly *post*-war because for Japan, there is no escaping its previous actions, especially actions of significant global consequence. The Japanese people have renounced the use of violence to build a vibrant, democratic, and wealthy nation, all the while sharing their surplus with the world. With climate change, rampant inequality and poverty, and rising nationalism as the primary threats to global peace and security, it is due time that the definition of "great power" changes. As a peace-loving nation, Japan is at the forefront for confronting the challenges of tomorrow, and here, it will secure an honored place in international society.

Guidelines for Japan-U.S. Defense Cooperation (Abridged)

Date	Key Points
1978 Guidelines	**Aim of Guidelines:** These draft guidelines shall not be construed as affecting the rights and obligations of Japan and the United States under the Japan-U.S. Security Treaty and its related arrangements. It is understood that the extension of facilitative assistance and support by Japan to the United States, which is described in the draft guidelines, is subject to the relevant laws and regulations of Japan.
	Basic Premises and Principles: Japan, as its defense policy will (1) will possess defense capability on an appropriate scale within the scope necessary for self-defense, (2) assure, in accordance with Status of Forces Agreement the stable and effective utilization of facilities and areas in Japan by U.S. Forces and the United States will maintain a nuclear deterrent capability and the forward deployments of combat-ready forces and other forces capable of reinforcing them
	Cooperation Framework: The U.S. and Japan will (1) conduct studies on joint defense planning, (2) undertake necessary joint exercises and training when appropriate, (3) study and prepare beforehand common procedures deemed necessary for operational needs in order jointly to undertake operations smoothly. Such procedures include matters related to operations,

intelligence, and logistics and (4) each nation is responsible for the logistics of its own forces

The Defense of Japan: Both nations will conduct closer liaison and will take necessary measures to ensure coordinated joint action and (1) In principle, Japan by itself will repel limited, small-scale aggression. When necessary, Japan will repel it with the cooperation of the U.S., (2) Japan will primarily conduct defensive operations of its territories and surrounding waters with the U.S. as support (3) Japan and the U.S. will work jointly and closely in operations, command and coordination, intelligence, and logistics, and (4) Japan will, in case of need, provide additional facilities to the U.S. in accordance with the U.S.-Japan Security Treaty.

Cooperation in Surrounding Areas that Influence Japan's Security: The Governments of Japan and the United States will (1) consult together from time to whenever changes in the circumstances so require and (2) conduct studies in advance on the scope and modalities of facilitative assistance to be extended to the U.S. Forces by Japan within the Japan-U.S. Security Treaty and related arrangements and agreements

1997 Guidelines   **Aim of Guidelines:** The aim of these Guidelines is to create a solid basis for more effective and credible U.S.-Japan cooperation under normal circumstances, in case of an armed attack against Japan, and in situations in areas surrounding Japan. The Guidelines also provided a general framework and policy direction for the roles and missions of the two countries and ways of cooperation and coordination, both under normal circumstances and during contingencies.

Basic Premises and Principles: (1) Upholds rights and obligations of U.S.-Japan Security Treaty, (2) Japan will conduct all actions within the limitations of its Constitution and maintain its exclusively defense-oriented policy and three non-nuclear principles, (3) all actions taken by the U.S. and Japan will be consistent with basic international law, and (4) the guidelines do not oblige either government to take legislative, administrative, or budgetary measures. However, the U.S. and Japan will establish an effective framework of cooperation.

Cooperation Framework: The U.S. and Japan will (1) increase information sharing and intelligence, (2) increase cooperation to promote regional and global security, and (3) both Governments will conduct bilateral defense planning in case of armed attack against Japan and mutual planning in situations in areas surround Japan.

The Defense of Japan: Both nations will cooperate as appropriate to ensure a coordinated response and (1) Japan will establish the basis for U.S. reinforcements, (2) Japan will have the primary responsibility for conducting operations for land, sea, and air defense (3) the U.S. will provide appropriate support for Japan, (4) Japan will, in case of need, provide additional facilities to the U.S. in accordance with the U.S.-Japan Security Treaty.

Cooperation in Surrounding Areas that Influence Japan's Security: (1) Both Governments in intensify information sharing and (2) cooperate in relief activities, search and rescue, activities ensuring effective sanctions, (3) establish common standards for preparation, (4) establish common procedures.

2015 Guidelines **Aim of Guidelines:** In order to ensure Japan's peace and security under any circumstances, from peacetime to contingencies, and to promote a stable, peaceful, and prosperous Asia-Pacific region and beyond, bilateral security and defense cooperation will emphasize: (1) seamless, robust, flexible, and effective bilateral responses, (2) synergy across the two governments' national security policies, (3) a whole-of-government Alliance approach, (4) cooperation with regional and other partners, as well as international organizations and (5) the global nature of the Japan-U.S. Alliance. Moreover, the two governments will continuously enhance the Japan-U.S. Alliance. Japan will possess defense capabilities according to the NSS and NDPG and the U.S. will continue to extend deterrence to Japan through the full range of capabilities, including U.S. nuclear forces.

Basic Premises and Principles: (1) Upholds rights and obligations of U.S.-Japan Security Treaty, (2) all actions taken by the U.S. and Japan will be consistent with basic international law, (3) all actions and activities undertaken by Japan and the United States will be in accordance with their respective constitutions, laws, and regulations then in effect, and basic positions on national security policy and Japan will maintain its exclusively national defense-oriented policy and non-nuclear principles, and (4) the Guidelines do not obligate either government to take legislative, budgetary, administrative, or other measures.

Cooperation Framework: The two governments will take advantage of all available channels to enhance information sharing and to ensure seamless and effective whole-of-government Alliance coordination that includes all relevant agencies. For this purpose, the two governments will establish a new, standing Alliance Coordination Mechanism, enhance operational coordination, and strengthen bilateral planning. The two governments will cooperate in (1) intelligence surveillance and reconnaissance (ISR), (2) air and missile defense, (3) maritime security, (4) asset protection, (5) training and exercises, (6) logistic support, and (7) use of facilities. Moreover, the two governments will develop and enhance bilateral cooperation in the areas of defense equipment and technology, intelligences and information security, and educational and research exchanges.

The Defense of Japan: The Alliance will respond to situations that influence Japan's peace and security; such situations cannot be confined geographically. Japan will establish and maintain the basis for its support of U.S. deployments. The preparations by the two governments may include but would not be limited to: joint/shared use of facilities and areas; mutual logistic support, including, but not limited to, supply, maintenance, transportation, engineering, and medical services; and reinforced protection of U.S. facilities and areas in Japan. Operations may include defending air space, counter ballistic missile attacks, defend maritime areas, counter ground attacks, and cross-domain operations.

Actions in Response to an Armed Attack of a Third Party: When Japan and the United States each decides to take actions involving the use of force in accordance with international law, including full respect for sovereignty, and with their respective Constitutions and laws to respond to an armed attack against the United States or a third country, and Japan has not come under armed attack, they will cooperate closely to respond to the armed attack and to deter further attacks. Bilateral responses will be coordinated through the whole-of-government Alliance Coordination Mechanism.

Cooperation for Regional and Global Peace and Security: Japan and the United States will take a leading role in cooperation with partners to provide a foundation for peace, security, stability, and economic prosperity in the Asia-Pacific region and beyond. The two governments will corporate closely and maximize interoperability in PKO, international HA/DR, maritime security, partner capability building, noncombatant evacuation operations, ISR, training and exercises, and logistic support. The governments will also promote and improve trilateral and multilateral security and defense cooperation. The government will also cooperate to secure the responsible, peaceful, and safe use of space. To help ensure the safe and stable use of cyberspace, the two governments will share information on threats and vulnerabilities in cyberspace in a timely and routine manner, as appropriate.

Source: Ministry of Defense, "The Guidelines for Japan-U.S. Defense Cooperation," accessed November 30, 2020, https://www.mod.go.jp/e/d_act/us/index.html#anpo.

Peace Museums and War History Museums in Japan

Peace Museum Name	Prefecture	Founded	Visitors (per year)
Hiroshima Peace Museum	Hiroshima	1955	1,758,746*
Nagasaki Atomic Bomb Museum	Nagasaki	1955	692,647*
Maruki Gallery	Saitama	1967	9,140*
Okinawa Prefectural Peace Memorial Museum	Okinawa	1975	339,631*
Daigo Fukuryū Maru (*Lucky Dragon No. 5*) Exhibition Hall	Tokyo	1976	111,594*
Peace Museum for the People	Fukuoka	1979	
Sōka Gakkai Toda Peace Memorial Hall	Kanagawa	1979	
Anne Frank Memorial House Japan	Hyōgo	1980	
Sendai Sensai Hukkou Memorial (Sendai Memorial on Postwar Rehabilitation)	Miyagi	1981	9,115*
Kobe City War Damages Exhibition Corner	Hyōgo	1981	6700
Japan Peace Museum	Tokyo	1983	
Life Is Treasure House	Okinawa	1984	5000
Osaka Human Rights Museum (Liberty Osaka)	Osaka	1985	
Peace Memorial Center	Hokkaidō	1985	
Hamamatsu Revival Memorial Center	Shizuoka	1988	
Ōkunoshima Poison Gas Museum	Hiroshima	1988	61,289*
Teranaka Art Museum	Wakayama	1988	
Maizuru Repatriation Memorial Museum	Kyoto	1988	85,406*

(*Continued*)

Peace Museum Name	Prefecture	Founded	Visitors (per year)
Grassroots House	Kōchi	1989	130 + (408)*ª
Himeyuri Peace Museum	Okinawa	1989	522,888*
Tanba Manganese Memorial Hall	Kyoto	1989	
Nakano Ward Peace Exhibition Hall	Tokyo	1989	
Aomori Air Raid War Damages Exhibition Hall	Aomori	1990	
Shoukokumin Museum (Museum of Children)	Nagasaki	1990	
Kōchi Liberty and People's Rights Museum	Kōchi	1990	51,583
Osaka International Peace Center (Peace Osaka)	Osaka	1991	4358
Taiji-cho Ishigaki Memorial Museum	Wakayama	1991	
Mirasaka Peace Museum of Art	Hiroshima	1991	
Suita Peace Memorial Center	Osaka	1992	8,839*
Kyoto Museum for World Peace	Kyoto	1992	
Kawasaki Peace Museum	Kanagawa	1992	37,838*
No More Hibakusha Hall	Hokkaidō	1992	
German Museum	Tokushima	1993	30,838*
Peace Museum of Saitama	Saitama	1993	37,754*
Sakima Art Museum	Okinawa	1993	30,000
Shizuoka Peace Center	Shizuoka	1993	
Human Rights and Peace Museum Fukuyama City	Hiroshima	1994	11,036*
Sakai City Peace and Human Rights Museum	Osaka	1994	14,478*
Oka Masaharu Memorial Nagasaki Peace Museum	Nagasaki	1995	3,391ᵇ
Takamatsu Civic Culture Centre: Peace Museum	Kagawa	1995	
Holocaust Education Center	Hiroshima	1995	
Pacific War History Museum	Iwate	1995	100
Setagaya Peace Gallery	Tokyo	1995	
Himeji Historical Peace Center	Hyōgo	1996	15,585*

Usui Peace Memorial Center	Fukuoka	1996	1000
Mugonkan Art Museum for Peace	Nagano	1997	
The Peace, Human Rights and Children Centre	Osaka	1997–2006	
Yawaragi: Peace Memorial in Saiki	Ōita	1997	4,451*
Kanagawa Plaza for Global Citizenship	Kanagawa	1998	427,492
Art Museum of Picture Books	Nagasaki	1999	3,995*
Chiune Sugihara Memorial Hall	Gifu	2000	
Auschwitz Peace Museum Japan	Fukushima	2000	
War Memorial Maritime Museum	Hyōgo	2000	3,303*
Yukinoshita Peace Culture Museum	Fukui	2001	
Korea Museum	Tokyo	2001	4,204*
The Center of the Tokyo Raids and War Damages	Tokyo	2002	
Gifu Peace Museum	Gifu	2002	70
Hiroshima National Peace Memorial Hall	Hiroshima	2002	379,163*
Kodomo Center Asahi	Osaka	2002	
Nishinomiya City Peace Center	Hyōgo	2002	13,071*
Fukuro-machi Elementary School Peace Museum	Hiroshima	2002	
Nagasaki National Peace Memorial Hall	Nagasaki	2003	147,467*
Nagasaki Peace Museum	Nagasaki	2003	
Nagaoka War Damages Center	Niigata	2003	14,492*
Kitakami Peace Memorial Hall	Iwate	2004	1,935*
Tsushima-maru Memorial Museum	Okinawa	2004	
Women's Active Museum on War and Peace	Tokyo	2005	
Peace Museum of Air-Raids on Okayama	Okayama	2005	38,007*
Wadatsumi no Koe Memorial Hall	Tokyo	2006	679
Chukiren Peace Memorial Museum	Saitama	2006	~200*
Peace Aichi	Aichi	2007	
Yamanashi Peace Museum	Yamanashi	2007	
Port of Humanity Tsuruga Museum	Fukui	2008	
Hanaoka Peace Memorial Museum	Akita	2010	587*
Shiga Peace Memorial Hall	Shiga	2012	28,004*
Choro-Kan (Morning Dew Museum)	Tochigi	2015	197*

(Continued)

War History Museum Name	Prefecture	Founded	Visitors (per year)
Yūshūkan Museum	Tokyo	1882	
Museum of Naval History	Hiroshima	1936	47,359*
Kaiten Memorial Museum	Yamaguchi	1968	12,446*
Kanoya Air Base Museum	Kagoshima	1973	
Tokushima Air Base Museum	Tokushima	1973	~850*
Kamikaze Special Attack Museum	Ehime	1979	Not open to public
Chiran Peace Museum	Kagoshima	1987	
Chikuzen-machi Tachiarai Peace Memorial Museum	Fukuoka	1987	100,494
Yokaren Museum	Ōita	1988	
Bansei Tokkō Peace Museum	Kagoshima	1993	11,523*
Hotaru Museum	Kagoshima	2001	
Ataka Exchange Center	Yamaguchi	2004	3,204*
Kure Maritime Museum (Yamato Museum)	Hiroshima	2005	908,353*
Yokaren Peace Memorial Museum	Ibaraki	2010	44,528*
Usa City Peace Museum	Ōita	2013	
Tsukuba Naval Air Group Museum	Ibaraki	2013	17,809*

Sources: Table created with information in part from Anzai Science & Peace Office's "List of Peace Museums," managed by Yamane Kazuyo, Katsura Ryotaro, and Anzai Ikuro, http://asap-anzai.com/2017/05/museums-for-peace-worldwide/; and information from Kamikaze Images museum website managed by Bill Gordan, http://www.kamikazeimages.net/museums/yokaren-oita/index.htm. Additional entries and visitor data gathered from personal correspondence with museums and research assistance from Nina Zhou and Hina Tanabe.

———

Notes:

In the last column, numbers with asterisks are from the year April 2019 to March 2020; those without are from April 2017 to March 2018.

[a]Grassroots House has limited recordkeeping due to human resource limitations. The venue is frequently used for special events, such as the summer 2019 "Thinking about War and Peace" event that was attended by 409 patrons.

[b]Data from October 2018 to September 2019.

Notes

1. JAPAN'S AGING PEACE

1. Scholars have predicted the return of Japan's "world power status" since the end of the Cold War, for example: Richard Betts, "Wealth, Power, and Instability: East Asia and the United States After the Cold War," *International Security* 18, no. 3 (1993): 34–77; Christopher Layne, "The Unipolar Illusion: Why New Great Powers Will Rise," *International Security* 17, no. 4 (1993): 5–51; and Kenneth Waltz, "Structural Realism After the Cold War," *International Security* 25, no. 1 (2000): 5–41.

2. In *Blueprint for a New Japan: The Rethinking of a Nation*, trans. Lousia Rubenfien (Tokyo: Kodansha International, 1994), 94–95, prominent Japanese politician Ozawa Ichirō argued that a "normal country" must be willing to shoulder the responsibilities of the international community and cooperate fully with other nations to "build prosperous stable lives for their people." The responsibilities to the international community were mainly military-related. Chapter 2 explores the variable meaning of "normalization" to illustrate how states pursue diverse security behaviors that they would consider normal. Realist scholars read Ozawa's normal as akin to U.S. great power politics, which was far more ambitious than he intended. Inoguchi Takashi, "Japan's Ambition for Normal Statehood," in *Between Compliance and Conflict: East Asia, Latin America, and the "New" Pax Americana*, ed. by Jorge I. Dominguez and Byung-kook Kim (New York: Routledge, 2005), 135–164, provides three models of normalcy that Japan could pursue in a changing international-security environment. See also Soeya Yoshihide, Tadokoro Masayuki, and David A. Welch, eds., *Japan as a 'Normal Country'?: A Nation in Search of Its Place in the World* (Toronto: University of Toronto Press, 2012), for a collection of essays on the contested meaning of "normal country" and its impact of foreign policy.

3. Thomas Berger, "From Sword to Chrysanthemum: Japan's Culture of Anti-Militarism," *International Security* 17, no. 4 (1993): 199–150; John Dower, *Embracing Defeat: Japan in the Wake of World War II* (New York: Norton, 1999); and Momose Hiroshi, "Democracy and Pacifism in Post-War Japan," in *Hiroshima & Peace*, ed. Carol Rinnert, Omar Farouk, and Inoue Yasuhiro (Hiroshima: Keisuisha, 2010), 113–130, provide detailed analyses

of the development of Japanese peace culture and postwar pacifism. It is important to recognize Berger's acknowledgment that Japan's antimilitarism could not exist if there were a grave threat to Japanese security and if the assurance of the durability of the U.S.-Japan Alliance was in question. Berger also contends that if Japan were to continue to not contribute to international security, its ability to abide by the antimilitarism norm would diminish. Yet, contrary to claims by Kawasaki Tsuyoshi, "Post-classical Realism and Japanese Security Policy," *Pacific Review* 14, no. 2 (2001): 221–240, constructivists are well aware that the conditions of the international environment impact the durability of norms.

4.   See Thomas Berger, *Cultures of Antimilitarism: National Security in Germany and Japan* (Baltimore, MD: John Hopkins University Press, 1998); Peter J. Katzenstein, *The Culture of National Security: Norms and Identity in World Politics*, (New York: Columbia University Press, 1996); and Andrew L. Oros, *Normalizing Japan: Politics, Identity, and the Evolution of Security Practice* (Stanford, CA: Stanford University Press, 2008).

5.   Brad Glosserman, *Peak Japan: The End of Great Ambitions* (Washington, DC: Georgetown University Press, 2019), provides a sobering account of the intractable problems and poor government leadership that have led to Japan's decline.

6.   See for example, Michael Green, *Japan's Reluctant Realism: Foreign Policy Challenges in an Era of Uncertain Power* (New York: Palgrave, 2001). Inoguchi Takahashi, "Japan as a Global Ordinary Power: Its Current Phase," *Japanese Journal of Political Science* 5, no. 1 (2008) has used the term "global ordinary power" in describing Japanese security policy, which balances between the responsibilities to the U.S.-Japan alliance and the demands of changing international conditions.

7.   Andrew L. Oros, *Japan's Security Renaissance: New Policies and Politics for the Twenty-First Century* (New York: Columbia University Press, 2017). The principles of the revolution in military affairs (RMA) have diffused throughout the world as states seek to decrease the financial and human costs of warfare. Japan is no exception. I acknowledge the modernization of the JSDF according to RMA precepts in "Japan and the Revolution in Military Affairs," *Journal of Asian Security and International Affairs* 5, no. 2 (2018): 172–196.

8.   Niccolò Machiavelli, *The Prince*, trans. Daniel Donno (New York: Bantam, 1981); and Hans Morgenthau, *Politics Among Nations: The Struggle for Power and Peace* (New York: Knopf, 1948).

9.   Nicolas Onuf, *World of Our Making: Rules and Rule in Social Theory and International Relations* (Abingdon, Oxon: Routledge/Taylor & Francis, 2013), 174.

10. Peer Schouten, "Theory Talk #70: Nicolas Onuf on the Evolution of Social Constructivism, Turns in IR, and a Discipline of Our Making," Theory Talks, July 2, 2015, http://www.theory-talks.org/2015/07/theory-talk-70.html.

11. Paul Midford, *Rethinking Japanese Public Opinion and Security: From Pacifism to Realism?* (Stanford, CA: Stanford University Press, 2011) provides a comprehensive analysis of public opinion polling data concerning the JSDF and Japanese security.

12. See Hidekazu Sakai and Yoichiro Sato, *Re-Rising Japan: Its Strategic Power in International Relations*, Asian Pacific Studies, vol. 1 (New York: Peter Lang, 2018), for a collection of essays discussing various causes of Japanese remilitarization.

13. The mutual constitution of the international and domestic environments addresses the agent-structure problem. International norms diffuse to domestic audiences and domestic actors can shape international norms. Rules situate agents and allow them to interpret and act in and upon the world. Nishimura Kuniyuki, "Worlds of Our Remembering: The Agent-Structure Problem as the Search for Identity," *Conflict and Cooperation* 46, no. 1 (2011): 96–112, has argued that it is memory and identity that allow agents to navigate change in the structure. Nishimura elaborates, arguing that structures do not linearly shift from one to another, but are revised and reformulated. Hence, changes to the structure and agents can be dramatic and gradual simultaneously.

14. Nicolas Onuf, *Making Sense, Making Worlds: Constructivism in Social Theory and International Relations* (London: Routledge, 2013), 9.

15. Oros, *Japan's Security Renaissance*, 13.

16. Vincent Pouliot, "The Essence of Constructivism," *Journal of International Relations and Development* 7, no. 2 (2004): 321.

17. Mahja Zehfuss, *Constructivism in International Relations: The Politics of Reality* (Cambridge: Cambridge University Press, 2002): 194; 194; 183.

18. An illustrative example of the varying degrees of coconstitution between the material and the ideational world is the relationship among money, food, and consumption. Money has value to the extent that is agreed upon by society. Social constructs also shape what is considered food, but some objects provide little nutrition or are naturally inedible. Regardless of what society agrees upon as money or food, the biological necessity of consumption does not change. Even if an individual chooses not to eat, the human body will still react to the lack of food. Social rules concerning money can determine how much food one can purchase, and therefore, influences the individual's interaction with food, and more broadly, the way one lives.

19. Onuf, *World of Our Making*, 64.

20. Onuf, *World of Our Making*; and Nicolas Onuf, "Rule and Rules in International Relations," *Erik Castrén Institute of International Law and Human Rights* (2014): 1–23.

21. Onuf, *World of Our Making*, 47; 59.

22. Onuf, "Rule and Rules," 2–4. Onuf's use of the term "rule" is analogous to speech acts. This book uses the terms "rule," "speech act," and "norm" interchangeably because they all institute rule and differ primarily in form. For more on norms, see Friedrich Kratochwil and John G. Ruggie, "International Organization: A State of the Art on an Art of the State, *International Organization* 40, no. 4 (1986): 753–775; and Audie Klotz and Cecelia Lynch, *Strategies for Research in Constructivist International Relations* (Armonk, NY: M. E. Sharpe, 2007).

23. For more on path dependence, see Paul Pierson, *Politics in Time: History, Institutions, and Social Analysis* (Princeton, NJ: Princeton University Press, 2004).

24. Although technology decreases the need for a large military, having a large pool of available conscripts increases the flexibility and quality of a country's armed forces. This is especially true for Japan, which relies on highly skilled personnel to make up for its lack of manpower. The MOD could be more discerning with recruitment if there were a larger population to draw from. Moreover, having a large military force diminishes the need

to make strategic sacrifices. All militaries must make sacrifices due to economic and personnel constraints, Japan more so than others. For example, due to the JSDF's limited size, the MOD has had to shift troops from the northern islands to defend the Senkaku Islands in the south. Ideally, Japan would be able to patrol both areas simultaneously.

25.   Tsuchiya Motohiro (Professor, Keio University), interview by author, Tokyo, December 26, 2018. The literal Japanese term for "four persons" is *yonin*. However, the *kondankai* intentionally used *yonjin* because all four keywords use "*jin*," i.e., *mujin, shōjin, rōjin,* and *fujin*.

26.   For more on postwar education and views of the military, see John Dower, *Embracing Defeat*; Sabine Frühstück, *Uneasy Warriors: Gender, Memory, and Popular Culture in the Japanese Army* (Oakland: University of California Press, 2007).

27.   These terms are functionally equivalent and differ primarily in the degree of codification.

28.   Onuf, *World of Our Making*, 58.

29.   Defense hawks frustrated with the difficulty of enacting security reform sometimes refer to the antimilitarism culture as *heiwa boke* (peace at any price). As the policy level, peace culture has been expressed as *sōgō anzen hoshō* (comprehensive security) and *senshu bōei* (exclusively defensive-defense).

30.   Satoh Haruko, "Rethinking Security in Japan: In Search of a Post-'Postwar' Narrative," in *Japan's Strategic Challenges in a Changing Regional Environment*, ed. Purnendra Jain and Lam Peng Er (Singapore: World Scientific, 2012), 286.

31.   Gun culture is almost nonexistent in contemporary Japan. Ueda Isamu (Kōmeitō) explains the relationship between the military, guns, and society, stating, "a lot of [Japanese] people feel very alienated, they feel very nervous when they see a lot of soldiers walking around a country when you go overseas." Ueda continues, "because we have not been used to military personnel presentation on the streets, and I think because the Japanese public, in general, does not carry weapons. We don't carry guns; we don't have guns at home. So that makes us uneasy when we see weapons, even if it is for self-defense purposes. So even the police forces are not armed in many cases" (interview by author, Tokyo, October 2014). Japan has some of the strictest gun-control laws and fewest guns per capita of any OECD country. The extensive background checks, education courses, mental health evaluations, drug tests, and penalties for illegal gun use have almost ritualized the taboo nature of gun ownership.

32.   For analysis of several major Japanese polls, see Tobias Harris's public opinion aggregator, "Japan Political Pulse," https://spfusa.org/category/japan-political-pulse/.

33.   Christoph O. Meyer and Eva Strickmann, "Solidifying Constructivism: How Material and Ideational Factors Interact in European Defense," *Journal of Common Market Studies* 49, no. 1 (2011): 68.

34.   Onuf, "Rules and Rules," 1–2.

35.   Kotani Tetsuo (Senior Research Fellow, The Japan Institute of International Affairs), interview by author, Tokyo, August 2015.

36.   Onuf, "Rules and Rules," 4.

37.   For more on the rise of nationalism in Japan, see Eugene A. Matthews, "Japan's New Nationalism," *Foreign Affairs* 82, no. 6 (2003): 74–90; and Cheol Hee Park, "Historical Memory and the Resurgence of Nationalism: A Korean Perspective," in *East Asia's*

Haunted Present: Historical Memories and the Resurgence of Nationalism, ed. Tsuyoshi Hasegawa and Kazuhiko Togo (Westport, CT: Praeger Security International, 2008), 190-204.

38. Onuf, *World of Our Making*, 281.

39. Onuf, *World of Our Making*, 281.

40. Martha Finnemore and Kathryn Sikkink, "International Norm Dynamics and Political Change," *International Organization* 52, no. 4 (1998): 895, have conceptualized norm life cycles as comprising three phases: (1) norm emergence, (2) norm cascade, and (3) norm internalization. The first and second stages are divided by a norm tipping point, where a critical mass of actors adopt the norm.

41. For a concise summation of core realist assumptions, see Jeffrey W. Legro and Andrew Moravcsik, "Is Anybody Still a Realist?" *International Security* 24, no. 1 (1999): 5-55. J. Samuel Barkin, *Realist Constructivism* (Cambridge: Cambridge University Press, 2010), argues for less paradigmatic rigidity, contending that a realist/constructivist synthesis addresses shortcomings of each school of thought. Barkin also claims that constructivism takes a "much clearer position on questions of the ontological relationship between individual society than on questions of the role of power in society" (7). This assessment neglects how rules and rule are fundamentally about the role of power in society. Constructivism has a direct methodological lineage to the analysis of power through Michel Foucault's *Discipline and Punish: The Birth of Prison*, trans. Alan Sheridan (London: Penguin, 1975); and Friedrich Nietzsche's *The Genealogy of Morals*, trans. Francis Golffing (Garden City, NY: Doubleday, 1956). For more on the different variants of constructivism, some of which are more complementary with classical realism, see Emanuel Adler, "Seizing the Middle Ground: Constructivism in World Politics," *European Journal of International Relations* 3, no. 3 (1997): 319-363.

42. Even if norms erode, they influence security policy by way of their erosion.

43. See Finnemore and Sikkink, "International Norm Dynamics," 400-401, for a discussion of norm entrepreneurs.

44. Many of these movements continue to the present day. The Teshima antidumping protests resulted in a settlement in 2000, but new waste was found in the original dump site, and protestors have restarted negotiations with the national government.

45. For more on the core tenets of structural realism, see Kenneth Waltz, *Theory of International Politics* (Reading, MA: Addison-Wesley, 1979); Stephen Walt, *The Origins of Alliances* (Ithaca, NY: Cornell University Press, 1987; and John J. Mearsheimer, *The Tragedy of Great Power Politics* (New York: Norton, 2001). Although not generally associated with realist school of thought, Samuel P. Huntington, "Why International Primacy Matters," *International Security* 43, no. 1 (1993): 93-126, argues that Japan will eventually seek international primacy due to its economic strength, which would eventually challenge U.S. hegemony.

46. See Christopher Hughes, " 'Super-sizing' the DPRK Threat: Japan's Evolving Military Posture and North Korea," *Asian Survey* 49, no. 2 (2009): 291-311; Michael Green, Zach Cooper, and Center for Strategic and International Studies, *Strategic Japan: New Approaches to Foreign Policy and the U.S.-Japan Alliance* (Washington, DC: Center for Strategic & International Studies, 2014); Jeffrey W. Hornung, "Japan's Growing Hard Hedge Against China," *Asian Security* 10, no. 2 (2014): 97-122; and Christopher W. Hughes,

"Japan's 'Resentful Realism' and Balancing China's Rise," *Chinese Journal of International Politics* 9, no. 2 (2016): 109-150.

47.   Kenneth Pyle, *Japan Rising: The Resurgence of Japanese Power and Purpose* (New York: Public Affairs), 2.

48.   Daniel Kliman, *Japan's Security Strategy in the Post-9/11 World: Embracing a New Realpolitik* (Westport, CT: Praeger), 2.

49.   Kenneth Waltz, "International Politics Is Not Foreign Policy," *Security Studies* 25, no. 1 (1996): 54-57.

50.   Layne, "The Unipolar Illusion," 5-51.

51.   Miyashita Akitoshi, "Where do Norms Come From? Foundations of Japan's Postwar Pacifism," *International Relations of the Asia-Pacific* 7, no. 1 (2007): 99-120.

52.   Jennifer M. Lind, "Pacifism or Passing the Buck? Testing Theories of Japanese Security Policy," *International Security* 29, no. 1 (2004): 93.

53.   Malcolm McIntosh, *Japan Re-Armed* (London: Pinter, 1986), 121.

54.   Under the JFY 2011-2015 Special Measures Agreement, Japan spends approximately ¥24.9 billion annually.

55.   Linus Hagström and Jon Williamsson, " 'Remilitarization,' Really?: Assessing Change in Japanese Foreign Security Policy," *Asian Security* 5, no. 3 (2009): 242-272.

56.   Paul Midford, "The Logic of Reassurance and Japan's Grand Strategy," *Security Studies* 11, no. 3 (2002): 1-43.

57.   Midford, *Rethinking Japanese Public Opinion*.

58.   Kawasaki, "Postclassical Realism," 224.

59.   Kawasaki, "Postclassical Realism," 225.

60.   Richard Samuels, *Securing Japan: Tokyo's Grand Strategy and the Future of East Asia* (Ithaca, NY: Cornell University Press, 2007), 5.

61.   Samuels, *Securing Japan*, 132.

62.   Hirata Keiko, "Who Shapes the National Security Debate? Divergent Interpretations of Japan's Security Role," *Asian Affairs* 35, no. 3 (2008): 123-151.

63.   David Arase, "Japan the Active State? Security Policy After 9/11," *Asian Survey* 47, no. 4 (2007): 561.

64.   Arase, "Japan the Active State?" 574. For more on the leadership's influence on security policy, see Gavan McCormack, "Remilitarizing Japan," *New Left Review* 29 (2004): 29-46.

65.   Kevin Cooney, *Japan's Foreign Policy Maturation: A Quest for Normalcy* (New York: Routledge, 2002), 144.

66.   Sasada Hironori, "Youth and Nationalism in Japan," *SAIS Review* 26, no. 2 (2006): 109.

67.   Sasada, "Youth and Nationalism in Japan," 109.

68.   This data point has received far more attention than warranted. The controversial *New History Textbook*, for example, is used in less than 1 percent of Japanese classrooms. See Daniel Chirot, Gi-Wook Shin, and Daniel Sneider, eds., *Confronting Memories of World War II: European and Asian Legacies* (Seattle: University of Washington Press, 2014), for more on historical war memory in Asia.

69.   Kevin M. Doak, "What is a Nation and Who Belongs? National Narratives and the Ethnic Imagination in Twentieth-Century Japan," *American Historical Review* 102, no. 2 (1997): 283-309.

70. Doak, "What is a Nation and Who Belongs?" 285.

71. Doak, "What is a Nation and Who Belongs?" 300.

72. Doak, "What is a Nation and Who Belongs?" 301.

73. Japan has long sought to have Article 53 and Article 107, also known as the "enemy clauses," removed from the United Nations Charter. Some believe the articles are an embarrassing reminder of Japan's World War II history and an obstacle to obtaining a seat on the UN Security Council.

74. It is important to recognize that the constructivist approach is not limited to the analysis of good norms. One of the objectives of this book is to investigate norms that legitimatize militarism and violence in settling international disputes.

75. Berger, "From Sword to Chrysanthemum," 120.

76. Dower, *Embracing Defeat*, 45.

77. Berger, "From Sword to Chrysanthemum," 120.

78. Andrew Oros, *Normalizing Japan*, 9.

79. Izumikawa Yasuhiro, "Explaining Japanese Antimilitarism: Normative and Realist Constraints on Japan's Security Policy," *International Security* 35, no. 2 (2010): 125.

80. Norman D, Levin, Mark A. Lorell, and Arthur J. Alexander, *The Wary Warriors: Future Directions in Japanese Security Policies* (Santa Monica, California: RAND, 1993).

81. Yamaguchi provides a detailed analysis of defense spending and the time it takes to implement technology in the following video, http://www.lowyinstitute.org/news-and-media/videos/chinas-rise-americas-pivot-and-japans-choice-lt-gen-noboru-yamaguchi.

82. The GOJ releases white papers annually, midterm defense programs (MTDP) approximately every five years, and NDPGs approximately every ten years.

83. Alexander L. George and Andrew Bennett, *Case Studies and Theory Development in the Social Sciences* (Cambridge, MA: MIT Press, 2005), 206. For more on process-tracing, see Jeffrey T. Checkel, "It's the Process Stupid! Process Tracing in the Study of European and International Politics," *ARENA Working Paper Series* 26 (2005): 1–29.

84. Pierson, *Politics in Time*, 55.

85. Tobias Harris, *The Iconoclast: Shinzō Abe and the New Japan* (United Kingdom: Hurst, 2020), provides the most exhaustive English account of Abe's career.

86. Cecelia Lynch, "Critical Interpretation and Interwar Peace Movements," in *Interpretation and Method: Empirical Research Methods and the Interpretive Turn*, ed. Dvora Yanow and Peregrine Schwarz-Shea (Armonk, NY: M. E. Sharpe, 2006), 294.

87. See Jutta Weldes, "High Politics and Low Data: Globalization Discourses in Popular Culture," in *Interpretation and Method: Empirical Research Methods and the Interpretive Turn*, ed. Dvora Yanow and Peregrine Schwarz-Shea (Armonk, NY: M. E. Sharpe, 2006), for a detailed analysis of the value of low data.

88. For more on discourse analysis, see Jennifer Milliken, "The Study of Discourse Analysis in International Relations: A Critique of Research and Methods," *European Journal of International Relations* 5, no. 2 (2009): 225–254. For an example of discourse and content analysis of Japanese security politics, see Amy Catalinac, *Electoral Reform and National Security in Japan* (New York: Cambridge University Press, 2016).

89. Richard Price, *The Chemical Weapons Taboo* (Ithaca, NY: Cornell University Press, 1993): 9.

2. MULTIPLE MILITARISMS

1.   Martin Shaw, "Twenty-First Century Militarism: A Historical-Sociological Framework," in *Militarism and International Relations: Political Economy, Security, Theory*, ed. Anna Stavrianakis and Jan Selby (London: Routledge, 2012).

2.   Cynthia Enloe, *The Curious Feminist: Searching for Women in a New Age of Empire* (Berkeley, CA: University of California Press, 2004), 219.

3.   Christopher B. Otley, "Militarism and Militarization in the Public Schools, 1900–1972," *British Journal of Sociology* 29, no. 3 (1978): 322.

4.   Cynthia Enloe, *Maneuvers: The International Politics of Militarizing Women's Lives* (Berkeley, CA: University of California Press, 2000), 3.

5.   See Seungsook Moon, "Trouble with Conscription, Entertaining Soldiers: Popular Culture and the Politics of Militarized Masculinity in South Korea," *Men and Masculinities* 8, no. 1 (2005): 64–92; Vron Ware, *Military Migrants: Fighting for Your Country* (Basingstoke, UK: Palgrave Macmillan, 2012); and Gladys Ganiel, "The Legacy of the Good Friday Agreement: Northern Irish Politics, Culture and Art after 1998," in *A Gender-Balanced Approach to Transforming Cultures of Militarism in Northern Ireland*, ed. Charles I. Armstrong, David Herbert, and Jan Erik Mustad (New York: Palgrave Macmillan, 2019), 133–152.

6.   Harry Harootunian, *Overcome by Modernity: History, Culture, and Community in Interwar Japan* (Princeton, NJ: Princeton University Press, 2000).

7.   Kevin Doak, "What is a Nation?"

8.   Takashi Fujitani, *Splendid Monarchy: Power and Pageantry in Modern Japan* (Berkeley, CA: University of California Press, 1996), 11.

9.   Fujitani, *Splendid Monarchy*, 51.

10.   Mikiso Hane, *Modern Japan: A Historical Survey* (Boulder, CO: Westview, 1992) 108.

11.   Andrew Gordon, *A Modern History of Japan: From Tokugawa Times to the Present* (New York: Oxford University Press, 2003), 88.

12.   Gordon, *A Modern History of Japan*, 66.

13.   Berger, "From Sword to Chrysanthemum," 145.

14.   Hane, *Modern Japan*, 97.

15.   Gordon, *A Modern History*, 66–67.

16.   Popular fiction has grossly exaggerated the military aspects of samurai and the influence of Bushido in Japanese society. By the end of the Tokugawa period, most samurai spent their time handling bureaucratic matters.

17.   Onuf, *Making Sense*, 5.

18.   Kozo Yamamura, "Success Illgotten? The Role of Meiji Militarism in Japan's Technological Progress," *Journal of Economic History* 37, no. 1 (1977): 113.

19.   Yamamura, "Success Illgotten?" 113.

20.   Yamamura, "Success Illgotten?" 114.

21.   Yamamura, "Success Illgotten?" 120.

22.   Gordon, *A Modern History*, 116.

23.   Gordon, *A Modern History*, 117.

24.   Gordon, *A Modern History*, 117.

25.   Gordon, *A Modern History*, 182.

26. Hane, *Modern Japan*, 246.

27. Kitaoka Shinichi, "How Should We View the Path the World and Japan Took During the 20th Century? What are the Lessons We Should Draw from the Experiences in the 20th Century?" in *Toward the Abe Statement on the 70th Anniversary of the End of World War II: Lessons from the 20th Century and a Vision for the 21st Century*, trans. Tara Cannon (Tokyo: Japan Publishing Industry Foundation for Culture, 2017), 15.

28. Onuf, *World of Our Making*, 85.

29. Kusunoki Ayako, "The Early Years of the Ground Self-Defense Forces, 1945–1960," in *The Japanese Ground Self-Defense Force: Search for Legitimacy*, ed. Robert D. Eldridge and Paul Midford (New York: Palgrave Macmillan, 2017), 59. In 2018, defense spending comprised less than 2 percent of the budget.

30. Hane, *Modern Japan*, 195.

31. Gordon, *A Modern History*, 175.

32. Hane, *Modern Japan*, 254.

33. Hane, *Modern Japan*, 254.

34. Hane, *Modern Japan*, 256.

35. Hane, *Modern Japan*, 257.

36. Gordon, *A Modern History*, 175.

37. Kitaoka, "How Should We View," 16.

38. Onuf, *World of Our Making*, 277.

39. Power transition theory cannot explain Japan's behavior because few among government and military elites believed Japan was capable of winning a war against the United States. Nor was it obvious that the United States was in decline. In other words, there was not an opportunity to exploit.

40. Naoki Sakai, "Subject and Substratum: On Japanese Imperial Nationalism," *Cultural Studies* 14, nos. 3–4 (2000): 462–530.

41. Sakai, "Subject and Substratum," 463.

42. John W. Dower, *War Without Mercy: Race and Power in the Pacific War* (New York: Pantheon, 1987), 263–264.

43. Robert Eskildsen, "Of Civilization and Savages: The Mimetic Imperialism of Japan's 1874 Expedition to Taiwan," *American Historical Review* 107 (2002): 389.

44. Gordon, *A Modern History*, 188.

45. Dower, *War Without Mercy*, 215.

46. Ito Takao, "Reading Resistance: The Record of Tsunesaburo Makiguchi's Interrogation by Wartime Japan's 'Thought Police,'" *Educational Studies* 45, no. 2 (2009): 138.

47. Ito, "Reading Resistance," 143.

48. Dower, *War Without Mercy*, 248.

49. Katarzyna Joanna Cwiertka, *Modern Japanese Cuisine: Food Power and National Identity* (London: Reaktion, 2006).

50. In *Daily Life in Wartime Japan, 1940–1945* (Lawrence, KS: University Press of Kansas, 2015), Samuel H. Yamashita provides a detailed history of the full mobilization of the public for war. In explaining the militarization of children through games, Sabine Frühstück, *Playing War: Children and the Paradoxes of Modern Militarisms in Japan* (Oakland, CA:

University of California Press, 2017), provides extensive examples of the relationship between society and war.

51.   Dower, *War Without Mercy*, 203.

52.   Dower, *War Without Mercy*, 208.

53.   The exact figures concerning the amount of ianfu varies wildly, but it is almost universally accepted that the Japanese government played some role in the operation of the comfort stations. Sarah C. Soh, *The Comfort Women: Sexual Violence and Postcolonial Memory in Korea and Japan* (Chicago: University of Chicago Press, 2008); and Tom P. Le, "Negotiating in Good Faith: Overcoming Legitimacy Problems in the Japan-South Korea Reconciliation Process," *Journal of Asian Studies* 78, no. 3 (2019): 621–644, provide further detail on the comfort women system and its impact on regional relations. Chapter 4 will discuss how the legacy of World War II creates political restraints on Japanese militarism.

54.   Dower, *War Without Mercy*, 296–297.

55.   Dower, *War Without Mercy*, 298.

56.   Shibata Masako, "The Politics of Religion: Modernity, Nationhood and Education in Japan," *Intercultural Education* 19, no. 4 (2008): 355.

57.   Robert Kisala, "Japanese Religions," in *Religion in the Modern World: Traditions and Transformations*, ed. Linda Woodhead (London: Routledge, 2002), 138.

58.   Shibata, "Politics of Religion," 357–358.

59.   Kisala, "Japanese Religions," 144.

60.   Akiko Takenaka, *Yasukuni Shrine: History, Memory, and Japan's Unending Postwar* (Honolulu: University of Hawaii Press, 2015), provides an in-depth history of the Yasukuni Shrine and its place in Japanese politics and society.

61.   The Yūshūkan is maintained by the Yasukuni Shrine but is not a religious site. Since 1946, the shrine has been privately funded and operated.

62.   William P. Woodard, *The Allied Occupation of Japan 1945–1952 and Japanese Religions* (Leiden, Netherlands: E. J. Brill, 1972), quoted in Masako Shibata, "Politics of Religion," 355.

63.   Post-War Constitution of Japan (1946), Chapter 1, art. I.

64.   Takashi Fujitani, "Electronic Pageantry and Japan's 'Symbolic Emperor,' " *Journal of Asian Studies* 41, no. 4 (1992): 827.

65.   Fujitani, "Electronic Pageantry," 830.

66.   Fujitani, "Electronic Pageantry," 841.

67.   Fujitani, "Electronic Pageantry," 847.

68.   Aurel Croissant, David Kuehn, Paul Chambers, and Siegfried O. Wolf, "Beyond the Fallacy of Coup-Ism: Conceptualizing Civilian Control of the Military in Emerging Democracies," *Democratization* 5, no. 5 (2010): 955.

69.   Croissant et al., "Beyond the Fallacy of Coup-Ism," 955.

70.   Aurel Croissant, "Civilian Control Over the Military in East Asia" (EAI Fellows Program Working Paper Series 31, Ruprecht-Karls-Universität, Heidelberg, 2011), 1–62.

71.   Croissant, "Civilian Control," 5.

72.   Hane, *Modern Japan*, 248.

73.   Ingo Trauschweizer, "On Militarism," *Journal of Military History* 76, no. 2 (2012): 512.

74.   Alfred Vagts, *A History of Militarism: Civilian and Military* (New York: Meridian, 1959), 17.

75.   Vagts, *A History of Militarism*, 13.

76.   Trauschweizer, "On Militarism," 542.

77.   Trauschweizer, "On Militarism," 525.

78.   Trauschweizer, "On Militarism," 527.

79.   Shaw, "Twenty-First Century Militarism," 20.

80.   Shaw, "Twenty-First Century Militarism," 20.

81.   Richard H. Kohn, "The Danger of Militarization in an Endless 'War' on Terrorism," *Journal of Military History* 73, no. 1 (2009): 177–208.

82.   Kohn, "The Danger of Militarization," 182.

83.   David Collier and Steven Levitsky, "Democracy 'with Adjectives': Conceptual Innovation in Comparative," *World Politics* 49, no. 3 (1997): 430–451.

84.   Collier and Levitsky, "Democracy 'with Adjectives,'" 442.

85.   Colin Elman, "Explanatory Typologies in Qualitative Studies in International Politics," *International Organization* 59, no. 2 (2005): 296.

86.   Elman, "Explanatory Typologies," 296–297.

87.   Akimoto Daisuke, *The Abe Doctrine: Japan's Proactive Pacifism and Security Strategy* (Singapore: Palgrave Macmillan, 2013).

88.   Bhubhindar Singh, *Japan's Security Identity: From a Peace State to an International State* (London: Routledge, 2013).

89.   Leif-Eric Easley, "How Proactive? How Pacifist? Charting Japan's Evolving Defense Posture," *Australian Journal of International Affairs* 71, no. 1 (2017): 63–87.

90.   Shaw, "Twenty-First Century Militarism."

91.   Andrew Bacevich, *The New American Militarism: How Americans are Seduced by War* (New York: Oxford University Press, 2005), xi.

92.   Michael Man, *Incoherent Empire* (London: Verso, 2003).

93.   Adrian Lewis, *The American Culture of War: The History of U.S. Military Force from World War II to Operation Iraqi Freedom*, 3rd ed. (New York: Routledge, 2017).

94.   Pierre Hassner, "Violence and Ethics: Beyond the Reason of State Paradigm," in *Ethics and International Affairs: Extent and Limits*, ed. Jean-Marc Coicaud and Daniel Warner (New York: United Nations University Press, 2001), 84–102.

3. WHO WILL FIGHT? THE JSDF'S DEMOGRAPHIC CRISES

1.   Howard Zinn, *A People's History of the United States* (New York: Harper & Row, 1980).

2.   James William Gibson, *The Perfect War: Technowar in Vietnam* (Boston: Atlantic Monthly Press, 2000), 23.

3.   Bjørn Møller, "The Revolution in Military Affairs: Myth or Reality?" *Peace Research Abstracts* 40, no. 5 (2003): 30.

4.   Government Official, interview by author, Zoom, June 2020.

5.   For more on RDT&E, see Ashley J. Tellis, Janice Bially, Christopher Layne, and Melissa McPherson, *Measuring National Power in the Postindustrial Age* (Santa Monica, CA: RAND, 2000).

6. The U.S. Department of Defense, *Dictionary of Military Terms* (New York: Skyhorse, 2009), 426, defines "power projection" as "the ability of a nation to apply all or some of its elements of national power—political, economic, informational, or military—by rapidly and effectively deploying and sustaining forces in and from multiple dispersed locations to respond to crises, to contribute to deterrence, and to enhance regional stability."

7. Thomas Robert Malthus, *An Essay on the Principle of Population: And a Summary View of the Principle Population*, ed. Andrew Flew (London: Penguin, 1988); and Garrett Hardin, "The Tragedy of the Commons," *Science* 162, no. 3859 (1968): 1243-1248.

8. Mark Haas, "A Geriatric Peace? The Future of U.S. Power in a World of Aging Populations," *International Security* 32, no. 1 (2007): 112-147.

9. Susan Yoshihara and Douglas A. Sylvia, *Population Decline and the Remaking of Great Power Politics* (Washington, DC: Potomac, 2011). Richard Jackson and Neil Howe, *The Graying of the Great Powers: Demography and Geopolitics in the 21st Century* (Washington, DC: Center for Strategic and International Studies, 2008), focus their attention on the developing world, arguing demographic transitions may lead to increased instability.

10. Valerie M. Hudson and Andrea Den Boar, "A Surplus of Men, a Deficit of Peace: Security and Sex Ratios in Asia's Largest State," *International Security* 26, no. 4 (2002): 5-38; and Max Abrahms, "What Terrorists Really Want: Terrorist Motives and Counterterrorism Strategy," *International Security* 32, no. 4 (2008): 78-105.

11. Ministry of Internal Affairs and Communications, Statistics Bureau of Japan. Between 1940 and 1945, the Japanese population declined by 541,625, or 0.7 percent. This decline can be attributed to World War II. Following the war, Japan, like many other industrialized countries, underwent massive economic growth fueled partly by a rapid increase in population size.

12. Yasukawa Masaaki and Hirooka Keijiro, "Estimates of Population Size and of the Birth- and Death-Rates in Japan, 1865-1920," *Keio Economic Studies* 11, no. 2 (1974): 41-66.

13. Government Official, interview by author, Zoom, June 2020

14. Ministry of Defense, "2020-Nendo Kamihanki no Kinkyū Hasshin Jisshi Jōkyō ni Tsuite" (About the Implementation of Scrambles in the First Half of FY2020), October 9, 2020.

15. Japan Coast Guard, "*Senkakushotō Shūhen Kaiiki ni Okeru Chūgoku Kōsentō no Dōkō to Wagakuni no Taishō*" (Trends in Chinese Government and Other Vessels in the Waters Surrounding the Senkaku Islands and Japan's Response), December 7, 2020. From December 2008 to November 2020, 940 vessels have entered Japan's territorial sea and 6,736 vessels have entered Japan's contiguous zone.

16. Suga Yoshihide, "Press Conference by the Chief Cabinet Secretary," Prime Minister of Japan and His Cabinet (website), June 13, 2017.

17. Self-Defense Forces Law, e-Gov, n.d.

18. According to Article 3 of the SDF Law, the JSDF major primary mission is the defense of Japan. This is followed by its primary mission, which is the maintenance of public order. The primary mission includes disaster relief, earthquake prevention dispatch, minesweeping, and several other traditional and nontraditional security activities. In practice, the JSDF is deployed far more often and in greater scale to nontraditional security missions. The JSDF also has an additional primary mission based on legislation other

than the SDF law, which includes international disaster relief and international peace cooperation activities. However, this primary mission cannot interfere with the other two primary missions. The JSDF's secondary mission includes engineering, education and training, cooperation for major athletic games, cooperation for Antarctic observation, transport of national guests, and bomb disposal.

19. Tomoyuki Sasaki, *Japan's Postwar Military and Civil Society: Contesting a Better Life* (London: Bloomsbury Academic, 2017).

20. Yoshizaki Tomonori, "The Military's Role in Disaster Relief Operations: A Japanese Perspective," in *International Symposium on Security Affairs. 14th Symposium* (Tokyo: National Diet Library, 2011), 71–89.

21. Yoshizaki, "The Military's Role," 71.

22. MOD Official, interview by author, Tokyo, September 2018. The MOD official notes that the military now has "a voice in national security policy formation," and the role of providing policy oversight by civilian officials has equally grown, however it is not a "zero sum game." Within their division, there are multiple military officers that help devise security policy. In a sense, *naikyoku* (internal bureau) are "in and of themselves, hybrid organizations."

23. Japan has the eleventh largest population in the world.

24. Ratio of military to civilian per 1,000 without including reserve forces: China (1.44:1,000); Japan (1.93:1,000); North Korea (50.21:1,000); Russia (6.25:1,000); South Korea (12.25:1,000); and Taiwan (9.10:1,000).

25. One government official concludes,

> We are pursuing two purposes with one policy. Improving the environment for women to work. Encouraging them to go to the workplace with a combination of some kind of financial assistance to families. On one side, it is a population policy. The other side is to bring more workforce to the labor market. Which is not precisely a policy aimed at increasing the birthrate. We are pursuing two goals. The public may be confused. The public may doubt how serious the government is about turning the birthrate. In economics theory, you can only achieve one objective with one policy. You need two policies for two objectives . . . If we are to be more serious about the population problem, a kind of single-mindedness is needed.
>
> Interview by Author, Zoom, June 2020.

26. Matsutani Akihiko, *Shrinking-Population Economics: Lessons from Japan*, trans. Brian Miller (Tokyo: International House of Japan, 2006), 4–5.

27. The 1.57 shock occurred in 1989 when Japan's fertility rate reached a record low. The fertility rate dropped twenty-one times over the next thirty years.

28. Ministry of Internal Affairs and Communications, *Statistical Handbook of Japan 2020*, 2020.

29. Oshio Takashi, "The Declining Birthrate in Japan," *Japan Economic Currents*, no. 69 (2008): 4.

30. Leonard Schoppa, "Japan's Declining Population: The Perspective of Japanese Women on the 'Problem' and the 'Solutions,'" in *Asia Program Special Report*, ed. Mark Mohr (Washington, DC: Woodrow Wilson Center for Scholars, 2008), 8.

31. Government Official, interview by author, Zoom, June 2020.

32. "Sexist Heckling Occurred at April Diet Committee Meeting: Female Diet Member," *Japan Times*, July 4, 2014.

33. Yashiro Naohiro (Economist, Showa Women's University), interview by author, Tokyo, October 2018.

34. Schoppa, "Japan's Declining Population," 10.

35. Sasaki Kaori, "Putting Families First," in *Reimagining Japan: The Quest for a Future that Works*, ed. Clay Chandler, Heang Chhor, and Brian Salsberg (San Francisco, CA: VIZ Media, 2011), 348.

36. Atoh Makoto, *Gendai Jinkōgaku, Shōshi Kōreishakai no Kiso Chishiki* (Contemporary Demography, Basic Knowledge on Low Fertility and Aging) (Tokyo: Nihon Hyōronsha, 2000). Atoh Makoto, "Very Low Fertility in Japan and Value Change Hypotheses," *Review of Population and Social Policy*, no. 10 (2001): 1–21, provides wide-reaching analysis of the various norms that lead to uneven household labor, and thus low fertility rates, such as views on sexuality, marriage, divorce, and childrearing.

37. Yashiro Naohiro, "Social Implications of Demographic Change in Japan," *Conference Series-Federal Reserve Bank of Boston*, no. 46 (2001): 299. For more on work-life balance and gender inequality, see Komuro Yoshie, "Japan's Next Balancing Act," in *Reimagining Japan: The Quest for a Future that Works*, ed. Clay Chandler, Heang Chhor, and Brian Salsberg (San Francisco, CA: VIZ Media, 2011), 343–346.

38. Yashiro Naohiro, interview by author, Tokyo, October 2018.

39. Yashiro, "Social Implications," 297.

40. Michael Strausz, *Help (Not) Wanted* (New York: SUNY Press, 2019), 7.

41. Strausz, *Help (Not) Wanted*, 9.

42. Ministry of Internal Affairs and Communications, *Statistical Handbook of Japan 2020*, 2020.

43. For more on exam passage rates and the difficulties faced by migrant nurses, see Ohno Shun, Setyowati Setyowati, Hirano O. Yoko, and Krisna Yetti, "Indonesian Nurses' Challenges for Passing the National Board Examination for Registered Nurse in Japanese: Suggestions for Solutions," *Southeast Asian Studies* 49, no. 4 (2012): 629–642.

44. Tabuchi Hiroko, "Japan Keeps a High Wall for Foreign Labor, *New York Times*, January 2, 2011.

45. JASSO, "International Students in Japan 2019," January 2019.

46. Strausz, *Help (Not) Wanted*, 135.

47. Strausz, *Help (Not) Wanted*, 135.

48. Miriam K. Kadia, "Repatriation But Not 'Return': A Japanese Brazilian Dekasegi Goes Back to Brazil," *Asia-Pacific Journal: Japan Focus* 13, no. 14 (2015): 1–15.

49. Tabuchi Hiroko, "Japan Pays Foreign Workers to Go Home," *New York Times*, April 22, 2009.

50. Sakanaka Hidenori, "The Future of Japan's Immigration Policy: A Battle Diary," trans. Andrew J. I. Taylor, *Asia-Pacific Journal: Japan Focus* 5, no. 4 (2005). In *Japan as an Immigration Nation: Demographic Change, Economic Necessity, and the Human Community Concept*, trans. Robert D. Eldridge and Graham B. Leonard (Lanham, MD: Lexington Books, 2020), Sasanaka argues only through sweeping immigration reform can Japan solve the population crisis.

51. Robert Dekle, *Land of the Setting Sun? Prosperity in Depth: Japan* (London: Legatum Institute, 2012), 9.

52. Sakanaka, "Future of Japan's Immigration," 4.

53. Yashiro Naohiro, interview by author, Tokyo, October 2018.

54. Matsutani, *Shrinking-Population Economics*, 1.

55. National Institute of Population and Social Security Research, "Population Projections for Japan," 2017.

56. For more on the impact of the aging population on healthcare, industry, and society, see Shiraishi Katsutaka and Matoba Nobutaka, eds., *Depopulation, Deindustrialisation & Disasters* (Cham, Switzerland: Palgrave Macmillan, 2019).

57. As much as Japan has a reputation as an export nation, domestic consumer spending comprises over 50 percent of the GDP.

58. Dekle, *Land of the Setting Sun*, 5.

59. Sasaki, *Japan's Postwar Military*.

60. Sasaki, *Japan's Postwar Military*.

61. Maeda Tetsuo, *The Hidden Army: The Untold Story of Japan's Military Forces*, ed. David J. Kenney, trans. Steven Karpa (Chicago: Edition Q, 1995), 260.

62. Morimoto Satoshi (Former Minister of Defense), interview by author, Tokyo, October 2018.

63. Linda Sieg and Miyazaki Ami, "Aging Japan: Military Recruiters Struggle as Applicant Pool Dries Up," *Reuters*, September 19, 2018.

64. United Nations, *World Urbanization Prospects* (Washington, DC: United Nations, 2014).

65. Tokuchi Hideshi (former Vice-Minister of Defense for International Affairs), interview by author, Tokyo, December 2018.

66. U.S. Bureau of Labor Statistics, "Labor Force Statistics from the Current Population Survey," May 30, 2020.

67. Statistics Bureau of Japan, "Labor Force Survey: Population Aged 15 Years Old and Over," e-Stat, January 31, 2020.

68. Ministry of Defense, *Defense of Japan* (Tokyo: Ministry of Defense, 2010), 406.

69. Self-Defense Force member (staff officer, ASDF), interview by author, Tokyo, October 2018.

70. The previous age band for recruits was eighteen to twenty-six.

71. Ministry of Defense, *Defense of Japan* (Tokyo: Ministry of Defense, 2019), 406.

72. Ministry of Defense, *Defense of Japan* (Tokyo: Ministry of Defense, 2020), 407.

73. Yamaguchi Noboru (Lieutenant General, GSDF, retired), interview by author, Tokyo, October 2018.

74. Susan Yoshihara, "The Setting Sun? Strategic Implications of Japan's Demographic Transition," in *Population Decline and the Remaking of Great Power Politics*, ed. Susan Yoshihara and Douglas A. Sylvia (Washington, DC: Potomac, 2012).

75. Ministry of Defense, *Defense of Japan* (Tokyo: Ministry of Defense, various years). Data for 2009 is excluded due to unavailability.

76. World Values Survey, 1981, 1990, 1995, 1999, 2010, 2017. The exact wording of the question is, "of course, we all hope that there will not be another war, but if it were to come to that, would you be willing to fight for your country?"

77. Tsukamoto Katsuya (Senior Research Fellow, National Institute for Defense Studies), interview by author, Tokyo, February 2015.

78. The most undesirable jobs in Japan are commonly referred to as "3K," or "3D" in English—*kitani, kiken, kitsui* (dirty, dangerous, and demanding). Members in the JSDF are proud of their work. However, their experiences are unknown to the general public, and thus, stereotypes of military service remain strong deterrents for potential recruits.

79. Michael Hoffman, "Japan Faces Up to the Prospect of Losing a Middle-Class War," *Japan Times*, April 14, 2018.

80. Sasaki, *Japan's Postwar Military*.

81. Tokuchi Hideshi, interview by author, Tokyo, December 2018.

82. Ono Keishi (Director, International Exchange and Libraries, National Institute for Defense Studies), interview by author, Tokyo, October 2018.

83. Morimoto Satoshi, interview by author, Tokyo, October 2018.

84. Robert D. Eldridge, *Jinkō Genshō to Jieitai* (Population Decline and the Self-Defense Forces) (Tokyo: Fusōsha Shinso, 2019), provides the most up-to-date analysis of the impact of population decline on the JSDF. Eldridge describes the decreasing competitiveness of JSDF salaries and perks, such as JSDF personnel having to pay for toiletries and utilities, as making the occupation less desirable.

85. Senior Official (Ministry of Defense), interview by author, Tokyo, October 2018.

86. Morimoto Satoshi, interview by author, Tokyo, October 2018.

87. Morimoto Satoshi, interview.

88. Officer (ASDF), interview by author, email, July 2020.

89. Shimoyachi Nao, "SDF Members Pursue Sense of Mission," *Japan Times*, February 5, 2004.

90. Ministry of Defense, "*Reiwa 2-Nendo Jiētai Junshoku Taiin Tsuitōshiki*" (2020 Memorial Ceremonies for JSDF Members Who Died on Duty), November 2020.

91. *Japan Press Weekly*, "40 SDF Members Dispatched Overseas Commit Suicide," July 9, 2014.

92. See U.S. Department of Veterans Affairs, "Suicide Among Veterans and Other Americans 2001–2014," Office of Mental Health and Suicide Prevention, August 3, 2016, for additional data on suicide in the U.S. Armed Forces.

93. Women can voluntarily serve in the armed forces but are not conscripted.

94. The Chinese Constitution (Article 55) states, "It is the sacred obligation of every citizen of the People's Republic of China to defend the motherland and resist aggression. It is the honorable duty of citizens of the People's Republic of China to perform military service and join the militia in accordance with the law."

95. Frühstück, *Uneasy Warriors*, 117.

96. For examples of MSDF recruitment ads, see: https://www.youtube.com/watch?v=rjHm-LAiCPDo and https://www.youtube.com/watch?v=k4WEGUuq_ck. For more on *moe* and the JSDF, see Yamamura Takayoshi, "Cooperation Between Anime Producers and the Japan Self-Defense Force: Creating Fantasy and/or Propaganda?" *Journal of War & Culture Studies* 12, no. 1 (2019): 8–23.

97. In "Women as Helpmates: The Japan Self-Defense Forces and Gender," *Critical Military Studies* (2018) and "Normalizing the Japan Self-Defense Forces via Marriage," *Journal of War & Culture Studies* (2019), Emma Dalton utilizes feminist theory to convincingly

demonstrate how matchmaking and marriage mobilizes women to be willing and unwilling supporters of the JSDF and the sanitization of its image.

98. Obinata Sumio, "The Establishment of the 'Imperial Army' and the Structure of Masculinity," *Jenda Shigaku* 2 (2006): 21–33.

99. Lisa Yoneyama, *Hiroshima Traces: Time, Space and the Dialects of Memory* (Berkeley: University of California Press, 1991), 191.

100. See Ministry of Defense, https://www.mod.go.jp/j/publication/book/mamor/ and https://www.mod.go.jp/j/kids/comic/index.html for a list of issues.

101. Staff Officer (ASDF), interview by author, Tokyo, October 2018.

102. Eric Schmitt, "Iraq-Bound Troops Confront Rumsfeld Over Lack of Armor," *New York Times*, December 8, 2004, https://www.nytimes.com/2004/12/08/international/middleeast/iraqbound-troops-confront-rumsfeld-over-lack-of.html.

103. Jonathan C. Goff (Colonel, USMC, U.S. Marine liaison to the JSDF), interview by author, Tokyo, August 2014.

104. Ministry of Defense, *Defense of Japan* (Tokyo: Ministry of Defense, various years). Data from 2009 is excluded due to unavailability.

105. Ministry of Defense, *Defense of Japan* (Tokyo: Ministry of Defense, 2011).

106. Ministry of Defense, *Defense of Japan* (Tokyo: Ministry of Defense, 2018).

107. Ministry of Defense, "Defense Programs and Budget of Japan," August 2019.

108. Harold Lasswell, *Politics: Who Gets What, When, How* (New York: Whittlesey House, 1936).

109. David Easton, *A Systems Analysis of Political Life* (New York: John Wiley & Sons, 1965).

110. Morimoto Satoshi, interview by author, Tokyo, October 2018.

111. Sato Fumika, "A Camouflaged Military: Japan Self-Defense Forces and Globalized Gender Mainstreaming," *Asia-Pacific Journal* 10, no. 3 (2012): 3.

112. Fumika, "A Camouflaged Military," 9.

113. Maya Eichler, "Militarized Masculinities in International Relations." *Brown Journal of World Affairs* 21, no. 1 (2014): 81.

114. Marcia Kovitz, "The Roots of Military Masculinity," in *Military Masculinities: Identity and the State*, ed. Paul R. Higate (Westport, CT.: Praeger, 2003): 1–14.

115. Sabine Frühstück, "The Modern Girl as Militarist: Female Soldiers in and Beyond Japan's Self-Defense Forces," in *Modern Girls on the Go: Gender, Mobility and Labor in Japan*, ed. Alisa Freedman, Laura Miller, and Christine R. Yano (Stanford, CA: Stanford University Press, 2013), 139.

116. Yashiro Naohiro, interview by author, Tokyo, October 2018.

117. Stephen Roach, "Asia's Sleeping Giant," in *Reimagining Japan: The Quest for a Future that Works*, ed. Clay Chandler, Heang Chhor, and Brian Salsberg (San Francisco, CA: VIZ Media, 2011), 100.

118. Dekle, *Land of the Setting Sun*, 7.

119. Dekle, *Land of the Setting Sun*, 7.

120. International Monetary Fund, "World Economic Outlook Database." www.imf.org.

121. Bank of Japan, "Bank of Japan Accounts December 10, 2020." https://www.boj.or.jp/en/statistics/boj/other/acmai/release/2020/ac201210.htm/.

122. Yashiro Naohiro, interview by author, Tokyo, October 2018.

123.   Morimoto Satoshi, interview by author, Tokyo, October 2018.

124.   Sato Fumika, "Why Have the Japanese Self-Defense Forces Included Women? The State's 'Nonfeminist Reasons,'" in *Militarized Currents: Toward a Decolonized Future in Asia and the Pacific*, ed. Shigematsu Setsu and Keith L. Camacho (Minneapolis: University of Minnesota Press), 251–276.

125.   Yashiro Naohiro, interview by author, Tokyo, October 2018.

4. TECHNICAL-INFRASTRUCTURAL CONSTRAINTS AND THE CAPACITY CRISES

1.   Ministry of Defense, *Defense of Japan* (Tokyo: Ministry of Defense, 2019), 548–559.

2.   Karl Gustafsson, Linus Hagström, and Ulv Hanssen, "Japan's Pacifism is Dead," *Survival* 60, no 6. (2018): 137–158; Christopher Hughes, *Japan's Re-Emergence as a "Normal" Military Power* (Oxford: Oxford University Press, 2004); Matthews, "Japan's New Nationalism"; and Denny Roy, "The Sources and Limits of Sino-Japanese Tensions," *Survival* 47, no. 2 (2005): 191–214.

3.   Hagström and Williamsson, "Remilitarization," 246.

4.   Nishida Jun (Ministry of Foreign Affairs), interview by author, Tokyo, February 2014.

5.   Lind, "Pacifism or Passing the Buck," 93.

6.   I would like to thank Paul Midford for this observation.

7.   Senior Official (Ministry of Defense), interview by author, Tokyo, October 2018.

8.   Ono Keishi, interview by author, Tokyo, October 2018. According to several experts and JSDF personnel interviewed for this book, there has been difficulty procuring parts for fighter aircraft, which has led to decreased flight rates.

9.   Ono Keishi (Director, International Exchange and Libraries, National Institute for Defense Studies), interview by author, Tokyo, October 2018. Ono, however, concludes that long-term costs of AI and robotics may be prohibitively expensive, stating, "The problem is whether we can maintain the purchasing power of the AI introduced in expensive equipment, and as the current situation is concerned, I think I have to say that the future of defense procurement in Japan is not so rosy. So far, more than half of equipment purchasing money is poured into system maintenance and renewing, not on the purchase of new equipment."

10.   Ono Keishi, interview by author, Tokyo, October 2018.

11.   Government Official, interview by author, Zoom, June 2020.

12.   Tokuchi Hideshi (former Vice-Minister of Defense for International Affairs), interview by author Tokyo, December 2018.

13.   See Sado Akihiro, *The Self-Defense Forces and Postwar Politics in Japan*, trans. Noda Makito (Tokyo: Japan Publishing Industry Foundation for Culture, 2017), for a detailed history of the JSDF, community relations, and bases. For more on community–base politics, see Alexander Cooley, *Base Politics: Demographic Change and the U.S. Military Overseas* (Ithaca, NY: Cornell University Press, 2008); Inoue Masamichi, *Okinawa and the U.S. Military: Identity Making in the Age of Globalization* (New York: Columbia University Press, 2017); and Katherine Moon, *Sex Among Allies: Military Prostitution in U.S.-Korea Relations* (New York: Columbia University Press, 1997).

14. Jonathan C. Goff (USMC, U.S. Marine liaison to the JSDF), interview by author, Tokyo, August 2014.

15. Staff Officer (ASDF), interview by author, Tokyo, October 2018.

16. Ministry of Defense, "Defense Programs and Budget of Japan," August 2019.

17. Staff officer (ASDF), interview by author, Tokyo, October 2018.

18. Ministry of Defense, "Defense Related Budget Request for JFY 2019;" and Ministry of Defense, "Defense Programs and Budget of Japan," August 2019.

19. Base commander (GSDF), interview by author, Tokyo, October 2018.

20. Per Christensson, "Firmware Definition," TechTerms, 2006.

21. To acquire combat experience would mean that deterrence and diplomacy have failed. The U.S.-Japan Alliance and ODA intend to avoid the scenarios where combat experience can be gained.

22. Captain (U.S. Navy), interview by author, January 2018.

23. Staff Officer (ASDF), interview by author, Tokyo, October 2018.

24. Ishizuka Katsumi, "Japan and UN Peace Operations," *Japanese Journal of Political Science* 5, no. 1 (2004): 67-86; and Aurelia G. Mulgan, "International Peace Keeping and Japan's Role: Catalyst or Cautionary Tale?" *Asian Survey* 35, no. 12 (1995): 1102-1117.

25. Ishizuka Katsumi, "Japan's Policy Towards UN Peacekeeping Operations," *International Peacekeeping* 12, no. 1 (2005): 153-154.

26. Lionel T. Fatton, " 'Japan is Back': Autonomy and Balancing Amidst an Unstable China-US-Japan Triangle," *Asia & the Pacific Policy Studies* 5, no. 2 (2018): 274.

27. Ministry of Foreign Affairs, "Japan's Contribution to UN Peacekeeping Operations (PKO): Outline of Japan's International Peace Contribution," May 14, 2015.

28. Yamaji Hideki (Director of Space and Maritime Security Policy Division), interview by author, Tokyo, May 2017.

29. Oros, *Normalizing Japan*, 90.

30. Ministry of Defense, "Strategy on Defense Production and Technological Bases: Toward Strengthening the Bases to Support Defense Forces and 'Proactive Contribution to Peace,' " June 2014, 1-30.

31. "Top 100 for 2019," *Defense News*, accessed December 16, 2020.

32. Mari Yamaguchi, "Japan Seeks to Expand Arms Deals with Southeast Asia," *Associated Press*, June 13, 2017.

33. Watanabe Tsuneo (Senior Research Fellow, Sasakawa Peace Foundation), interview by author, Tokyo, May 2017.

34. Kubota Yukari, "Japan's Industrial Base in Danger of Collapse," *AJISS*, no. 90 (2010): 1-4.

35. Kubota, "Japan's Industrial Base," 1-4.

36. Kubota, "Japan's Industrial Base," 1-4.

37. "Toshiba Seeks 9.3 Bil. Yen from Defense Ministry over F-13 Modifying," *Mainichi Daily News*, October 31, 2011; and "Toshiba Hit with F-15 Countersuit," *Japan Times*, November 27, 2012.

38. Morimoto Satoshi (former Minister of Defense), interview by author, Tokyo, October 2018.

39. Tokuchi Hideshi, interview by author, Toyoko, December 2018.

40. Masuda Masayuki (Senior Fellow, National Institute for Defense Studies), interview by author, Tokyo, May 2017.

41. Kotani Tetsuo (Senior Fellow, National Institute for Defense Studies), interview by author, Tokyo, August 2015.

42. David McNeill, "Japanese Scientists Fight U.S.-Style Ties Between Universities and Military," *Chronicle of Higher Education*, March 23, 2015.

43. David Cryanoski, "Japanese Scientists Call for Boycott of Military Research," *Nature*, April 6, 2017.

44. Science Council of Japan, "Statement on Research for Military Security," March 24, 2017.

45. Onuf, *World of Our Making*, 98.

46. McNeill, "Japanese Scientists."

47. Official (Ministry of Defense), interview by author, Tokyo, May 2017.

48. Tokuchi Hideshi, interview by author, Tokyo, December 2018.

49. Professor, interview by author, Tokyo, February 2015.

50. Morimoto Satoshi, interview by author, Tokyo, October 2018.

51. See appendix A for a summary of the Three Principles on Arms Exports, 1976 Principles, 2014 Principles, and related laws.

52. Upper House Diet member (LDP), interview by author, Tokyo, September 2014.

53. Craig Agena (colonel, U.S. Army), interview by author, Tokyo, April 2014.

54. Nishida Jun, interview by author, Tokyo, August 2014.

55. Fujisaki Ichirō (former Japanese Ambassador to the United States), interview by author, Tokyo, February 2015.

56. Craig Agena (Colonel, U.S. Army, retired), interview by author, email, August 2015.

57. Satake Tomohiko (Senior Fellow, National Institute for Defense Studies), interview by author, Tokyo, February 2015.

58. Ueda Isamu (Kōmeitō), interview by author, Tokyo, October 2014.

59. Jonathan C. Goff (USMC, U.S. Marine liaison to the JSDF), interview by author, Tokyo, August 2014.

60. Masuda Masayuki, interview by author, Tokyo, May 2017.

61. Haraguchi Kazuhiro (Democratic Party of Japan), interview by author, Tokyo, May 2017.

62. Watanabe Tsuneo, interview by author, Tokyo, May 2017.

63. Tsuruoka Michito (Professor, Keio University), interview by author, Tokyo, May 2017.

64. Executive (American defense contractor), interview by author, telephone, January 2018.

65. Yashiro Naohiro (Economist, Showa Women's University), interview by author, Tokyo, October 2018.

66. Staff Officer (ASDF), interview by author, Tokyo, October 2018.

67. Tsukamoto Katsuya (Senior Research Fellow, National Institute for Defense Studies), interview by author, Tokyo, February 2015.

68. Morimoto Satoshi, interview by author, Tokyo, October 2018.

69. Mitsubishi Heavy Industries, *MHI Report 2018* (Tokyo: Mitsubishi Heavy Industries Group, 2018), 1–76.

70. Stephen Biddle, "Explaining Military Outcomes," in *Creating Military Power: The Sources of Military Effectiveness*, ed. Risa A. Brooks and Elizabeth A. Stanley (Stanford, CA: Stanford University Press): 208.

71. Captain (U.S. Navy), interview by author, Skype, January 2019.

72. Senior Official (Ministry of Defense), interview by author, Tokyo, October 2018.

5. ANTIMILITARISM AND THE POLITICS OF RESTRAINT

1. Onuf, *World of Our Making*, 116.
2. Yamaji Hideki (Director of Space and Maritime Security Policy Division), interview by author, Tokyo, May 2017.
3. Yamaji Hideki, interview by author, Tokyo, May 2017.
4. Midford, *Rethinking Japanese Public Opinion*, 32.
5. Roni Sarig, "Sadako Sasaki and Anne Frank: Myths in Japanese and Israeli Memory of the Second World War," in *War and Militarism in Modern Japan: Issues of History and Identity*, ed. Guy Podeler (Folkestone: Global Oriental, 2009), 167.
6. Kurino Ohtori, "Challenge and Dilemma for Peace Movements in Japan," *Hiroshima Peace Science* 10 (1987): 167.
7. Kawasaki Akira (Peace Boat), interview by author, Tokyo, May 2014.
8. Hane, *Modern Japan*, 341.
9. Gordon, *A Modern History*, 225.
10. Dower, *Embracing Defeat*, 199.
11. Midford, *Rethinking Japanese Public Opinion*, 30.
12. Midford, *Rethinking Japanese Public Opinion*, 30.
13. Dower, *War Without Mercy*, 307.
14. Tanaka Terumi, interview by author, Tokyo, February 2015.
15. Dower, *Embracing Defeat*, 489.
16. Dower, *Embracing Defeat*, 489.
17. Robert Eskildsen, "Of Civilization"; Mark E. Caprio, *Japanese Assimilation Policies in Colonial Korea, 1910–1945* (Seattle: University of Washington Press, 2009); and Allen S. Christy, "The Making of Imperial Subjects in Okinawa," *Positions: East Asia Cultures Critique* 1, no. 3 (1993): 607-639.
18. Fujisaki Ichirō (former Japanese Ambassador to the United States), interview by author, Tokyo, February 2015.
19. Fujisaki Ichirō, interview by author, Tokyo, February 2015.
20. Berger, "From Sword to Chrysanthemum," 174.
21. Momose, "Democracy," 115.
22. Hane, *Modern Japan*, 338.
23. Midford, *Rethinking Japanese Public Opinion*, 51.
24. Berger, "From Sword to Chrysanthemum," 136.
25. Dower, *Embracing Defeat*, 196.
26. Anne Allison, *Millennial Monsters: Japanese Toys and the Global Imagination* (Berkeley: University of California Press, 2006), 45.
27. Hirano Keiji, "Legacy of 1960 Protest Movement Lives On," *Japan Times*, July 11, 2010.
28. Kurino, "Challenge and Dilemma," 171.
29. Jon Mitchell, "Battle Scars: Okinawa and the Vietnam War," *Japan Times*, March 7, 2015.
30. Nakashima Takeshi, interview by author, Hiroshima, October 2014.
31. Sorpong Peou, *Peace and Security in the Asia-Pacific: Theory and Practice* (Santa Barbara, CA: Praeger Security International, 2010), 147.
32. Midford, *Rethinking Japanese Public Opinion*, 180.
33. Diet Member, interview by author, Tokyo, September 2014.

34. Tsukamoto Katsuya (Senior Research Fellow, National Institute for Defense Studies), interview by author, Tokyo, February 2015.
35. Onuf, *World of Our Making*, 127.
36. Dower, *Embracing Defeat*, 250.
37. RENGO Officer, interview by author, Tokyo, August 2014.
38. Kawai Kimiaki (Director of Peace and Human Rights, Soka Gakkai International), interview by author, Tokyo, May 2014.
39. Chalmers A. Johnson, *Japan in Search of a "Normal" Role* (La Jolla, CA: IGCC, 1992), 24.
40. Dower, *Embracing Defeat*, 249.
41. Cabinet Office polls are retrieved from: https://survey.gov-online.go.jp/index.html.
42. Cabinet Office, "Overview in the Public Opinion on Diplomacy," December 2018. https://gov-online.go.jp/eng/pdf/summaryg18.pdf.
43. Steve Leeper (former Chairperson of the Hiroshima Peace Culture Foundation), interview by author, Hiroshima, April 2014.
44. Komizō Yasuyoshi (Chairperson of the Hiroshima Peace Culture Foundation), interview by author, Hiroshima, April 2014.
45. Komizō Yasuyoshi, interview by author, Hiroshima, April 2014.
46. Kusunoki, "The Early Years," 60.
47. Onuf, *World of Our Making*, 214.
48. Kawasaki, "Postclassical Realism," 223.
49. Midford, "Logic of Reassurance," 33.
50. Louis D. Hayes, *Japan and the Security of Asia* (Lanham, MD: Lexington Books, 2001), 183.
51. Komizō Yasuyoshi, interview by author, Hiroshima, April 2014.
52. Nishida Jun (Ministry of Foreign Affairs), interview by author, Tokyo, August 2014.
53. Nishida Jun, interview by author, Tokyo, August 2014.
54. Pew Research Center, "Japanese Public's Mood Rebounding, Abe Highly Popular: China and South Korea Very Negative Toward Japan," July 11, 2013.
55. Pew Research Center, "How Asians View Each Other," July 14, 2014, https://www.pewresearch.org/global/2014/07/14/chapter-4-how-asians-view-each-other/.
56. Genron NPO, "The 15th Joint Public Opinion Poll: Japan-China Public Opinion Survey 2019," October 2019; and Genron NPO, "The 7th Japan-South Korea Joint Opinion Poll: Analysis Report on Comparative Data," June 2019.
57. Pew Research Center, "How Asians View Each Other."
58. Genron NPO, "The 15th Joint Public Opinion Poll."
59. Nagashima Akihisa (Democratic Party of Japan), interview by author, Tokyo, June 2014.
60. Nishida Jun, interview by author, Tokyo, August 2014.
61. Abe Shinzō, "Press Conference During His Visit to Southeast Asia," Prime Minister of Japan and His Cabinet, July 27, 2013.
62. Abe, "Press Conference," July 27, 2013.
63. Abe Shinzō, "Press Conference," Prime Minister of Japan and His Cabinet, June 24, 2014.
64. Abe Shinzō, "Press Conference," Prime Minister of Japan and His Cabinet, July 1, 2014.
65. Onuf, *World of Our Making*, 131.
66. Koizumi Junichiro, "Press Conference," January 4, 2005.

67.   Koizumi Junichiro, "Press Conference," April 27, 2001.

68.   Midford, *Rethinking Japanese Public Opinion*, 26

69.   Inoguchi Takashi, "A North-East Asian Perspective," *Australian Journal of International Affairs* 55, no. 2 (2001): 199–212.

70.   Allen S. Whiting, "China and Japan: Politics Versus Economics," *Annals of the American Academy of Political and Social Science* 519, no. 1 (1992): 39–51. For more on East Asian attitudes concerning Japanese remilitarization, see Hugo Dobson, *Japan and United Nations Peacekeeping: New Pressures and New Responses* (London: Routledge Curzon, 2003).

71.   Jack Kim, Sui-Lee Wee, and Linda Sieg, "South Korea, China Warn Japan Not to Backtrack on Apology Over Wartime Past," Reuters, January 27, 2015.

72.   Yoshida Reiji, "Murayama, Kono Assail Revisionism, Urge Abe to Uphold Their Apologies in Entirety," *Japan Times*, June 9, 2015.

73.   Yoshida Reiji, "South Korea, China Warn Japan not to Backtrack on Apology Over Wartime Past," Reuters, January 27, 2015.

74.   Stephen McDonell, "China Criticizes Japan's Revision of Pacifist Constitution," ABC.net, July 2, 2014.

75.   John Ruwitch, "China Envoy Urges Japan to Stick to Apology Script," Reuters, March 13, 2015.

76.   Amy King, "China's Response to Japan's Constitutional Reinterpretation, *East Asia Forum*, July 27, 2014.

77.   Nagashima Akihisa, interview by author, Tokyo, June 2014.

78.   Komizō Yasuyoshi, interview by author, Hiroshima, April 2014.

79.   Nishida Jun, interview by author, Tokyo, August 2014.

80.   Konō Tarō (Liberal Democratic Party), interview by author, Tokyo, May 2014.

6. PEACE CULTURE AND NORMATIVE RESTRAINTS

1.   In this section, I use the term "norms" (until it cannot be used), instead of the more encompassing and accurate term "rules." I have yet to find the terms "rule" and "rules" used in the East Asia security academic literature. Security studies have all but ignored the foundational constructivist literature.

2.   Christopher W. Hughes, *Japan's Remilitarisation* (Oxon, UK: Routledge for International Institute for Strategic Studies, 2009).

3.   Miyashita, "Where Do Norms Come From?" and Lind, "Pacifism or Passing the Buck?"

4.   Some may argue that gaming a rule could reduce, if not eliminate, its behavioral impact over time. Such exploitive tactics are within the agency of actors. However, actors still need to probe and prod the extent they can game rules without sanctions. Moreover, by exploiting a rule, actors reinforce that there are legitimate and illegitimate behaviors.

5.   Onuf, *World of Our Making*, 66.

6.   Kusunoki, "Early Years," 60.

7.   Kusunoki, "Early Years," 60. See also Paul Midford, "The GSDF's Quest for Public Acceptance and the 'Allergy' Myth," in *The Japanese Ground Self-Defense Force: Search for Legitimacy*, ed. Robert D. Eldridge and Paul Midford (New York: Palgrave Macmillan, 2017), 297–346, for an explanation of how the GSDF built legitimacy with the public through disaster relief

activities. Midford makes it clear that as early as the 1960s, Japanese public opinion saw "military power as having utility for defending national territory, but not possessing utility as a foreign policy instrument for advancing national interest overseas" (300).

8.   Japan has provided financial assistance to hosting the U.S. Armed Forces in Japan since 1987. In the most recent five-year HNS agreement (2016–2020), Japan agreed to spend $1.6 billion annually. Since 1997, SACO-related expenses have ranged from $100 million to $3 billion annually, or equal to 8 percent of the entire defense budget. The social cost of hosting bases in Japan, especially in Okinawa, is incalculable.

9.   Midford, *Rethinking Japanese Public Opinion.*

10. Government Official, interview by author, Zoom, June 2020.

11. Onuf, *World of Our Making*, 76.

12. For more on shame in the Japanese context, see Tamamoto Masaru, "Japan's Politics of Cultural Shame," *Global Asia* 2, no. 1 (2007); Nassrine Azimi, "An Admirable Culture of Shame," *New York Times*, June 7, 2010; and Takada Akira, "Socialization Practices Regarding Shame in Japanese Caregiver-Child Interactions," *Frontiers in Psychology* 10 (2019): 1–14. Pauline Kent, "Shame as a Social Sanction in Japan: Shameful Behavior as Perceived by the Voting Public," *Japan Review*, no. 3 (1992): 97–130, provides a masterful breakdown of debates over Japanese shame culture in the academic literature.

13. Kim Mikyoung, "Memory and Reconciliation: Culturally Embedded Memories of Japan and Korea," in *Hiroshima & Peace*, ed. Carol Rinnert, Omar Farouk, and Inoue Yasuhiro (Hiroshima: Keisuisha, 2010), 147–165.

14. Genron NPO, "The 15th Joint Public Opinion Poll; and Genron NPO, "The 7th Japan-South Korea Joint Opinion Poll."

15. Tim Kelly and Nobuhiro Kobu, "Gulf War Trauma Began Japan's Retreat from Pacifism," *Reuters*, December 19, 2015.

16. Ienaga Saburō, for example, was a professor at Tokyo University who dedicated his postwar life to revealing Japan's colonial atrocities. Ienaga famously won a thirty-two-year lawsuit against the Japanese government over textbook censorship. Ienaga expressed shame for not resisting war propaganda as a high school teacher during the war. See Nozaki Yoshiko and Inokuchi Hiromitsu, "Japanese Education, Nationalism, and Ienaga Saburo's Court Challenges," *Bulletin of Concerned Asian Scholars* 30, no. 2 (1998): 37–46.

17. Nihon Hidankyō's website can be accessed at http://www.ne.jp/asahi/hidankyo/nihon /index.html.

18. Tanaka Terumi, interview by author, Tokyo, February 2015.

19. Ministry of Health, Labour, and Welfare, "*Hibakushasū (Hibakusha Kenkō Techō Shojishasū) Heikin Nenrei (2019)*" [Number of A-Bomb Survivors (Health Notebook Holders) Average Age (2019)], accessed November 19, 2020.

20. Ministry of Health, Labour, and Welfare, "*Hibakusha (Hibakusha Kenkō Techō Shojisha) Sū no Suii*" [Changes in the Number of A-bomb Survivors (Health Notebook Holders)], accessed November 19, 2020.

21. Ministry of Foreign Affairs, "Youth Communicator for a World Without Nuclear Weapons," 2013.

22. Kanazaki Yumi (Reporter, Chugoku Shimbun), interview by author, Hiroshima, June 2014.

23. Taue Tomihisa (Mayor of Nagasaki), interview by author, email, July 2014.

24.   Taue Tomihisa, interview by author, email, July 2014.

25.   Taue Tomihisa, "Nagasaki Peace Declaration," 2018.

26.   Matsui Kazumi, "Peace Declaration," Hiroshima, Japan, August 6, 2018.

27.   Egawa Yusuke, Mizukawa Kyousuke, and Niiyama Kyoko, "Hiroshima Mayor Avoids Calling for Ratification of Nuclear Treaty in Peace Declaration," *Chugoku Shimbun*, August 7, 2018.

28.   Komizō Yasuyoshi (Chairperson of the Hiroshima Peace Culture Foundation), interview by author, Hiroshima, April 2014.

29.   John W. Treat, *Writing Ground Zero: Japanese Literature and the Atomic Bomb* (Chicago: University of Chicago Press, 1995), 301.

30.   Tanaka Terumi (Secretary General, Nihon Hidankyo), interview by author, Tokyo, February 2015.

31.   Hamai Shinso, *A-Bomb Mayor: Warnings and Hope from Hiroshima*, trans. Elizabeth W. Baldwin (Hiroshima, Japan: Publication Committee for the English Version of A-Bomb Mayor, 2010), 65.

32.   Morishita Yusuke (Sales Planning Department, fan service section), interview by author, Hiroshima, August 2016.

33.   The Kyūshū shinkansen line is scheduled to connect to Nagasaki in 2023. Hiroshima received its first shinkansen in 1975, which connected the city to Tokyo through Osaka via the Sanyo shinkansen line.

34.   Jodai Miyako, "The 69th Nagasaki Peace Ceremony Pledge for Peace," Nagasaki, Japan, August 9, 2014, https://www.youtube.com/watch?v=kueL3VCoEZQ.

35.   Jodai Miyako, "69th Nagasaki Peace Ceremony," Nagasaki, Japan, August 9, 2014.

36.   Abe Shinzō, "Address at the Hiroshima Peace Memorial Ceremony," Prime Minister of Japan and His Cabinet, August 6, 2017.

37.   Onuf, *World of Our Making*, 135.

38.   Onuf, *World of Our Making*, 135.

39.   Onuf, *World of Our Making*, 135.

40.   See Thomas Berger, *War, Guilt, and World Politics after World War II* (New York: Cambridge University Press, 2012); and Jennifer Lind, *Sorry States: Apologies in International Politics* (Ithaca, NY: Cornell University Press, 2008).

41.   Saito Hiro, *The History Problem: The Politics of War Commemoration in East Asia* (Honolulu: University of Hawai'i Press, 2017), 4.

42.   See Mark Langager, "Elements of War and Peace in History Education in the US and Japan: A Case Study Comparison," *Journal of Peace Education* 6, no. 1 (2009): 119–136, for more on peace education.

43.   Taue Tomihisa (mayor of Nagasaki), interview by author, email, July 2014.

44.   Peter van den Dungen and Yamane Kazuyo, "Peace Education Through Peace Museums," *Journal of Peace Education* 12, no. 3 (2015): 213.

45.   Roy Tamashiro and Ellen Furnari, "Museums for Peace: Agents and Instruments of Peace Education," *Journal of Peace Education* 12, no. 3 (2015). I use the term "peace museums," but some scholars use the more encompassing term "museums for peace," which includes museums that are not solely focused on peace education. See Clive Barrett and Joyce Apsel, *Museums for Peace: Transforming Cultures* (The Hague: International Network of

Museums for Peace, 2012), for a collection of informative essays on peace museums and education.

46. Tamashiro and Furnari, "Museums for Peace," 224.

47. Tamashiro and Furnari, "Museums for Peace," 224–225.

48. For more on the Network of Peace Museums, see *Muse* magazine. Available at http://www.tokyo-sensai.net/muse/index.htm.

49. The price of admission for the museums is ¥200/$1.60. Admission is free on August 6 and 9.

50. Shiga Kenji (Hiroshima Peace Memorial Museum director), interview by author, Hiroshima, July 2016; and Hiroshima Peace Media Center, "Editorial: Removal of Mannequins from Museum," Hiroshima Peace Memorial Center, October 23, 2013.

51. Statistics Bureau of Japan, "*Gakkō Kihon Chōsa*" (School Basic Survey), 2019.

52. Ministry of Land, Infrastructure, Transport, and Tourism, "Transition of the Number of Passengers Using Domestic Airlines," 2012; and Ministry of Land, Infrastructure, Transport, and Tourism, "Transition of the Number of Passengers Using International Airlines." 2012.

53. City of Hiroshima, "*Shūgakuruokō-tō Dantai no Chiiki Betsu Nyūkanshasū FY2017-FY2019*" (Number of School Trips and Such Visitors by Region), 2018.

54. Matthew Allen and Rumi Sakamoto, "War and Peace: War Memories and Museums in Japan," *History Compass* 11, no. 12 (2013): 1054.

55. WAM. https://wam-peace.org/en/about.

56. Van den Dungen and Yamane, "Peace Education," 217.

57. This book does not include the kamikaze museums in its list of peace museums. However, the museums' information pamphlets and exhibitions express the desire for "everlasting peace" so that events such as World War II never occur again. There is no agreement within the peace studies community on what constitutes a peace museum.

58. Philip Seaton, "Kamikaze Museums and Contents Tourism," *Journal of War & Culture Studies* 12, no. 1 (2019): 67–84.

59. See "Introduction," Chiran Peace Museum, accessed November 25, 2020, http://www.chiran-tokkou.jp/english/about/heiwakaikan/index.html.

60. Seaton, "Kamikaze Museums and Contents," 75.

61. Todaka Kazushige (Director, Kure Maritime Museum), interview by author, Kure, July 2014.

62. Todaka Kazushige, interview by author, Kure, July 2014.

63. Tamashiro and Furnari, "Museums for Peace," 224.

64. Coincidentally, Shōwakan is just a 650 meter walk to the Yasukuni Jinja. In recent years, far-right groups have developed a troubled relationship with the imperial family. Although Hirohito reigned during the most intense period of Japanese expansion, following the war, Hirohito was forced to reject his divine status and boycotted the Yasukuni Shrine until his death. Hirohito's successor, Akihito, has never visited the Yasukuni Shrine and, along with current emperor Naruhito, has at times breached protocol to express antimilitarism sentiments. In 2015, Naruhito stated, "I hope this year will be an opportunity to take the preciousness of peace to heart and renew our determination to pursue peace," concluding that Japan's peace and prosperity was built on Japan's

Constitution. "Crown prince turns 55, calls for accounts of history to be passed down correctly," *Japan Times*, February 23, 2015, https://www.japantimes.co.jp/news/2015/02/23/national/crown-prince-turns-55-calls-accounts-history-passed-correctly.

65. "Planned War Museum in Kumamoto Prefecture Criticized for Tourism Focus," *Japan Times*, July 27, 2018.

66. Yoshida Takashi, "Revising the Past, Complicating the Future: The Yushukan War Museum in Modern Japanese History," *Asia-Pacific Journal: Japan Focus* 5, no.12 (2007): 3.

67. Allen and Sakamoto, "War and Peace," 1049.

68. Yoshida Reiji, "Yasukuni Shrine's Chief Priest Forced to Quiet After Criticizing Emperor for Not Visiting War-Linked Shrine," *Japan Times*, October 11, 2018.

69. Allen and Sakamoto, "War and Peace," 1049.

70. Allen and Sakamoto, "War and Peace," 1049.

71. Abe Shinzō, "Pledge for Everlasting Peace," Statement, Ministry of Foreign Affairs of Japan, December 26, 2013.

72. Friedrich Kratochwil, "The Force of Prescriptions," *International Organization* 38, no. 4 (1984): 700.

73. Abe Shinzō, "Pledge for Everlasting Peace."

74. Allen and Sakamoto, "War and Peace," 1054.

75. Van den Dungen and Yamane, "Peace Education."

76. For more on peace museums and peace education, see the essential work of Yamane Kazuyo, *Grassroots Museums for Peace in Japan: Unknown Efforts for Peace and Reconciliation* (Saarbrüden, Germany: VDM Verlag Dr. Müller, 2009); "Moving Beyond the War Memorial Museum," *Peace Forum* 24, no. 34 (2009): 75–85; and "Japanese Peace Museums: Education and Reconciliation," in *Peace Studies in the Chinese Century*, ed. Alan Hunter (London: Routledge, 2017), 85–113.

77. RENGO Officer, interview by author, Tokyo, August 2014.

78. Kawai Kimiaki, interview by author, Tokyo, May 2014.

79. Kawai Kimiaki, interview by author, Tokyo, May 2014.

80. See Erica Baffelli, "Sōka Gakkai and Politics in Japan," *Religion Compass* 4, no. 12 (2010): 746–756; and Anne M. Fisker-Nielson, *Religion and Politics in Contemporary Japan: Soka Gakkai Youth and Komeito* (London: Routledge, 2013) for more on Kōmeitō and Sōka Gakkai's influence in Japanese politics.

81. Tsujimoto would join the House of Representatives in 2005.

82. "We Are," Peace Boat, accessed December 19, 2020, https://peaceboat.org.

83. Robin Lewis (Peace Boat), interview by author, Tokyo, June 2016.

84. Kawasaki Akira (Peace Boat), interview by author, Tokyo, May 2014.

85. For more information, see http://www.article-9.org/jp/index.html.

86. For more information, see the Nuclear Free Now website: http://npfree.jp/index.html.

87. Kawasaki Akira, interview by author, Tokyo, May 2014.

88. Mayors for Peace website. For more information, see http://www.mayorsforpeace.org/jp/.

89. Watanabe Tomoko (Executive Director, ANT-Hiroshima), interview by author, Hiroshima, March 2014.

90. Ogura Keiko (Hiroshima Interpreters for Peace), interview by author, Hiroshima, March 2015.

91. Mito Kosei (Free and Informative Guides), interview by author, Hiroshima, March 2014 and January 2015.

92. Yokoyama Motonobu (Director of Peace Programs, Hiroshima City), interview by author, Hiroshima, March 2015.

93. Yamaoka Michiko (Free and Informative Guides), interview by author, Hiroshima, November 2014.

94. Osaki Tomohiro, "Thousands Rally Outside Diet Against Abe's Security Bills," *Japan Times*, June 6, 2015.

95. Tokuchi Hideshi (former Vice-Minister of Defense for International Affairs), interview by author, Tokyo, December 2018.

96. Yoshida Reiji and Osaki Tomohiro, "Fiery Suicide Bid Shocks Shinjuku on Eve of Historic Security Decision," *Japan Times*, June 30, 2014.

97. Kanazaki Yumi, interview by author, Hiroshima, June 2014.

98. Parliamentarian ((Liberal Democratic Party)), interview by author, Tokyo, September 2014.

99. Steve Leeper, interview by author, Hiroshima, April 2014.

100. Tanaka Terumi, interview by author, Tokyo, February 2015.

101. Tanaka Terumi, interview by author, Tokyo, February 2015.

102. Robin Lewis, interview by author, Tokyo, June 2016.

103. Steve Leeper, interview by author, Hiroshima, April 2014.

104. Yokoyama Motonobu, interview by author, Hiroshima, March 2015.

105. Watarida Masahiro (Activist), interview by author, Hiroshima, August 2015.

106. Watarida Masahiro, interview by author, Hiroshima, August 2015.

107. Onuf, *World of Our Making*, 136.

108. Post-War Constitution of Japan, "Chapter 2."

109. Parliamentarian, interview by author, Tokyo, September 2014.

110. Hirose Shunsuke, "Shinzo Abe's Biggest Enemy: The LDP," *Diplomat*, April 14; and Yoshida Reiji, "Ishin No To Leader Lashes Abe Over Security Bills," *Japan Times*, June 17, 2015.

111. Onuf, *World of Our Making*, 22.

112. Arase, "Japan, the Active State?"

113. Nishikawa Toshiyuki, "The Future of the Japanese Constitution: From the 'MacArthur Constitution' to What?" *Journal of Comparative Law Culture*, no. 17 (2008): 51–79.

114. "Nikkei Regular Telephone Opinion Poll," *Nikkei Shimbun*, trans. the Maureen and Mike Mansfield Foundation, April 2005.

115. "April 2009 Public Opinion Poll on the Constitution," *Asahi Shimbun*, trans. the Maureen and Mike Mansfield Foundation, May 1, 2009.

116. "April 2010 Regular Public Opinion Poll," *Asahi Shimbun*, trans. the Maureen and Mike Mansfield Foundation, April 19, 2010.

117. "48 percent in Favor of Constitutional Amendment: Mainichi Survey," *Mainichi*, May 3, 2017.

118. "Regular Public Opinion Poll," *Asahi Shimbun*, trans. the Maureen and Mike Mansfield Foundation April 21, 2014.

119. "Regular Public Opinion Poll," *Asahi Shimbun*, trans. the Maureen and Mike Mansfield Foundation, May 26, 2014.

120. "Regular Public Opinion Poll," *Asahi Shimbun*, trans. the Maureen and Mike Mansfield Foundation, May 19, 2015.

121. Asaoka Masatoshi, "Japanese Public Opinion on Constitutional Revision in 2006," Council on Foreign Relations, August 1, 2016.

122. NHK, "Yoron Chōsa: Nihonjin to Kenpō 2017" (Public Opinion Poll: Japanese and the Constitution 2017)," 2017.

123. Okudaira Yasuhiro, "Forty Years of the Constitution and its Various Influences: Japanese, American, and European, *Law and Contemporary Problems* 53, no. 1 (1990): 18.

124. Asaoka, "Japanese Public Opinion."

125. Onuf, *World of Our Making*, 80.

126. Taue Tomihisa, interview by author, email, July 2014.

127. "Yomiuri Shimbun March 2008 Opinion Polls," *Yomiuri Shimbun*, trans. the Maureen and Mike Mansfield Foundation, accessed November 21, 2020.

128. Tsuchiya Motohiro (Professor, Keio University), interview by author, Tokyo, December 2018.

129. NHK, "Yoron Chōsa."

130. Onuf, *World of Our Making*, 85.

131. See Musashi Katsuhiro, "The Ground Self-Defense Force and Civilian Control," in *The Japanese Ground Self-Defense Force: Search for Legitimacy*, ed. Robert D. Eldridge and Paul Midford (New York: Palgrave Macmillan, 2017), for more on civilian control of the JSDF.

132. See Chaihark Hahm and Kim Sung Ho, *Making We the People: Democratic Constitutional Founding in Postwar Japan and South Korea* (New York: Cambridge University Press, 2015), for more on the history of the Constitution of Japan.

133. Onuf, *World of Our Making*, 60.

134. Ueda Isamu (Kōmeitō), interview by author, Tokyo, October 2014.

135. Sado, *The Self-Defense Forces*, 208.

136. Morimoto Satoshi (former Minister of Defense), interview by author, Tokyo, October 2018.

137. Iwaya Takeshi, "Ministerial Press Conference (as recorded)," Ministry of Defense, Tokyo, Japan, October 2, 2018.

138. Iwaya Takeshi, "Ministerial Press Conference (10:45–11:31 p.m.)," Ministry of Defense, Tokyo, Japan, October 2, 2018.

139. Government Official, interview by author, Zoom, June 2020.

140. Morimoto Satoshi, interview by author, Tokyo, October 2018.

141. Kitagawa Keizō (Captain, MSDF), interview by author, Tokyo, May 2017.

142. Tsuruoka Michito (Professor, Keio University), interview by author, Tokyo, May 2017.

143. Richard Samuels, " 'New Fight Power!' Japan's Growing Maritime Capabilities and the East Asian Security," *International Security* 32, no. 3 (2007/2008): 84–112, has argued, "The modernization and expansion of the JCG enhance not only Japan's power projection capabilities but also Japan's ability to project influence—and it does so without destabilizing consequences that a shift in the formal defense budget may entail." Power projection may be even more limited than Samuels concludes because, although the JCG's budget increased by approximately 13 percent between 2008 and 2018, personnel costs accounted for over 50 percent of the budget. Capital equipment purchases and maintenance fees never rose above 20 percent.

144.   Morimoto Satoshi, interview by author, Tokyo, October 2018.

145.   Ministry of Finance, "Highlights of the Draft FY 2019 Budget," December 13, 2019.

146.   Etel Solingen, *Nuclear Logics: Contrasting Paths in East Asia and the Middle East* (Princeton, NJ: Princeton University Press, 2007); and Nina Tannenwald, *The Nuclear Taboo: The United States and the Non-Use of Nuclear Weapons since 1945* (Cambridge: Cambridge University Press, 2007).

147.   Abe Nobuyasu, "No First Use: How to Overcome Japan's Great Divide," *Journal for Peace and Nuclear Disarmament* 1, no. 1 (2018): 137–151; and Thomas E. Doyle II, "Hiroshima and Two Paradoxes of Japanese Nuclear Perplexity," *Critical Military Studies* 1, no. 2 (2015): 160–173.

148.   "No Need to Review Three Non-nuclear Principles, Kono Says," *Japan Times*, September 8, 2017.

149.   Kōno Tarō, "Foreign Policy Speech by Foreign Minister Kono to the 198th Session of the Diet," Ministry of Foreign Affairs of Japan, Tokyo, January 28, 2019.

150.   Hiroshima Prefecture and Japan Institute of International Affairs, "Hiroshima Report: Evaluation of Achievement in Nuclear Disarmament, Non-Proliferation and Nuclear Security in 2014," *Hiroshima Report* (2015): 1–189.

151.   Rebecca Davis Gibbons, "The Humanitarian Turn in Nuclear Disarmament and the Treaty on the Prohibition of Nuclear Weapons," *Nonproliferation Review* 25, no. 1–2 (2018): 11–36.

152.   "Top 30 Attractions in Japan by International Travelers 2020," Trip Advisor (website), April 28, 2020.

153.   Otley, "Militarism," 322.

7. CRAFTING PEACE AMONG MILITARISMS

1.   Bhubhindar Singh, "Japan's Security Policy, From a Peace State to an International State," *Pacific Review* 21, no. 3 (2008): 305.

2.   Onuf, *World of Our Making*, 5.

3.   Kurusu Kaoru and Rikki Kersten, "Japan as an Active Agent for Global Norms: The Political Dynamism behind the Acceptance and Promotion of 'Human Security,' " *Asia-Pacific Review* (2011): 115–116.

4.   Nicholas Onuf, "Everyday Ethics in International Relations," *Millennium-London-London School of Economics* 27, no. 3 (1998): 676.

5.   Ministry of Foreign Affairs, "Cabinet Decision on Development of Seamless Security Legislation to Ensure Japan's Survival and Protect Its People," July 1, 2014.

6.   Onuf, *World of Our Making*, 76.

7.   Onuf, *World of Our Making*, 77.

8.   Nicholas Onuf, *International Legal Theory: Essays and Engagements, 1966–2006* (Abingdon, VA: Routledge-Cavendish, 2008), 304.

9.   Fukushima Akiko, "Multilateralism Recalibrated: Japan's Engagement in Institution Building in the Past 70 Years and Beyond," (Washington, DC: Center for Strategic & International Studies, 2016), 5

10.   Akira Iriye, *Japan and the Wider World: From the Mid-Nineteenth Century to the Present* (London: Routledge, 2014), 188.

11. David Arase, *Buying Power: The Political Economy of Japan's Foreign Aid* (Boulder, CO: Lynne Reinner, 1995); and Giuseppe A. Stavale, "The GSDF During the Post-Cold War Years, 1989-2015," in *The Japanese Ground Self-Defense Force: Search for Legitimacy*, ed. Robert D. Eldridge and Paul Midford (New York: Palgrave Macmillan, 2017)

12. Cooney, *Japan's Foreign Policy.*

13. Hane, *Modern Japan*, 410.

14. Singh, "Japan's Security Policy," 313.

15. Ministry of Foreign Affairs, "Japan's Contribution."

16. Robert Eldridge and Paul Midford, eds., *The Japanese Ground Self-Defense Force: Search for Legitimacy* (New York: Palgrave Macmillan, 2017), 4.

17. Ministry of Defense, "About International Peace Cooperation Activities," https://www .mod.go.jp/e/d_act/kokusai_heiwa/about.html.

18. Futori Hideshi, "Japan's Disaster Diplomacy: Fostering Military Cooperation in Asia," *Pacific Bulletin*, no. 213 (May 13, 2013).

19. Kitagawa Keizō (Captain, MSDF), interview by author, Tokyo, May 2017.

20. Ministry of Foreign Affairs, "Diplomatic Bluebook 2013 Summary," November 11, 2013; and Cabinet Office, "*Gaikō ni Kansuru Yoron Chōsa*" (Public Opinion Poll on Diplomacy), October 2019.

21. Singh, "Japan's Security Policy," 310.

22. Shiozaki Yasuhisa, "Speech at the 42nd Munich on Security Policy," Hotel Bayerisher Hof, Munich, Germany, February 5, 2006.

23. Ozawa, *Blueprint*, 94-95.

24. Ozawa, *Blueprint*, 94-95.

25. Itoh Mayumi, "Japanese Constitutional Revision: A Neo-Liberal Proposal for Article 9 in a Comparative Perspective," *Asian Survey* 41, no. 2 (2001): 312.

26. Koizumi Junichiro, "Policy Speech to the 151st Session of the Diet," Ministry of Foreign Affairs of Japan, May 7, 2001.

27. Koizumi Junichiro, "Policy Speech to the 164th Session of the Diet," Ministry of Foreign Affairs of Japan, January 20, 2006.

28. Ashizawa Kuniko, "Japanese Assistance in Afghanistan: Helping the United States, Acting Globally, and Making a Friend," *Asia Policy* 17, no. 1 (2014): 59.

29. Machimura Nobutaka, "Statement on the Adoption of the United Nations Security Council Resolution on the Extension of the Mandate on the ISAF (International Security Force) in Afghanistan," Ministry of Foreign Affairs of Japan, September 20, 2007.

30. Kōmura Masahiko, "Japan: A Builder of Peace," Ministry of Foreign Affairs of Japan, January 4, 2008.

31. Fukuda Yasuo, "Policy Speech to the 169th Session of the Diet," Prime Minister of Japan and His Cabinet, January 18, 2008.

32. Ashizawa, "Japanese Assistance," 60.

33. Alex J. Bellamy and Sara E. Davies, "The Responsibility to Protect in the Asia-Pacific Region," *Security Dialogue* 40, no. 6 (2009): 551.

34. Bellamy and Davies, "The Responsibility to Protect," 551.

35. Ban Ki-Moon, "Implementing the Responsibility to Protect," Report of the Secretary General, United Nations, January 12, 2009, 4.

36. Ban, "Implementing the Responsibility," 15.

37. Bellamy and Davies, "The Responsibility to Protect," 550.

38. Honna Jun, "Japan and the Responsibility to Protect: Coping with Human Security Diplomacy," *Pacific Review* 25, no. 1 (2012): 98.

39. Honna, "Japan and the Responsibility," 100.

40. Honna, "Japan and the Responsibility," 100.

41. Honna, "Japan and the Responsibility," 100.

42. Iwami Tadashi, "Understanding Japan's Peacebuilding in Concept and Practice," *East Asia: International Quarterly* 33, no. 2 (2016): 111–132.

43. Fukushima Akiko, "Japan's Proactive Contribution to Peace: A Mere Political Label?" Tokyo Foundation for Policy Research, June 19, 2014.

44. Murakami Tomoaki, "The GSDF and Disaster Relief Dispatches," in *The Japanese Ground Self-Defense Force: Search for Legitimacy*, ed. Robert D. Eldridge and Paul Midford (New York: Palgrave Macmillan, 2017).

45. Murakami, "The GSDF and Disaster Relief Dispatches," 267.

46. Onuf, "Everyday Ethics," 687.

47. Ministry of Foreign Affairs, "Japan Disaster Relief Teams Deployed from 1987 to 2019," n.d. https://www.mofa.go.jp/files/000207528.pdf.

48. Abe Shinzō, "Address at the Ministry of Defense and the Self-Defense Forces 60th Anniversary Air Review," Prime Minister of Japan and His Cabinet October 26, 2014.

49. Fukushima, "Japan's Proactive Contribution."

50. Futori, "Japan's Disaster Diplomacy."

51. Futori, "Japan's Disaster Diplomacy."

52. United Nations, *Hyōgo Framework for Action 2005–2015: Building the Resilience of Nations and Communities to Disasters* (New York: United Nations Office for Disaster Risk Reduction, 2007), 1–25.

53. United Nations, *Sendai Framework for Disaster Risk Reduction 2015–2030* (New York: United Nations Office for Disaster Risk Reduction, 2015), 7.

54. "Japan to Dispatch SDF to Nepal, Part of Multifaceted Aid Effort," *Japan Times*, April 28, 2015.

55. Hiroshima Peace Builders Center Website. For more information on HPBC activities, see http://www.peacebuilderscenter.jp/eng/about_e.html.

56. Tomodachi Initiative, *Annual Report*, 2019.

57. Yamaguchi Noboru (Lieutenant General, GSDF, retired), interview by author, Tokyo, October 2018.

58. Ministry of Defense, *Defense of Japan* (Tokyo: Ministry of Defense, 2011), 443.

59. Yezi Yeo, "De-Militarizing Military: Confirming Japan's Self-Defense Forces' Identity as a Disaster Relief Agency in the 2011 Tohoku Triple Crisis," *Asia Journal of Global Studies* 5, no. 2 (2012): 78.

60. Yeo, "De-Militarizing Military," 78.

61. Yeo, "De-Militarizing Military," 78.

62. "World Values Survey," 1981; 1990; 1995; 2000; 2005; and 2010.

63. Cabinet Office, "*Jietai Bōeimondai ni Kansuru Seronchōsa*" (Public Opinion Poll on the Self-Defense Forces and Defense Issues), January 2017, https://survey.gov-online.go.jp /h29/h29-bouei/index.html.

64. NHK, "Yoron Chōsa: Nihonjin to Kenpō 2017" (Public Opinion Poll: Japanese and the Constitution 2017)," 2017.

65. Yeo, "De-Militarizing Military," 72.

66. The use of the concept of affirmative essentialisms in this book borrows from Elissa Helms, "Women as Agents of Ethnic Reconciliation? Women's NGOs and International Intervention in Postwar Bosnia-Herzegovina," *Women Studies International Forum* 26, no. 1 (2003): 15–33. Helms explains how language meant to portray women positively, such as "peacemaker" and "nurturer," risks "closing off women's potential for influence in the formal (male) political sphere." The JSDF's use of anime imagery and emphasis on its nontraditional security operations influences the public's perception of the appropriate responsibilities of the JSDF.

67. Singh, "Japan's Security Policy," 318.

68. Cabinet Office, "*Gaikō ni Kansuru Yoron Chōsa*" (Public Opinion Poll), October 2004.

69. Cabinet Office, "*Gaikō ni Kansuru Yoron Chōsa*."

70. Cabinet Office, "Overview of the Public Opinion Survey on Diplomacy," December 2018.

71. Kōsai Yutaka, "Contributions, Yes, But Geared to the Complex Needs of a Complex World," in *Japan, Internationalism and the UN*, ed. Ronald Dore (London: Routledge, 1997), 152.

72. Yoshimura Shinsuke, "To Die for High Principle?" in *Japan, Internationalism and the UN*, ed. Ronald Dore (London: Routledge, 1997), 158.

73. Yoshimura, "To Die," 56.

74. Yoshimura, "To Die," 156.

75. Watanabe Tomoko (Executive Director, ANT-Hiroshima), interview by author, Hiroshima, March 2014.

76. Watanabe Tomoko, interview by author, Hiroshima, March 2014.

77. Watarida Masahiro (Activist), interview by author, Hiroshima, August 2015.

78. Yoshimura, "To Die," 158.

79. OECD, "Official Development Assistance 2018–Preliminary Data." Accessed November 27, 2020.

80. Fukushima, "Japan's Proactive Contribution."

81. For detailed information, see United Nations Development Group website at: http://mptf.undp.org/factsheet/fund/ITF00.

82. Abe Shinzō, "Statement by Mr. Shinzo Abe," United Nations Sustainable Summit 2015," September 27, 2015.

83. Ministry of Defense, *Defense of Japan* (Tokyo: Ministry of Defense, 2005), 55.

84. Ministry of Foreign Affairs, "Cabinet Decision on the Development Cooperation Charter," February 10, 2015.

85. Ministry of Foreign Affairs, "Cabinet Decision," February 10, 2015.

86. Ministry of Foreign Affairs, "Official Development Assistance (ODA): Rebuttal Statement Against the Editorial of *Japan Times* 'Aid That Could Foment Conflict,' " March 8, 2015.

87. Jochen Prantl and Nakano Ryoko, "Global Norm Diffusion in East Asia: How China and Japan Implement the Responsibility to Protect," *International Relations* 25, no. 2 (2011): 216.

88. Cabinet Office, "Overview of the Public Opinion Survey on Diplomacy," December 2018.

89. Honna, "Japan and the Responsibility to Protect," 96.

90.   Paul Midford, "The GSDF's Quest," 297–298.

91.   Amitav Acharya, "How Ideas Spread: Whose Norms Matter? Norm Localization and Institutional Change in Asian Regionalism," *International Organization* 58, no. 2 (2004): 239–275.

92.   Pantl and Nakano, "Global Norm Diffusion," 217.

93.   Ministry of Defense, "National Defense Program Guidelines for FY 2019 and Beyond," December 18, 2018.

94.   Abe Shinzō, "Toward an Alliance of Hope—Address to a Joint Meeting of the U.S. Congress by Prime Minister Shinzo Abe,'" Washington DC, April 29, 2015.

95.   Abe, "Toward an Alliance of Hope."

96.   Abe Shinzō and Barack Obama, "Remarks by President Obama and Prime Minister Abe of Japan in Joint Press Conference," Washington DC, April 28, 2015.

97.   Abe and Obama, "Remarks by President Obama and Prime Minister Abe."

98.   Koizumi Junichiro, "Press Conference by Prime Minister Junichiro Koizumi," January 4, 2006.

99.   John Kerry, Chuck Hagel, Kishida Fumio, and Onodera Itsunori, "Joint Statement of the Security Consultative Committee: Toward a More Robust Alliance and Greater Shared Responsibilities," October 3, 2013.

100.   Matsuyama Yukio, "The Need to Wait for a Generation Change," in *Japan, Internationalism and the UN*, ed. Ronald Dore (London: Routledge, 1997), 163.

101.   There is an extensive body of literature that explains the various norms that regulate alliances. See Charles W. Kegly and Gregory A. Raymond, "Alliance Norms and War: A New Piece in an Old Puzzle," *International Studies Quarterly* 26, no. 4 (1982): 572–595; and Stephanie C. Hofmann and Andrew I. Yeo, "Business as Usual: The Role of Norms in Alliance Management," *European Journal of International Relations* 21, no. 2 (2015): 377–401, for such examples.

102.   Cabinet Office, "Overview of the Public Opinion Survey on Diplomacy," December 2016,

103.   Cabinet Office, "Overview of the Public Opinion Survey on Diplomacy," December 2017.

104.   Cabinet Office, "Overview of the Public Opinion Survey on Diplomacy," December 2018.

105.   Bruce Stokes and Kat Devlin, "View of the U.S. and President Trump," Pew Research Center, November 12, 2018, https://www.gov-online.go.jp/eng/pdf/summaryg18.pdf.

106.   Craig Kafura, "Public Opinion and the US-Japan Alliance at the Outset of the Trump Administration," Chicago Council on Global Affairs, February 8, 2017.

107.   Yamaguchi Noboru, "Redefining the Japan-US Alliance," Nippon.com, May 11, 2012.

108.   Matsuyama, "The Need to Wait," 163.

109.   James J. Pryzstup, National Defense University Press, and National Defense University, "The U.S.-Japan Alliance: Review of the Guidelines for Defense Cooperation," *Strategic Perspectives*, no. 18 (2015), 10.

110.   Kotani Tetsuo (Senior Research Fellow, The Japan Institute of International Affairs), interview by author, Tokyo, August 2015.

111.   Kameda Masaaki, "Abe: Japan Won't Slide into US War Despite Collective Defense Loophole," *Japan Times*, May 14, 2015.

112.   Nagashima Akihisa, interview by author, Tokyo, June 2014.

113.   Advisory Panel on Reconstruction of the Legal Basis for Security, "Report of the Advisory Panel on Reconstruction of the Legal Basis for Security," May 15, 2014, 5.

114.   Government Official, interview by author, Zoom, June 2020.

115.   Nancy Snow, "The Abe Administration's Arrogance of Power Moment," *Japan Times*, July 16, 2015; Asahi Shimbun, "Students, Professors Getting Political over Security Bills," *Asahi Shimbun*, July 19, 2015; and Japan Times, "Thousands Rally Outside Diet Against Abe's Security Bills," *Japan Times*, June 15, 2015.

116.   "Asahi Poll: Constitutional Scholars Almost Unanimous That Bills Are Unconstitutional," *Asahi Shimbun*, July 11, 2015.

117.   "Asahi Poll: 63 percent Oppose Abe's Attempt to Lift Ban on Collective Self-Defense," *Asahi Shimbun*, April 7, 2014.

118.   "Asahi Poll: Nonsupport Rate for Abe Cabinet Jumps to 42 percent, Exceed Support," *Asahi Shimbun*, July 13, 2015.

119.   Ministry of Defense, "National Defense Program Guidelines for FY 2014 and Beyond," December 17, 2013, 7.

120.   Ministry of Defense, "National Defense Program Guidelines for FY 2014," 10.

121.   Ministry of Defense, "National Security Strategy," December 17, 2013.

122.   Ministry of Foreign Affairs, "Cabinet Decision on Development of Seamless Security."

123.   Nagashima Akihisa, interview by author, Tokyo, June 2014.

124.   Paul Midford and Robert D. Eldridge, "Introduction," in *The Japanese Ground Self-Defense Force: Search for Legitimacy*, ed. Robert D. Eldridge and Paul Midford (New York: Palgrave Macmillan, 2017), 4.

125.   Cabinet Office, "Overview of the Public Opinion Survey on Diplomacy," December 2018.

126.   Craig Agena (Colonel, U.S. Army), interview by author, Tokyo, April 2014.

8. AGING GRACEFULLY

1.   Sheila A. Smith, *Japan Rearmed: The Politics of Military Power* (Cambridge, MA: Harvard University Press, 2019), provides an informative summation of how the Japanese government has responded to the changing regional security context and became more comfortable with the use of the military for statecraft. Although Smith acknowledges the public's skepticism of military power, the work focuses primarily on elite politics and perceptions, particularly of Prime Minister Abe.

2.   Christopher Hughes, *Japan's Foreign and Security Policy Under the "Abe Doctrine": New Dynamism or New Dead End?* (Basingstoke, UK: Palgrave Macmillan, 2015), 8.

3.   Onuf, "Everyday Ethics," 670.

4.   See Paul Midford, "Abe's Pro-Active Pacifism and Values Diplomacy: Implications for EU-Japan Political and Security Cooperation," in *The EU-Japan Partnership in the Shadow of China: The Crisis of Liberalism*, ed. Alex Berkofsky, Christopher W. Hughes, Paul Midford, and Marie Söderberg (Abingdon, UK: Routledge, 2018), 40–58; and Akimoto, *The Abe Doctrine*, for a detailed discussion of the origins of the term "proactive pacifism."

5.   Abe Shinzō, "Address at the Opening Session of the Sixth Tokyo International Conference on African Development (TICAD VI), Kenyatta International Convention Center (KICC), Nairobi, August 27, 2016.

6.   See chapter 1 for a discussion of alleged watershed moments. H. D. P. Envall, "The 'Abe Doctrine': Japan's New Regional Realism," *International Relations of the Asia-Pacific* 20, no. 1 (2018), contends the Abe doctrine is not a radical shift toward militarism but modifies Japan's realist tradition, which was predominately a regional focus. Envall concludes, however, that the changing security environment is "nudging Japanese foreign and security policy in new, and maybe unexpected, directions" (51).

7.   Fatton, " 'Japan is Back,' " 265.

8.   Hugo Dobson, "Is Japan Really Back? The 'Abe Doctrine' and Global Governance," *Journal of Contemporary Asia* 47, no. 2 (2017): 217.

9.   Abe Shinzō, "Japan is Back," Policy Speech, Center for Strategic and International Studies (CSIS), Washington, DC, February 22, 2013.

10. Christopher Hughes, "Japan's Strategic Trajectory and Collective Self-Defense: Essential Continuity or Radical Shift?" *Journal of Japanese Studies* 43, no.1 (2017): 98.

11. The Peace and Security Legislation Development Act was a package of amendments to existing laws that allowed for collective self-defense and modest increases to the JSDF responsibilities in PKOs. The International Peace Cooperation Act allowed for the JSDF to use "small arms" in necessary cases. Collective self-defense does not allow for the defense of a foreign country. The use of force is allowed only under the following three conditions: (1) when an armed attack against Japan occurs or when an armed attack against a foreign country that is in a close relationship with Japan occurs and as a result threatens Japan's survival and poses a clear danger to fundamentally overturn people's right to life, liberty, and pursuit of happiness; (2) when there is no other appropriate means available to repel the attack and ensure Japan's survival and protect its people; and (3) use of force limited to the minimum extent necessary (Ministry of Defense, *Defense of Japan*, 2016). Adam Liff, "Policy by Other Means: Collective Self-Defense and the Politics of Japan's Postwar Constitutional Reinterpretations," *Asia Policy* 24 (2017): 193–172, concludes that collective self-defense is "evolutionary rather than revolutionary."

12. Ministry of Defense, "Overview and Fundamental Concepts of National Defense," May 20, 1957.

13. Ministry of Defense, "National Security Strategy."

14. Adam Liff, "Japan's National Security Council: Policy Coordination and Political Power," *Japanese Studies* 38, no. 2 (2018): 9.

15. Jonathan Berkshire Miller, "How Will Japan's NSC Work?" *Diplomat*, January 29, 2014.

16. According to the NSS, "gray zone" scenarios are situations that are "neither pure peacetime nor contingencies over territorial sovereignty and interests." The debate concerning gray zones illustrates how antimilitarism differs from pacifism. There are no gray zones for pacifists because the use of force is illegitimate under all circumstances.

17. Abe Shinzō, "Confluence of the Two Seas," Speech, Parliament of the Republic of India, August 22, 2007.

18. For a history of the Arc of Freedom and Prosperity, see Hosoya Yuichi, "The Rise and Fall of Japan's Grand Strategy: The 'Arc of Freedom and Prosperity' and the Future Asian Order," *Asia-Pacific Review* 18, no. 1 (2011): 13–24.

19. Abe Shinzō, "Address at the Seventy-Third Session of the United Nations General Assembly," United Nations Headquarters, New York City, September 25, 2018.

20. Abe, "Address at the Seventy-Third Session."

21. Abe Shinzō, "Press Conference by Prime Minister Shinzo Abe Following His Attendance at the APEC Economic Leaders' Meeting, ASEAN-related Summit Meetings, and Other Related Meetings," Prime Minister of Japan and His Cabinet, November 14, 2017.

22. Abe Shinzō, "Policy Speech by Prime Minister Shinzo Abe to the 198th Session of the Diet," Prime Minister of Japan and His Cabinet, January 28, 2019.

23. Abe Shinzō, "Press Conference by Prime Minister Shinzo Abe Following His Attendance at the APEC Economic Leaders' Meeting."

24. Abe, "Address by Prime Minister Abe at the Ministry of Defense."

25. Abe, "Address by Prime Minister Abe at the Ministry of Defense."

26. Dower, *Embracing Defeat*, 65.

27. Tara Cannon, *Toward the Abe Statement on the 70th Anniversary of the End of World War II: Lessons from the 20th Century and a Vision for the 21st Century for Japan*, trans. Tara Cannon (Tokyo: Japan Publishing Industry Foundation for Culture, 2017), 41.

28. Abe Shinzō, "Statement," Prime Minister of Japan and His Cabinet, August 14, 2015.

29. Cannon, *Toward the Abe Statement*, 35.

30. Cannon, *Toward the Abe Statement*, 49.

31. Cannon, *Toward the Abe Statement*, 49.

32. Abe Shinzō, "Statement," Prime Minister of Japan and His Cabinet, August 14, 2015. https://japan.kantei.go.jp/97_abe/statement/201508/0814statement.html.

33. Abe Shinzō, "New Year's Press Conference," Prime Minister of Japan and His Cabinet, January 5, 2015.

34. Satake Tomohiko (Senior Fellow, National Institute for Defense Studies), interview by author, Tokyo, February 2015.

35. Midford, "Abe's Pro-Active Pacifism."

36. Iwami, "Understanding Japan's Peacebuilding."

37. Dower, *Embracing Defeat*, 64.

38. Yamaguchi Noboru (Lieutenant General, GSDF, retired), interview by author, Tokyo, October 2018.

39. Stephen G. Cecchetti, M. S. Mahoney, and Fabrizio Zampolli, "The Future of Public Debt: Prospects and Implications," *BIS Working Papers* 300 (2010): 1–22.

40. Nicholas Eberstadt, "Demography and Japan's Future," in *Reimagining Japan: The Quest for a Future that Works*, ed. Clay Chandler, Heang Chhor, and Brian Salsberg (San Francisco, CA: VIZ Media, 2011).

41. Workingdays.org, "Working days in Japan," https://japan.workingdays.org/#a28, accessed December 12, 2020.

42. OECD, "Gender wage gap," https://data.oecd.org/earnwage/gender-wage-gap.htm.

43. Ministry of Internal Affairs and Communications, *Statistical Handbook of Japan 2020*, 2020.

44. Japan Student Services Organization, "Heisei 30-Nendo Kyōtei-tō ni Motodzuku Nihonjin Gakusei Ryūgaku Jōkyō Chōsa Kekka" (FY2018 Japanese Student Study Abroad Survey Results), April, 2019.

45. Ministry of Health, Labour, and Welfare, "Reiwa Nendo Koyō Kintō Kihon Chōsa" (Basic Survey on Equal Employment, 2018), https://www.mhlw.go.jp/toukei/list/71-r01.html.

46.   Matt Alt, *Pure Invention: How Japan's Pop Culture Conquered the World* (New York: Crown, 2020), argues that Japan experienced a rebirth during the Lost Decade through the staggering expansion of its soft power. Although the Japanese economy remained stagnant, cool Japanese goods such as video games, manga, the Walkman, and karaoke machines became commonplace in homes and businesses throughout the world. David Leheny, *Empire of Hope: The Sentimental Politics of Japanese Decline* (Ithaca, NY: Cornell University Press, 2018), provides an additional perspective of Japan's decline through a novel framework of sentimental politics. Leheny complicates popular culture and events and argues that it had more value for domestic narratives on the state of the nation than as a measurement of Japan's influence abroad.

47.   Cental Intelligence Agency, *World Factbook*, "Total Fertility Rate." Accessed on December 26, 2020, https://www.cia.gov/library/publications/the-world-factbook/fields/356.html.

48.   World Economic Forum, "Gender Gap Report 2020," December 16, 2019. http://www3 .weforum.org/docs/WEF_GGGR_2020.pdf.

49.   In discussing Japan's 1 percent cap on defense spending, Watanabe Tsuneo reveals how the realist logic leads states to pursue security policies to the detriment of domestic human security. Watanabe doubts Japan will increase its defense spending, stating, "I keep telling my Chinese friends, you need to save money. You're going to have big trouble. You are Asian like Japan and your economic growth will stop. Stagnate. You should save money for social security costs. That is more important for regime survival" (interview by author, Tokyo, May 2017).

50.   See Bruce W. Jentleson and Ely Ratner, "Bridging the Beltway–Ivory Tower Gap," *International Studies Review* 13, no. 1 (2011): 6–11; Joseph Nye Jr., "International Relations: The Relevance of Theory to Practice," in *Oxford Handbook of International Relations*, ed. Christian Reus-Smit and Duncan Snidal (Oxford: Oxford University Press, 2008): 648–660; Steve Smith, "Six Wishes for a More Relevant Discipline of International Relations," in *Oxford Handbook of International Relations*, ed. Christian Reus-Smit and Duncan Snidal (Oxford: Oxford University Press, 2008), 725–732; Paul C. Avey and Michael C. Desch, "What Do Policymakers Want From Us? Results of a Survey of Current and Former Senior National Security Decision Makers," *International Studies Quarterly* 58, no. 2 (2014): 227–246; and Michael C. Desch, "How Political Science Became Irrelevant," *Chronicle of Higher Education*, February 27, 2019.

51.   Sakai, "Subject and Substratum," 483.

52.   Lanny Ebenstein, *Chicagonomics: The Evolution of Chicago Free Market Economics* (New York: St. Martin's Press, 2015); and Paul Krugman, "How Did Economists Get it so Wrong?" *New York Times*, September 2, 2009.

53.   Ido Oren's groundbreaking article titled, "Is Culture Independent of National Security? How America's National Security Concerns Shaped 'Political Culture' Research,' " *European Journal of International Relations* 6, no. 4 (2000): 543–573, calls attention to the reverse problem of state interests influencing academic research.

54.   Onuf, *World of Our Making*, 288.

55.   Notable examples include former Minister of Economy, Trade and Industry Motegi Toshimitsu, who received a master of public policy from the Harvard Kennedy School of

Government. Former Chief Cabinet Secretary Shiozaki Yasuhisa also attended the Kennedy School. Nishimura Yasutoshi graduated from the University of Maryland's Graduate School of Public Policy.

56. Onuf, *World of Our Making*.
57. See Aram Hur, "Adapting to Democracy: Identity and the Political Development of North Korean Defectors," *Journal of East Asian Studies* 18, no. 1 (2018): 97–115; Darcie Draudt, "South Korea's National Identity Crisis in the Face of Emerging Multiculturalism," *Georgetown Journal of International Affairs* 18, no. 1 (2016): 12–19; Minseon Ku, "The Role of Identity in South Korea's Policies Towards Japan," *Korean Social Science Journal* 43 (2016): 75–94; Kristin Vekasi, "Transforming Geopolitical Risk: Public Diplomacy of Multinational Firms for Foreign Audiences," *Chinese Journal of International Politics* 10, no. 1 (2017): 95–129; and Mary Alice Haddad, "Environmental Advocacy: Insights from East Asia," *Asian Journal of Political Science* 25, no. 3 (2017): 401–419, for some examples of stellar scholarship that takes into account variables that impact domestic and regional security beyond a power balancing framework.

Bibliography

Abe, Nobuyasu. "No First Use: How to Overcome Japan's Great Divide." *Journal for Peace and Nuclear Disarmament* 1, no. 1 (2018): 137–151. https://doi.org/10.1080/25751654.2018.1456042.

Abe, Shinzō. "Address at the Hiroshima Peace Memorial Ceremony." Prime Minister of Japan and His Cabinet, August 6, 2017. https://japan.kantei.go.jp/97_abe/statement/201708/1223996_11583.html.

——. "Address at the Ministry of Defense and the Self-Defense Forces 60th Anniversary Air Review." Prime Minister of Japan and His Cabinet, October 26, 2014. http://japan.kantei.go.jp/96_abe/statement/201410/1026kunji.html.

——. "Address at the Opening Session of the Sixth Tokyo International Conference on African Development (TICAD VI)." Speech, Nairobi, August 27, 2016. https://www.mofa.go.jp/afr/af2/page4e_000496.html.

——. "Address at the Seventy-Third Session of the United Nations General Assembly." Speech, United Nations Headquarters, New York City, September 25, 2018. https://japan.kantei.go.jp/98_abe/statement/201809/_00005.html.

——. "Confluence of the Two Seas." Speech, Parliament of the Republic of India, August 22, 2007. https://www.mofa.go.jp/region/asia-paci/pmv0708/speech-2.html.

——. "Japan is Back." Speech, Center for Strategic and International Studies (CSIS), Washington, DC, February 22, 2013. https://japan.kantei.go.jp/96_abe/statement/201302/22speech_e.html.

——. "New Year's Press Conference." Prime Minister of Japan and His Cabinet, January 5, 2015. https://japan.kantei.go.jp/97_abe/statement/201501/05newyear.html.

——. "Pledge for Everlasting Peace." Statement, Ministry of Foreign Affairs of Japan, December 26, 2013. https://www.mofa.go.jp/a_o/rp/page24e_000021.html.

——. "Policy Speech by Prime Minister Shinzō Abe to the 198th Session of the Diet." Prime Minister of Japan and His Cabinet, January 28, 2019. https://japan.kantei.go.jp/98_abe/statement/201801/_00003.html.

——. "Press Conference." Prime Minister of Japan and His Cabinet, June 24, 2014. http://japan.kantei.go.jp/96_abe/statement/201406/0624kaiken.html.

——. "Press Conference," Prime Minister of Japan and His Cabinet, July 1, 2014. http://japan.kantei.go.jp/96_abe/statement/201407/0701kaiken.html.

—. "Press Conference During His Visit to Southeast Asia." Prime Minister of Japan and His Cabinet, July 27, 2013. http://japan.kantei.go.jp/96_abe/statement/201307/27kaiken_e.html.

—. "Press Conference Following His Attendance at the APEC Economic Leaders' Meeting, ASEAN-Related Summit Meetings, and Other Related Meetings." Prime Minister of Japan and His Cabinet, November 14, 2017. https://japan.kantei.go.jp/98_abe/statement/201711/_00007.html.

—. "Statement." Prime Minister of Japan and His Cabinet, August 14, 2015. https://japan.kantei.go.jp/97_abe/statement/201508/0814statement.html.

—. "Statement by Mr. Shinzō Abe." United Nations Sustainable Development Summit 2015, New York, September 27, 2015. https://www.mofa.go.jp/files/000101404.pdf.

—. "Toward an Alliance of Hope." Speech, Washington, DC, April 29, 2015. http://japan.kantei.go.jp/97_abe/statement/201504/uscongress.html.

Abe, Shinzō, and Barack Obama. "Remarks by President Obama and Prime Minister Abe of Japan in Joint Press Conference," Washington DC, April 28, 2015. https://obamawhitehouse.archives.gov/the-press-office/2015/04/28/remarks-president-obama-and-prime-minister-abe-japan-joint-press-confere.

Abrahms, Max. "What Terrorists Really Want: Terrorist Motives and Counterterrorism Strategy." *International Security* 32, no. 4 (2008): 78–105. https://doi.org/10.1162/isec.2008.32.4.78.

Acharya, Amitav. "How Ideas Spread: Whose Norms Matter? Norm Localization and Institutional Change in Asian Regionalism." *International Organization* 58, no. 2 (2004): 239–275. https://doi.org/10.1017/S0020818304582024.

Acquisition, Technology & Logistics Agency. "Chūō Chōtatsu no Gaikyō" (Central Procurement Overview). July 19, 2019. https://www.mod.go.jp/atla/souhon/ousho/pdf/ousho_total.pdf.

Adler, Emanuel. "Seizing the Middle Ground: Constructivism in World Politics." *European Journal of International Relations* 3, no. 3 (1997): 319–363. https://doi.org/10.1177/1354066197003003003.

Advisory Panel on Reconstruction of the Legal Basis for Security. "Report of the Advisory Panel on Reconstruction of the Legal Basis for Security." May 15, 2014. https://www.kantei.go.jp/jp/singi/anzenhosyou2/dai7/houkoku_en.pdf.

Akimoto, Daisuke. *The Abe Doctrine: Japan's Proactive Pacifism and Security Strategy*. Singapore: Palgrave Macmillan, 2018.

Allen, Matthew and Rumi Sakamoto. "War and Peace: War Memories and Museums in Japan." *History Compass* 11, no. 12 (2013): 1047–1058. https://doi.org/10.1111/hic3.12108.

Allison, Anne. *Millennial Monsters: Japanese Toys and the Global Imagination*. Berkeley: University of California Press, 2006.

Alt, Matt. *Pure Invention: How Japan's Pop Culture Conquered the World*. New York: Crown, 2020.

Anzai Science and Peace Office. "List of Museums for Peace Worldwide." May 5, 2017. http://asap-anzai.com/2017/05/museums-for-peace-worldwide/.

Arase, David. *Buying Power: The Political Economy of Japan's Foreign Aid*. Boulder, CO: Lynne Reinner, 1995.

—. "Japan, the Active State? Security Policy after 9/11." *Asian Survey* 47, no. 4 (2007): 560–583. https://doi.org/10.1525/as.2007.47.4.560.

Asahi Shimbun. "April 2009 Public Opinion Poll on the Constitution." Translated by the Maureen and Mike Mansfield Foundation, May 1, 2009. https://web.archive.org/web/20160603223722; http://mansfieldfdn.org/backup/polls/2009/poll-09-11.htm.

——. "April 2010 Regular Public Opinion Poll." Translated by the Maureen and Mike Mansfield Foundation, April 19, 2010. https://web.archive.org/web/20160604035657/; http://mansfieldfdn .org/backup/polls/2010/poll-10-12.htm.

——. "Asahi Poll: Constitutional Scholars Almost Unanimous That Bills Are Unconstitutional." July 11, 2015, https://web.archive.org/web/20150713013050; http://ajw.asahi.com/article/behind _news/politics/AJ201507110046.

——. "Asahi Poll: Nonsupport Rate for Abe Cabinet Jumps to 42 percent, Exceed Support," *Asahi Shimbun*, July 13, 2015, https://web.archive.org/web/20150809084649/; http://ajw.asahi.com /article/behind_news/politics/AJ201507130088.

——. "Asahi Poll: 63 percent Oppose Abe's Attempt to Lift Ban on Collective Self-Defense." April 7, 2014. https://web.archive.org/web/20140426132021; http://ajw.asahi.com/article/behind _news/politics/AJ201404070067.

——. "Regular Public Opinion Poll." Translated by the Maureen and Mike Mansfield Foundation, April 21, 2014. https://web.archive.org/web/20141109061257; http://mansfieldfdn.org /program/research-education-and-communication/asian-opinion-poll-database/listofpolls /2014-polls/.

——. "Regular Public Opinion Poll," Translated by the Maureen and Mike Mansfield Foundation, May 26, 2014. https://web.archive.org/web/20141109061257; http://mansfieldfdn.org/program /research-education-and-communication/asian-opinion-poll-database/listofpolls/2014-polls/.

——. "Regular Public Opinion Poll." Translated by the Maureen and Mike Mansfield Foundation, May 19, 2015. https://web.archive.org/web/20150715223223; http://mansfieldfdn.org/program /research-education-and-communication/asian-opinion-poll-database/asahi-shimbun-regular -public-opinion-poll-05192015/.

——. "Students, Professors Getting Political over Security Bills." July 19, 2015. https://web .archive.org/web/20150930055750; http://ajw.asahi.com/article/behind_news/social_affairs /AJ201507190012.

Asaoka, Masatoshi. "Japanese Public Opinion on Constitutional Revision in 2006." Council on Foreign Relations, August 1, 2016. https://www.cfr.org/blog/japanese-public-opinion-constitutional -revision-2016.

Ashizawa, Kuniko. "Japanese Assistance in Afghanistan: Helping the United States, Acting Globally, and Making a Friend." *Asia Policy* 17, no. 1 (2014): 59–65. https://doi.org/10.1353/asp .2014.0011.

Atoh, Makoto. *Gendai Jinkōgaku, Shōshi Kōreishakai no Kiso Chishiki* (Contemporary Demography, Basic Knowledge on Low Fertility and Aging). Tokyo: Nihon Hyōronsha, 2000.

——. "Very Low Fertility in Japan and Value Change Hypotheses." *Review of Population and Social Policy*, no. 10 (2001): 1–21.

Avey, Paul C. and Michael C. Desch. "What Do Policymakers Want from Us? Results of a Survey of Current and Former Senior National Security Decision Makers." *International Studies Quarterly* 58, no. 2 (2014): 227–246. https://doi.org/10.1111/isqu.12111.

Azimi, Nassrine. "An Admirable Culture of Shame." *New York Times*, June 7, 2010. https://www .nytimes.com/2010/06/08/opinion/08iht-edazimi.html.

Bacevich, Andrew. *The New American Militarism: How Americans are Seduced by War*. New York: Oxford University Press, 2005.

Baffelli, Erica. "Sōka Gakkai and Politics in Japan." *Religion Compass* 4, no. 12 (2010): 746–756. https://onlinelibrary.wiley.com/doi/abs/10.1111/j.1749-8171.2010.00252.x.

Ban, Ki-moon. "Implementing the Responsibility to Protect." Report of the Secretary General, United Nations, January 12, 2009. https://www.un.org/ruleoflaw/files/SG_reportA_63_677_en.pdf.

Bank of Japan. "Bank of Japan Accounts December 10, 2020." https://www.boj.or.jp/en/statistics/boj/other/acmai/release/2020/ac201210.htm/.

Barkin, J. Samuel. *Realist Constructivism*. Cambridge: Cambridge University Press, 2010.

Barrett, Clive, and Joyce Apsel. *Museums for Peace: Transforming Cultures*. The Hague: International Network of Museums for Peace, 2011.

Bellamy, Alex J., and Sara E. Davies. "The Responsibility to Protect in the Asia-Pacific Region." *Security Dialogue* 40, no. 6 (2009): 547–574. https://doi.org/10.1177/0967010609349907.

Berger, Thomas U. *Cultures of Antimilitarism: National Security in Germany and Japan*. Baltimore, MD: Johns Hopkins University Press, 1998.

——. "From Sword to Chrysanthemum: Japan's Culture of Anti-Militarism." *International Security* 17, no. 4 (1993): 119–150. http://doi.org/10.2307/2539024.

——. *War, Guilt, and World Politics After World War II*. New York: Cambridge University Press, 2012.

Betts, Richard K. "Wealth, Power, and Instability: East Asia and the United States After the Cold War." *International Security* 18, no. 3 (1993): 34–77. https://doi.org/10.2307/2539205.

Biddle, Stephen. "Explaining Military Outcomes." In *Creating Military Power: The Sources of Military Effectiveness*, ed. Risa A. Brooks and Elizabeth A. Stanley, 207–227. Stanford, CA: Stanford University Press, 2007.

Cabinet Office. "Gaikō ni Kansuru Yoron Chōsa" (Public Opinion Poll on Diplomacy). October 2004. https://web.archive.org/web/20130123052605; http://www8.cao.go.jp/survey/h16/h16-gaikou/3.html.

——. "Gaikō ni Kansuru Yoron Chōsa" (Public Opinion Poll on Diplomacy). October 2019. https://survey.gov-online.go.jp/r01/r01-gaiko/zh/z22.html.

——. "Jiētai Bōeimondai ni Kansuru Yoron Chōsa" (Public Opinion Poll on the Self-Defense Forces and Defense Issues). January 2017. https://survey.gov-online.go.jp/h29/h29-bouei/index.html.

——. "Overview of the Public Opinion Survey on Diplomacy." December 2016. https://www.gov-online.go.jp/eng/pdf/summaryg16.pdf.

——. "Overview of the Public Opinion Survey on Diplomacy." December 2017. https://www.gov-online.go.jp/eng/pdf/summaryg17.pdf.

——. "Overview of the Public Opinion Survey on Diplomacy." December 2018. https://www.gov-online.go.jp/eng/pdf/summaryg18.pdf.

Cannon, Tara. *Toward the Abe Statement on the 70th Anniversary of the End of World War II: Lessons from the 20th Century and a Vision for the 21st Century for Japan*. Translated by Tara Cannon. Tokyo: Japan Publishing Industry Foundation for Culture, 2017.

Caprio, Mark E. *Japanese Assimilation Policies in Colonial Korea, 1910–1945*. Seattle: University of Washington Press, 2009.

Catalinac, Amy. *Electoral Reform and National Security in Japan: From Pork to Foreign Policy*. New York: Cambridge University Press, 2016.

Cecchetti, Stephen G., M. S. Mahoney, and Fabrizio Zampolli, "The Future of Public Debt: Prospects and Implications." *BIS Working Papers* 300 (2010): 1–22. https://www.bis.org/publ /othp09.pdf.

Checkel, Jeffrey T. "It's the Process Stupid! Process Tracing in the Study of European and International Politics." *ARENA Working Papers Series* 26 (2005): 1–29.

Chiran Peace Museum. "Introduction." Accessed November 25, 2020. http://www.chiran-tokkou.jp /english/about/heiwakaikan/index.html.

Chirot, Daniel, Gi-Wook Shin, and Daniel Sneider, eds. *Confronting Memories of World War II: European and Asian Legacies.* Seattle: University of Washington Press, 2014.

Christensson, Per. "Firmware Definition." TechTerms, 2006. http://techterms.com/definition /firmware.

Christy, Alan S. "The Making of Imperial Subjects in Okinawa." *Positions: East Asia Cultures Critique* 1, no. 3 (1993): 607–639. https://doi.org/10.1215/10679847-1-3-607.

Central Intelligence Agency. *World Factbook 2020–2021.* New York: Skyhorse, 2020.

——. "Total Fertility Rate." Accessed on December 26, 2020. https://www.cia.gov/library/publications /the-world-factbook/fields/356.html.

City of Hiroshima. "Hiroshima-shi Kankō Gaikyō" (Hiroshima City Tourism Overview). Hiroshima City Economic and Tourism Bureau. 2018. https://www.city.hiroshima.lg.jp/uploaded /attachment/107329.pdf.

——. "Nendo Betsu Sō Nyūkanshasū Oyobi Gaikokujin Nyūkanshasū-tō" (Total Number of Visitors and Foreign Visitors and Such by Fiscal Year). April 7, 2020. https://www.city.hiroshima.lg.jp /uploaded/attachment/112311.pdf.

——. "Shūgakuryokō-tō Dantai no Chiiki Betsu Nyūkanshasū FY2017-FY2019" (Number of School Trips and Such Visitors by Region FY2017–FY2019). April 7, 2020. https://www.city.hiroshima .lg.jp/uploaded/attachment/112309.pdf?fbclid=IwAR029fshrOmcgt769eSUqG-V31vTPoyps _6T_VttscOzWJbshkrjbwq_vvI.

——. "Sō Nyūkanshasū Oyobi Shūgakuryokō-tō Dantai Nyūkanshasū-to" (Total Number of Visitors and Such and Number of Student Group Excursions and Such), accessed November 30, 2020. https://www.city.hiroshima.lg.jp/uploaded/attachment/112310.pdf.

City of Nagasaki. "Genbaku Shiryōkan Nendo Betsu Nyūkanshasū (FY1955~)" (Number of Visitors to the Atomic Bomb Museum from FY1955~). N.d.

Collier, David, and Steven Levitsky. "Democracy 'with Adjectives': Conceptual Innovation in Comparative." *World Politics* 49, no. 3 (1997): 430–451. https://www.jstor.org/stable/25054009.

Cooley, Alexander. *Base Politics: Demographic Change and the U.S. Military Overseas.* Ithaca, NY: Cornell University Press, 2008.

Cooney, Kevin J. *Japan's Foreign Policy Maturation: A Quest of Normalcy.* New York: Routledge, 2002.

Croissant, Aurel. "Civilian Control Over the Military in East Asia." EAI Fellows Program Working Paper Series 31, Ruprecht-Karls-Universität, Heidelberg, 2011, 1–62. http://www.eai.or.kr /data/bbs/eng_report/20111151042365.pdf.

Croissant, Aurel, David. Kuehn, Paul. Chambers, and Siegfried. O. Wolf. "Beyond the Fallacy of Coup-ism: Conceptualizing Civilian Control of the Military in Emerging Democracies." *Democratization* 17, no. 5 (2010): 950–975. https://doi.org/10.1080/13510347.2010.501180.

Cryanoski, David. "Japanese Scientists Call for Boycott of Military Research." *Nature*, April 6, 2017. https://www.nature.com/news/japanese-scientists-call-for-boycott-of-military-research-1.21779.

Cwiertka, Katarzyna J. *Modern Japanese Cuisine: Food, Power and National Identity*. London: Reaktion, 2006.

Dalton, Emma. "Normalizing the Japan Self-Defense Forces via Marriage." *Journal of War & Culture Studies* (2019). https://doi.org/10.1080/17526272.2020.1738680.

——. "Women as Helpmates: The Japan Self-Defense Forces and Gender." *Critical Military Studies* (2018). https://doi.org/10.1080/23337486.2019.1707496.

Defense News. "Top 100 for 2019." Accessed November 19 2020. https://people.defensenews.com/top-100/.

Dekle, Robert. *Land of the Setting Sun?—Prosperity in Depth: Japan*. London: Legatum Institute, 2012.

Department of State. "Visits by Foreign Leaders." Office of the Historian. Accessed November 30, 2020. https://history.state.gov/departmenthistory/visits.

Desch, Michael C. "How Political Science Became Irrelevant." *Chronicle of Higher Education*, February 27, 2019. https://www.chronicle.com/article/How-Political-Science-Became/245777?cid=wcontentgrid_40_2.

Doak, Kevin M. "What Is a Nation and Who Belongs? National Narratives and the Ethnic Imagination in Twentieth-Century Japan." *American Historical Review* 102, no. 2 (1997): 283–309. https://doi.org/10.1086/ahr/102.2.283.

Dobson, Hugo. "Is Japan Really Back? The 'Abe Doctrine' and Global Governance." *Journal of Contemporary Asia* 47, no. 2 (2017): 199–224. https://doi.org/10.1080/00472336.2016.1257044.

——. *Japan and United Nations Peacekeeping: New Pressures and New Responses*. London: Routledge Curzon, 2003.

Dower, John. W. *Embracing Defeat: Japan in the Wake of World War II*. New York: Norton, 1999.

——. *War Without Mercy: Race and Power in the Pacific War*. New York: Pantheon, 1987.

Doyle II, Thomas E. "Hiroshima and Two Paradoxes of Japanese Nuclear Perplexity." *Critical Military Studies* 1, no. 2 (2015): 160–173. https://doi.org/10.1080/23337486.2015.1050266.

Draudt, Darcie. "South Korea's National Identity Crisis in the Face of Emerging Multiculturalism." *Georgetown Journal of International Affairs* 18, no. 1 (2016): 12–19. http://doi.org/10.1353/gia.2016.0003.

Easley, Leif-Eric. "How Proactive? How Pacifist? Charting Japan's Evolving Defense Posture." *Australian Journal of International Affairs* 71, no. 1 (2017): 63–87. https://doi.org/10.1080/10357718.2016.1181148.

Easton, David. *A Systems Analysis of Political Life*. New York: John Wiley, 1965.

Ebenstein, Lanny. *Chicagonomics: The Evolution of Chicago Free Market Economics*. New York: St. Martin's, 2015.

Eberstadt, Nicholas. "Demography and Japan's Future." In *Reimagining Japan: The Quest for a Future That Works*, ed. Clay Chandler, Heang Chhor, and Brian Salsberg, 82–87. San Francisco: VIZ Media, 2011.

Egawa, Yusuke, Mizukawa Kyousuke, and Niiyama Kyoko. "Hiroshima Mayor Avoids Calling for Ratification of Nuclear Treaty in Peace Declaration." *Chugoku Shimbun*, August 7, 2018. http://www.hiroshimapeacemedia.jp/?p=86527.

Eichler, Maya. "Militarized Masculinities in International Relations." *Brown Journal of World Affairs* 21, no. 1 (2014): 81–94. http://bjwa.brown.edu/21-1/militarized-masculinities-in-international -relations/.

Eldridge, Robert D. *Jinkō Genshō to Jieitai* (Population Decline and the Self-Defense Forces). Tokyo: Fusōsha Shinso, 2019.

Eldridge, Robert D., and Paul Midford, eds. *The Japanese Ground Self-Defense Force: Search for Legitimacy*. New York: Palgrave Macmillan, 2017.

Elman, Colin. "Explanatory Typologies in Qualitative Studies of International Politics." *International Organization* 59, no. 2 (2005): 293–326. https://doi.org/10.1017/S0020818305050101.

Enloe, Cynthia. *The Curious Feminist: Searching for Women in a New Age of Empire*. Berkeley: University of California Press, 2004.

—. *Maneuvers: The International Politics of Militarizing Women's Lives*. Berkeley: University of California Press, 2000.

Envall, H. D. P. "The 'Abe Doctrine': Japan's New Regional Realism." *International Relations of the Asia-Pacific* 20, no. 1 (2020): 31–59. https://doi.org/10.1093/irap/lcy014.

Eskildsen, Robert. "Of Civilization and Savages: The Mimetic Imperialism of Japan's 1874 Expedition to Taiwan." *American Historical Review* 107, no. 2 (2002): 388–418. https://doi.org /10.1086/ahr/107.2.388.

Fatton, Lionel P. " 'Japan is Back': Autonomy and Balancing Amidst an Unstable China–US–Japan Triangle." *Asia & the Pacific Policy Studies* 5, no. 2 (2018): 264–278. https://doi.org/10.1002 /app5.240.

Finnemore, Martha, and Kathryn Sikkink. "International Norm Dynamics and Political Change." *International Organization* 52, no. 4 (1998): 887–917. https://doi.org/10.1162/002081898550789.

Fisker-Nielson, Anne M. *Religion and Politics in Contemporary Japan: Soka Gakkai Youth and Komeito*. London: Routledge, 2013.

Foucault, Michel. *Discipline and Punish: The Birth of Prison*. Translated by Alan Sheridan. London: Penguin, 1975.

Frühstück, Sabine. "The Modern Girl as Militarist: Female Soldiers in and Beyond Japan's Self-Defense Forces." In *Modern Girls on the Go: Gender, Mobility and Labor in Japan*, ed. Alisa Freedman, Laura Miller, and Christine R. Yano, 131–148. Stanford, CA: Stanford University Press, 2013.

—. *Playing War: Children and the Paradoxes of Modern Militarism in Japan*. Oakland: University of California Press, 2017.

—. *Uneasy Warriors: Gender, Memory, and Popular Culture in the Japanese Army*. Berkeley: University of California Press, 2007.

Fujitani, Takashi. "Electronic Pageantry and Japan's "Symbolic Emperor' " *Journal of Asian Studies* 51, no. 4 (1992): 824–850. https://doi.org/10.2307/2059038.

—. *Splendid Monarchy: Power and Pageantry in Modern Japan*. Berkeley: University of California Press, 1996.

Fukuda, Yasuo. "Policy Speech to the 169th Session of the Diet." Prime Minister of Japan and His Cabinet, January 18, 2008. http://japan.kantei.go.jp/hukudaspeech/2008/01/18housin_e.html.

Fukushima, Akiko. "Japan's 'Proactive Contribution to Peace': A Mere Political Label?" Tokyo Foundation for Policy Research, June 19, 2014. https://www.tkfd.or.jp/en/research/detail .php?id=344.

——. *Multilateralism Recalibrated: Japan's Engagement in Institution Building in the Past 70 Years and Beyond.* Washington, DC: Center for Strategic & International Studies, 2016, 1–35. https://csis-website-prod.s3.amazonaws.com/s3fs-public/160401_Multilateralism_Recalibrated.pdf.

Futori, Hideshi. "Japan's Disaster Diplomacy: Fostering Military Cooperation in Asia." *Pacific Bulletin*, no. 213 (May 13, 2013). https://www.eastwestcenter.org/system/tdf/private/apb213.pdf?file=1&type=node&id=34057.

Ganiel, Gladys. "The Legacy of the Good Friday Agreement: Northern Irish Politics, Culture and Art After 1998." In *A Gender-Balanced Approach to Transforming Cultures of Militarism in Northern Ireland*, ed. Charles I. Armstrong, David Herbert, and Jan Erik Mustad, 133–152. New York: Palgrave Macmillan, 2019.

Genron NPO. "The 7th Japan-South Korea Joint Public Opinion Poll (2019): Analysis Report on Comparative Data." June 2019. https://www.genron-npo.net/en/7th-Japan-South%20Korea-JointOpinionPoll.pdf.

——. "The 15th Joint Public Opinion Poll: Japan-China Public Opinion Survey 2019." October 2019. https://www.genron-npo.net/en/archives/191024.pdf.

George, Alexander L., and Andrew Bennett. *Case Studies and Theory Development in the Social Sciences.* Cambridge, MA: MIT Press, 2005.

Gibbons, Rebecca Davis. "The Humanitarian Turn in Nuclear Disarmament and the Treaty on the Prohibition of Nuclear Weapons." *Nonproliferation Review* 25, no. 1–2 (2018): 11–36. https://doi.org/10.1080/10736700.2018.1486960.

Gibson, James William. *The Perfect War: Technowar in Vietnam.* Boston: Atlantic Monthly Press, 2000.

Glosserman, Brad. *Peak Japan: The End of Great Ambitions.* Washington, DC: Georgetown University Press, 2019.

Gordon, Andrew. *A Modern History of Japan: From Tokugawa Times to the Present.* New York: Oxford University Press, 2003.

Green, Michael. *Japan's Reluctant Realism: Foreign Policy Challenges in an Era of Uncertain Power.* New York: Palgrave, 2001.

Green, Michael, Zach Cooper, and Center for Strategic and International Studies (Washington, DC). *Strategic Japan: New Approaches to Foreign Policy and the U.S.–Japan Alliance*, ed. Michael Green and Zach Cooper. Washington, DC: Center for Strategic & International Studies, 2015.

Gustafsson, Karl, Linus Hagström and Uly Hanssen. "Japan's Pacifism is Dead." *Survival* 60, no. 6 (2018): 137–158. https://doi.org/10.1080/00396338.2018.1542803.

Haas, Mark L. "A Geriatric Peace? The Future of US Power in a World of Aging Populations." *International Security* 32, no. 1 (2007): 112–147. https://doi.org/10.1162/isec.2007.32.1.112.

Haddad, Mary Alice. "Environmental Advocacy: Insights from East Asia." *Asian Journal of Political Science* 25, no. 3 (2017): 401–419. https://doi.org/10.1080/02185377.2017.1352526.

Hagström, Linus, and Jon Williamsson. " 'Remilitarization,' Really? Assessing Change in Japanese Foreign Security Policy." *Asian Security* 5, no. 3 (2009): 242–272. https://doi.org/10.1080/14799850903178980.

Hahm, Chaihark, and Kim Sung Ho. *Making We the People: Democratic Constitutional Founding in Postwar Japan and South Korea* (Comparative Constitutional Law and Policy). New York: Cambridge University Press, 2015.

Hamai, Shinso. *A-Bomb Mayor: Warnings and Hope from Hiroshima*. Translated by Elizabeth W. Baldwin. Hiroshima, Japan: Publication Committee for the English Version of A-Bomb Mayor, 2010.

Hane, Mikiso. *Modern Japan: A Historical Survey*. Boulder, CO: Westview, 1992.

Hardin, Garrett. "The Tragedy of the Commons." *Science* 162, no. 3859 (1968): 1243–1248. http://doi.org/10.1126/science.162.3859.1243.

Harootunian, Harry D. *Overcome by Modernity: History, Culture, and Community in Interwar Japan*. Princeton, NJ: Princeton University Press, 2000.

Harris, Tobias. *The Iconoclast: Shinzō Abe and the New Japan*. London: Hurst, 2020.

Hassner, Pierre. "Violence and Ethics: Beyond the Reason of State Paradigm." In *Ethics and International Affairs: Extent and Limits*, ed. Jean-Marc Coicaud and Daniel Warner, 84–102. New York: United Nations University Press, 2001.

Hayes, Louis D. *Japan and the Security of Asia. Studies of Modern Japan*. Lanham, MD: Lexington, 2001.

Helms, Elissa. "Women as Agents of Ethnic Reconciliation? Women's NGOs and International Intervention in Postwar Bosnia-Herzegovina." *Women's Studies International Forum* 26, no. 1 (2003): 15–33. https://doi.org/10.1016/S0277-5395(02)00352-7.

Hirano, Keiji. "Legacy of 1960 Protest Movement Lives On." *Japan Times*, July 11, 2010. http://www.japantimes.co.jp/news/2010/06/11/national/legacy-of-1960-protest-movement-lives-on/#.VXl6mGD4tFL.

Hirata, Keiko. "Who Shapes the National Security Debate? Divergent Interpretations of Japan's Security Role." *Asian Affairs: An American Review* 35, no. 3 (2008): 123–151. https://www.tandfonline.com/doi/abs/10.3200/AAFS.35.3.123-151.

Hirose, Shunsuke. "Shinzō Abe's Biggest Enemy: The LDP." *Diplomat*, April 14, 2014. https://thediplomat.com/2014/04/shinzo-abes-biggest-enemy-the-ldp/.

Hiroshima Peace Media Center. "Editorial: Removal of Mannequins from Museum." Hiroshima Peace Memorial Center, October 23, 2013. http://www.hiroshimapeacemedia.jp/?p=20531.

Hiroshima Prefecture and Japan Institute of International Affairs. *Hiroshima Report: Evaluation of Achievement in Nuclear Disarmament, Non-Proliferation and Nuclear Security in 2014*. 2015, 1–189.

Hoffman, Michael. "Japan Faces Up to the Prospect of Losing a Middle-Class War." *Japan Times*, April 14, 2018. https://www.japantimes.co.jp/news/2018/04/14/national/media-national/japan-faces-prospect-losing-middle-class-war/#.XISc2y2ZN24.

Hofmann, Stephanie C., and Andrew I. Yeo. "Business as Usual: The Role of Norms in Alliance Management." *European Journal of International Relations* 21, no. 2 (2015): 377–401. https://doi.org/10.1177/1354066114533978.

Honna, Jun. "Japan and the Responsibility to Protect: Coping with Human Security Diplomacy." *Pacific Review* 25, no. 1 (2012): 95–112. https://doi.org/10.1080/09512748.2011.632968.

Hornung, Jeffrey W. "Japan's Growing Hard Hedge Against China." *Asian Security* 10, no. 2 (2014): 97–122. https://doi.org/10.1080/14799855.2014.914497.

Hosoya, Yuichi. "The Rise and Fall of Japan's Grand Strategy: The 'Arc of Freedom and Prosperity' and the Future Asian Order." *Asia-Pacific Review* 18, no. 1 (2011): 13–24. https://doi.org/10.1080/13439006.2011.582677.

Hudson, Valerie M., and Andrea Den Boar. "A Surplus of Men, a Deficit of Peace: Security and Sex Ratios in Asia's Largest State." *International Security* 26, no. 4 (2002): 5-38. https://doi .org/10.1162/016228802753696753.

Hughes, Christopher W. *Japan's Foreign and Security Policy Under the "Abe Doctrine": New Dynamism or New Dead End?* (Palgrave Pivot), Basingstoke, UK: Palgrave Macmillan, 2017.

——. *Japan's Re-Emergence as a "Normal" Military Power.* Oxford: Oxford University Press for the International Institute of Strategic Studies, 2004.

——. *Japan's Remilitarisation.* Oxon, UK: Routledge for International Institute for Strategic Studies, 2009.

——. "Japan's 'Resentful Realism' and Balancing China's Rise." *Chinese Journal of International Politics* 9, no. 2 (2016): 109-150. https://doi.org/10.1093/cjip/pow004.

——. "Japan's Strategic Trajectory and Collective Self-Defense: Essential Continuity or Radical Shift?" *Journal of Japanese Studies* 43, no. 1 (2017): 93-126. https://doi.org/10.1353/jjs.2017.0005.

——. "'Super-Sizing' the DPRK Threat: Japan's Evolving Military Posture and North Korea." *Asian Survey* 49, no. 2 (2009): 291-311. https://doi.org/10.1525/as.2009.49.2.291.

Huntington, Samuel P. "Why International Primacy Matters." *International Security* 17, no. 4 (1993): 68-83. https://doi.org/10.2307/2539022.

Hur, Aram. "Adapting to Democracy: Identity and the Political Development of North Korean Defectors." *Journal of East Asian Studies* 18, no. 1 (2018): 97-115. https://doi.org/10.1017/jea.2017.30.

Inoguchi, Takashi. "A North-East Asian Perspective." *Australian Journal of International Affairs* 55, no. 2 (2001): 199-212. https://doi.org/10.1080/10357710120066894.

——. "Japan's Ambition for Normal Statehood." In *Between Compliance and Conflict: East Asia, Latin America, and the "New" Pax Americana*, ed. Jorge I. Domínguez, and Byung-kook Kim, 135-164. New York: Routledge, 2005.

——. "Japan as a Global Ordinary Power: Its Current Phase." *Japanese Studies* 28, no. 1 (2008): 3-13. https://doi.org/10.1080/10371390801939047.

Inoue, Masamichi S. *Okinawa and the U.S. Military: Identity Making in the Age of Globalization, with a New Preface.* New York: Columbia University Press, 2017.

International Institute for Strategic Studies. *The Military Balance.* London: Routledge, various years.

International Monetary Fund. "World Economic Outlook Database."

Iriye, Akira. *Japan and the Wider World: From the Mid-Nineteenth Century to the Present.* London: Routledge, 2014.

Ishizuka, Katsumi. "Japan and UN Peace Operations." *Japanese Journal of Political Science* 5, no. 1 (2004): 137-157. https://doi.org/10.1017/S1468109904001355.

——. "Japan's Policy Towards UN Peacekeeping Operations." *International Peacekeeping* 12, no. 1 (2005): 67-86. https://doi.org/10.1080/1353331042000286568.

Ito, Takao. "Reading Resistance: The Record of Tsunesaburo Makiguchi's Interrogation by Wartime Japan's 'Thought Police.'" *Educational Studies* 45, no. 2 (2009): 133-145. https://doi.org /10.1080/00131940902762169.

Itoh, Mayumi. "Japanese Constitutional Revision: A Neo-Liberal Proposal for Article 9 in a Comparative Perspective." *Asian Survey* 41, no. 2 (2001): 310-327. https://doi.org/10.1525/as.2001 .41.2.310.

Iwami, Tadashi. "Understanding Japan's Peacebuilding in Concept and Practice." *East Asia: An International Quarterly* 33, no. 2 (2016): 111–132. https://doi.org/10.1007/s12140-016-9255-9.

Iwaya, Takeshi. "Press Conference" (as recorded). Ministry of Defense, Tokyo, Japan, October 2, 2018. https://www.mod.go.jp/e/press/2018/10/02a.html.

——. "Press Conference (10:45–11:31 p.m.)." Ministry of Defense, Tokyo, Japan. October 2, 2018. https://www.mod.go.jp/e/press/2018/10/02b.html.

Izumikawa, Yasuhiro. "Explaining Japanese Antimilitarism: Normative and Realist Constraints on Japan's Security Policy." *International Security* 35, no. 2 (2010): 123–160. https://doi.org/10.1162/ISEC_a_00020.

Jackson, Richard, and Neil Howe. *The Graying of the Great Powers: Demography and Geopolitics in the 21st Century.* Washington, DC: Center for Strategic and International Studies, 2008.

Japan Coast Guard. "*Senkakushotō Shūhen Kaiiki ni Okeru Chūgoku Kōsentō no Dōkō to Wagakuni no Taisho*" (Trends in Chinese Government and Other Vessels in the Waters Surrounding the Senkaku Islands and Japan's Response). July 9, 2020. https://www.kaiho.mlit.go.jp/mission/senkaku/senkaku.html.

Japan Press Weekly. "40 SDF Members Dispatched Overseas Commit Suicide." July 9, 2014. http://www.japan-press.co.jp/modules/news/index.php?id=7370.

Japan Student Services Organization (JASSO). "Heisei 30-Nendo Nihonjin Gakusei Ryūgaku Jōkyō Chōsa Kekka" (FY2018 Japanese Student Study Abroad Survey Results). April, 2019. https://www.studyinjapan.go.jp/ja/_mt/2020/08/date2018n.pdf.

——. "International Students in Japan 2019." January 2019. https://www.jasso.go.jp/en/about/statistics/intl_student/data2018.html.

Japan Times. "Crown Prince Turns 55, Calls for Accounts of History to be Passed Down Correctly." February 23, 2015. https://www.japantimes.co.jp/news/2015/02/23/national/crown-prince-turns-55-calls-accounts-history-passed-correctly/.

——. "Japan to Dispatch SDF to Nepal, Part of Multifaceted Aid Effort." April 28, 2015. https://www.japantimes.co.jp/news/2015/04/28/national/japan-send-110-troops-nepal-join-quake-relief-operations/.

——. "No Need to Review Three Non-Nuclear Principles, Kono Says." September 8, 2017. https://www.japantimes.co.jp/news/2017/09/08/national/no-need-review-three-non-nuclear-principles-kono-says/#.XuxaFS2z125.

——. "Planned War Museum in Kumamoto Prefecture Criticized for Tourism Focus. July 27, 2018. https://www.japantimes.co.jp/news/2018/07/27/national/planned-war-museum-kumamoto-prefecture-criticized-tourism-focus/.

——. "Sexist Heckling Occurred at April Diet Committee Meeting: Female Diet Member." July 4, 2014. http://www.japantimes.co.jp/news/2014/07/04/national/politics-diplomacy/sexist-heckling-occurred-april-diet-committee-meeting-female-diet-member/.

——. "Thousands Rally Outside Diet Against Abe's Security Bills." June 15, 2015. https://web.archive.org/web/20150617214736; http://www.japantimes.co.jp/news/2015/06/15/national/politics-diplomacy/thousands-rally-outside-diet-abes-security-bills/.

——."Toshiba Hit with F-15 Countersuit." November 27, 2012. https://www.japantimes.co.jp/news/2012/11/27/national/toshiba-hit-with-f-15-countersuit/#.XwuUyi2z124.

Jentleson, Bruce W., and Ely Ratner. "Bridging the Beltway–Ivory Tower Gap." *International Studies Review* 13, no. 1 (2011): 6–11. https://doi.org/10.1111/j.1468-2486.2010.00992.x.

Jodai, Miyako. "The 69th Nagasaki Peace Ceremony Pledge for Peace." Nagasaki, Japan, August 9, 2014. https://www.youtube.com/watch?v=kueL3VC0EZQ.

Johnson, Chalmers A. *Japan in Search of a "Normal" Role.* La Jolla, CA.: IGCC, 1992.

Kadia, Miriam. K. "Repatriation but Not 'Return': A Japanese Brazilian Dekasegi Goes Back to Brazil." *Asia-Pacific Journal: Japan Focus* 13, no. 14 (2015): 1–15. https://apjjf.org/2015/13/13/Miriam-Kingsberg/4304.html.

Kafura, Craig. "Public Opinion and the US-Japan Alliance at the Outset of the Trump Administration." Chicago Council on Global Affairs, February 8, 2017. https://www.thechicagocouncil.org/publication/public-opinion-and-us-japan-alliance-outset-trump-administration.

Kameda, Masaaki. "Abe: Japan Won't Slide into US War despite Collective Defense Loophole." *Japan Times*, May 14, 2015. https://www.japantimes.co.jp/news/2015/05/14/national/politics-diplomacy/abe-says-new-security-bills-are-not-war-legislation/#.XvmRcy2z124.

Katzenstein, Peter J. *The Culture of National Security: Norms and Identity in World Politics* (New Directions in World Politics). New York: Columbia University Press, 1996.

Kawasaki, Tsuyoshi. "Postclassical Realism and Japanese Security Policy." *Pacific Review* 14, no. 2 (2001): 221–240. https://doi.org/10.1080/09512740110037361.

Kegly, Charles W., and Gregory A. Raymond. "Alliance Norms and War: A New Piece in an Old Puzzle." *International Studies Quarterly* 26, no. 4 (1982): 572–595. https://doi.org/10.2307/3013963.

Kelly Tim, and Kobu, Nobuhiro. "Gulf War Trauma Began Japan's Retreat from Pacifism." Reuters, December 19, 2015. https://www.reuters.com/article/us-japan-military-history-insight/gulf-war-trauma-began-japans-retreat-from-pacifism-idUSKBN0U300D20151220.

Kent, Pauline. "Shame as a Social Sanction in Japan: Shameful Behavior as Perceived by the Voting Public." *Japan Review*, no. 3 (1992): 97–130. https://www.jstor.org/stable/25790914.

Kerry, John, Chuck Hagel, Kishida Fumio, and Onodera Itsunori. "Joint Statement of the Security Consultative Committee: Toward a More Robust Alliance and Greater Shared Responsibilities." U.S. Department of State, October 3, 2013. https://2009-2017.state.gov/r/pa/prs/ps/2013/10/215070.htm.

Kim, Jack, Sui-Lee Wee, and Linda Sieg. "South Korea, China Warn Japan Not to Backtrack on Apology over Wartime Past." Reuters, January 27, 2015. https://www.reuters.com/article/us-southkorea-japan-abe/south-korea-china-warn-japan-not-to-backtrack-on-apology-over-wartime-past-idUSKBN0L00QO20150128..

Kim, Mikyoung, "Memory and Reconciliation: Culturally Embedded Memories of Japan and Korea." In *Hiroshima & Peace*, ed. Carol Rinnert, Omar Farouk, and Inoue Yasuhiro, 147–165. Hiroshima: Keisuisha, 2010.

King, Amy. "China's Response to Japan's Constitutional Reinterpretation." *East Asia Forum*, July 27, 2014. http://www.eastasiaforum.org/2014/07/27/china-responds-to-japans-constitutional-reinterpretation/.

Kisala, Robert. J. "Japanese Religions." In *Religion in the Modern World Traditions and Transformations*, ed. Linda. Woodhead, 127–148. London: Routledge, 2002.

Kitaoka, Shinichi, "How Should We View the Path the World and Japan Took During the 20th Century? What are the Lessons We Should Draw from the Experiences in the 20th Century?" In *Toward the Abe Statement on the 70th Anniversary of the End of World War II: Lessons from the 20th Century and a Vision for the 21st Century.* Translated by Tara Cannon. Tokyo: Japan Publishing Industry Foundation for Culture, 2017.

Kliman, Daniel M. *Japan's Security Strategy in the Post-9/11 World Embracing a New Realpolitik.* Westport, CT: Praeger, 2006.

Klotz, Audie, and Cecelia Lynch. *Strategies for Research in Constructivist International Relations.* Armonk, NY: M. E. Sharpe, 2007.

Kohn, Richard H. "The Danger of Militarization in an Endless 'War' on Terrorism." *Journal of Military History* 73, no. 1 (2009): 177–208. https://doi.org/10.1353/jmh.0.0216.

Koizumi, Junichiro. "Policy Speech to the 151st Session of the Diet." Ministry of Foreign Affairs of Japan, May 7, 2001. http://www.mofa.go.jp/announce/pm/koizumi/speech0105.html.

——. "Policy Speech to the 164th Session of the Diet." Ministry of Foreign Affairs of Japan, January 20, 2006. https://japan.kantei.go.jp/koizumispeech/2006/01/20speech_e.html.

——. "Press Conference." Warp Web Archiving Project, April 27, 2001. https://warp.ndl.go.jp/info:ndljp/pid/11236451/www.kantei.go.jp/jp/koizumispeech/2001/0427kisyakaiken.html.

——. "Press Conference." Ministry of Foreign Affairs of Japan, January 4, 2005. https://www.mofa.go.jp/announce/pm/koizumi/press0501.html.

——. "Press Conference." Ministry of Foreign Affairs of Japan, January 4, 2006. http://www.mofa.go.jp/announce/pm/koizumi/speech0105.htmlhttp://japan.kantei.go.jp/koizumispeech/2006/01/04press_e.html.

Kōmura, Masahiko. "Japan: A Builder of Peace." Ministry of Foreign Affairs of Japan, January 24, 2008. http://www.mofa.go.jp/policy/un/pko/speech0801.html.

Komuro, Yoshie. "Japan's Next Balancing Act." In *Reimagining Japan: The Quest for a Future That Works*, ed. Clay Chandler, Heang Chhor, and Brian Salsberg, 343–346. San Francisco: VIZ Media, 2011.

Kōno, Tarō. "Foreign Policy Speech by Foreign Minister Kono to the 198th Session of the Diet." Ministry of Foreign Affairs of Japan, Tokyo, January 28, 2019. https://www.mofa.go.jp/fp/unp_a/page3e_000987.html.

Kōsai, Yutaka. "Contributions, Yes, But Geared to the Complex Needs of a Complex World." In *Japan, Internationalism and the UN*, ed. Ronald Dore, 148–155. London: Routledge, 1997.

Kovitz, Marcia. "The Roots of Military Masculinity." In *Military Masculinities: Identity and the State*, ed. Paul R. Higate, 1–14. Westport, CT.: Praeger, 2003.

Kratochwil, Friedrich. "The Force of Prescriptions." *International Organization* 38, no. 4 (1984): 685–708. https://doi.org/10.1017/S0020818300026916.

Kratochwil, Friedrich, and John G. Ruggie. "International Organization: A State of the Art on an Art of the State." *International Organization* 40, no. 4 (1986): 753–775. https://doi.org/10.1017/S0020818300027363.

Krugman, Paul. "How Did Economists Get it so Wrong?" *New York Times*, September 2, 2009. https://www.nytimes.com/2009/09/06/magazine/06Economic-t.html.

Ku, Minseon, "The Role of Identity in South Korea's Policies Towards Japan." *Korean Social Science Journal* 43 (2016): 75–94. https://doi.org/10.1007/s40483-016-0033-5.

Kubota, Yukari. "Japan's Defense Industrial Base in Danger of Collapse." *AJISS*, no. 90 (2010): 1–4. https://www.jiia.or.jp/en_commentary/pdf/AJISS-Commentary90.pdf.

Kurino, Ohtori. "Challenge and Dilemma for Peace Movements in Japan." *Hiroshima Peace Science* 10 (1987): 167–185. https://doi.org/10.15027/15180.

Kurusu, Kaori, and Rikki Kersten. "Japan as an Active Agent for Global Norms: The Political Dynamism Behind the Acceptance and Promotion of 'Human Security.' " *Asia-Pacific Review* 18, no. 2 (2011): 115–137. https://doi.org/10.1080/13439006.2011.630854.

Kusunoki, Ayako, "The Early Years of the Ground Self-Defense Forces, 1945–1960." In *The Japanese Ground Self-Defense Force: Search for Legitimacy*, ed. Robert D. Eldridge and Paul Midford. New York: Palgrave Macmillan, 2017.

Langager, Mark. "Elements of War and Peace in History Education in the US and Japan: A Case Study Comparison." *Journal of Peace Education* 6, no. 1 (2009): 119–136. https://doi.org/10.1080/17400200802677985.

Lasswell, Harold. *Politics: Who Gets What, When, How.* New York: Whittlesey House, 1936.

Layne, Christopher. "The Unipolar Illusion: Why New Great Powers Will Rise." *International Security* 17, no. 4 (1993): 5–51. https://doi.org/10.2307/2539020.

Le, Tom P. "Japan and the Revolution in Military Affairs." *Journal of Asian Security and International Affairs* 5, no. 2 (2018): 172–196. https://doi.org/10.1177/2347797018783112.

——. "Negotiating in Good Faith: Overcoming Legitimacy Problems in the Japan-South Korea Reconciliation Process," *Journal of Asian Studies* 78, no. 3 (2019): 621–644. https://doi.org/10.1017/S0021911819000664P.

Legro, Jeffrey. W., and Andrew Moravcsik. "Is Anybody Still a Realist?" *International Security* 24, no. 2 (1999): 5–55. https://doi.org/10.1162/016228899560130.

Leheny, David. *Empire of Hope: The Sentimental Politics of Japanese Decline.* Ithaca, NY: Cornell University Press, 2018.

Levin, Norman D., Mark A. Lorell, and Arthur J. Alexander. *The Wary Warriors: Future Directions in Japanese Security Policies.* Santa Monica, CA: Rand, 1993.

Lewis, Adrian. *The American Culture of War: The History of U.S. Military Force from World War II to Operation Iraqi Freedom.* 3rd ed. New York: Routledge, 2017. https://doi-org.ccl.idm.oclc.org/10.4324/9781315544021.

Liff, Adam P. "Japan's National Security Council: Policy Coordination and Political Power." *Japanese Studies* 38, no. 2 (2018): 253–279. https://doi.org/10.1080/10371397.2018.1503926.

——. "Policy by Other Means: Collective Self-Defense and the Politics of Japan's Postwar Constitutional Reinterpretations." *Asia Policy* 24 (2017): 139–172. https://doi.org/10.1353/asp.2017.0035.

Lind, Jennifer M. "Pacifism or Passing the Buck? Testing Theories of Japanese Security Policy." *International Security* 29, no. 1 (2004): 92–121. https://doi.org/10.1162/0162288041762968.

——. *Sorry States Apologies in International Politics.* Ithaca, NY: Cornell University Press, 2008.

Lynch, Cecelia. "Critical Interpretation and Interwar Peace Movements: Challenging Dominant Narratives." In *Interpretation and Method: Empirical Research Methods and the Interpretive Turn*, ed. Dvora Yanow and Peregrine Schwartz-Shea, 291–299. Armonk, NY: M. E. Sharpe, 2006.

Machiavelli, Niccolò. *The Prince.* Translated.by Daniel Donno. New York: Bantam, 1981.

Machimura, Nobutaka. "Statement on the Adoption of the United Nations Security Council Resolution on the Extension of the Mandate of the ISAF (International Security Assistance

Force) in Afghanistan." Ministry of Foreign Affairs of Japan, September 20, 2007. http://www.mofa.go.jp/announce/announce/2007/9/1175558_834.html.

Maeda, Tetsuo. *The Hidden Army: The Untold Story of Japan's Military Forces*. Ed. David J. Kenney. Translated by Steven Karpa. Chicago: Edition Q, 1995.

Mainichi Daily News, "Toshiba Seeks 9.3 Bil. Yen from Defense Ministry over F-13 Modifying." October31,2011.https://web.archive.org/web/20111103025202;http://mdn.mainichi.jp/mdnnews/business/news/20111031p2g00m0bu108000c.html.

Mainichi Shimbun. "48 percent in Favor of Constitutional Amendment: Mainichi Survey." May 3, 2017, https://mainichi.jp/english/articles/20170503/p2a/00m/0na/005000c.

Malthus, Thomas Robert. *An Essay on the Principle of Population: And a Summary View of the Principle Population*. Ed. Andrew Flew. London: Penguin, 1988.

Man, Michael. *Incoherent Empire*. London: Verso, 2003.

Matsui, Kazumi. "Peace Declaration." Speech. Hiroshima, Japan, August 6, 2018. https://www.city.hiroshima.lg.jp/uploaded/attachment/32395.pdf.

Matsutani Akihiko. *Shrinking-Population Economics: Lessons from Japan*. Translated by Brian Miller. Tokyo: International House of Japan, 2006.

Matsuyama, Yukio. "The Need to Wait for a Generation Change." In *Japan, Internationalism and the UN*, ed. Ronald Dore, 162–168. London: Routledge, 1997.

Matthews, Eugene A. "Japan's New Nationalism." *Foreign Affairs* 82, no. 6 (2003): 74–90. https://doi.org/10.2307/20033758.

McCormack, Gavan. "Remilitarizing Japan." *New Left Review*, no. 29 (2004): 29–46. https://newleftreview.org/issues/ii29/articles/gavan-mccormack-remilitarizing-japan.

McDonell, Stephen. "China Criticizes Japan's Revision of Pacifist Constitution." *ABC.net*, July 2, 2014. http://www.abc.net.au/news/2014-07-02/china-slams-japan-military-shift/5565630.

McIntosh, Malcolm. *Japan Re-Armed*. London: Pinter, 1986.

McNeill, David. "Japanese Scientists Fight U.S.-Style Ties Between Universities and Military." *Chronicle of Higher Education*, March 23, 2015. https://www.chronicle.com/article/Japanese-Scientists-Fight/228663.

Mearsheimer, John J. *The Tragedy of Great Power Politics*. New York: Norton, 2001.

Meyer, Cristoph. O., and Eva Strickmann. "Solidifying Constructivism: How Material and Ideational Factors Interact in European Defense." *Journal of Common Market Studies* 49, no. 1 (2011): 61–81. https://doi.org/10.1111/j.1468-5965.2011.02129.x.

Midford, Paul. "Abe's Pro-Active Pacifism and Values Diplomacy: Implications for EU-Japan Political and Security Cooperation." In *The EU-Japan Partnership in the Shadow of China: The Crisis of Liberalism*, ed. Alex Berkofsky, Christopher W. Hughes, Paul Midford, and Marie Söderberg, 40–58. Abingdon, UK: Routledge, 2018.

——. "The GSDF's Quest for Public Acceptance and the 'Allergy' Myth." In *The Japanese Ground Self-Defense Force: Search for Legitimacy*, ed. Robert D. Eldridge and Paul Midford, 297–346. New York: Palgrave Macmillan, 2017.

——. "The Logic of Reassurance and Japan's Grand Strategy." *Security Studies* 11, no. 3 (2002): 1–43. https://doi.org/10.1080/714005337.

——. *Rethinking Japanese Public Opinion and Security: From Pacifism to Realism?* Stanford, CA: Stanford University Press, 2011.

Midford, Paul, and Robert D. Eldridge. "Introduction." In *The Japanese Ground Self-Defense Force: Search for Legitimacy*, ed. Robert D. Eldridge and Paul Midford, 3–17. New York: Palgrave Macmillan, 2017.

Miller, J. Berkshire. "How Will Japan's New NSC Work?" *Diplomat*, January 29, 2014. http://thediplomat.com/2014/01/how-will-japans-new-nsc-work/.

Milliken, Jennifer. "The Study of Discourse Analysis in International Relations: A Critique of Research and Methods." *European Journal of International Relations* 5, no. 2 (2009): 225–254. https://doi.org/10.1177/1354066199005002003.

Ministry of Defense. "About International Peace Cooperation Activities." N.d. https://www.mod.go.jp/e/d_act/kokusai_heiwa/about.html.

——. *Bōei Hakusho*. Tokyo: Ministry of Defense, 1970–2020.

——. *Defense of Japan*. Tokyo: Ministry of Defense, various years.

——. "Defense Programs and Budget of Japan: Overview of JFY 2020 Budget." 2019. https://www.mod.go.jp/e/d_act/d_budget/pdf/200330a.pdf.

——. "Defense Related Budget Request for JFY 2019." September 2018. https://www.mod.go.jp/e/d_act/d_budget/pdf/300914.pdf.

——. "Guidelines for Japan-U.S. Defense Cooperation." Accessed November 30, 2020, https://www.mod.go.jp/e/d_act/us/index.html#anpo.

——. "National Defense Program Guidelines for FY 2014 and Beyond." December 17, 2013. https://www.mod.go.jp/j/approach/agenda/guideline/2014/pdf/20131217_e2.pdf.

——. "National Defense Program Guidelines for FY 2019 and Beyond." December 18, 2018. https://www.mod.go.jp/j/approach/agenda/guideline/2019/pdf/20181218_e.pdf.

——. "National Security Strategy." December 17, 2013. http://japan.kantei.go.jp/96_abe/documents/2013/__icsFiles/afieldfile/2013/12/17/NSS.pdf.

——. "Overview and Fundamental Concepts of National Defense." May 20, 1957. https://www.mod.go.jp/e/d_act/d_policy/.

——. "Reiwa 2-Nendo Jiētai Junshoku Taiin Tsuitōshiki" [2020 Memorial Ceremonies for JSDF Members Who Died on Duty]. November 2020. https://www.mod.go.jp/j/press/news/2020/11/06a.html.

——. "Strategy on Defense Production and Technological Basis: Toward Strengthening the Bases to Support Defense Forces and 'Proactive Contribution to Peace,' " June 2014, 1–30. https://www.mod.go.jp/atla/soubiseisaku/soubiseisakuseisan/2606honbuneigo.pdf.

——. "Statistics on Scrambles through FY 2019." April 9, 2020. https://www.mod.go.jp/js/Press/press2020/press_pdf/p20200409_02.pdf.

——. "2020-Nendo Kamihanki no Kinkyū Hasshin Jisshi Jōkyō ni Tsuite" (About the Implementation of Scrambles in the First Half of FY2020). October 9, 2020. https://www.mod.go.jp/js/Press/press2020/press_pdf/p20201009_01.pdf.

Ministry of Finance. "Highlights of the Draft FY 2019 Budget." December 13, 2019. https://www.mof.go.jp/english/budget/budget/fy2019/01.pdf.

Ministry of Foreign Affairs. "Cabinet Decision on Development of Seamless Security Legislation to Ensure Japan's Survival and Protect Its People." July 1, 2014. https://www.mofa.go.jp/fp/nsp/page23e_000273.html.

——. "Cabinet Decision on the Development Cooperation Charter." February 10, 2015. https://www.mofa.go.jp/files/000067701.pdf.

——. "Diplomatic Blue Book 2013 Summary." November 11, 2013. https://www.mofa.go.jp/policy/page22e_000013.html.

——. "Japan Disaster Relief Teams Deployed from 1987 to 2019." N.d. https://www.mofa.go.jp/files/000207528.pdf.

——. "Japan's Contribution to UN Peacekeeping Operations (PKO): Outline of Japan's International Peace Cooperation." 2015. https://www.mofa.go.jp/fp/ipc/page22e_000683.html.

——. "Official Development Assistance (ODA): Rebuttal Statement Against the Editorial of *Japan Times* 'Aid that Could Foment Conflict.' " March 8, 2015. https://www.mofa.go.jp/policy/oda/page_000139.html.

——. "White Paper on Development Cooperation." 2017. https://www.mofa.go.jp/files/000406627.pdf.

——. "Youth Communicator for a World Without Nuclear Weapons." 2013. https://www.mofa.go.jp/files/000149237.pdf.

Ministry of Health, Labour, and Welfare. "Basic Survey on Equal Employment, 2018" [Reiwa Nendo Koyō Kintō Kihon Chōsa." December 26, 2019. https://www.mhlw.go.jp/toukei/list/71-r01.html

——. "Hibakushasū (Hibakusha Kenkō Techō Shojishasū) Heikin Nenrei (2019)" (Number of A-Bomb Survivors [Health Notebook Holders] Average Age [2019]). Accessed January 4, 2021. https://www.mhlw.go.jp/stf/newpage_13411.html.

——. "Hibakusha (Hibakusha Kenkō Techō Shojisha) Sū no Suii" [Changes in the Number of A-bomb Survivors (Health Notebook Holders)]. Accessed January 4, 2021. https://www.mhlw.go.jp/stf/newpage_13419.html.

——. *Outline of Health, Labor and Welfare Statistics*, 2019. https://www.mhlw.go.jp/toukei/youran/aramashi/all.pdf.

Ministry of Land, Infrastructure, Transport, and Tourism. "Transition of the Number of Passengers Using Domestic Airlines." 2012. http://www.mlit.go.jp/koku/15_hf_000118.html.

Mitchell, Jon. "Battle Scars: Okinawa and the Vietnam War." *Japan Times*, March 7, 2015. https://www.japantimes.co.jp/news/2015/03/07/national/history/forgotten-history-okinawa-vietnam-war/#.VXmHXGD4tFI.

Mitsubishi Heavy Industries. *MHI Report 2018*. Tokyo: Mitsubishi Heavy Industries Group, 2018, 1–76.

Miyashita, Akitoshi. "Where Do Norms Come From? Foundations of Japan's Postwar Pacifism." *International Relations of the Asia-Pacific* 7, no. 1 (2007): 99–120. https://doi.org/10.1093/irap/lci135.

Møller, Bjørn. "The Revolution in Military Affairs: Myth or Reality?" *Peace Research Abstracts* 40, no. 5 (2003): 1–94.

Momose, Hiroshi, "Democracy and Pacifism in Post-War Japan." In *Hiroshima & Peace*, ed. Carol Rinnert, Omar Farouk, and Inoue Yasuhiro, 113–130. Hiroshima: Kseisuisha, 2010.

Moon, Katherine. *Sex Among Allies: Military Prostitution in U.S.-Korea Relations*. New York: Columbia University Press, 1997.

Moon, Seungsook. "Trouble with Conscription, Entertaining Soldiers: Popular Culture and the Politics of Militarized Masculinity in South Korea." *Men and Masculinities* 8, no. 1 (2005): 64–92. https://doi.org/10.1177/1097184X04268800.

Morgenthau, Hans J. *Politics Among Nations: The Struggle for Power and Peace*. New York: Knopf, 1948.

Mulgan, Aurelia G. "International Peacekeeping and Japan's Role: Catalyst or Cautionary Tale?" *Asian Survey* 35, no. 12 (1995): 1102–1117. https://doi.org/10.2307/2645833.

Murakami, Tomoaki. "The GSDF and Disaster Relief Dispatches." In *The Japanese Ground Self-Defense Force: Search for Legitimacy*, ed. Robert D. Eldridge and Paul Midford, 265–296. New York: Palgrave Macmillan, 2017.

Musashi, Katsuhiro. "The Ground Self-Defense Force and Civilian Control." In *The Japanese Ground Self-Defense Force: Search for Legitimacy*, ed. Robert D. Eldridge and Paul Midford, 233–264. New York: Palgrave Macmillan, 2017.

National Institute of Population and Social Security Research. "Population Projections for Japan." 2017. http://www.ipss.go.jp/pp-zenkoku/e/zenkoku_e2017/g_images_e/pp29gt0203e.htm.

——. "Social Security in Japan 2014." Accessed November 30, 2020. http://www.ipss.go.jp/s-info/e/ssj2014/001.html.

National People's Congress of the People's Republic of China. "Constitution." March 14, 2014. http://www.npc.gov.cn/zgrdw/englishnpc/Constitution/node_2825.htm.

NHK. "Yoron Chōsa Nihonjin to Kenpō 2017" (Public Opinion Poll: Japanese and the Constitution 2017). 2017. https://web.archive.org/web/20190405201453; https://www3.nhk.or.jp/news/special/kenpou70/yoron2017.html.

Nietzsche, Friedrich. *The Birth of Tragedy and the Genealogy of Morals*. Translated by Francis Golffing. Garden City, NY: Doubleday, 1956.

Nikkei Shimbun. "Regular Telephone Opinion Poll." Translated by the Maureen and Mike Mansfield Mansfield Foundation, April 2005. https://web.archive.org/web/20160604043230; http://mansfieldfdn.org/backup/polls/2005/poll-05-8.htm.

Nishikawa, Toshiyuki. "The Future of the Japanese Constitution: From the 'MacArthur Constitution' to What?" *Journal of Comparative Law* Culture, no. 17 (2008): 51–79. https://doi.org/10.15004/00000410.

Nishimura, Kuniyuki. "Worlds of Our Remembering: The Agent-Structure Problem as the Search for Identity." *Cooperation and Conflict* 46, no. 1 (2011): 96–112. https://doi.org/10.1177/0010836710396836.

Nozaki, Yoshiko, and Inokuchi Hiromitsu. "Japanese Education, Nationalism, and Ienaga Saburo's Court Challenges." *Bulletin of Concerned Asian Scholars* 30, no. 2 (1998): 37–46. https://doi.org/10.1080/14672715.1998.10411042.

Nye, Joseph S., Jr. "International Relations: The Relevance of Theory to Practice." In *Oxford Handbook of International Relations*, ed. Christian Reus-Smit and Duncan Snidal, 648–660. Oxford: Oxford University Press, 2008. http://doi.org/10.1093/oxfordhb/9780199219322.003.0037.

Obinata, Sumio. "The Establishment of the 'Imperial Army' and the Structure of Masculinity." *Jenda Shigaku* 2 (2006): 21–33. https://doi.org/10.11365/genderhistory.2.21.

OECD. "Gender Wage Gap." N.d. https://data.oecd.org/earnwage/gender-wage-gap.htm Accessed on January 2, 2021.

——. "Official Development Assistance 2018—Preliminary Data." Accessed November 27, 2020. https://www1.compareyourcountry.org/en.

Ohno, Shun, Setyowati Setyowati, Hirano O. Yoko, and Krisna Yetti. "Indonesian Nurses' Challenges for Passing the National Board Examination for Registered Nurse in Japanese: Suggestions for Solutions." *Southeast Asian Studies* 49, no. 4 (2012): 629–642.

Okudaira, Yasuhiro. "Forty Years of the Constitution and Its Various Influences: Japanese, American, and European." *Law and Contemporary Problems* 53, no. 1 (1990): 17–49. https://doi .org/10.2307/1191824.

Onuf, Nicholas. "Everyday Ethics in International Relations." *Millennium—London—London School of Economics* 27, no. 3 (1998): 669–694.

—. *International Legal Theory: Essays and Engagements, 1966–2006.* Abingdon, VA: Routledge-Cavendish, 2008.

—. *Making Sense, Making Worlds: Constructivism in Social Theory and International Relations.* London: Routledge, 2013.

—. "Rule and Rules in International Relations." *Erik Castrén Institute of International Law and Human Rights*: 1–23, 2014.

—. *World of Our Making: Rules and Rule in Social Theory and International Relations* (The New International Relations Series). Abingdon, Oxon: Routledge/Taylor & Francis, 2013.

Oren, Ido. "Is Culture Independent of National Security? How America's National Security Concerns Shaped 'Political Culture' Research." *European Journal of International Relations* 6, no. 4 (2000): 543–573. https://doi.org/10.1177/1354066100006004004.

Oros, Andrew L. *Japan's Security Renaissance: New Policies and Politics for the Twenty-First Century* (Contemporary Asia in the World). New York: Columbia University Press, 2017.

—. *Normalizing Japan: Politics, Identity, and the Evolution of Security Practice.* Stanford, CA.: Stanford University Press, 2008.

Osaki Tomohiro. "Thousands Rally Outside Diet Against Abe's Security Bills." *Japan Times*, June 6, 2015. https://www.japantimes.co.jp/news/2015/08/30/national/thousands-protest-abe-security -bills-diet-rally/.

Oshio, Takashi. "The Declining Birthrate in Japan." *Japan Economic Currents*, no. 69 (2008): 1–10.

Otley, Christopher B. "Militarism and Militarization in the Public Schools, 1900–1972." *British Journal of Sociology* 29, no. 3 (1978): 321–339. https://doi.org/10.2307/590104.

Ozawa, Ichirō. *Blueprint for a New Japan: The Rethinking of a Nation.* Translated by Lousia Rubenfien. Tokyo: Kodansha International, 1994.

Park, Cheol Hee. "Historical Memory and the Resurgence of Nationalism: A Korean Perspective." In *East Asia's Haunted Present: Historical Memories and the Resurgence of Nationalism*, ed. Tsuyoshi Hasegawa, and Kazuhiko Togo, 190–204. Westport, CT: Praeger Security International, 2008.

Peace Boat. "We Are," accessed November 25, 2020. https://peaceboat.org/english/.

Peou, Sorpong. *Peace and Security in the Asia-Pacific: Theory and Practice.* Santa Barbara, CA: Praeger Security International, 2010.

Pew Research Center. "How Asians View Each Other." July 14, 2014. https://www.pewresearch .org/global/2014/07/14/chapter-4-how-asians-view-each-other/.

—. "Japanese Public's Mood Rebounding, Abe Highly Popular: China and South Korea Very Negative Toward Japan." July 11, 2013. https://www.pewresearch.org/global/2013/07/11/japanese-publics -mood-rebounding-abe-strongly-popular/.

Pierson, Paul. *Politics in Time: History, Institutions, and Social Analysis.* Princeton, NJ: Princeton University Press, 2004.

Post-War Constitution of Japan. November 3, 1946. https://www.refworld.org/docid/3ae6b4ee38 .html.

Pouliot, Vincent. "The Essence of Constructivism." *Journal of International Relations and Development* 7, no. 3 (2004): 319–336. https://doi.org/10.1057/palgrave.jird.1800022.

Prantl, Jochen and Nakano Ryoko. "Global Norm Diffusion in East Asia: How China and Japan Implement the Responsibility to Protect." *International Relations* 25, no. 2 (2011): 204–223. https://doi.org/10.1177/0047117811404450.

Price, Richard M. *The Chemical Weapons Taboo*. Ithaca, NY: Cornell University Press, 2007.

Przystup, James J., National Defense University Press, and National Defense University, Institute for National Strategic Studies. "The U.S.-Japan Alliance: Review of the Guidelines for Defense Cooperation." *Strategic Perspectives*, no. 18 (2015).

Pyle, Kenneth. *Japan Rising: The Resurgence of Japanese Power and Purpose*. New York: Public Affairs, 2007.

Roach, Stephen. "Asia's Sleeping Giant." In *Reimagining Japan: The Quest for a Future That Works*, ed. Clay Chandler, Heang Chhor, and Brian Salsberg, 96–101. San Francisco: VIZ Media, 2011.

Roy, Denny. "The Sources and Limits of Sino-Japanese Tensions." *Survival* 47, no. 2 (2005): 191–214. https://doi.org/10.1080/00396330500156495.

Ruwitch, John. "China Envoy Urges Japan to Stick to Apology Script: China Daily." Reuters, March 13, 2015. https://www.reuters.com/article/us-china-japan/china-envoy-urges-japan-to-stick-to-apology-script-china-daily-idUSKBN0M905020150313.

Sado, Akihiro. *The Self-Defense Forces and Postwar Politics in Japan*. Translated by Noda Makiko. Tokyo: Japan Publishing Industry Foundation for Culture, 2017.

Sakai, Hidekazu, and Yochiro Sato, eds. *Re-Rising Japan: Its Strategic Power in International Relations*. New York: Peter Lang, 2018.

Sakai, Naoki. "Subject and Substratum: On Japanese Imperial Nationalism." *Cultural Studies* 14, nos. 3-4 (2000): 462–530. https://doi.org/10.1080/09502380050130428.

Samuels, Richard J. " 'New Fight Power!' Japan's Growing Maritime Capabilities and the East Asian Security." *International Security* 32, no. 3 (2007/2008): 84–112. https://www.jstor.org/stable/30130519.

——. *Securing Japan: Tokyo's Grand Strategy and the Future of East Asia*. Ithaca, NY: Cornell University Press, 2007.

Sasada, Hironori. "Youth and Nationalism in Japan." *SAIS Review of International Affairs* 26, no. 2 (2006): 109–122. https://doi.org/10.1353/sais.2006.0044.

Sasaki, Kaori. "Putting Families First." In *Reimagining Japan: The Quest for a Future That Works*, ed. Clay Chandler, Heang Chhor, and Brian Salsberg, 347–348. San Francisco: VIZ Media, 2011.

Sasaki, Tomoyuki. *Japan's Postwar Military and Civil Society: Contesting a Better Life* (Paperback ed., SOAS Studies in Modern and Contemporary Japan). London: Bloomsbury Academic, 2017.

Sakanaka, Hidenori. "The Future of Japan's Immigration Policy: A Battle Diary." Abridged translation by Andrew J. I. Taylor. *Asia-Pacific Journal: Japan Focus* 5, no. 4 (2005). http://www.japanfocus.org/-sakanaka-hidenori/2396/article.html.

——. *Japan as an Immigration Nation: Demographic Change, Economic Necessity, and the Human Community Concept*. Translated by Robert D. Eldridge and Graham B. Leonard. Lanham, MD: Lexington, 2020.

Saito, Hiro. *The History Problem: The Politics of War Commemoration in East Asia*. Honolulu: University of Hawai'i Press, 2017.

Sarig, Roni. "Sadako Sasaki and Anne Frank: Myths in Japanese and Israeli Memory of the Second World War." In *War and Militarism in Modern Japan*, ed. Guy Podeler. Folkestone, UK: Global Oriental, 2009.

Sato, Fumika. "Why Have the Japanese Self-Defense Forces Included Women? The State's 'Nonfeminist Reasons.' " In *Militarized Currents: Toward a Decolonized Future in Asia and the Pacific*, ed. Shigematsu Setsu and Keith L. Camacho, 251–276. Minneapolis: University of Minnesota Press, 2010.

——. "A Camouflaged Military: Japan's Self-Defense Forces and Globalized Gender Mainstreaming." *Asia-Pacific Journal* 10, no. 36 (2012): 1–23. https://apjjf.org/2012/10/36/Fumika-Sato/3820/article.html.

Satoh, Haruko, "Rethinking Security in Japan: In Search of a Post-'Postwar' Narrative." In *Japan's Strategic Challenges in a Changing Regional* Environment, ed. Purnendra Jain and Lam Peng Er, 273–296. Singapore: World Scientific, 2012.

Schmitt, Eric. "Iraq-Bound Troops Confront Rumsfeld Over Lack of Armor." New York Times, December 8, 2004. https://www.nytimes.com/2004/12/08/international/middleeast/iraqbound-troops-confront-rumsfeld-over-lack-of.html.

Schoppa, Leonard J. "Japan's Declining Population: The Perspective of Japanese Women on the 'Problem' and the 'Solutions.' " In *Asia Program Special Report*, ed. Mark Mohr, 6–10. Washington, DC: Woodrow Wilson Center for Scholars, 2008.

Schouten, Peer. "Theory Talk #70: Nicholas Onuf on the Evolution of Social Constructivism, Turns in IR, and a Discipline of Our Making." Theory Talks, July 2, 2015. http://www.theory-talks.org/2015/07/theory-talk-70.html.

Science Council of Japan. "Statement on Research for Military Security." March 24, 2017. http://www.scj.go.jp/ja/info/kohyo/pdf/kohyo-23-s243-en.pdf.

Seaton, Philip. "Kamikaze Museums and Contents Tourism." *Journal of War & Peace Studies* 12, no. 1 (2019): 67–84. https://doi.org/10.1080/17526272.2018.1424432.

Self-Defense Forces Law. e-Gov, n.d. https://elaws.e-gov.go.jp/search/elawsSearch/elaws_search/lsg0500/detail?lawId=329AC0000000165_20180413_430AC0000000013&openerCode=1.

Shaw, Martin. "Twenty-First Century Militarism: A Historical-Sociological Framework." In *Militarism and International Relations: Political Economy, Security, Theory*, ed. Anna Stavianakis and Jan Selby, 19–32. London: Routledge, 2012.

Shibata, Masako. "The Politics of Religion: Modernity, Nationhood and Education in Japan." *Intercultural Education* 19, no. 4 (2008): 353–361. https://doi.org/10.1080/14675980802376879.

Shimoyachi, Nao. "SDF Members Pursue Sense of Mission." *Japan Times*, June 30, 2004. https://web.archive.org/web/20040825180241; http://www.japantimes.co.jp/cgi-bin/getarticle.pl5?nn20040630f1.htm.

Shiozaki, Yasuhisa. "Speech at the 42nd Munich Conference on Security Policy." Hotel Bayerischer Hof, Munich, Germany, February 5, 2006. https://www.mofa.go.jp/policy/security/speech0602.html.

Shiraishi, Katsutaka, and Matoba Nobutaka, eds. *Depopulation, Deindustrialisation & Disasters*. Cham, Switzerland: Palgrave Macmillan, 2019.

Sieg, Linda, and Miyazaki Ami. "Aging Japan: Military Recruiters Struggle as Applicant Pool Dries Up." *Reuters*, September 19, 2018. https://www.reuters.com/article/us-japan-ageing-military-recruits/aging-japan-military-recruiters-struggle-as-applicant-pool-dries-up-idUSKCN1LZ14S.

Singh, Bhubhindar. *Japan's Security Identity: From a Peace State to an International State* (Sheffield Centre for Japanese Studies/Routledge Series, 45). London: Routledge, 2013.

——. "Japan's Security Policy: From a Peace State to an International State." *Pacific Review* 21, no. 3 (2008): 303–325. https://doi.org/10.1080/09512740802134141.

Smith, Sheila A. *Japan Rearmed: The Politics of Military Power.* Cambridge, MA: Harvard University Press, 2019.

Smith, Stevie. "Six Wishes for a More Relevant Discipline of International Relations." In *Oxford Handbook of International Relations*, ed. Christian Reus-Smit and Duncan Snidal, 725–732. Oxford: Oxford University Press, 2008.

Snow, Nancy. "The Abe Administration's Arrogance of Power Moment." *Japan Times*, July 16, 2015. http://www.japantimes.co.jp/opinion/2015/07/16/commentary/japan-commentary/abe -administrations-arrogance-power-moment/#.ValgY3j4tFL.

Soeya, Yoshihide, Tadokoro Masayuki, and David A. Welch, eds. *Japan as a 'Normal Country'?: A Nation in Search of Its Place in the World.* Toronto: University of Toronto Press, 2012.

Soh, Sarah C. *The Comfort Women: Sexual Violence and Postcolonial Memory in Korea and Japan.* Chicago: University of Chicago Press, 2008.

Solingen, Etel. *Nuclear Logics: Contrasting Paths in East Asia and the Middle East* (Princeton Studies in International History and Politics). Princeton, NJ: Princeton University Press, 2007.

Statistics Bureau of Japan. "Labor Force Survey: Population Aged 15 Years Old and Over." e-Stat, January 31, 2020. https://www.e-stat.go.jp/en/stat-search/files?page=1&layout=datalist &toukei=00200531&tstat=000000110001&cycle=7&year=20190&month=0&tclass1 =000001040276&tclass2=000001040283&tclass3=000001040284&result_back=1.

——. *"Nihon no Tōkei 2020"* (Statistics of Japan 2020). March 2019. https://www.stat.go.jp/data /nihon/pdf/20nihon.pdf.

Stavale, Giuseppe A. "The GSDF During the Post-Cold War Years, 1989–2015." In *The Japanese Ground Self-Defense Force: Search for Legitimacy*, ed. Robert D. Eldridge and Paul Midford, 183–230. New York: Palgrave Macmillan, 2017.

Stockholm International Peace Research Institute. "SIPRI Arms Industry Database." Accessed November 30, 2020. https://www.sipri.org/databases/armsindustry.

——. "SIPRI Military Expenditure Database." Accessed November 30, 2020. https://www.sipri .org/databases/milex.

Stokes, Bruce, and Kat Devlin. "Views of the U.S. and President Trump." Pew Research Center, November 12, 2018. http://www.pewglobal.org/2018/11/12/views-of-the-u-s-and-president-trump/.

Strausz, Michael. *Help (Not) Wanted.* New York: SUNY Press, 2019.

Suga, Yoshihide. "Press Conference by the Chief Cabinet Secretary." Prime Minister of Japan and His Cabinet (website), June 13, 2017. https://japan.kantei.go.jp/tyoukanpress/201706/13_p .html.

Tabuchi, Hiroko. "Japan Keeps a High Wall for Foreign Labor." *New York Times*, January 2, 2011. http://www.nytimes.com/2011/01/03/world/asia/03japan.html.

——. "Japan Pays Foreign Workers to Go Home." *New York Times*, April 22, 2009. http://www .nytimes.com/2009/04/23/business/global/23immigrant.html.

Takada, Akira. "Socialization Practices Regarding Shame in Japanese Caregiver-Child Interactions." *Frontiers in Psychology* 10 (2019): 1–14. https://doi.org/10.3389/fpsyg.2019.01545.

Takenaka, Akiko. *Yasukuni Shrine: History, Memory, and Japan's Unending Postwar*. Honolulu: University of Hawaii Press, 2015.

Tamamoto, Masaru. "Japan's Politics of Cultural Shame." *Global Asia* 2, no. 1 (2007). https://globalasia.org/v2no1/cover/japans-politics-of-cultural-shame_masaru-tamamoto.

Tamashiro, Roy, and Ellen Furnari. "Museums for Peace: Agents and Instruments of Peace Education." *Journal of Peace Education* 12, no. 3 (2015): 223-235. https://doi.org/10.1080/17400201.2015.1092712.

Tannenwald, Nina. *The Nuclear Taboo: The United States and the Non-Use of Nuclear Weapons since 1945* (Cambridge Studies in International Relations, 87). Cambridge: Cambridge University Press, 2007.

Taue, Tomihisa. "Nagasaki Peace Declaration." Speech. Nagasaki, Japan, August 9, 2018. https://www.wagingpeace.org/2018-nagasaki-peace-declaration/.

Tellis, Ashley J., Janice Bially, Christopher Layne, and Melissa McPherson. *Measuring National Power in the Postindustrial Age*. Santa Monica, CA: RAND, 2000.

Tomodachi Initiative. *Annual Report*. 2019. http://usjapantomodachi.org/wp/wp-content/uploads/2020/06/TOMODACHI-2019-Annual-Report-Final-Spreads.pdf.

Trauschweizer, Ingo. "On Militarism." *Journal of Military History* 76, no. 2 (2012): 507-543.

Treat, John W. *Writing Ground Zero: Japanese Literature and the Atomic Bomb*. Chicago: University of Chicago Press, 1995.

Trip Advisor. "Top 30 Attractions in Japan by International Travelers 2020." April 28. 2020. https://tg.tripadvisor.jp/news/ranking/best-inbound-attractions/.

United Nations. *Hyōgo Framework for Action 2005–2015: Building the Resilience of Nations and Communities to Disasters*. New York: United Nations Office for Disaster Risk Reduction, 2007, 1-25. https://www.preventionweb.net/files/1037_hyogoframeworkforactionenglish.pdf.

——. *Sendai Framework for Disaster Risk Reduction 2015–2030*. New York: United Nations Office for Disaster Risk Reduction, 2015, 1-39. https://www.preventionweb.net/files/43291_sendai-frameworkfordrren.pdf.

——. *World Urbanization Prospects*. Washington, DC: United Nations, 2014. https://esa.un.org/unpd/wup/publications/files/wup2014-highlights.pdf.

United Nations Peacekeeping. "Troop and Police Contributors." Accessed November 30, 2020. https://peacekeeping.un.org/en/troop-and-police-contributors.

U.S. Bureau of Labor Statistics. "Labor Force Statistics from the Current Population Survey." May 30, 2020. https://data.bls.gov/timeseries/LNS14000000.

U.S. Department of Defense. *Dictionary of Military Terms*. New York: Skyhorse, 2009.

U.S. Department of Veterans Affairs. "Suicide Among Veterans and Other Americans 2001-2014." Office of Mental Health and Suicide Prevention, August 3, 2016. https://www.mentalhealth.va.gov/docs/2016suicidedatareport.pdf.

Vagts, Alfred. *A History of Militarism: Civilian and Military*. New York: Meridian, 1959.

Van den Dungen, Peter, and Yamane Kazuyo. "Peace Education Through Peace Museums." *Journal of Peace Education* 12, no. 3 (2015). https://doi.org/10.1080/17400201.2015.1103393.

Vekasi, Kristin. "Transforming Geopolitical Risk: Public Diplomacy of Multinational Firms for Foreign Audiences." *Chinese Journal of International Politics* 10, no. 1 (2017): 95-129. https://doi.org/10.1093/cjip/pow017.

Walt, Stephen M. *The Origins of Alliances*. Ithaca, NY: Cornell University Press, 1987.

Waltz, Kenneth N. "International Politics Is Not Foreign Policy." *Security Studies* 6, no. 1 (1996): 54–57. https://doi.org/10.1080/09636419608429298.

——. "Structural Realism After the Cold War." *International Security* 25, no. 1 (2000): 5–41. https://doi.org/10.1162/016228800560372.

——. *Theory of International Politics*. Reading, MA: Addison-Wesley, 1979.

Ware, Vron. *Military Migrants: Fighting for Your Country*. Basingstoke, UK: Palgrave Mcmillan, 2012).

Weldes, Jutta. "High Politics and Low Data: Globalization Discourses in Popular Culture." In *Interpretation and Method: Empirical Research Methods and the Interpretive Turn*, ed. Dvora Yanow and Peregrine Schwartz-Shea, 176–186. Armonk, NY: M. E. Sharpe, 2006.

Whiting, Allen S. "China and Japan: Politics Versus Economics." *The Annals of the American Academy of Political and Social Science* 519, no. 1 (1992): 39–51. https://doi.org/10.1177/0002716292519001004.

Woodard, William P. *The Allied Occupation of Japan 1945–1952 and Japanese Religions*. Leiden, Netherlands: E. J. Brill, 1972.

Workingdays.org. "Working days in Japan." N.d. https://japan.workingdays.org/#a28.

World Economic Forum. "Gender Gap Report 2020." December 16, 2019. http://www3.weforum.org/docs/WEF_GGGR_2020.pdf.

World Values Survey. "World Values Survey" (data file and code book). Various years. https://www.worldvaluessurvey.org/wvs.jsp.

Yamaguchi, Mari. "Japan Seeks to Expand Arms Deals with Southeast Asia." *Associated Press*, June 13, 2017. https://apnews.com/148468bcf20e4dbd9973417e92c2e167.

Yamaguchi, Noboru. "Redefining the Japan-US Alliance." Nippon.com, May 11, 2012. http://www.nippon.com/en/features/c00204/.

Yamamura, Kozo. "Success Illgotten? The Role of Meiji Militarism in Japan's Technological Progress." *Journal of Economic History* 37, no. 1 (1977): 113–135. https://doi.org/10.1017/S0022050700096777.

Yamamura, Takayoshi. "Cooperation Between Anime Producers and the Japan Self-Defense Force: Creating Fantasy and/or Propaganda?" *Journal of War & Culture Studies* 12, no. 1 (2019): 8–23. https://doi.org/10.1080/17526272.2017.1396077.

Yamane, Kazuyo. *Grassroots Museums for Peace in Japan: Unknown Efforts for Peace and Reconciliation*. Saarbrüden, Germany: VDM Verlag Dr. Müller, 2009.

——. "Moving Beyond the War Memorial Museum." *Peace Forum* 24, no. 34 (2009): 75–84.

——. "Japanese Peace Museums: Education and Reconciliation." In *Peace Studies in the Chinese Century*, ed. Alan Hunter, 85–113. London: Routledge, 2017.

Yamashita, Samuel H. *Daily Life in Wartime Japan, 1940–1945* (Modern War Studies). Lawrence, KS: University Press of Kansas, 2015.

Yashiro, Naohiro. "Social Implications of Demographic Change in Japan." *Conference Series—Federal Reserve Bank of Boston* 46 (2001): 297–304.

Yasukawa, Masaaki, and Hirooka Keijiro. "Estimates of Population Size and of the Birth- and Death-Rates in Japan, 1865–1920." *Keio Economic Studies* 11, no. 2 (1974): 41–66.

Yeo, Yezi. "De-Militarizing Military: Confirming Japan's Self-Defense Forces' Identity as a Disaster Relief Agency in the 2011 Tohoku Triple Crisis." *Asia Journal of Global Studies* 5, no. 2 (2012): 71–80. http://www.aags.org/journal/ajgs-2013-volume-5-issue-2-issn-1884-0264.

Yomiuri Shimbun. "March 2008 Opinion Polls." Translated by the Maureen and Mike Mansfield Foundation. Accessed November 21, 2020. https://web.archive.org/web/20160604012119; http://mansfieldfdn.org/backup/polls/2008/poll-08-06.htm.

Yoneyama, Lisa. *Hiroshima Traces: Time, Space and the Dialects of Memory.* Berkeley: University of California Press, 1991.

Yoshida, Reiji. "Ishin No To Leader Lashes Abe Over Security Bills." *Japan Times*, June 17, 2015. http://www.japantimes.co.jp/news/2015/06/17/national/politics-diplomacy/ishin-no-to -leader-lashes-abe-over-security-bills/#.VYW-OGD4tFK.

——. "Murayama, Kono Assail Revisionism, Urge Abe to Uphold Their Apologies in Entirety." *Japan Times*, June 9, 2015. http://www.japantimes.co.jp/news/2015/06/09/national/politics -diplomacy/murayama-kono-assail-revisionism-urge-abe-uphold-apologies-entirety/#. VYW-PWD4tFJ.

——. "South Korea, China Warn Japan not to Backtrack on Apology Over Wartime Past." Reuters, January 27, 2015. http://www.reuters.com/article/2015/01/27/us-southkorea-japan-abe -idUSKBN0L00QO20150127.

——. "Yasukuni Shrine's Chief Priest Forced to Quit after Criticizing Emperor for Not Visiting War-Linked Shrine." *Japan Times*, October 11, 2018. https://www.japantimes.co.jp/news/2018 /10/11/national/yasukuni-shrines-chief-priest-forced-quit-criticizing-nonvisiting-emperor/.

Yoshida, Reiji, and Osaki Tomohiro. "Fiery Suicide Bid Shocks Shinjuku on Eve of Historic Security Decision." *Japan Times*, June 30, 2014. http://www.japantimes.co.jp/news/2014/06/30 /national/fiery-suicide-bid-shocks-shinjuku/#.VXqlY2D4tFI.

Yoshida, Takashi. "Revising the Past, Complicating the Future: The Yushukan War Museum in Modern Japanese History." *Asia-Pacific Journal: Japan Focus* 5, no. 12 (2007): 1–8.

Yoshihara, Susan. "The Setting Sun? Strategic Implications of Japan's Demographic Transition." In *Population Decline and the Remaking of Great Power Politics*, ed. Susan Yoshihara and Douglas A. Sylva, 137–158. Washington, DC: Potomac, 2012.

Yoshihara, Susan and Douglas A. Sylvia. *Population Decline and the Remaking of Great Power Politics.* Washington, DC: Potomac, 2011.

Yoshimura, Shinsuke. "To Die for High Principle?" In *Japan, Internationalism and the UN*, edited Ronald Dore, 156–159. London: Routledge, 1997.

Yoshizaki, Tomonori. "The Military's Role in Disaster Relief Operations: A Japanese Perspective." In *International Symposium on Security Affairs. 14th Symposium* (Tokyo: National Diet Library, 2011), 71–89. https://dl.ndl.go.jp/info:ndljp/pid/10314991?itemId=info%3Andljp%2Fpid%2F10314991 &_lang=en.

Zehfuss, Maja. *Constructivism in International Relations: The Politics of Reality* (Cambridge Studies in International Relations, 83). Cambridge: Cambridge University Press, 2002.

Zinn, Howard. *A People's History of the United States.* New York: Harper & Row, 1980.

Index

Page numbers in *italics* indicate figures or tables.

CONTEMPORARY ASIA IN THE WORLD

David C. Kang and Victor D. Cha, Editors

Nation at Play: A History of Sport in India, Ronojoy Sen, 2015

The China Boom: Why China Will Not Rule the World, Ho-fung Hung, 2015

Japan's Security Renaissance: New Policies and Politics for the Twenty-First Century, Andrew L. Oros, 2017

Japan, South Korea, and the United States Nuclear Umbrella: Deterrence After the Cold War, Terrence Roehrig, 2017

GMO China: How Global Debates Transformed China's Agricultural Biotechnology Policies, Cong Cao, 2018

Dying for Rights: Putting North Korea's Human Rights Abuses on the Record, Sandra Fahy, 2019

Japan's New Regional Reality: Geoeconomic Strategy in the Asia-Pacific, Saori N. Katada, 2020

GPSR Authorized Representative: Easy Access System Europe, Mustamäe tee
50, 10621 Tallinn, Estonia, gpsr.requests@easproject.com

www.ingramcontent.com/pod-product-compliance
Lightning Source LLC
Chambersburg PA
CBHW022132020426
42334CB00015B/861